Housing Policies in the Socialist Third World

Housing Policies
in the Socialist Third World

edited by Kosta Mathéy

Profil Verlag
München

MANSELL

LONDON AND NEW YORK

Published jointly 1990 in the United Kingdom by

Mansell Publishing Limited, *A Cassell Imprint*
Villiers House, 41–47 Strand, London WC2N 5JE, England
125 East Street, Suite 300, New York 10010, USA

and in Germany by

Profil Verlag GmbH, Schwanthalerstraße 10
8000 München 2, Germany

© Kosta Mathéy and the contributors 1990

British Library Cataloguing in Publication Data
Housing policies in the socialist Third World.
  1. Developing Socialist countries. Housing. Policies of Governments
  I. Mathéy, Kosta
  363.556091724

  ISBN 0 7201 2049 7

Library of Congress Cataloging–in–Publication Data

  [applied for]

Deutsche Bibliothek Cataloguing–in–Publication Data
Housing policies in the socialist Third World / ed. by Kosta Mathéy.
– London; New York: Mansell; München: Profil–Verl., 1990
  ISBN 3–89019–254–8 (Profil–Verl.)
NE: Mathéy, Kosta [Hrsg.]

This book has been printed and bound in Great Britain, by Biddles Ltd, Guildford and King's Lynn from camera–ready copy supplied by the volume editor.

The printing of this book was subsidized by the German Research Foundation (DFG).

TP

Contents

The Contributors   vii

Part I: Background

Introduction   3
Kosta Mathéy

Socialist Housing: Some Key Issues   13
Kosta Mathéy

Socialism in the Periphery   19
Reinhart Kößler

Part II: Country Studies

Cuba   35
Jill Hamberg

Nicaragua   71
Kosta Mathéy

Guinea Bissau   97
Julio Davila

Cape Verde   121
Christina von Schweinichen

Angola   129
Otto Greger

Mozambique   147
Paul Jenkins

Tanzania   181
Karin Nuru

Zimbabwe   197
Ann Schlyter

Ethiopia   227
Sabine Wendt, Sabine Wähning, Kosta Mathéy, Matteo Scaramelli

Algeria   249
Djaffar Lesbet

Vietnam   275
Ngyên Duc Nhuân and Kosta Mathéy

China   289
Richard Kirkby

Albania   315
Lena Magnusson

Index   323

The Contributors

Julio D. Dávila, BSc, Dip., MSc (Econ), holds a postgraduate diploma and an MSc (Econ) in urban development planning from the University of London, and a first degree in civil engineering from the Universidad de los Andes, in his native Bogotá, Colombia. He worked with Colombia's National Planning Agency as part of a team in charge of preparing the first national housing plan. Since 1984, as a researcher with the International Institute for Environment and Development (IIED), based in London and Buenos Aires, he has carried out research on housing and human settlements issues, particularly in Guinea Bissau and Latin America. His working experience also includes teaching at post–graduate level at the University of London. He is co–author of an annotated bibliography on the subject of small and medium-sized cities in Third World development and a co–editor of the journal *Environment and Urbanization*. Mr Dávila is currently writing a PhD thesis on the spatial dynamics of manufacturing in the metropolitan region of Bogotá.

Otto Greger, Dipl.-Ing., is a German architect and professor at the Faculty of Engineering's Department of Architecture, University Agostinho Neto, P.R. Angola. He was previously attached to the Technical University of Berlin engaged in research and teaching planning and building in the developing world. His practical experience includes architectural projects in Egypt, Angola, Brazil, and the Cape Verde Islands. Greger is a co–founder of TRIALOG, the German journal on Planning and Building in the Third World. His publications include, among others, 'Architektur und Stadtgestalt in Kairo: Die Bedeutung der Tradition für die Gegenwart' (jointly with F. Steinberg and L. Christians), Berlin 1987, and 'Transformations of Formal Housing: Unintended Evolutionary Developments as Inspiration for Innovative Design' in *Open House Intl.*, vol. 13, no. 3, 1988.

Jill Hamberg is an urban planner whose work in recent years has included writing and consulting on housing and homeless issues and community needs assessments. She has taught at universities in Latin America and in the New York City area. At present, she is completing a doctoral dissertation on Cuban housing and urban planning.

vii

Paul Jenkins is currently employed as architect and planner on a U.N.C.H.S. (Habitat) project to assist the ministry of construction and water affairs of the People's Republic of Mozambique in the elaboration in a national housing policy. He has worked continuously in the areas of housing and planning at local and central government levels in Mozambique since 1980, having previously worked in Malawi and Botswana in the central and southern African region. His professional experience includes architectural design and urban planning, development of appropriate construction technologies and training programmes, and the promotion of low–cost housing and self–help/community based construction activities.

Richard Kirkby, PhD, was director of the Chinese Services Centre at Sheffield City Polytechnic at the time of writing the chapter reproduced within this volume. In 1990 he was appointed lecturer in Planning in Developing Countries at the University of Liverpool and Editor of the *Third World Planning Review.* Over the past two decades he has pursued a research interest in China's urban and regional development. Dr Kirkby is author of 'Urbanization in China – Town and Country in a Developing Economy 1949–2000 AD' (1985).

Reinhart Kößler holds a PhD in Sociology and teaches at the University of Münster, West Germany. He is founding member and co–editor of 'Peripherie', a radical journal on Third World problems, and a board member of ISSA, the Information Centre on Southern Africa in Bonn. He is the author of the books *Dritte Internatio- nale Bauernrevolution* and *Arbeitskultur im Industrialisierungsprozeß* (1982) (forthcoming). Other publications include topics such as sociology of development, sociology of work and industrialization, liberation movements on South Africa, Eastern Europe and China, and Marxist Theory.

Djaffar Lesbet, an Algerian researcher, is professor of sociology at the Institute of Urbanism of the University of Paris VIII. He has widely published on spatial development and housing in Algeria. His monographs include *Les 1000 Villages Socialistes en Algerie* (1983), *La Casbah d'Alger – Gestion Urbaine et Vide Social.*

Lena Magnusson, geographer, is a research officer at the National Swedish Institute for Building Research in Gävle, Sweden. Her research deals with residential mobility, housing market interaction, and vacancy chain models. Having focused on the Swedish case initially it has now been extended to Eastern Europe. Ms. Magnusson is investigating the Albanian case in this context.

Kosta Mathéy, Dipl.–Ing., Dip.Grad.Hons (AA), architect and planner, has taught at the Universities of Darmstadt, Ife, and Kassel, West Germany. He is also founder and co–editor of the journal *TRIALOG,* and president of the Association for Research into Housing, Planning and Building in the Developing World. He has conducted research on self–help housing in Cuba, Nicaragua, and Venezuela. His publications on the housing issues include 5 books and some 50 chapters in edited books or articles in scientific journals. He is currently preparing a PhD on housing in Cuba, and editing a book on self–help housing in Europe, Asia, Africa, and the Americas.

Karin Nuru, Dipl.–Ing., is an architect teaching Design in the Tropics at the Postgraduate Department of the Building Academy in Weimar, German Democratic Republic. She was a practising architect in Tanzania between 1980 and 1985, and specializes in rural building and infrastructure provision. She has written several articles on Tanzanian housing and architecture, of which some were published in the *Wissenschaftliche Zeitschrift der Hochschule für Architektur und Bauwesen.*

Ngyên Duc Nhuân, PhD, is a Vietnamese researcher based at the Third World Laboratory, University of Paris V. He has published widely on settlement issues and general politics in Vietnam.

Matteo Scaramella is an architect–planner now living and working in Rome. He has been involved in urban projects and housing policies and programmes in several African countries: Ethiopia, Mozambique, Togo, Burkina Faso, Senegal, Nigeria, and taught Urban and Regional Planning at the University of Ife. In Addis Ababa he worked as architect in the planners' team preparing the city's master plan.

Ann Schlyter, PhD, is an architect and researcher based at the National Swedish Institute for Housing Research in Lund. Affiliated to the University of Zimbabwe she carried out a study in Harare 1985–1989 focusing on housing policy and households headed by women. In other research projects she has been following the long term development of shanty towns and improvement areas in Lusaka, Zambia, and is continuing to research housing and gender in Southern Africa.

Christina von Schweinichen, Dipl.–Ing., has studied architecture and planning in Venice, Edinburgh, and Bruges. She has worked as a researcher and consultant for several international agencies, including the UNESCO, and non–governmental organizations (NGOs) in Venice, the USA, Ethiopia, and the Cape Verde Islands. At present she is responsible for aid to development projects in Latin America for an Italian NGO.

Sabine Wähning, Dipl.–Ing., is an architect who graduated at Hamburg, West Germany. She has worked as architect and researcher into development and environmental impact studies in Ethiopia, Germany, Belgium, and Italy. At present she is associate architect with the UN High Commission for Refugees (UNCHR) in Geneva.

Sabine Wendt, Dr.–Ing., is professor of architecture specializing in building in the Developing World at the University of Weimar, German Democratic Republic. She taught Basic Design and Housing at Addis Ababa University from 1980 to 1983, and has published several articles on architecture in Ethiopia.

Part I: Background

Introduction

Since the writings of Friedrich Engels the socialist project has always promised to offer a solution to the 'housing question' – and solutions are particularly needed in the Third World today, with millions of homeless. Here, the prevailing capitalist social formations are regularly being held responsible for the ever worsening housing conditions of the urban and rural poor, and for the recurrent failures of all policy attempts to guarantee a right to shelter for everyone. Exploitative labour conditions with incomes below subsistence level, corruption, land and housing speculation mark the wider social context within which even a socially oriented government is restricted in enforcing its declared policies, and there are some who opine that capitalist governments could do much more to provide housing for the masses. Therefore, one might assume that those Third World countries which underwent a revolution and claim to build socialist societies would provide better favourable preconditions for the formulation and implementation of efficient housing policies, and might demonstrate how a thoughtful housing policy can permanently improve the living conditions of the masses.

From a theoretical perspective, it must be possible to make housing cheaper in a socialist economy through the elimination of speculation, capital cost (interest), landlords' gains, and profits in the construction industry. Affordability can be increased through better balanced income distribution, and through rent pooling. Access to housing will become more social if based on need instead of ability to pay. Maximum security of tenure can be achieved when houses belong to the state or to the occupier instead of to private landlords and estate agents. Housing consumption can incorporate a larger variety of collective activities and amenities, and can overcome the many problems associated with living in nuclear families, if the economic system is not based upon consumerism, individualism, alienation, and personal competition.

There is, of course, a difference between theory and practice. Some socialist regimes in the Third World were able to turn their knowledge and theoretical promises into practice, so that shelter conditions improved. In some cases, however, they worsened due to revolution, and housing remained sparse for many years. The reasons for the widespread ignorance lay partly in the difficulties in obtaining official and/or reliable data. Foreign experts generally needed special permission to conduct

3

research in socialist countries, and were often not allowed to collect the data on their own, to conduct qualitative interviews, or to take written documents out of the country. Also, on the part of West European and North American funding institutions, there was to be less support for research into these countries because of the lack of underlying trade or business interests. Additionally, scientific co-operation and exchange with these countries was often further discouraged for political consider-ations (i.e. in the cases of Nicaragua, Cuba, Vietnam).

In the last few years, however, the frontiers have become more open and information has begun to flow in both directions. Influenced by the Soviet *perestro-ika*, experts and politicians in the socialist Third World are beginning to speak more openly about their problems, and reports about success stories cannot simply be rated as propaganda alone and disregarded.

The majority of the reports revealed, however, little evidence that real socialism in the Third World had been more successful in conquering the typical phenomena of overcrowding, lack of urban services, and unfit or substandard structures. Annual construction figures have lagged far behind those recommended by the United Nations. But a deeper look revealed that at least some nations have dealt better with the quantitative aspect of the problem and do not manifest open homelessness, have no extensive rims of shanty towns around their cities, and provide better legal protection for tenants. Other socialist states have implemented innovative and alternative policies that would be unthinkable in pure market oriented economies, and have seriously attacked the most universal problems in the areas of housing, including land speculation, the imbalance between town and countryside, uncontrolled migration and urban growth, just to name a few examples. Often, these experiments were discontinued for reasons rooted in other sectors of the economy, in the worsening of international terms of trade, in tribal conflicts and the like. But this does not mean that the discarded policy elements will not work more successfully in a different place, or at another point in time. Generally there were not enough human and financial resources to analyze the reasons and implications behind both success stories and failures for each of them, and to understand the full potential of individual pro-grammes and projects in a long-term perspective.

The situation in socialist Third World states was never more difficult than today. The validity of the socialist concept has been fundamentally questioned, and real socialism in Eastern Europe has disintegrated overnight. The full impact of this development in Europe on socialist Third World nations is still unknown, but it is unlikely that they can continue with past and present policies without radical reforms. First, increasing popular pressure for social change is probable, and improvements in housing provision have always been considered an efficient instrument to gain popular support by right and leftist governments alike (Castells, 1976; Rodriguez, 1972, Schmidt-Relenberg, 1980, and others). Second, and most importantly, some of the countries' previous allies are not only converting one after another to a different political system but they would also be unable to support Third World countries through 'fair trade' arrangements and all kind of subsidies anyway, because they are close to bankruptcy themselves.

Space for manoeuvre is too narrow for any outstanding reforms. Several of these countries had given up socialist positions – in practice, if not in rhetoric – already before the spectacular changes in the former COMECON states in late 1989. However, considering that it still remains to be demonstrated that by adopting capitalist social relations Eastern European countries can really attain similar levels of wealth as enjoyed by their western neighbours, the chances that this can happen are even more remote in the Third World with a much less industrialized economy. There are already too many states in the periphery who have chosen the capitalist path to development without being able to improve their situation. Instead, the absolute poverty among their populations spiralled, while the moderate but stable indigenous economies were replaced with economically (and ecologically) uncontrollable export–oriented farming and second–hand industries.

If following the Eastern European path does not appear to be a viable proposition for the Developing World, the notion of 'self–reliance' may become the last resort, rather than a political slogan like so often in the past. Therefore it is time to take stock now, to scrutinize experiences of past and present policies at home, and with neighbouring countries. The reports collected in this book may provide a useful resource for doing so in discussing, comparing, and evaluating alternative shelter strategies, achievements and failures.

The conceptual and personal basis for this book was developed in 1985, when five European research institutions (TRIALOG in Germany, GRET in France, IIED in Britain, the 'Dipartimento di Urbanistica' of Venice University in Italy, and LCHS in Sweden) jointly organized a seminar on 'Shelter Policies in Socialist Third World Nations' in Kleve, West Germany. The event became the first meeting of this kind worldwide, and set the foundations for an informal but expanding network of specialists with a common interest in this topic. The amount and quality of the original material collected and presented at the seminar exceeded all expectations by the organizers, who felt that access to this information should not remain restricted to the 45 experts who met in Kleve, but should be made accessible to the wider public – particularly to our colleagues and politicians in the Third World and the countries concerned. This book, although containing a completely new and up–to–date set of essays, was compiled in this spirit, even if the majority of its authors were not participants in that first seminar.

The organization of this volume reflects the experience of the Kleve Seminar in many respects. The first chapter, **'Socialist Housing: Some Key Issues'**, outlines those topics which were considered the most critical determinants of a 'socialist housing policy' in the preparatory debates among the seminar's organizers. The same set of issues was presented to the authors of this volume as a guide for structuring the country reports, and to facilitate a comparison between the individual cases for the reader. Of course, our list of key questions was far too long to be covered comprehensively in all the presentations of this volume. Therefore the authors were advised to select and concentrate on those issues which they considered the most characteristic or outstanding elements within the particular national context. The selection of topics was, of course, further influenced by the author's personal work and research experience in that country and by the availability of information.

It was not easy to decide on the selection of the countries to be included in this volume. Some interesting, if not exotic, cases for socialist housing policies, like North Korea, Guyana, Burma had to be skipped because no competent author was available. More fundamental, however, was the question where to draw the line between socialist states and market economies. In the second chapter, '**Socialism in the Periphery**', *Reinhart Kößler* points to differences between anti–colonial liberation movements and leftist revolutions, and highlights some typical difficulties that Third World states face in defining a socialist development that departs from the classical 'Soviet' model relying on heavy industrialization. The case of the Soviet Union also differs because it can draw on a large hinterland to make it less dependent on international trade to satisfy its population's basic needs.

In the light of the fact that there is no uniform definition of a 'socialist country'[1], a decision was eventually taken to adopt the respective government's own claim to follow a socialist path as a pragmatic criterion to decide whether a country study should be considered in the making of this book.

The first country case is **Cuba,** presented by *Jill Hamberg.* Being one of the oldest socialist states in the 'Developing World' it offers much better housing conditions to the population than almost all other countries in Latin America. Although space standards are modest, nobody is sleeping in the street, and there are almost no slums and squatter settlements to be found in and around the towns. Nearly 100 per cent of the population are owners of the dwellings they live in, the cost of loans is modest, and land speculation is unknown. A particularly interesting way of house building is the *microbrigadas* – an authentic Cuban innovation. With a labour force of almost 40,000 these represent the most important contribution to new housing construction, renovation, and maintenance today, and thus constitute a model of popular participation and de–institutionalization which – by not depending on the individual's initiative and proficiency – appears to be superior to the current trend for privatization, and to passing unpopular government functions to 'Non–Governmental Organizations' (NGOs) which seems to be the trend in other Third World countries.

Nicaragua, covered in the following chapter by *Kosta Mathéy,* adopted some of the Cuban concepts, but, as a mixed economy, relies much more on individual initiative and private investment. A socially oriented housing policy provides free access to land with security of land tenure for all. The majority of the poor have become owner–occupiers in the ten years since the revolution. However, with the national economy dismantled by the war, the US embargo, and by the worsening terms of trade for its main export products coffee, bananas and cane, the margin for direct state intervention and investment is minimal. The recent liquidation of the huge Ministry of Housing seems to be both a logical and symptomatic measure advisable also to certain other countries which have started revolutionary reconstruction by establishing an ambitious state bureaucracy. The war situation has obliged residential communities to organize themselves for the satisfaction of certain basic neighbourhood needs. It can be hoped that this experience provides a sound basis for the future success of concept of society that incorporates strong elements of grass roots democracy.

---

1) A useful approach for definition approach is the Modes of Production concept, which suggests that each social formation comprises a number of different forms of production, but of which one is dominant over the others and could then be referred to as a label for the economic system. (Ruccio, 1988)

Guinea Bissau, entering independence in a rather unprepared situation after the departure of the Portuguese in 1974, presents a case of 'patch–work and fire–brigade'–type housing policies as *Julio Dávila* suggests in his chapter. As one of the world's thirty–eight poorest countries it cannot afford to insist on ideologically burdened shelter policies. Therefore, the adopted approach was rather pragmatic, catering for the loudest (say: urban) claims first, and accepting almost all international aid offers for different, and possibly contradictory, types of projects. The bitter lesson of this *flexibility approach* is the country's political dependence today, and its suffering under the IMF's and World Bank's standard requirements for structural adjustment, including the cancellation of most social services which were initially won as an achievement of the revolution. The experience calls for a discussion of 'minimal economic conditions' for conceiving a socialist housing policy (or any housing policy at all).

The case of **Cape Verde** is discussed by *Christina von Schweinichen.* The country, historically closely linked to Guinea Bissau, is in a slightly better situation since the country is so small that even little projects can make an impact. However, long lasting ecological mismanagement has led to recurrent famines which triggered off migration towards the towns and abroad. The large number of Cape Verdeans now living outside the country, mostly in the USA, guarantee a certain income in foreign exchange but make the country economically dependent from abroad. However, this situation differs from the case of Guinea Bissau where the powers lie with the international organizations: in the case of Cape Verde the interests of *individuals* have to be taken into account. For example, the nationalization of land and houses of absentee landlords would be a risky decision, because the mostly affected emigrated nationals would then withdraw their financial support and cause a nation–wide economic disaster.

Angola, outlined here by *Otto Greger,* gained independence at the same time as the previous two countries, but then suffered from the consequences of a long–lasting civil war – the so–called 'second liberation war' against South African (backed) troops. Even more than in the Nicaraguan case, this led to massive internal migration from rural areas towards the towns where the refugees felt safer. This spontaneous movement thwarted all anti–urbanization policies initially conceived by planners and politicians, but enforced, together with the frequent interruption of the country's communication lines, imaginative strategies for regional (and urban) self–sufficiency in food and other basic needs. The functioning of its strategy would be unthinkable without wide popular participation, and implies collective self–help in the housing sector, and the revival of traditional building technologies (the latter more for need than for conviction). Unlike Guinea Bissau, Angola as a non–borrower was not directly affected by economic interventions on behalf of the large international organizations; but it received military and development aid from Cuba, from where certain planning and housing concepts such as prefabricated building systems have been imported (often without much success). This assistance, however, was not conditional on any economic or social reforms – a positive model for South–South partnership.

Mozambique shares many of Angola's experiences, as *Paul Jenkins* explains. It was also hit by a civil war fuelled by the South African regime, and the cities were periodically de–linked from their hinterland. Popular mobilization and self–help (though more of the individual than collective type) are important elements in housing provision. The organization of neighbourhood concerns is handled through a highly decentralized political administration, incorporating the *dynamizing groups* and *bairros* as typical elements. In respect to international allies, Mozambique was less isolated than Angola and obtained considerable assistance from West European countries (by government and non–government organizations alike), and from international organizations (the World Bank). In line with this decision, certain early 'socialist' experiments in housing provision are bound to be replaced by conventional market solutions.

Tanzania, presented in the chapter by *Karin Nuru*, is an interesting case because it 'invented' the concept of *African Socialism*, which claims to offer a political alternative outside capitalism and the Eastern–European type of Real Socialism. Self–reliance was the guiding principle, and was tested in practice in the new *Ujamaa*-villages, for example. In urban areas there were early attempts at replacing slum areas and to guarantee high housing standards to everyone, but the financial limitations for implementing such programmes had to be recognized. A long–term achievement remains the nationalization of land, which is linked to a system of free and non–tradable user rights.

The chapter on **Zimbabwe** was written by *Ann Schlyter*. Being a former British colony Zimbabwe has inherited an urbanistic pattern marked by clear social/spatial segregation, and an elaborate planning and administrative structure, in a similar way to Tanzania. Initially inspired by a *social housing* supply policy, the government soon realized that it lacked the necessary funds to carry out such policies on a large scale, and opted for a cost–recovery approach which privileged the middle classes. It was hoped that the poorer population will eventually benefit, too, through a filtering down process, and through subletting opportunities in particular. A revolutionary element were the *building brigades* in Zimbabwe, introduced by inspiration from the Cuban *microbrigadas,* but – being rather a variation of municipal direct labour departments than of collective self–help – they proved unfit to compete with the private construction industry or the informal sector, and never made a quantitatively significant contribution. Also *building co–operatives,* another imported programme type, remained a marginal activity in Zimbabwe due to bureaucratic hindrances and the lack of convincing benefits to those joining them. However, in spite of questionable outcomes of its housing strategies, the Zimbabwean government has so far resisted – at least verbally – pressures from the World Bank to abandon the principle of housing as a social right and to adopt a market oriented approach instead.

Ethiopia, a country covered in a collective paper by *Sabine Wendt, Sabine Wähning, Kosta Mathéy,* and *Matteo Scaramella,* has, in pursuing an orthodox Marxist policy, achieved a number of perceivable housing improvements since the revolution in 1974. Among the most important advancements are the absolute security of tenure for all, and the elimination of land speculation. It has embarked on a villagization programme which, as in Tanzania and Algeria, turned out to be highly controversial, though for different reasons: in Ethiopia the rights and interests of ethnic minorities are often frustrated by these programmes, and vulnerable ecosystems are being destroyed for short–sighted benefits. Apart from the villagization programme hardly any other new housing has been built on a large scale over the last 25 years; bad building maintenance and overcrowding are rampant. Very recently the government signalled a departure from its austere communist ideology and invited the private sector and international organizations (including the World Bank) to invest in housing construction. It is, however, too early to assess the results of this policy shift.

The chapter on **Algeria** was written by *Djaffar Lesbet*. It shows how the country, after its liberation from French occupation in 1962, underwent a turbulent development. Initially rich revenues from the sale of crude oil provided the necessary finance to initiate an ambitious villagization programme, and to import prefabricated building systems to offer almost free accommodation to every Algerian in the country. However, an escalating urbanization process soon grew beyond control, the oil revenue ceased, and the need for maintenance of both the new mass housing and of the historical stock in the old parts of the cities exceeded the financial, administrative and cultural capacities of the government. Many of the new villages were left without the necessary infrastructure thus making them useless for their intended inhabitants. The state had second thoughts about accepting the overall responsibility to provide housing and changed its mind. Most housing responsibilities were passed on to the private sector. At the same time it became impossible to control speculation – which had devastating results for the poor. With one of the world's highest rates of population growth (3.1 per cent), continuing rural–urban migration, and a police force that suppresses any attempts of squatting, overcrowding has become a common feature; empty dwellings are traded on the black market and for foreign exchange only.

Vietnam, discussed in a joint paper by *Ngyên Duc Nhuân* and *Kosta Mathéy*, was, like Algeria, a former French colony and gained independence in the same period. However, a continuing and devastating war caused similar handicaps for development as in Nicaragua, Angola or Mozambique. The government was not in the position to guarantee, in practice, the right to housing that it had prescribed in the constitution. Apart from various villagization programmes of varying success, (central) state intervention in housing remained rather restrictive and included, for example, severe migration controls within the country to discourage uncontrolled urban growth. Simultaneously, the traditional custom of far–reaching local government powers was respected by the new regime and extended to many housing issues, too.

The spirit of local autarchy also became a leading contribution in the historical discussion about parasite cities, which were hoped to be avoidable through the demarcation of green belts to allow at least partial urban food–self–sufficiency. Apparently the housing and urbanization situation remained under control until 1986, when the orthodox political leadership was replaced by younger cadres, who ventured a political U–turn and instituted the concept of 'market socialism' in the national economy. Free personal movement was now tolerated countrywide, and provoked first appearances of squatting and pavement dwellers the streets and railway stations in the biggest Vietnamese cities. Commercial construction enterprises and private house building are being encouraged in the aspiration that investment by nationals living abroad can be attracted (the 'Cape Verdean model'), but the immediate result was the appearance of land speculation. Also subletting is now tolerated, but has not yet led to excessive 'hidden rents' like in Algeria, for example.

China – apart from Cuba the oldest socialist regime in the developing world and analyzed here by *Richard Kirkby* – experienced a series of radical (and partly contradictory) policy shifts in respect to housing and urban development. In particular the preferred location and executing agency for mass housing provision changed several times. But as a constant feature the state accepted a responsibility to provide housing for its citizens as part of the social wage, at least for the urban population, for more than thirty years. At the village level, the principle of local self–sufficiency equally remained a rather continuous feature.

There were recurrent though fruitless attempts to raise the average floor space per person. The financial and administrative resources set aside to maintain and expand the immense state owned housing stock were not enough to catch up with the increasing public demand for better housing and living conditions. New concepts were eventually tested from the mid–1980s onwards. Cost rents and private house ownership were the most outstanding features of a policy turn, that coincided with commodification and privatization strategies in other socialist countries.

Albania is the last country study in this volume, and was written by *Lena Mag–nusson*. The country also has a relatively long 'socialist' history, and represents an interesting case because for over forty years it followed its own, independent development path, remaining even relatively isolated within the socialist bloc. Although *private ownership* was banned from many aspects of daily life, housing was not affected – possibly a reflection of rural traditions. Migration and urban development, however, was strictly controlled with definitive *limits for expansion* defined by the so–called 'yellow lines' – the border between city and countryside.

It is more than tempting to search for common positive or negative experiences and prevailing present trends in the presented cases, and some observations are evident – like, for example, failures of villagization programmes or in attempts to achieve benefits of scale through industrialized building systems. There is a common emphasis on social mobilization and *collective* self–help housing activities, a recent trend towards privatization, commodification and inviting foreign funding from international agencies or from the Western bloc. The latter aspect is, of course, linked to the decline of Soviet financial assistance after *perestroika* and of former allies in Eastern Europe.

The specific circumstances of the individual countries are, however, much more complex than the short chapters in this volume suggest, and a large amount of important information necessary for a serious and systematic comparison could not be included for lack of space. Therefore a second seminar with the authors of the country studies, and with some additional researchers specializing on particular sectoral topics, will be organized following the publication of this book. The main objective of that coming event will be the comparison of decisive sectoral housing and settlement issues across the countries, and to assess the impact of the dramatic changes in Eastern Europe during 1989 and 1990 for future housing policies in Third World countries with a socialist perspective. We hope to be able to document the results of that analysis in a forthcoming second volume to this publication.

A book like this could never be produced by one person alone. Apart from the authors of the different chapters I want to thank my colleagues Yves Cabannes and Guillaume Chantry from GRET (Paris), Julio Dávila and David Satterthwaite from IIED (London), Daniele Pini and Marcello Balbo from DU (Venezia), and Lars Reuterswärd from the University of Lund, who were all co–organizers of the Kleve seminar and conceived together with myself the idea of a book like this in the first place. David Barkin, Joachim Brech, Mark Gimson, Brian Higgins, Per Ivansson, Birgit Krantz, Ronaldo Ramirez, Dorothy M. Rerrich, Farida Sheriff, and Nigel Thrift contributed, among many others, valuable help and ideas at particular stages in the preparation of the book. Last but not least I am grateful to John Duncan for the stylistic editing of most of the chapters and for his advice on all production matters. The German Research Foundation provided a grant which made it possible to invite the participants to the Kleve seminar in 1985, being the initial impetus for this joint effort.

February, 1990   *Kosta Mathéy*

References and further reading

Burgess, Rod, 1982. 'The Politics of Urban Residence in Latin America', *International Journal of Urban and Regional Research, no. 4 vol. 6,* London/GB, Pp. 465–467.

Burgess, Rod, 1984. 'The Limits of State Self–Help Housing Programs', In: Bruno, E., Körte, A. & Mathéy, K. (Eds.). *Development of Urban Low Income Neighbourhoods in the Third World,* Darmstadt, Pp. 15–60.

Castells, Manuel, 1976. 'Theoretical Propositions for an Experimental Study of Urban Social Movements', In: Pickvance, C. G. (Ed.). *Urban Sociology, Critical Essays,* London.

Engels, Friedrich, 1975. *The Housing Question,* Moscow: Progress.

Forbes, Dean & Thrift, Nigel (Eds.) 1987. The *Socialist Third World. Urban Development and Territorial Planning.*

Jameson, Kenneth P. & Wilber, Charles K. (Eds.), 1981: 'Socialist Models of Development'. Special Issue of: *World Development,* vol. 9, No. 9/10. Oxford: Pergamon.

Pradilla Cobos, Emilio (Ed.), 1982. *Ensayos sobre el problema de la vivienda en América Latina,* Mexico: Universidad Autonoma Metropolit., Pp. 472.

Ruccio, David F. & Simon, Lawrence H., 1986. 'Methodological Aspects of a Marxian Approach to Development: An Analysis of the Modes of Production School', *World Development,* no. 2 vol. 14, Oxford, Pp. 211–222.

Schmidt-Relenberg, N., Kärner, H. & Köhler, V., 1980. *Selbstorganisation der Armen,* Frankfurt: Vervuert.

White, G., Murray, R., & White, C. (Eds.), 1983: *Revolutionary Socialist Development in the Third World.* Brighton: Wheatsheaf Books.

White, Gordon & Elisabeth Croll (Eds.), 1985. Agriculture in Socialist Development. Special issue of: *World Development, vol. 13, No.1.* Oxford: Pergamon.

Socialist Housing

Some Key Issues

Kosta Mathéy

Looking at the built environment of both the West and the East, it is difficult to spot a convincing difference between a 'socialist house' and a 'capitalist' one. Although the organization of everyday life, the relationship between the sexes, the provision of communal services, and the percentage of people living below the poverty line should, and probably do differ theoretically in these two social systems, the basic need for housing is more dependent on climatic conditions and biological needs than political and economic parameters. It can be also said that the social formation of any country under consideration will invariably include some compromise and thereby combine elements found in either socialist or capitalist political principles.

However, the best way of responding to and satisfying the housing need is a highly political question. Since the access and distribution of such scare resources as land and the protection of the environment are matters which concern the whole nation, a co–ordinated effort is required among a larger number of people than just a family. It is also necessary to consider whether housing should be allowed to exist as an instrument for human exploitation, for such matters ought to be handled differently in a society which supposedly tries to satisfy the needs of the workers rather than to maximize profits.

At the point when they became liberated, a few countries – Cuba and Algeria, for instance – had a considerable and well–maintained housing stock available for distribution because of the exodus of the previous bourgeoisie. But the majority of countries – Nicaragua being one of them – were in the opposite position. They had to deal with a housing deficit accumulated by many years of capitalist rule and aggravated by damage caused by the war of liberation.

The typical situation after a successful liberation struggle or revolution was that almost no systematic research and co–ordination of popular issues could be made by the new leaders. But in the young socialist state there is a need drastically to revise the previous policies. Given also that there is usually a very young and inexperienced 'crew' of policy makers, advice is often sought from other socialist states. They, however, often recommend their own approach which is, all too often, adopted without major changes.

The evaluation of a housing policy should, therefore, identify those parts of the policy which serve the specific needs of the country, recognize those parts which have been too readily acquired and transplanted out of a different context, and look for aspects which could be recommended elsewhere under certain conditions.

National Development and Housing

Given the backlog of industrial development in all developing states and the typical burden of foreign debt, state expenditure tends to give priority to investments in the productive sector before raising the level of popular consumption. It remains a continuing debate in socialist states as to whether housing can be considered part of the productive sector, or whether it is a purely consumptive item. The necessity to rely on a healthy and locally concentrated labour force would strengthen the first argument, and has led to interlinked development of factories or agricultural centres and housing, for which certain projects by the Nicaraguan Ministry of Agriculture or China at particular periods can be cited as examples.

In capitalist states housing remains and is seen as a commodity, which should be provided by the market. Socialist countries, on the other hand, view housing as a social service, which must compete with other social services. For example, Nicaragua demonstrates that a greater number of people will benefit by government investment in a literacy campaign than if the same investment was made in house building. How far the state feels responsible for housing provision should, thus, be examined, bearing in mind the relationship between housing expenditure and other areas of production or social services.

The Land Issue

Land is a scarce resource and thus it is an easy target for speculation in societies with high population growth rates. The extracted rent on the land is not based on the input of labour by the landlord, and contradicts socialist principles. Bearing this in mind most socialist states have nationalized land, or at least attempted to control the transfer of land, in order to safeguard the optimum use of the land and in turn serve the social needs of the community.

It has been particular in places, where inflation rates were high before the liberation, for parts of the middle class to invest their savings in land. This has been done without necessarily intending to speculate and make a profit on the possible sale later on. Expropriation is problematic in such a case, since it would tend to threaten the government's support from a significant portion of the population. On the other hand buying the land at the market price and paying cash compensation to all those small land owners is largely beyond the means of a young socialist nation. Often nationalization and reprivatization of former large landholdings is the adopted practice. The government can in turn build up popular support, particularly among the rural population. However, this policy may prove to be short-sighted, for problems in the future will arise when plots need to be divided among a deceased owner's heirs, for example.

It may be concluded that, in many socialist countries, nationalization of all land may not be possible, and is probably not necessary either. It should be questioned, however, whether the state can succeed in controlling the transfer of land ownership and in prohibiting the practice of land speculation.

Administrative Structure and Popular Mobilization

Bureaucracy is a problem almost everywhere in the world, and even more so in economies which rely on centralist planning. On the other hand a population which has successfully led a liberation struggle has gained a certain degree of experience of self administration. A well–organized community can have the potential to offset the deficiencies of bureaucratic structures that it inherited from the pre–liberation administration or that have developed since. Most countries have established a community representation structure at a grass roots level, thus with the intention for greater participation in both decision–making and the execution of communal tasks. However, a typical problem seems to be a working link between the community level of grass roots democracy and the central bodies of the national government. Centralized co–ordination and planning is indispensable to facilitate balanced development. But decision–making from the top down must be avoided if local resources are to be mobilized and local needs effectively met.

Housing Production Programmes and Targets

The traditional approach by socialist states to housing needs was to provide mass housing. Particularly in Eastern Europe, and to a certain degree in Cuba, a considerable proportion of the population could be provided with high standard dwellings. With a well–organized state construction sector (direct labour), a qualified labour force could be steadily maintained and the production targets could be programmed well in advance.

In the Third World, however, mass housing has always been too expensive to build in great quantity leaving aside such oil–producing states as Algeria. Also the 'cheap recipe' of Sites–and–Services and Slum Upgrading, promoted as it is by the international agents, does not offer a solution which can be implemented on a large scale at affordable cost to the residents.

In the socialist Third World states, two specific kinds of programme in particular have been developed, which are not conceivable in a capitalist state. One of them is in the form of the 'building brigades' (or *microbrigadas* as a Cuban particularity) who try to mobilize community labour for housing production. The other is in the form of the Nicaraguan *Urbanizaciones Progresivas,* who work on the basis of skipping the requirement of cost recovery and land cost for the very poor.

The questions to ask, in relation to housing programmes and targets, however, are more fundamental:

1. Is there a need for specific 'programmes' and 'projects', since they invariably must represent an exception from the standard rule? Are there better means to achieve equally good housing conditions for the whole population?

2. The example of Hungary demonstrates that it is possible to produce an impressive number of housing units unparalleled in the other countries. But it is apparent that very little effort has been spent on improving the quality. Does the desire to fulfil a plan preclude a continuation of the 'numbers game'?

Housing Distribution: Access, Finance and Tenure

In capitalist states access to housing is generally regulated through the market, which from the user's point of view is segregated into either owner occupation or rented accommodation. In the rented sector the rent is intended to pay back the initial construction cost, but after the depreciation period the landlord continues to collect the rent which then becomes his profit. However, in the situation where the landlord is the state or a co–operative, this profit can be 'socialized', in which case that extra rent will be utilized to make payments towards new housing for other members of the community.

This very simple thought has led many socialist countries to opt for, and make available, state rental housing. This socializing of the cost of housing makes it possible, therefore, not to establish a direct link between the construction of the individual dwelling and the rent collected from the user (cost recovery), but to relate the rent to the income of the tenant (frequently fixed at about 10 per cent of the salary). In a situation where the state is both the landlord and the employer, the rent, it is suggested, could be made nominal or scrapped altogether (bearing in mind that the rent has to come out of the salary). In any case, affordability is eliminated as the necessary mechanism in the distribution of housing. Dwellings may then be allocated according to need.

The criterion and methods of allocating the houses can vary greatly, being administered through the bureaucracy workplace, or community representation. Sometimes merit was introduced as an additional criterion for allocation. It should be asked whether access to housing functions without discrimination according to need, and what other parameters can interfere.

Production Process and Technology

There are two aspects which deserve particular attention. One is the choice of technology in relation to the absolute cost of a building. The other is the matter of self–help construction (self–building), generally assumed to increase affordability to the user.

Following standard economic debate, the cost of any product may be reduced through increasing division of labour and industrialization. Most socialist governments consider this rule to be valid for housing as much as it is for other commodities. On the other hand, experience even from the most industrialized countries demonstrates that there are particular conditions in the production of housing which apparently inhibit such gains. Socialist states, such as Cuba, have also experienced that industrialized building can be more expensive than conventional building methods. Nevertheless, they often continue high technology housing production, hoping that due to the resulting increased productivity (relationship of labour to fixed capital) more workers can be employed in other sectors. Or else, the total production could be increased and the housing deficit more rapidly reduced on the basis of the same number of construction workers. Sometimes, the already–installed machinery–producing industrialized building elements (often gifts from other countries), cannot be left to lie idle.

The whole argument as to whether to industrialize the building industry is relevant to those countries with highly nationalized economies and high absorption rates of the effective labour force into the state employment system. However, the majority of countries moving towards socialism still have high rates of unemployment with the result that the application of labour–intensive technology is more appropriate.

Industrialized building systems tend to be highly dependent on imports, which ought to be substituted in order to save foreign exchange. Conventional construction methods often still use local building materials, or can be adjusted to their use with the help of appropriate technology. By the same token, small components made of local materials can be prefabricated in decentralized workshops. The Sandino system, used in Cuba, Angola, Mozambique and Nicaragua, is a good example for this possibility. However, it has been reported from Angola that the system does not meet the climatic requirements in certain regions.

One common argument about self–help housing holds that the user can contribute part of the building cost through his own unpaid labour, and also through the mobilization of private savings of his family and friends. However, since self–help labour is an unqualified form of labour by its very definition, such output of work thereby tends not to be very time–efficient. In the capitalist context a calculation of productivity on the national level is never made, because the economy is based on the 'in–house calculation' of individual enterprises. Extra labour spent by the worker in his 'free' time is not taken into account, or may even be calculated in such a way as to help to reduce his wage. However, in a socialist context, since a more complete calculation can be made, few arguments should theoretically exist in favour of self–built housing. Nevertheless, many socialist states rely increasingly upon the self–help contribution (though preferably of the collective type), but for a different reason: namely, to reduce the high expense of maintenance work and administration that would come from a central agency together with any consequential interference from the bureaucracy. There is a danger that both industrialized building and self–building could both become myths and be promoted on an ideological bias, originating from the context of different social formations.

Socialism in the Periphery

Reinhart Kößler

Experiments in socialism have taken place up to now almost exclusively in the periphery of the capitalist world market. Even the Soviet Union, the second largest industrial power in the world, originated from a revolution in a country that was marked by grossly uneven development, but above all, by backwardness, a large foreign debt, heavy foreign capital investments in the key industries and a tiny proletariat in relation to the 'peasant sea' that engulfed the industrial islands of Petrograd, Moscow and the Ukraine.

Victories of socialist revolutions not in the centres of capitalist accumulation but in relatively backward countries have formed a central and most unexpected feature of twentieth century history. This has fostered grave repercussions, above all for the concept and legitimacy of socialism itself. By being implanted into an environment where to 'catch up and overtake' appeared to be the order of the day, socialism was transformed into basically a modernist ideology. Development of productive forces, regardless of the meaning of the concrete working of machinery for the working-life of the direct producers, took precedence over considerations of how the aims of socialism could be advanced (see also Kößler/Muchie). For this reason, I prefer the term 'Soviet-type societies' to a misuse of the term 'socialism' or even to 'really existing socialism', which denotes in some criticisms that in actual fact no such thing was taken to exist at all.

The performance of socialist experiments has been ambivalent at best, and today socialists experience a seeming or real retreat the world over. But such a state of things ought to provoke questions rather than write off the entire project in melancholy resignation. These questions necessarily have to refer back to the roots of the socialist project; we are compelled to take stock of what has become of socialism on account of the unforeseen developments of our century; there is a need to understand the crises as well as the current or imminent changes in erstwhile 'model' societies such as the Soviet Union, China or Cuba; finally, there is a

19

legitimate interest in mapping out future avenues of development that might measure up to socialist standards.

Of course, it is quite impossible to cover all these aspects in a brief introductory chapter. I shall, therefore, limit the discussion to a few salient features in the recent fate of Third World socialism, along with some closing remarks on current trends and transformations. Before we review some of the problems associated with 'socialism in the periphery', it will be useful to recall how the historical foundation for this notion has evolved, namely the advent of regimes laying claim to socialism in the course of decolonization and national liberation struggles after World War II.

The Three Waves of Socialism in the Periphery

Developing countries claiming to build socialism have come into existence by a variety of processes. Roughly, there were three waves, each of which exhibits some distinctive features, although chronological overlaps are obvious.

A first wave may be located in the aftermath of World War II. These developments were marked by the *presence of Communist Parties* with a history usually reaching back into the founding years of the Comintern in the early 1920s. These parties had struck roots in their respective societies to quite different degrees. Above all in China and Vietnam, they had succeeded, in the wake of Japanese occupation, in becoming the legitimate representatives not only of social, but also of national aspirations, probably forming majorities in their societies. The most important development was the capture of central state–power by the Chinese Communists in 1949. This victory was the result of an autochthonous process where decisive groups inside the CCP gradually came to terms with Chinese reality, often in defiance of Comintern dogma. Above all, reliance on the peasantry assigned to the urban proletariat a much less conspicuous role than called for by Marxist theory. Soon after their accession to state power, the Chinese Communists, and in a different fashion also the North Koreans, entered into heavy criticism of Soviet principles of planning that contributed to the 'split in world communism' and culminated in military encounters. But this also gave rise to specific development strategies.

From early on, development strategies in the People's Republic of China tended towards a shift in emphasis from industry to agriculture, in contradistinction to the Soviet approach. Above all, being cut off from the urban proletarian milieu for over twenty years had caused decisive groups in the CCP to establish intimate contact with the peasants and to gain a deeper understanding of their potential for development. Yet, as has become apparent by now, basic problems associated with an early adaption to Soviet methods of planning and administration have not been set off by such a shift of emphasis. Latest developments will be discussed below.

In China, North Korea and then North Vietnam, internal developments and especially bloc orientation may be taken as predetermined by the ascendancy of the respective Communist parties. The situation is totally different in the case of societies that have attained formal sovereignty in the course of de–colonization during the late 1950s and early 1960s. Apart from the Indian states of Kerala and West Bengal,

Communist Parties did not come to power in a 'pure' and direct manner in Third World countries after 1949. In Chile, President Allende's government alliance included the CP, but it was not the dominant partner; in Afghanistan, the Democratic People's Party came to power in April 1978 in the wake of a military coup. In Cuba and Ethiopia, ruling Communist parties were formed many years after the respective regimes had been installed.

In comparison to the more or less 'orthodox' background of former member parties of the Comintern, socialist endeavours that got under way, especially on the African continent since about 1960, offer a colourful sight. As a common starting point they claim to follow a *'third road'*, independent of either the Soviet model or Western capitalism. In this group, a number of development strategies were conceived that have in common a quest to preserve autochthonous social structures; these were claimed to be more egalitarian and solidary than the conditions induced by colonial rule.

In most cases, 'African socialism' presents itself as a patchwork of sheer demagogy, designed to camouflage, through socialist rhetoric, a socio–economic and political situation in which little had happened apart from changing the skin–colour of the ruling clique. On the other hand, figures like Kwame Nkrumah of Ghana exert powerful influences even long after their deposition from power; and Tanzania's strategy of *ujamaa* has for a long time attracted considerable international interest and sympathy. In other cases, such as Benin or the People's Republic of Congo, military rulers have at some stage declared their 'socialist' aspirations; but little was changed by that except endeavours to tighten up state control over markets or opposition movements. There have been apparent exceptions, such as Burkina Faso under Colonel Sankara, or Maurice Bishop's 'revo' in Grenada, both of which foundered tragically on dissent among the ruling group. A notable exception of quite a different sort is, of course, Ethiopia where in 1974, a military coup forestalled what might have become a popular revolution, only to declare, after considerable bloody infights, the socialist orientation of the regime (Markakis and Ayele, 1978).

In practical terms, the search for a 'third road' addresses a real and urgent problem. It once promised, at least on the level of written programmes, a chance to overcome the industrialist bias inherent in the notion of modern socialism elsewhere. These strategies, while brandishing the banner of 'self–reliance', were not in themselves capable to overcome the material bonds linking their respective countries to a world market ruled by highly industrialized capitalist economies. This, apart from internal blunders, has to be considered as one of the strategic barriers to any attempt at social and economic self–determination.

The process of decolonization reached a new quality with the victories of *national liberation movements*. Defeats of colonial powers or neo–colonial regimes, attained after long years of armed struggle, led to diverse developments as exemplified by Cuba, Algeria, Vietnam, Cambodia, Laos, Guinea Bissau, Cape Verde, Mozambique, Angola, Nicaragua and Zimbabwe. They all have in common a broad coalition of social classes and strata, and also of political groupings or currents, all of which contributed towards the overthrow of the old regime. Generally at their inception, and in part even on their accession to power, these movements showed little 'socialist' aspirations. This holds true, for instance, for the movement of 26th of July in Cuba or the liberation movements in the former Portuguese colonies in Africa. Here, a socialist option emerged only in the course of the struggle or, as in the Cuban case, after victory had been achieved.

On the whole, national liberation movements followed a similar pattern. Fundamental social and economic change was effectively put on the political agenda. This would call, as a minimum, for effective agrarian reform and national – though not necessarily state – control over natural resources as well as over finance and any existing industry. By the U.S.A. and generally by the O.E.C.D. countries, such aims were perceived as a threat to their international hegemony and thus met with stiff resistance, including military intervention. This opposition is still present today, more than a decade after 1975, the year of the victory of the Vietnamese people and of independence for the former Portuguese colonies in Africa. It may be illustrated by the U.S. refusal to assist Vietnam in rebuilding a country destroyed by the war machine of the Western superpower or in the isolation of Cuba persisting over almost three decades; and it is present in the U.S.–backed destabilization strategy of South Africa, against the surrounding sovereign African states.

Under such circumstances liberation movements in power experience extreme hindrance in formulating and implementing their development strategies. But their obvious failure in most cases to 'deliver the goods' in terms of a better and more self determined life for the bulk of the population cannot be attributed solely to the external causes of isolation, world market hierarchy and state terrorism. Current difficulties are also homemade in decisive aspects; they arise from specific policy decisions generating or aggravating structural problems. Before reviewing some of these questions in greater detail, a closer look at the country that has served as a model for most subsequent experiences, even where these did not adhere slavishly to its precepts, may serve as a useful point of reference.

The Soviet Model for Development

For a long time, socialism and, above all, its Marxist tendency has been associated with the class politics of, or in many cases for, the proletariat. This implied a positive or even enthusiastic appraisal of modernity and industrialism. The *Communist Manifesto* saw the bourgeoisie not just as the exploiter of the working class under capitalism but, at the same time, it extolled the bourgeoisie as the class whose advent to power has removed medieval fetters that previously had tied down social and material progress, the class whose action had made all solid and stagnant social relations 'melt into air' (Berman, 1987, ch. 2).

By this dialectic, Marxism denoted industrial capitalism as the last decisive step to make human liberty a realistic proposition for society at large. The novel problematic posed by the revolutions of the twentieth century is their 'untimeliness' in terms of the trajectory envisaged by classical theory. Most societies that experienced revolution were backward in terms of industrial development: the proletariat, which Marxist revolutionaries had viewed as the main historic agent, represented but a small minority.

At the close of the Russian Civil War, Lenin formulated the problem in quite drastic terms when he said that 'the industrial proletariat in our country . . . is declassed, meaning it is thrown off its class rails and *has ceased to exist as a proletariat'* (Lenin, 1964, p. 116; my emphasis). In other words, a class that had made up some 3 per cent in 1917, had vanished altogether three years later. Lenin drew a most fateful conclusion. He envisaged the Communist party not just to represent and lead, but to *substitute* itself *for* the proletariat (Deutscher, 1987). This 'substitutism', to be sure, was only conceived as a temporary arrangement, but it contained grave dangers for the revolution. In Lenin's view, this situation had to be overcome by the very process of rebuilding and further developing Russian industry which was hoped to 'produce' a new proletariat and thus a class base, as well as justification, for proletarian dictatorship (di Leo, 1973, ch. 1). Deferred industrialization was thus given a new historical content.

It was precisely Russia that had experienced, during the last decades of Tsarism, a truly ruthless drive towards industrialization and modernization of the economy. In this effort, little heed was given to the needs of a population pushed close to starvation by relentless export offensives (von Laue, 1963). But this attempt to catch up with the West at considerable cost was very conservative in terms of the intended impact on the social fabric of Russian society. More than other late industrializers, Tsarism took particular care to preserve its structural base, conceived as the village commune and the absence of a strong urban working class. However, within a short time, the appearance on the stage of the working class and the demise of the village commune as a means of effective control over large masses of the rural population had proved this strategy futile (Zelnik, 1971; Shanin, 1985).

Soviet industrialization contrasted its Tsarist precedent decisively. The creation and growth of a numerous industrial working class was one of the foremost objectives, not only in economic, but, above all, in political terms. Although more successful than its predecessor, the Soviet experiment faced similar obstacles which persist even today – not only for 'socialist' developing countries, but even for the Soviet Union. The structure of trade with the developed capitalist industrial countries is indicative: speaking broadly, high–level technology goes one way, raw materials or half–processed goods go in the opposite direction. Thus, the Soviet Union today, regardless of its great advances in fields like military and space technology, still is only a secondary industrial power when it comes to competing in the world market. The watchword to 'catch up and overtake', sounded by Khrushchev for the last time, never has materialized. Today, fundamental overhaul of the longest–standing socialist experiment once again amounts to adapting to the pace of Western capitalism.

For a long time, Soviet methods of planning and administration have appeared as the epitome of a socialist path of development or even as the only conceivable one to most socialists as well as non–socialists. Thus, whenever national liberation struggles had brought Communist Parties into power, such as in China, there simply was no ready alternative to the Soviet model for overcoming the most pressing aspects of underdevelopment (Menzel, 1978, p. 81).

For a clearer understanding, we may recall the most significant features of the Soviet model. There was enthusiasm and some measure of demonstrable success in the huge build–up of industry during the first two five–year plans in the 1930s. Only recent research has shown the waste and disorganization engendered by forcing through such mammoth projects as the steel combines of Magnitogorsk or Kuznetsk (cf. Kirstein, 1984). Such giant projects were given absolute priority in resource allocation. They were justified by the quest for self–sufficiency and by the fear of renewed foreign military intervention. The latter was kept constantly alive as an important source of legitimacy for the Stalinist regime. Besides the apparent triumph of industrialization, there was the historic victory of the Soviet people over the German Nazi invasion. Lastly, Stalinism acquired a virtual monopoly in representing revolutionary Marxism as a result of Comintern policies aiming at the 'Bolshevization' of non–Soviet parties and establishing a monopoly for the CPSU leadership in the 1920s and 1930s, but also from the advance of fascism in Europe, which blotted out important dissenting traditions.

The Soviet experience thus almost out of necessity appeared to represent a tested alternative to capitalist development, above all in the periphery. It constituted the notion of socialism as a strategy for late industrialization and 'development', although this contradicted the overwhelming majority of traditional socialist programmes, Marxian and non–Marxian alike. The ascendancy of this approach was enhanced further by the fact that after World War II, anti–colonial and national liberation movements found it increasingly difficult to win allies in the West, once decoloniz–ation appeared to be detrimental to the short–run interest of the United States and its allies. The liberation movements in the former Portuguese colonies are salient examples; another case is Vietnam whose people had to fight a thirty years' war, less for socialism than for the chance of real national self–determination.

To be sure, no one spoke of simply copying Soviet experience; from 1956 onwards, alternatives emerged in China and Cuba leading to serious rifts in World Communism and certainly projecting a plurality little known for some time before. In a few former colonies, national paths to socialism were proclaimed, including 'African' socialism.

On account of long–term performance at home, there seems little substance today for a Soviet claim to hold out a model for socialist development. Nevertheless, the going notion of socialism is still associated with the socio–political and economic reality that pertained in Eastern Europe up to the mid–1980s. This implies large–scale industrial projects; a bias towards the development of heavy industry; drives for rationalization of the countryside favouring big agricultural enterprises; controls on and curtailment of market mechanism; centralized planning vested in a strong, vertically controlled state; and a one–party system underpinning political monopoly. Significantly, grass roots participation by workers or peasants has been absent from this list for a long time. Debate has raged over various methods of planning, over regionalization, over the autonomy of plant managers and 'moral' versus 'material' incentives. Yet until quite recently, the basic set–up has not been questioned. Rather, the system has been adopted, by and large, for post–colonial societies as well.

This may be exemplified by the policy pursued by Mozambique's Frelimo vis–à–vis industrial workers. In line with Lenin's position, Frelimo defined these workers both as the nucleus of the *future* social basis in its own development strategy and as a target for education including harsh disciplinary action in the realm of industrial relations. This was expressed with particular clarity by the late Samora Machel at the founding congress of the Mozambican trade union OTM in October 1983. Machel stressed the historical identity of interest between the working class and the 'whole people *(povo)'*. On these grounds, he denied to the union a role as an 'instrument of confrontation', for instance, in wage conflicts (Machel, 1983, p. 26). Instead, he assigned it the task of 'schools where we acquire the competence, the efficiency, the aptitude, the devotion and the love for work'. At the same time, Samora Machel stressed that the working class had to 'win and procure' its 'leading role' through achievements in production and by actually creating the coalition with the peasantry (1983, pp. 22, 24).

In Search of Alternatives

At present, all societies with socialist pretensions without exception find themselves in crisis. The crisis of socialism comprises both the societal project and the political programme. 'Socialism' in the sense just outlined has failed as a development strategy, has not brought a 'steep rise' in economic growth rates (Baran, 1957, ch. 8). In general, it has also failed in giving people a better chance to determine their own lives. In some cases at least, regimes with socialist pretensions actually have deflated mass activity and popular movements. Thus, it has been said that the military coup that set Congo–Brazzaville onto the road to 'socialism' in 1968 'overthrew . . . the most potentially democratic regime the Congo has ever known' and has resulted in 'the complete demobilization of the masses of the people' (Wamba, 1987, p. 106).

Above all, victorious liberation movements have shown a tendency to exert their newly–won control of the central state apparatus in a quest for rapid development. A salient case is once more Mozambique. Here, Frelimo, reconstituted as the Marxist–Leninist Party of labour, in 1980 proclaimed the overcoming of underdevelopment within only ten years. This was hoped to be achieved by the installment of large–scale enterprises ranging from steelmills to agricultural estates. This grand plan foresaw economic self–sufficiency (Saul, 1985, pp. 106–10), relying on large–scale transfers from agriculture for financing the programme of industrialization (Schoeller, 1981). However, neglect of the small peasant sector and pressure for large–scale, supposedly 'higher' forms of organization such as large village *nuclei (aldeais communais)* has not only led to losses in vital production potential, but has also entailed political cost that can hardly be measured in mere figures: an example is the estrangement of peasants even in former liberated zones (Adam, 1988; Rudebeck, 1988). This policy has been recognized by now as unrealistic *gigantismo* which superseded an incipient structure of 'people's power' after liberation in 1975 (Egerö, 1986, p. 135). Currently, the country is pressed by problems of a totally different order, due to the devastating effects of South African destabilization strategies (Hanlon, 1984, part 7). But even now, persisting consequences of *gigantismo* may be identified in squandered resources for ill–conceived and futile projects to the detriment of existing and viable forms of production.

A number of African states with socialist pretensions have attempted to remodel the countryside by a strategy of villagization, implying the development of large settlement nuclei which would improve the accessibility of public health and schooling facilities. This policy has in fact resulted in large–scale and sometimes forced resettlement in very many cases. Examples are Mozambique, Tanzania, Algeria and Ethiopia. In Tanzania, villagization was originally a central element in the programme for a self–reliant socialist economy laid down in the Arusha Declaration of 1967. After initial successes of *ujamaa*–villages organized on a voluntary basis, a nation–wide villagization programme produced deleterious results during the 1970s: uprooting most of the peasant population in a huge effort to re–organize the countryside led to large–scale losses in productive potential and has contributed decisively towards turning the country into a net importer of foodstuffs (von Freyhold, 1979, pp. 58f, 109). In the long run, villagization in Tanzania has offset the significant advances in education and public health that had been gained up to the crisis of the 1980s and that had served, to a large extent, to legitimize the programme.

In the cities, the Tanzanian experience may stand as an example for other countries. It is marked by tight state controls on the trade union movement legislated as early as 1962 (Shivji, 1986, pp. 229–35). While initially, urban wages were reduced in relation to farm income, both fell steeply in the late 1970s, with peasants hardest hit by the crisis (Bevan, 1988, pp. 79–82). What is more, the avowedly socialist policies of state–sponsored industrialization have reproduced colonial patterns of valorization, especially of the peasant economy; further, the attempts to introduce rigid state control over a whole range of products has fostered a burgeoning parallel economy (Biermann, 1988).

The deep crisis of the Tanzanian experiment in transforming a post–colonial society in line with principles of socialism and self–reliance confirms a general problem. Attempts to overcome the existing dependence on a world market dominated by the Western industrial countries and to achieve self–reliance have failed so far, and options for individual countries are very limited in a hierarchically structured world economy, as the present debt crisis demonstrates with brutal clarity (Hein, 1982). The same applies to various attempts by groups of Third World nations to join efforts, be it in the case of successive UNCTAD conferences where the Group of 77 has hardly succeeded in winning guarantees against vacillating prices and deteriorat–ing terms of trade for their exports; be it under the banner of 'collective self–reliance' and South–South cooperation. Ventures such as the Southern African Conference on Co–operation and Development (SADCC) which brings together various countries confronting South African regional economic control and military intervention have proved utterly dependent on grants from international or unilateral donors (Amin, 1987). The imposition of IMF programmes on countries like Tanzania underscore the actual power relations that exist in the world today. But the existence of a home–made crisis has to be acknowledged as well. It is no surprise when radical African scholars today stress the need for more popular participation as opposed to a reality in which 'socialist' aspirations have above all implied the strengthening of the central state apparatus and extension of state control over almost each and everything. This state dominated concept which stems from the Soviet model is now increasingly recognized to paralyze popular initiative which is so vital for any sustained effort to overcome the effects of underdevelopment and dependence (Goulbourne, 1987).

The 'Market' versus 'Socialism'?

Apparent failures of the Soviet model and of self-reliance strategies along with successive governments succumbing to the conditions set by the IMF and the World Bank have given rise to fears (or hopes) that legalization of existing market relationships, such as of small peasants, may be taken as a signal for an impending victory for 'capitalism' in 'socialist' Third World countries. Besides mixing up a whole range of diverging aspects of the situation, such interpretations seem to be based upon a misconception of both socialism and the market. The underlying conceptional debate over the market certainly indicates a deep crisis not only of the Soviet model but of all variations of 'real existing socialism'. At present, a hegemony of conserva-tive–cum–liberal arguments and concomitant solutions is evident. It has to be seen, among other things, also as an outcome of this very crisis.

The most celebrated example both of first an attempt at forced transformation and then of stepping back to seemingly modest concepts of social transformation is the People's Republic of China. Of course, China can hardly be compared with the medium–sized and impoverished African countries referred to above. But its recent experience is of interest precisely because here new policies were not just a form of crisis management. Obviously, these policies have been introduced in the verge of the disastrous experiments of the cultural revolution. But at the same time, the 'four modernizations' were conceived also as a grand strategy for further industrial development, albeit with important changes in favour of consumer needs, a more balanced industrial strategy, intensive instead of extensive growth and an opening–up towards the outside world (Wu, 1985, pp. 251–53).

After more than a decade of reforms and set–backs, significant changes have been achieved, although fresh problems have been generated as well. In the countryside, the change to commodity production and exchange has meant a shift from a policy of local or regional self–sufficiency to commodity exchange, and thereby, towards a resurgence of markets. There has been a decisive rise in productivity, largely attributable to new incentive systems (Kosta, 1987, p. 161); rural real incomes have risen significantly, but there is also the danger of increased stratification (Quaisser, 1987, p. 190). Similarly, in the city the abandoning of the 'iron rice bowl', symboliz-ing a basic level of provision for regularly employed industrial workers, has brought into the open unemployment especially among young people, thinly veiled by the phrase of 'those who are waiting for work' (Kosta, 1987, p. 166). In the countryside, underemployment is a major problem. The loosening of price controls and rising wages have fostered inflation (Kosta, 1987, p. 165) which today forms a persistent problem. The strengthening of market mechanisms has also facilitated the apparent spread of corruption in the state apparatus and parallel market structures.

It would appear that the Chinese leadership have to a large extent succeeded in achieving the aims originally envisaged by Lenin's New Economic Policy: to harness indigenous productive potential and also foreign capital to the industrialization effort while controlling the whole process from the 'commanding heights' of the economy, big industry and the financial system. At the same time, strictly centralist control remains the key feature of the state apparatus. However, the success of wiping out the danger of famine for the time being does not necessarily justify all the reform measures. The dynamics of this system are still unknown; current developments in Yugoslavia certainly demonstrate that the 'market' is not a safe remedy to the pitfalls of the 'plan', with destructive contests among firms pursuing the particularist aims of individual collectives.

Whether reforms like those undertaken in China may justly be interpreted as harnessing *capitalism* to a socialist perspective is quite questionable. Capitalism, to be sure, requires more than a market. As a socio–economic system, it implies above all the valorization of capital on a level where this forges all basic social relations. Markets, on the other hand, can exist under almost any form of society. It is therefore *not* necessarily a step towards capitalism when peasant farmers are allowed to market their harvest surplus or even their cash crops instead of hiding or smuggling it out of the country, selling it on the black market or simply not producing it at all.

The question of the market may be viewed from two interrelated angles. The market serves as a decision–making device by mediating between otherwise isolated producers. For a long time, it has been almost a dogma in socialist and, more specifically, in Marxist programmes to replace this mechanism by a central plan. Today, after some sixty years' experience with central planning, encompassing in principle everything down to single nails and screws, it is obvious that such a 'conscious' form of steering the economy does not necessarily imply a more rational use of resources. Apart from its distributive aspect, the market acts as a control mechanism in respect to the quality of the goods produced as well as to the satisfaction of existing needs. So far, non–market industrializing economies have not found an adequate substitute for these control functions. Instead, their being taken over by an almighty administrative apparatus has contributed largely to what has aptly been termed the 'dictatorship over needs' (Heller, 1985).

All this said, it should be remembered that the concept of socialism always has contained so much more than the elimination of market disproportions. Taken seriously, it includes the principles of radical democracy in the sense of empowering people to control and determine their own lives. In this perspective, Gorbachev's programme of reforms addresses the most germane shortcoming of a historical experience that has rendered socialism almost synonymous with central state control and political monopoly of the ruling party. Participation and democratic structures have become indispensable today for a number of reasons, including, for instance, new forms of industrial work processes which require consent and discussion among workers.

Under such circumstances, the widening of market structures may, to varying degrees according to the concrete reform project, not only afford some breathing space to rural and also to urban producers, but also to intellectuals, to people worrying about regional problems or about the ecology or to such nationalities who have found it particularly difficult to acquiesce in the cultural as well as material consequences of centralism and of *gigantismo* which tends to be a regular attribute of statism. In most cases, 'the market' implies de–centralization in the first place, a decisive move away from the centralist state, a step which to me is a prerequisite for any advance on the road towards socialism. To be sure, countries such as Mozambique or Angola, confronting continuous and vicious attacks by South African destabilization and state terror, will find it difficult to de-centralize under present conditions. War and the military call for centralism, and it is as hard to retrieve local control after so many years of war as it is to eradicate militarist modes of thinking from people's minds.

But still, the majority of countries laying claim to socialism today do have a certain manoeuvring space. An indicative feature is the wide variety of responses to the Soviet reform movement. In assessing the current situation, it has also to be noted that contrary even to, say, 1975, 'conventional' socialism has lost much of its attraction due to failed experiments, the atrocities committed by the Khmer Rouge, the war between China and Vietnam and, above all, by the Soviet intervention in Afghanistan. 'Socialist' development strategies seem to have failed in winning (or preserving) the backing by the majority of the population in many of the countries concerned. These setbacks restrict democratization processes along socialist lines and represent a historical mortgage weighing heavily upon any socialist project. The controlled introduction of a set of market elements thus may be suitable to create preconditions for future advances both on the level of material progress and on that of political culture.

Consumerism and Late Industrialization

Whereas the introduction of participatory and even of new market elements may be seen as part of a way out of the impasse of present–day 'socialist' experiments, the phenomenon of consumerism is of a different nature. But it is also closely related to the problematic of late industrialization, whether capitalist or socialist. Despite a growing awareness of environmental problems and of the limitations of disposable natural resources, development still stands for industrialization to the minds of an overwhelming majority, and socialist development still is synonymous with non–capitalist industrialization above everything else. The fundamental cause may be that modern industrial capitalism still is the dominant power in today's world. Its dominance is expressed not only in economic strength, unequal terms of trade and the debt crisis, or even in military strength embracing the entire globe. Industrial capitalism is the dominant and technically most advanced model of development today and projects its typical cultural patterns as the epitome of progress and the good life. This is the meaning of Coca–Cola in Beijing or McDonald's in Red Square, even though both these ciphers of dominant Western culture may not convince us of their healthiness or sophistication, let alone their being 'cultured'. Yet they symbolize cultural hegemony of Western consumerism which is intimately linked to the 'Fordist' model of accumulation (Lipietz, 1986).

The ideological linkage between Fordist industrialization and consumption patterns applies for socialist industrialization projects as well. Since Fourier and Marx, the dominant tendencies in socialist thought always have associated their aims with the latest and highest technological standards as guarantees for future generalized affluence. This has been an important premise of Soviet industrialization (Süss, 1985). After all, the 'dictatorship over needs' has consisted of defining the legitimacy of needs and thereby *denying* to the population at large a huge portion of the fruits of their work and maintaining high rates of investment in heavy industry and the military instead.

The legitimate wish to participate in consumption patterns that are propagated around the world as the very epitome of the good life gives a great deal of legitimacy to drives for late industrialization. At the same time, the 'positional character of industrialization' (Altvater, 1987, p. 36) makes it difficult for late industrializers, capitalist and non-capitalist alike, actually to catch up with the countries that have embarked earlier upon this road and are still advancing along the same trail. Ecological considerations aggravate these doubts. Industrialization along the lines of the 'overdeveloped' economies of today is not feasible on a global scale considering both the limited supplies of natural resources and the nature of outputs, such as industrial waste. Precisely because the development of present-day industrialized countries has rested decisively on the transfer of values and goods from today's 'underdeveloped' countries, it seems most unlikely that this experience can be repeated *ad infinitum.* A perspective of egalitarian development on a world scale, if realistic, therefore has to be conceived beyond the industrialist model (Caldwell, 1977). But at the same time, 'today, there does not exist a viable alternative to the Fordist form of industrialization' (Altvater, 1987, p. 53). In other words, having stated the difficulties of late industrialization in the sense of actually catching up, we still confront the sweeping hegemony of the Fordist model.

The absence of an effective alternative model of development is demonstrated also by current reform policies of the few 'socialist' countries that still have preserved sovereign power to decide over their own courses of action. Reform strategies both in the Soviet Union and China now centre around Fordist consumption patterns that had not been attained by central planning. The reform process has not implied basic shifts away from the hegemonic pattern of development. So far, it has favoured individual over collective use of long-term consumer goods, individual motorization on the road over public transport systems, especially over rail-based ones, while 'social consumption', which once figured large in the more successful 'socialist' experiments, has frequently been curtailed.

In the periphery, the dominance of the image of Western, and thereby of urban modes of living certainly has contributed largely to rapid urbanization. It is in the large urban centres, above all in the capital cities, where funds for development aid arrive, where they are distributed and in most cases, where they are disbursed. A strong bias in resource allocation towards the city has even been found in a country such as Guinea Bissau, where the liberation movement had, before its advent to power in 1973, strongly propagated the favouring of rural sectors (Schiefer, 1982). The urban and the industrial biases are obviously closely linked to each other and to a concept of development geared to the aim of achieving the economic profile of the most 'advanced' countries.

References

Adam, Yussuf, 1988. 'Kollektive ländliche Entwicklung und Genossenschaften in Mozambique – Die Lage in den alten "befreiten Gebieten"'. In Meyns, 1988.

Altvater, Elmar, 1987. *Sachzwang Weltmarkt. Verschuldungskrise, blockierte Industrialisierung, ökologische Gefährdung – der Fall Brasilien.* Hamburg.

Amin, Samir, Derrick Chitala, Ibbo Mandaza (eds.), 1987. *SADCC. Prospects for Disengagement and Development in Southern Africa.* London and New Jersey.

Baran, Paul, 1957. *The Political Economy of Growth.* New York.

Berman, Marshall, 1987. *All That Is Solid Melts Into Air. The Experience of Modernity.* London.

Bevan, D. L., et al., 1988. 'Incomes in the United Republic of Tanzania During the "Nyerere Experiment" '. In Wouter van Ginneken (ed.), *Trends in Employment and Labour Incomes. Case studies on developing countries.* Geneva, pp.61–84.

Biermann, Werner, 1988. 'Ökonomische Optionen durch Strukturanpassungin afrikanischen Transformationsgesellschaften am Beispiel Tanzanias.' *Peripherie* 33/34.

Caldwell, Malcolm, 1977. *The Wealth of Some Nations.* London.

Deutscher, Isaac, 1987. *The Prophet Armed: Trotsky 1879–1921.* Oxford (1954).

Egerö, Bertil, 1986. 'People's Power: The Case of Mozambique'. In Barry Munslow (ed.), *Africa: Problems in the Transition to Socialism.* London and New Jersey.

von Freyhold, 1979. *Ujamaa Villages in Tanzania. Analysis of a social experiment.* London.

Gey, Peter et al. (eds.), 1985. *Sozialismus und Industrialisierung/Socialism und Industrialization. A Comparison of the Economic Systems Poland, Yugoslavia, China und Cuba.* Frankfurt am Main and New York.

Gey, Peter et al. (eds.), 1987. *Crisis and Reform in Socialist Economies.* Boulder and London.

Goulbourne, Harry, 1987. 'The State, Development and the Need for Participatory Democracy in Africa'. In Nyong'o 1987.

Gorbachev Mikhail, 1987. *Perestroika.* New York.

Hanlon, Joseph, 1984. *Mozambique: The Revolution Under Fire.* London.

Hein, Wolfgang, 1982. 'Globale Vergesellschaftung im kapitalistischen Weltsystem und die Grenzen eigenständiger nationaler Entwicklung'. *Peripherie* 10/11.

Heller, Agnes et al., 1985. *Dictatorship over Needs. Analysis of Soviet Societies.* London.

Kirstein, Tatjana, 1984. *Die Bedeutung von Durchführungsentscheidungen in dem zentralistisch verfaßten Entscheidungssystem der Sowjetunion. Eine Analyse des stalinistischen Entscheidungs- systems am Beispiel des Aufbaus von Magnitogorsk (1928–1932).* Berlin und Wiesbaden.

Kößler, Reinhart, and Mammo Muchie, forthcoming. 'American Dreams and Soviet Realities: Taylorism and Socialism.' *(Capital and Class).*

Kosta, Jiri, 1987. 'The Chinese Economic Reform: Approaches, Results and Prospects'. In Gey, 1987.

Von Laue, Th. H., 1963. *Sergei Witte and the Industrialization of Russia.* New York and London.

Lenin, V.I. 1964. 'Novaya ekonomicheskaya politika i zadachi politprosvetov'. In Lenin, *Polnoe sobranie sochineniy* vol. 44, Moscow.

di Leo, Rita, 1973. *Die Arbeiter und das sowjetische System. Die Entwicklung von Klassenstrukturen in der UdSSR.* München (Italian ed., Bari, 1970).

Lipietz, Alain, 1986. *Mirages et miracles. Problèmes de l'industrialisation dans le tiers monde.* Paris.

Machel, Samora, 1983. 'Sindicatos: Contra o fome, contra a nudez'. *Tempo* (Maputo) No. 685.

Markakis, John, and Nega Ayele, 1978. *Class and Revolution in Ethiopia.* Nottingham.

Menzel, Ulrich, 1978. *Wirtschaft und Politik im modernen China.* Opladen.

Meyns, Peter (ed.), 1988. *Agrargesellschaften im portugiesischsprachigen Afrika.* Saarbrücken and Fort Lauderdale.

Nyong'o, Peter Anyang' (ed.), 1987. *Popular Struggles for Democracy in Africa.* London and Tokyo.

Rudebeck, Lars, 1988. 'Entwicklung und Demokratie – Notizen zur Volksmacht in Mozambique'. In Meyns, 1988.

Quaisser, Wolfgang, 1987. 'The New Agricultural Reform in China: From the People's Communes to Peasant Agriculture'. In Gey, 1987.

Saul, John, 1985. 'Mozambique: An Overview'. In Saul (ed.), 1985: *A Difficult Road. The Transition to Socialism in Mozambique.* New York.

Schiefer, Ulrich, 1982. 'Guiné-Bissau. Probleme beim 'nationalen Wiederaufbau' eines befreiten Landes. Essay über die Möglichkeit des Scheiterns'. *Peripherie* 10/11.

Schoeller, Wolfgang, 1981. 'Zur ökonomischen Entwicklung Mosambiks seit der Unabhängigkeit'. *Peripherie* 5/6.

Shanin, Teodor, 1985. *Russia as a 'Developing' Society.* Vol. I: *The Roots of Otherness: Russia's Turn of Century.* Basingstoke.

Shivji, Issa, 1986. *Law, State and the Working Class in Tanzania, c. 1920–1964.* London, Dar es Salaam, and Portsmouth.

Süss, Walter, 1985. *Die Arbeiterklasse als Maschine. Ein industrie–soziologischer Beitrag zur Sozialgeschichte des aufkommenden Stalinismus.* Wiesbaden.

Ticktin, Hillel, 1973. 'Towards a Political Economy of USSR'. *Critique* 1.

Wamba-dia-Wamba, E., 1987. 'The Experience of Struggle in the People's Republic of Congo'. In Nyong'o, 1987.

Wu Jiang-Lian, 1985. 'The Chinese Economy: The Shift of Development Strategy and the Reform of the Economic System' In Gey, 1985.

Zelnick, Reginald E., 1971. *Labor and Society in Tsarist Russia. The Factory Workers of St. Petersburg 1855–1870.* Stanford.

Part II: Country Studies

Cuba

Jill Hamberg

Introduction[1]

During the three decades after its 1959 revolution, Cuba occupied a nearly unique place in the overlapping space of the two worlds of which it was a part – the developing Third World and the more developed socialist world – and its housing policies in many ways reflected this particular situation.

At the time of its revolution, Cuba shared with most other Third World nations a highly distorted, export–oriented and import–dependent economy. Three–quarters of what little industry it had was concentrated in Havana, the capital, which accounted for more than a fifth of the nation's population. Living conditions in rural areas were not unlike those in most other Latin American societies.

But at the same time, Cuba had many of the attributes of a developed country: more than half its population lived in urban areas; the majority of both its urban and rural labour force was composed of wage earners, most of whom were unionized; and by some measures, its standard of living, especially in the largest cities, rivalled that of southern Europe.

On 1 January 1959, those who made the Cuban revolution took over a country with its economic and residential infrastructure largely intact, unlike the massive destruction faced by most other socialist governments that came to power in the wake of world wars, protracted rebellions, or natural disasters. Cuba has remained the target of unrelenting military, economic, and political aggression by the United States for the last 30 years. But the physical damage and loss of life were relatively less severe than that experienced in the years after progressive and socialist governments

---

1) Some of the material in this chapter was originally compiled for an article on Cuba in *International Handbook of Housing Policies and Practices,* edited by Willem Van Vliet, Westport, CT, Spring 1990: Greenwood Press. Copyright © by Willem van Vliet. Reprinted with permission.

Country Profile: Cuba

National territory: 114,524 km²
Population: 10.38 million; 66% 'white', 22% 'mixed', 12% 'black' (according to 1981 census)
Population density: 87 inhab/sq.km
Labour force: 3,987,000 (1985), 61% male, 38.3% female (1988)
    22.2% in industry, 17.6% in agriculture & fishing, 46% in services.
Unemployment: 3.4% (1981)
Urbanization rate: 68%
Capital: Havana; 2,036,800 inhabitants
Estimated natural growth rate: 0.7% (1973–1984)
Estimated urban growth rate:
Life expectancy: 72.2 years for men; 75.8 years for women
Infant mortality: 1.6%
Illiteracy rate: 2.2%
Religion: Official atheism, mainly Catholic and Afro–Cuban syncretic religions
Language: Spanish
Educational expenditure: 30.1 % of budget (1984)
Military expenditure: 10% of budget (1984)
Major export products: sugar 75%, petroleum products 11%, metal 5%, fruit 2%, fish 2%
Major markets: Soviet Union 54%, Iraq 30%, China 4%, Canada 3%, Japan 3%
Foreign assistance: $ 708.4 million (1984); sources: over 90% CMEA, 9.7 % World Food
    Programme, 1% OECD

Some important dates:
1492   First arrival of Columbus
1514   Foundation of La Habana
1899   Liberation from Spanish occupation, first US intervention
1925   Foundation of Communist Party
1952   Military coup and beginning of Batista dictatorship
1953   (26 of July) First attempt led by Fidel Castro to overthrow the Batista regime
1959   Defeat of the Batista regime, Castro becoming head of state
1961   Revolution declared "communist"; defeated US invasion (Playa Giron)
1964   Beginning of OAS embargo
1976   Socialist constitution of Cuba implying, among other reforms, new administrative re-
    gions, direct votes, decentralized government

Sources: Die Länder der Erde, Köln: Pahl–Rugenstein, 1982. Third World Guide, Montevideo: Third World Editors, 1988. Jean Stubbs: CUBA, the Test of Time. London: Latin American Bureau, 1989. Map from: Wilde, Cuba Hand-buch. Rielasingen: Unterwegs Verlag, 1988.

assumed power in other Third World countries such as Nicaragua, Vietnam, and the former Portuguese African colonies. These factors would influence the Cuban revolution's early measures and aspirations regarding housing.

Stages in Cuban Housing

Before discussing specific aspects of Cuban housing, it would be useful first to review the situation at the time of the 1959 Cuban revolution and summarize highlights of housing policy since then.[2] Further details are provided in later sections.

Before the revolution: Cuba's prerevolutionary housing situation reflected the country's general level of development and its history of dependence on foreign powers, first as a Spanish colony and, after 1898, as a neocolony of the United States. The country's enormous sugar earnings and its role as the center of Spain's declining empire meant that Cuba urbanized earlier and accumulated relatively greater wealth than most other Latin American nations. Much of this wealth was channeled into public and private building in urban areas, initially as an expression of Spanish colonial power, and then in the twentieth century as a major investment arena, with rampant real estate speculation after World War II.

At the time of the revolution, between 650,000 and 750,000 units were considered substandard, that is, about half of the total stock of 1.4 million units. The vast differences between city and countryside were also evidenced in housing. In 1953 (the year of the last prerevolutionary census), more than four–fifths of the rural dwellings consisted of thatched roof huts with dirt floors, known as *bohíos,* and less than 10 percent of rural houses had electricity or plumbing (IUA 1963; Fernández Núñez 1976). Six percent of Havana's population lived in shantytowns, a relatively low proportion compared to other Latin American countries.

In the two decades before the revolution, tenants – who in 1953 represented nearly three–fifths of urban households and three–quarters of those in Havana (IUA 1963) – acquired a series of protections and rights more advanced than in most Third World countries and even a number of industrialized ones. Cuba instituted rent control in 1939 and continued it in one form or another until the revolution. It included rent freezes and reductions and a right to permanent occupancy, although evictions for nonpayment were common and rents averaged over a quarter of tenants' income.

1959–1963: Housing–related legislation in the first years after the revolution halted evictions and rolled back most rents by up to 50 percent. The government did not nationalize urban land as such but did curtail land speculation by requiring

---

2) For more information on the history of Cuban housing since the revolution and its landmark housing laws, see Acosta and Hardoy 1971, Agüero 1980, Björklund 1989, Castex 1986, Eckstein 1977, Estévez 1984, Fernández Núñez 1976, Fields 1985, Hamberg 1986, IUA 1963, Mace 1979, Ortega Morales et al. 1987, Roca 1979, Segre 1980, and Vega Vega 1962, 1986. Note that most of these sources do not discuss self–built housing; official statistics did not begin to reflect accurately such units until the mid–1980s.

private owners to sell sites at low uniform prices to anyone willing to start construction within six months. Most urban land coming into government hands was taken from speculators under a different law permitting confiscation of property of those leaving the country. Cuba's two agrarian reform laws nationalized 60 percent of agricultural land and granted small farms to thousands of landless peasants.

The landmark October 1960 Urban Reform Law converted more than half of the urban tenants into homeowners. Most former owners were fully compensated and many even received lifetime pensions. The rest of the tenants – those living in slum tenement buildings – were eventually given long–term rent–free leases, but their former landlords received no compensation. Households were permitted to own no more than one primary residence and one vacation home. Almost all private renting and subletting were prohibited. All units built or distributed by the government after 1961 were assigned with long–term leases (under the legal concept of 'usufruct') at no more than 10 percent of household income.

The government experimented with an array of programmes for new residential construction in the early 1960s, until the U.S.–inspired economic embargo and other construction priorities took their toll on housing. The lottery was transformed into a mechanism to finance housing. The largest and worst shantytowns were demolished; their residents built replacement housing through the short–lived Self–Help and Mutual Aid programme. An extensive programme of new construction in rural areas was initiated. Loans and technical assistance were made available for private construction by owner–occupants. Latrines and cement floors were provided to more than 100,000 rural dwellings, and electricity and other urban infrastructure were extended to thousands of houses in low–income urban neighbourhoods.

1964–1970: During the rest of the 1960s, central government policy concentrated almost exclusively on new state housing construction, mostly in rural areas, although little was actually built. Instead, resources were concentrated on developing agriculture as well as the economic and social infrastructure.

1971–1975: After a major campaign, the 1970 sugar harvest set a record, but the effort severely disrupted the economy and also failed to attain its target of 10 million tons. It had the positive effect of provoking a profound reassessment of almost all aspects of Cuban life, including housing. The 1970 census indicated that central government agencies had created only a quarter of the houses and apartments constructed since 1959 (see *Table 1*). The rest had been self–built, often with some degree of informal local government support. Although most of these units were of poor quality, it demonstrated tremendous pent–up demand and people's willingness to take action to provide their own shelter. A labour shortage in construction and other industries, coupled with disguised unemployment, led to the creation of the 'microbrigades.' In this system, a group of employees from a given workplace formed brigades to build housing. During this period, state housing construction nearly tripled and partially shifted back to cities (see *Table 2*).

1976–1985: Many of the changes initiated in the early 1970s came to fruition in the second half of the decade. The 1976 constitution established a system of elections

Table 1: Total Public and Self-Built Construction of Houses and Apartments: 1959-88*

Period	Total Public and and Private Total Units	Percent	Government Housing Total Units	Percent	Estimated Self-Built Housing Total Units	Percent
1959-1970	416,400 (a)	100	99,600 (b)	24	316,800 (d)	76
1971-1975	212,000 (a)	100	81,000 (c)	38	131,000 (d)	62
1976-1980	246,000 (a)	100	82,000 (c)	33	164,000 (d)	67
1981-1985	342,000 (e)	100	135,000 (e)	39	207,000 (e)	61
1986-1988	302,000 (e)	100	85,000 (e)	42	118,000 (e)	58
Total	1,419,400	100	482,600	34	936,800	66

* *Bohíos,* units in tenements (i.e., rooms without exclusive use of sanitary services) and improvised housing not included.

Sources:
(a) CEE (1984a). Based on houses and apartments occupied in 1981 by year of construction.
(b) Fernández Núñez (1976).
(c) CEE (1980). Note that only 6,000 units were built in 1971, but annual construction averaged 18,000 from 1972 to 1975.
(d) Total minus government construction. Thirty percent of the self-built units 1970-1980 were subdivisions or reconstructions of existing units or adaptations of nonresidential structures (Medina 1984).
(e) CEE (1986); INV (1988). Government construction includes permanent units built in agricultural cooperatives and by the military. See footnote 4 for exclusions to self-built units for 1981-88.

(secret ballot, competitive) of officials to governing bodies on the municipal, provincial, and national levels. Moreover, the country's geographic and administrative structures were reorganized and decentralized. The new Economic Management and Planning System, approved in 1975 and gradually implemented starting several years later, introduced self-financing in most workplaces, decentralized some economic decision making, instituted one- and five-year plans, and legalized a small self-employed sector.

In the housing field, major trends included growing attention to maintenance and repair of existing housing, greater quantity and quality of informal self-building, and the slow decline of the microbrigades.

After nearly a quarter century of dispersed and uncoordinated housing laws, policies, and institutions and widespread public discontent about housing, Cuba's national legislature undertook the country's first comprehensive study of housing policy, culminating in the landmark 1984 housing law. It recognized the importance of self-building and attempted to resolve tenure, maintenance, inheritance, mobility,

Table 2: Average Annual Public and Self-Built Construction of Houses and Apartments: 1959-88*

Period	Total Public and and Private Total	Per 1000 Pop.**	Government Housing Total	Per 1000 Pop.**	Estimated Self-Built Housing Total	Per 1000 Pop.**
1959-1970	34,700 (a)	4.5	8,300 (b)	1.1	26,400 (d)	3.4
1971-1975	42,400 (a)	4.7	16,200 (c)	1.8	26,200 (d)	2.9
1976-1980	49,200 (a)	5.1	16,400 (c)	1.7	32,800 (d)	3.4
1981-1985	68,500 (e)	6.9	27,000 (e)	2.7	41,500 (e)	4.2
1986-1988	67,600 (e)	6.8	28,300 (e)	2.8	39,500 (e)	3.9

* *Bohíos,* units in tenements (i.e., rooms without exclusive use of sanitary services) and improvised housing not included.
** Population at mid-point of period (CEE 1986).

Sources: See Table 1.

and payment issues. It converted leaseholders living in government–owned housing into homeowners, permitted limited short–term private rentals, fostered self–built housing construction, and updated existing legislation regulating housing management, maintenance and repair, evictions, and the buying and selling of land and housing.

1986–1989: By the mid–1980s, Cuba had experienced a labour situation partially reminiscent of the early 1970s: a construction labour shortage coupled with unemployment, both disguised (overstaffed workplaces) and open (teens and young adults born during the 1960s baby boom). This situation coincided with economic difficulties precipitated by a sharp decline in hard currency to purchase imports and by distortions in the wake of the previous decade's economic reforms. At the same time, housing construction and repair enterprises, despite having greater resources, were proving woefully inadequate to meet the growing demand and expectations unleashed by the 1984 housing law.

The microbrigades, weakened but hardly moribund, were called upon to help address most of these problems. They were reorganized, revived, and given new tasks to such an extent that they became a central pillar of the reform process known as 'rectification.' In 1988 a new housing law was approved, retaining most of the basic policies of the 1984 law, but incorporating refinements contained in subsequent regulations and reflecting the new role of the microbrigades.

Overview of the Housing Stock and Urban Growth

Quantity and quality of the housing stock

By 1988, Cuba's 10 million people lived in some 2.75 million housing units.[3] As of 1981, the date of the most recent census, two–thirds of all units were single–family houses; 15 percent were apartments (21 percent in urban areas); nearly 5 percent (mostly in Havana) were tenement units known as *cuarterías, casas de vecindad, ciudadelas,* and *solares* (inner–city slum housing where households live in one or two small rooms and share sanitary facilities); and 13 percent were *bohíos,* representing two–fifths of all units in rural areas. More than half of the apartments and single–family houses were built since 1959, and two–thirds of them were self–built (see *Table 1*).[4]

---

3) Sources for this section include BNC–BPA–INV 1989; CEE 1980, 1983, 1984a, 1984b, 1986; and DCE 1976. See also BPA (Banco Popular de Ahorro) 1988; and Luzón 1988.

4) *Bohíos,* which are impermanent structures (usually rebuilt every eight to ten years), and tenements (almost all of which were constructed before the revolution) are not included in this figure. The 1980–1988 figures in Tables 1 and 2 also exclude two other categories: (1) units with walls of wood and roofs of tar paper or thatch (25,000 built during the 1981–1983 period); and (2) units with walls of adobe, mud, or palm leaf or board; and roofs of tile, metal, fibrocement, thatch, or tar paper (38,000 in the same period) (CEE 1983).

Ill. 1: A Cuban 'bohío' — the traditional rural one-room house built by the owner.
(Drawing by Michael Wilkens)

Between 1958 and 1988 the number of housing units increased by 87 percent, outpacing the 58 percent growth in population. Average household size dropped from 4.6 in 1953 (year of the last prerevolutionary census) to 4.2 in 1981. The decline was sharpest in rural areas (5.4 in 1953 to 4.4 in 1981) but almost imperceptible in urban areas. Average household size actually increased in some localities, especially Havana, the nation's capital. In 1981 the average number of persons per room was 1.03 (excluding bathrooms, but including eat–in kitchens), and per sleeping room, 2.07, although on both measures the averages were somewhat higher for urban tenements and rural *bohíos*.

The decrease in average household size is related to the fact that Cuba's rate of population growth has declined significantly since the mid–1960s and is among the lowest in the developing world. But in the early 1980s, the nation began to experience a veritable explosion in housing demand when the 1960s baby–boom generation started forming households. Continued rural to urban migration and the trend toward smaller families and a greater variety of household composition due to an aging population and low birth and high divorce rates have also increased overall demand.

The quality of housing as a whole has improved since 1959 but not at the same rate in all regions or for all measures. In 1981 virtually all urban housing had electricity (as opposed to 84 percent in 1953). Rural electrification dramatically jumped from 9 percent in 1953 to 46 percent in 1981 but was still deficient in remote mountain areas. In the 1980s, substantial progress was made in closing this gap, in some cases by constructing small hydroelectric systems or installing local generators to provide current for a few hours a day until these remote settlements can be incorporated into the national electric system. By 1990 all rural settlements are expected to have access to some form of electric service.

Water and sanitation have also improved but not quite as dramatically. In 1953 only one–third of all households had exclusive use of indoor piped water coming from a water main. By 1981 the proportion had increased to one–half (two–thirds in urban areas). A quarter obtained their water from wells (three–fifths in rural areas) and the remainder from rivers and streams. The proportion of urban units with exclusive use of indoor toilets increased from 45 percent in 1953 to 61 percent in 1981. In 1953 only 45 percent of rural houses had access to any kind of sanitary facilities, but this had risen by 1981 to 80 percent, mostly in the form of outdoor latrines.

Despite the fact that Cuba is still deficient in providing complete indoor plumbing, it enjoys a remarkably low infant mortality rate, 11.9 per thousand live births in 1988, perhaps the lowest among developing nations and lower than a number of European countries (*Juventud Rebelde,* 22 January 1989). Mortality and morbidity rates from diseases associated with poor sanitary conditions are also among the lowest in the Third World, a reflection of Cuba's advances in providing universal access to adequate nutrition and medical care.

Housing and Urban Growth

Cuba has been almost uniquely successful among developing nations in channelling most internal migration away from the capital and toward provincial capitals and other cities and towns, a feat accomplished largely *without* direct administrative measures to control internal migration.[5] Before the revolution, Havana absorbed 52 percent of internal migration, in contrast to only 12 percent between 1970 and 1981. In that same period, towns between 2,000 and 20,000 population grew at an annual rate of 3.4 percent and cities from 20,000 to 500,000 inhabitants at 2.3 percent, in contrast to Havana (0.7 percent) and the country as a whole (1.1 percent). Industrial location policy and improved living standards throughout the country have been the main factors responsible for this shift.

One key aspect of this strategy has been to urbanize rural areas by creating communities large enough to support social and consumer services. Four types of rural settlements have sprung up: (1) agricultural new towns (more than 400) for workers employed in the associated state farms (in many cases peasants were assigned these units after selling their land to the government) (Agüero 1980); (2) housing developments for sugar workers in or near to existing sugar mill towns; (3) new communities associated with agricultural co–operatives; and (4) new or enlarged hamlets, growing spontaneously or with deliberate government support.[6]

Although many of these types of settlement have been 'planned,' they have not always been planned in relation to each other or to the broader urban system. Hence

---

5) For foreign views on Cuban urban and regional planning see Acosta and Hardoy 1971, Díaz–Briquets 1988, Barkin 1978, Gugler 1980, Landstreet 1981, Slater 1982, and Susman 1987. For Cuban views, see Morejón Seijas et al. 1988 for a comprehensive review of migration, urbanization, and development, and IPF 1985 for an overview of urban and regional planning.

6)   Medina 1984; and Deas Martínez and Ginarte 1988.

the size of many communities may have been appropriate for their related farms, but they are not large enough to sustain an adequate level of urban services. Moreover, over time household members find jobs elsewhere, retire, marry, divorce, and so on, often leaving few of the community's residents working in the associated agricultural or industrial enterprise. Some planners have argued for larger settlements housing people employed in a range of local activities, rather than the more dispersed and segmented approach common up until recently.

Despite the relative success of urban and regional policies, Cuba has yet to achieve fully balanced regional development (Perdomo and Montes 1980). Mountainous areas, especially in the eastern provinces, have lagged behind, resulting in substantial out–migration and labour shortages in key agricultural crops. For that reason an intensive programme was launched in the early 1980s to increase social, economic, and recreational services and infrastructure in these areas. By the late 1980s out–migration had begun to decline and some areas even experienced in-migration (Deas Martínez and Ginarte 1988).

Even successes have not been without their problems. Neglecting Havana in favour of other areas may have suppressed its growth, but it is now paying the cost in severely deteriorated buildings. Other cities grew more rapidly but often in problematic ways. Since 1959 the populations of Cuba's largest cities have doubled but their land areas have tripled, a result both of uncontrolled growth and of planned developments occupying more land than necessary (Estévez 1984). Moreover, burgeoning urban settlements of all sizes have encroached on valuable agricultural land (Rodríguez Bello 1985).

Although direct administrative measures to regulate migration – such as residence permits or an internal passport system of the sort common in parts of Eastern Europe until very recently – continue to be rejected, indirect forms are being explored. The Isle of Youth, one of Cuba's previously underpopulated 'growth poles,' was so successful in attracting new inhabitants that since 1987 officials have been seeking effective ways to stem migration until sufficient housing and other needed services and jobs can be provided. Regulations issued in 1989 governing exchanges of housing units (see below) strengthen or reintroduce requirements for prior government approval for moves to the cities of Havana and Santiago, the Isle of Youth, certain neighbourhoods within Havana, and tourist or other specified areas.

Housing Construction and Technology

The National Housing Institute, established by the 1984 housing law, develops and coordinates housing policy on a national level and monitors the work of provincial and municipal housing departments. The Ministry of Construction, several other ministries, the microbrigades, and local government agencies are responsible for building state–sponsored housing. The People's Savings Bank provides loans for private self–building and repairs. Local government agencies sell materials, run housing repair companies, and establish and enforce building and zoning regulations.

Total housing expenditures are not known, partially because the value of self-built units has not been calculated. But figures are available on spending by construction agencies, although they underestimate the total since other entities also build housing. In 1986, 9.3 percent of the value created by construction enterprises was allocated to new housing construction and related urban infrastructure and another 3.1 percent to residential maintenance and repair (CEE 1986). The construction and operation of state–built housing and all community services (e.g., garbage collection, street cleaning, etc.) accounted for 6.6 percent of the national budget for that same year (*Granma Weekly Review,* 12 January 1986). The overall housing and construction budgets are prepared by the Central Planning Board and approved by the national legislature.

There are basically two types of housing construction: state–sponsored and self-built. An overview of these is presented here, with further discussion below of microbrigades and self–building.

State–sponsored housing

The term 'state–sponsored' covers a number of different programmes and institutions:

State brigades: Since the early 1960s, roughly half of all government–built units have been erected by 'state' brigades, which consist of regular employees of the Ministry of Construction (MICONS). These brigades concentrate on building housing in labour–scarce agricultural or industrial new towns and more complex high–rise dwellings in large cities.

Microbrigades:[7] Microbrigades consist of teams of thirty–three employees from one or more workplaces. Sixty percent of the units are then distributed to their workplace labour force, and the other 40 percent is reserved for employees of workplaces without microbrigades and for households living in buildings that are uninhabitable or otherwise slated for demolition. Allocation of units within each workplace is decided in workers' meetings. Priority is given to those with outstanding job performance who need housing, but brigade members are not necessarily selected. Those remaining at the workplace agree to maintain production levels, and many also spend time on the construction project in the evening or weekends. Nearly half of the microbrigade members are assigned to build community facilities, while the rest erect housing.

In addition to workplace–based microbrigades, neighbourhood–level 'social microbrigades' have also been organized. Variations include residents of shantytowns

---

7) Microbrigades are listed here under state–sponsored rather than self–built housing for several reasons. Cuban construction, housing, and statistical agencies consider microbrigade housing to be state–built. Funds are budgeted centrally, brigade members are paid wages out of the state budget, and the production process is organized by state enterprises. But there is controversy about whether microbrigade housing should more properly be considered a form of "collective self–help" (see discussion of this debate in Mathéy 1988).

building new housing and unemployed youth, housewives, and retired construction workers providing maintenance and repair services for deteriorated units in their own neighbourhoods.

Other workplace-related or institutional housing: Aside from the Ministry of Construction, a limited number of other ministries – primarily the armed forces and the sugar and agriculture ministries – directly build housing to ensure a labour force in labour-scarce or remote areas. In addition, some self-building is workplace-related. Examples include agricultural cooperatives where members form informal building brigades and when enterprises, such as sugar mills, occasionally provide land, materials, and blueprints to their best workers. Twenty percent of agricultural land remains privately owned, 65 percent of which has been voluntarily incorporated into agricultural cooperatives since the late 1970s.

Local government: Since the 1976 decentralization of many functions to local government – and to some extent before that step – local authorities have played an increasingly active role in different phases of housing construction, including establishing local materials industries, assigning land, and building urban infrastructure. Local governments also directly build housing with their own resources. More important has been their role in enforcing building codes and land-use regulations and providing technical assistance, land, materials, and equipment for self-building. Administrative responsibility for the microbrigades has been transferred from MICONS to local government in some provinces, and some other MICONS functions may be decentralized as well.

Self-built housing

Under the 1984 law, low-interest bank loans are available to cover a wide range of building costs: materials for construction or repairs, land, architectural and other technical assistance, equipment rental, and contracted labour. Land or the right to build on roofs may be purchased at free market prices from private individuals, and permanent surface rights to state-owned land can be bought at lower 'legal prices.'

The term 'self-built' is used here to refer to informal actions initiated and largely organized by individual households to distinguish such activities from more formal self-help schemes. In practice, however, this kind of housing is rarely completely 'self-built'; the household usually receives assistance from family, friends, and contracted labour.

Building technology, productivity, and design

The quantitative and qualitative aspects of housing are intimately related to choices about construction technology and building standards and design.[8] During the wave of housing construction in the early 1960s, units were built to generous space and design standards using conventional construction methods. In rural areas single-family detached dwellings were erected on relatively large lots. Most urban units were in single-family detached residences or four-story walk-up apartment buildings. The exception was Habana del Este, an ambitious 2,300-unit development organized around the neighbourhood unit concept and the superblock, which combined high-rise and walk-up residential buildings with community facilities and commercial areas.

But by 1963 events soon forced a reevaluation of this approach. Materials for house building – most of which had been imported – became scarce due to the 1961 U.S.-imposed trade embargo, and even those available were soon diverted to more pressing needs.

For a variety of practical, and to some degree ideological, reasons, officials soon came to believe that they had no choice but to industrialize construction and to do so through the development of prefabrication. Conventional methods were hindered by the scarcity of imported wood to build forms for casting concrete. A construction worker shortage emerged, and it was especially difficult to find skilled craftsmen outside Havana. In the early 1960s Cuban officials estimated that 100,000 units a year would be necessary to relieve the housing shortage, and thus it was believed that the solution had to be a massive and speedy one. They perceived industrialized construction as being rapid, requiring less labour, humanizing arduous tasks, and using far less scarce wood than conventional methods. Industrialization was also seen as congruent with the 'scientific–technical revolution' and socialist planning.

Before the revolution Cuba already had some experience with a domestically developed lightweight prefabrication system, later renamed the Sandino system. In the early 1960s Cuba began developing its own and importing more advanced large-panel systems from Western and Eastern Europe. By the late 1970s, Cuba was using some ten systems. In international conferences, Cuban delegates waxed evangelical about what they saw as the advantages of industrialized construction – as opposed to 'appropriate' and 'intermediate' technology – for both the developed *and* the developing world (Glazer 1989, Sección Cubana FPAA 1979). They predicted that in Cuba even lightweight and semiprefabricated systems would soon be phased out in favour of the 'more productive' large-panel systems.

But in reality Cuba has experienced a highly mixed system all along. Self-built houses were and still are being built with traditional methods employed for generations, with occasional use of the Sandino system. Moreover, throughout the revo-

---

8)   For more information on construction technology, urban renewal, historic preservation, and other housing design matters, see Coyula 1985, 1989; Glazer 1989; and the Cuban professional journals *Arquitectura Cuba* and *Arquitectura y Urbanismo*.

Ill. 2: Low–rise walk–up blocks in Habana del Este, a well designed residential quarter east of the capital city. *(Foto by K. Mathéy)*

lutionary period there have also been active proponents of using traditional systems and materials.

The state–built sector has increasingly been dominated by the use of large–panel prefabricated systems, but expected productivity gains have materialized only sporadically. Cuban officials and publications have repeatedly denounced construction delays due to materials bottlenecks caused by poor coordination and a perpetual tendency to start more projects than available resources can support. Cranes and other scarce heavy equipment and vehicles are vulnerable to breakdown, and both equipment and labour are often diverted to higher priority projects. The installation of water and sewer lines is often delayed, and finishing materials are in short supply, leaving otherwise completed units vacant for months or even years. Even when new units are occupied, basic infrastructure and community facilities and services often lag far behind or are completely ignored. End–of–the–year round–the–clock building 'marathons' produce poor-quality structures, causing innumerable maintenance problems later. All these problems, plus a persistent lack of cost control, lead to projects wasting large amounts of materials and turning out much more costly than planned.

Numerous past attempts have been made to remedy these long–recognized problems, but the shakeup in the construction industry provoked by the microbrigade revival may bear some fruits. The new policy is to finish projects before starting others, and more emphasis is being placed on completions than value produced. More effective cost–control mechanisms and greater attention to materials storage are resulting in projects being completed more rapidly and at a lower cost. Services and infrastructure are to be built at the same time as housing, especially in the newly

Ill. 3: The small scale prefabricated 'Sandino' construction system is widely used in Cuba, and was also exported to other countries.   (Foto by K. Mathéy, Drawing by F. Martinez)

created 'Comprehensive Development Zones.' The demand for construction resources is pump priming the building materials industry, which is increasing productivity, adding extra shifts, and launching major investments to produce additional equipment and substitute imports (which represent 14 percent of building materials). Some transportation–induced losses and delays may be avoided, and quality enhanced, by the projected use of more on–site prefabrication.

Aside from construction–related problems, apartment building and housing development designs have also come under fire for their monotony and generally poor site planning. Although planners agree on the need to achieve high densities, they debate the best ways to achieve this goal. Officials have noted with irony the apparent contradiction of policies promoting four– and five–story structures in rural new towns (to preserve agricultural land), while both planned and uncontrolled growth in cities has perpetuated urban sprawl.

High–rise buildings have been put forth as the appropriate solution but have been criticized in recent years because of their higher per–unit cost (extra reinforcement for high winds and earthquakes), greater use of imported materials (elevators, structural elements), increased energy drain, and greater maintenance cost. Even many of those who support a judicious use of high–rise structures in large cities, and then only in downtown areas, on principal streets, and at major intersections, resist the policy – often sought by local officials – of building high rises in smaller cities and towns. Although the policy of building high–rise structures in a limited number of areas continues – in part to employ existing prefabrication capacity – a shift from structures of 18 to 26 stories to those of 8 to 12 floors is slowly beginning.

Critics have argued that sufficient densities can better be achieved by constructing high–density low–rise buildings, 'in–fill' housing, and second stories on existing structures. New approaches to building design, construction, and site planning have emerged from lessons learned from historic preservation and urban renewal projects, and a new appreciation of positive features of prerevolutionary housing (coinciding with similar trends in other countries). The decentralization of certain design respon-sibilities to the municipal level has fostered closer ties between architects, builders, and users. For instance, in Havana, 'bulky' walk–up buildings for small lots are being designed to blend into the surrounding area, including varying facades to avoid monotony. Building in rural areas is shifting back to one– and two–story units, usually with backyards.

Architects are striving to apply similar concepts in new construction, including aspects such as mixed–use buildings, compact site plans, varied building heights, and maintaining the street as the focal point (unlike the 'tower–in–the–park' super-block). Such designs seek to overcome the monotony in current design and site planning and also to respond to studies indicating that undifferentiated open space tends to be poorly used and maintained. Generous space standards between buildings, borrowed from cold European climates, are not well adapted to tropical conditions, where shade is of the utmost importance.

In response to the rapid decay and near collapse of sectors of older urban areas, officials moved to protect historic districts and develop plans to deal with other deteriorating neighbourhoods. In the late 1970s Old Havana was declared a national landmark, thereby halting indiscriminate demolition; a comprehensive plan was

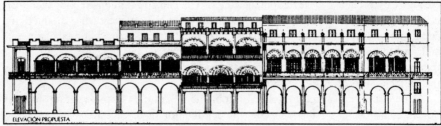

Ill. 4: Old Havana, granted the status of 'world cultural heritage' by UNESCO, is now being restored. Most houses will accommodate flats for the already present population and premises for social and cultural use.

completed; and greater resources were allocated for rehabilitating the main squares and their connecting streets. Furthermore, UNESCO granted Old Havana 'world cultural heritage' status in late 1982. Architects have thus been challenged to find ways to preserve not only Old Havana's hundreds of landmark buildings but also thousands of other structures in the historic district. They have also become interested in preserving other older areas, whether of historic value or not (Coyula 1985). Indeed, the concept of 'preservation' has been broadened to cover conserving most of the existing stock as well (Medina 1988).

Most Cuban policymakers are still committed to the long–term development of industrialized construction, although they believe that the shift from traditional methods will take much longer than originally envisioned, and debate still continues on the shape and speed of the transition. Attempts are underway to adapt the installed prefabrication capacity to more varied design solutions. The need to mass produce materials for traditional self–built construction and repair has led to greater emphasis on industrializing the manufacture of items such as bricks, cement blocks, and roof tiles, a form of industrialization relatively ignored in the past.[9]

Housing Tenure, Distribution, and Finance[10]

Tenure

When the 1984 housing law was passed, slightly more than half of Cuba's 2.5 million households were owner–occupants, and another one–fifth lived in government–owned units for which they paid no more than 10 percent of their income in rent.

---

9)   In her generally favourable discussion of Cuba's experience in industrializing construction, Jill Wells (1986) noted that the essence of industrialization is standardization and repetition, not necessarily full–scale prefabrication.

10)   For more information on the 1984 housing law and its regulations, discussed in this and other sections, see 'Ley No. 48: Ley General de la Vivienda' 1984, Vega Vega 1986, and the entire July–September 1987 issue of the *Revista Cubana de Derecho,* which contains relevant articles as well as regulations regarding multiple dwellings, workplace–related housing, tenements, pricing, sales, and others. For the 1988 law, see 'Ley No. 65: Ley General de la Vivienda,' 1989. For information on housing finance, see BNC–BPA–INV 1989.

The rest fell into a number of different categories. Many of these households held rent–free leases, including over 45,200 households living in rural new towns, 117,000 residing in urban tenements, and 23,000 very low–income families. Those who had built on land purchased in illegal or semilegal ways, or who simply squatted, were usually in a more ambiguous tenure situation.

One of the goals of the 1984 housing law was to establish a dominant and uniform tenure status by converting leaseholders into homeowners and legalizing most ambiguous or illegal situations. By the end of 1988, 450,000 former leaseholders had become owners, and their 'rents' were amortizing the purchase price of their dwellings. Another 330,000 – mostly self–builders – had been granted title at no cost. A minority of households did not immediately become homeowners, including families receiving public assistance and those continuing to live in tenements and grossly substandard shantytowns, all of whom still retain rent–free leases.

The tenure status of residents of the 145,000 units owned by or 'tied' to work-places received special treatment in the law. They represent only 6 percent of the total stock, but nearly a third of units built by the state since the revolution. Residents of workplace–related units are considered 'renters' and their monthly payments are only half of what owners pay for equivalent units (see below). Additional rent reductions of 5 to 30 percent are made for residents of 'tied' units in mountainous or otherwise remote areas. After 20 years residents can become owners with previously paid rents fully amortizing the purchase price.

The 1988 housing law further extended the concept of 'renting.' By late 1988, some 25,000 households eligible to become owners had not yet taken steps to acquire their units. They can choose to remain as renters, paying less monthly than new owners, or they can convert to homeownership within two years. Furthermore, in special districts, such as tourist areas, the government can assign units as rentals rather than in ownership.

Management, Maintenance, and Repairs

Another purpose of the 1984 housing law was to clarify responsibility for man-agement and ordinary maintenance and major repairs. Residents of single–family dwellings (no matter what their tenure status) continue to have responsibility for maintenance and repair of their units. Multifamily buildings, which are owned as condominiums, have been divided into two categories. Some 33,000 low–rise structures are self–managed by residents' councils. Municipal housing departments and residents' councils jointly manage 650 high–rise elevator buildings, almost all in Havana. All residents belong to these councils and are required to contribute a low monthly maintenance fee, which is reduced or waived for low–income house-holds. Local governments pay an additional subsidy to help maintain the more expensive elevator high–rise structures.

These residents' councils have followed in a long tradition of neighbourhood activism since the revolution. Local block clubs, called Committees for the Defence of the Revolution (CDR), are active in local cleanup and beautification campaigns, as well as citizen anticrime patrols, blood drives, and other kinds of voluntarism. The

Cuban Women's Federation is also organized on the block level. Most apartment buildings had residents' councils for many years – some more active than others—but they received little consistent support from government agencies.

Since the late 1970s much greater attention has been paid to maintenance, repair, and rehabilitation of the existing housing stock. As a result, the quantity of materials sold directly to residents has increased dramatically. The right to buy scarce items is allocated by local elected neighbourhood committees.

But it was not until the late 1980s that serious attention again turned to urban slum housing. Cuba's remaining shantytowns and inner–city slums are quite small compared to those in other developing countries, but they nevertheless represent a starkly visible reminder of the legacy of underdevelopment and the lack of adequate maintenance and repair. In 1985, Cuba had 117,000 tenement units accommodating 322,800 people; 416 shantytowns (61 of which were in Havana) where 300,000 people lived; 355,000 *bohíos*; 93,000 units shored up, of which 50,000 can be rehabilitated; and 11,445 households containing 45,300 individuals – almost all in Havana – lodged in units declared dangerously inhabitable or in shelters (BPA, 1988). Frequent building collapses, with their related deaths and injuries, have led Havana officials to expand their existing shelter capacity of 3,800 beds in fifty shelters to accommodate another 2,500 people.

The neighbourhood–based social microbrigades grew out of several local efforts in Havana's slums and shantytowns initiated by neighbourhood activists and local elected officials, who were able to garner resources and support first from municipal repair enterprises and eventually from national officials.

Housing Distribution and Redistribution

There are essentially two types of housing distribution: the 'primary' allocation of units (and the right to buy materials and state–owned land) by local governments, workplaces, and other organizations; and the 'secondary' redistribution of the existing units, land, and materials through sales, exchanges, and inheritance.

Primary allocation: Cuban policy makers have striven to balance different objectives in distributing housing: economic development, equity, and improving conditions for those in the worst situations. They have also sought to combat corruption, or the appearance of it, by fostering collective, public forms of allocation. But balancing all of these objectives has been no easy task.

In the early years, 'need' – always defined in terms of living conditions rather than income – was the main determinant in urban areas for allocating units confiscated from people leaving Cuba. But when 150,000 applications were received for 7,000 vacant units, unduly raising expectations and making a fair choice impossible, the government handed the units over to trade unions to distribute among their members based on need. By the mid–1960s the number of Havana residents living in buildings on the verge of collapse had mushroomed. Therefore, the selection process was transferred back to local administrators using a municipal list of those in dangerous situations, thus opening the way for what would appear to be corruption.

The establishment of the microbrigade system in the early 1970s coincided with a broader movement to increase productivity and deal with the apparent labour shortage through a variety of measures, including a law combating absenteeism and 'loafing.' Microbrigade housing, as well as other scarce consumer durable goods, were distributed in a public and collective fashion in workplace assemblies. But the criteria were based not only on need but also on 'merit,' which translated into good job performance and generally positive social behaviour. Between 1971 and 1985, 40 percent of all state-built housing was distributed by the microbrigades. Most microbrigade housing is still allocated according to these criteria, as is a portion of the elements needed for self-building.

About a third of government-built housing has been constructed primarily in labour-scarce areas and largely distributed by workplaces. In agricultural new towns units have gone to former peasants and salaried rural workers. The National Association of Small Farmers allocates materials among agricultural cooperatives, and the members of each cooperative determine who will receive the completed units. Only in new industrial areas, existing cities and towns in underdeveloped regions, and occasionally the outskirts of major cities has an explicit bias sometimes existed toward managers, skilled workers, technicians, and professionals. Although seen as necessary to ensure balanced regional development in the absence of restrictions on internal migration and significant wage differentials, this policy has been criticized, and greater occupational balance in allocation is increasingly common in such areas.

Unlike state-distributed housing, the range in housing quality and user costs in self-built units has reflected ability to pay to a much greater degree. Deliberate allocation of resources for self-building occurs when state-owned land and the right to buy materials are assigned. New regulations attempt to enforce minimum construction standards and prevent overbuilding. But in the countryside, the political and economic consequences of differences in housing quality are already apparent. The new homes of agricultural cooperative members tend to be of higher quality than the salaried cane cutters' new 'low-cost housing.' Small farmers, who have earned huge sums selling their produce in the short-lived legal farmers' markets or on the black market, have built even more elaborate abodes. This, in turn, discourages them from joining cooperatives.

The danger of corruption in housing distribution is always present – a danger that the collective and public microbrigade distribution process is designed to thwart. Indeed, a number of well-publicized instances have come to light of high-level or well-connected officials illicitly obtaining housing resources for themselves, relatives, friends, or lovers. But while the political cost of both revealed and rumoured corruption can be high, such situations probably represent a minute portion of new housing and an even smaller share of the total housing stock.

It is on the other end of the spectrum – those who are deliberately denied better housing – that other problems have also arisen. In the revolution's first years the worst shantytowns were cleared and their residents relocated to new housing, as a matter of simple justice and on the assumption that job opportunities and new housing would eliminate perceived antisocial behaviour of some of their residents.

The early Self–Help and Mutual Aid programme (run by the Welfare Ministry rather than the one dealing with construction) relocated former shantytown dwellers together in communities each averaging 100 families scattered throughout the largest cities. But this strategy was soon abandoned in favour of dispersing former residents of these settlements and other urban slum areas throughout new and existing housing to more fully integrate them into society and avoid stigmatizing them as former slum dwellers.[11]

After 1970 this approach changed markedly. Rewarding slackers with coveted housing was seen as being just as demoralizing to industrious workers as paying loafers the same wages whether or not they came to work. A process of 'creaming' the most active and hard–working families from the worst slums appears to have occurred, leaving behind those believed to have social problems. Indeed, each successive wave of concern about preventing juvenile delinquency and crime – still low by international standards – has been accompanied by studies of specific neighbourhoods where antisocial behaviour is thought to be concentrated. The new emphasis on rehabilitating slums, replacing shantytowns with new housing, and distributing a portion of microbrigade units to those in the worst housing is beginning to reverse this situation.

The 'secondary' market: Before the 1984 law, private sales of land and housing were legal but only under very limited circumstances. Government permission was required, and the state had first option to buy, having only to pay the 'legal' price as determined under the Urban Reform Law. The selling price between private parties was also limited to the 'legal' price. Because of these restrictions, unauthorized sales at free–market prices were common, leaving many households without proper title to their dwellings or land. Even when carried out with government permission, under–the–table payments were frequent.

The 1984 law attempted to legalize and control what was occurring anyway. Provisions were made to legalize most previously illegal situations, and free–market prices were permitted for sales of land and houses. The state retained its right of first refusal, but apparently mostly as a form of land banking for future public projects and preventing housing from being erected in unsuitable areas. Within a year and a half after the law went into effect, overt speculation was so rampant that the government clamped down and began requiring that most sales be directly to the state, except in the case of property transfers to close relatives. Speculators included private farmers who sold produce at high prices on the short–lived farmers' markets, self–employed individuals, and black marketeers. Government agencies and state–owned companies also got into the bidding war, further pushing up prices.

Because of all of these problems with buying and selling, the most common way that Cuban families move is by exchanging their units. Before the 1984 law, the parties to the exchange retained the tenure status – leaseholders or homeowners – they previously held in their former residences. Hence it was not unusual to find

---

11) See Butterworth 1980; and Lewis, Lewis and Rigdon 1977, 1978, for 1970 studies of relocated slum dwellers.

'state-owned' housing developments partially occupied by people 'owning' their own units. Since the new law converted the vast majority of households into owners, this is less of a problem. Regulations have been issued dealing with house swaps between households with different tenure status and units of different value.

Since home loans are personal loans, not mortgages, when families trade dwellings, they normally take their debt obligations with them. However, the 1984 law permits the parties to exchange their debt or one party to assume the debt on both dwellings. In many cases additional payments reflecting free-market prices are made, which remains perfectly legal despite the crackdown on private sales. Most people exchanging their units do not need prior government approval, but the 1988 law allows any of the parties involved, or the government, to challenge any specific trade. However, prior government approval is required under 1989 house swap regulations to monitor moves to certain areas such as Havana, Santiago, the Isle of Youth, and tourist and other specified areas.

Houses for exchange are announced in classified advertisements, a system replacing the cumbersome Housing Exchange Offices in the late 1970s. People also put up signs on their houses, at bus stops, and in grocery stores. Some individuals have taken on an informal broker function, often organizing exchange 'chains,' a sequence of interrelated transfers among three or more households.

Another form of 'redistribution' is inheritance. Privately owned homes may be inherited, but a distinction is made between the right to occupy the dwelling and to

BOLETIN DE CLASIFICADOS DE LA DIRECCION PROVINCIAL DE VIVIENDAS EN C. DE LA HABANA ●

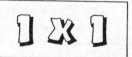

OFREZCO: Apto. a una cuadra Manzana de Gómez de 3/4, sala-comedor, cocina, baño, 2 balcones calle, agua, gas y telf. (todo amplio).
NECESITO: Casa o apto. en Ciudad Habana o Rpto. cercano, puedo reducirme, imprescindible gas y telf. Inf: 61-4545 Después 3 pm. Caridad (2).

NECESITO: Apto 2 1/2 hab. telf, gas, agua, Vedado o Playa. Inf: 30-6328 (14)

OFREZCO: Apto 2/4, sala-comedor, baño, cocina, telf, int. 1er piso.
NECESITO: Apto o casa 3/4, similares condiciones, telf, Vedado, Stos Suárez, Víbora o Playa. Inf: 30-3457 Después 6 pm (15)

OFREZCO: Apto moderno, pintado y nuevo de 1/4 chico y otro grande, sala-comedor, cocina, baño, balcón, gas calle, 2do piso.

OFREZCO: Casa en bajos, entrada de carro, sala grande, comedor aparte, hall, 3/4, cocina, baño y patio.
NECESITO: Casa independiente, 2 1/2 ó 3/4 c/garaje o posibilidad de hacerlo, Víbora, Sevillano o Rpto cercano. Inf: 30-2534 Jorge o Zulema, Calle 8 609-B e/ 25 y 27, Vedado, Plaza. (28)

OFREZCO: Apto moderno, vista calle, 1/4, sala-comedor, baño, cocina, patiecito, agua, luz y gas siempre.
NECESITO: Ampliarme en lugar no apartado. Inf: Clavel

Ill. 5: The Newspaper "Permutas" exclusively publishes advertisements of people wanting to swap dwellings.

receive its value. The current occupants, if they had lived with the now–deceased occupant for at least two years if close relatives, and five years if not, cannot be thrown out whether or not they are heirs. These occupants amortize the value of the dwelling over a period of time to the government, which, in turn, reimburses the heirs.

Financing and Payment

Since the revolution there has been an evolution in thinking about what, if anything, residents should pay for housing. The 1960 Urban Reform Law established several types of payment. Some existing homeowners with mortgage debt had their principal reduced by up to a third and interest on the debt was eliminated. The more than 200,000 tenant households who were converted into owners amortized the value of their units by continuing to pay their rents (most already rolled back in 1959) for between five and twenty years, depending on the age of the building. Hence by the 1980s virtually all of these households owned their units free and clear. Indeed, by 1972 only 10 percent of all households were still making some kind of amortization payment (BNC 1975).

Leaseholders in most housing built or distributed by the government paid no more than 10 percent of income, although in practice the range was between 3 and 7 percent since rents were rarely adjusted upward when incomes increased or additional household members took a job. Residents of microbrigade housing built before the 1984 housing law paid a maximum of 6 percent of income to reflect the 'surplus work' contributed either as microbrigade members or by working more on their regular jobs. Although the goal of eventually making housing free, proclaimed in the Urban Reform Law, was never fully attained, rent–free leases were granted to tenement dwellers and those living in rural new towns. Starting in the early 1970s very low income households were also exempted from paying rent.

The costs and form of payment for self–built housing varied widely, depending on a number of things: Was land obtained legally or illegally; at no cost, at the low legal cost, or at high free–market prices? Were materials obtained from nature, purchased from public agencies, received free, stolen, or bought on the black market? Was the unit a substandard shack or an oversized, high–quality residence? As a stopgap measure, in 1971 people who had already built on land they did not own were granted rent–free leases to their sites, but in all such future situations households were expected to pay 10 percent of their incomes for land rent in addition to any expenses of building their own dwellings.

By the late 1970s, the whole tenure and rent–setting system began to appear unfair. Only homeowners acquired equity and could sell and bequeath their property. Whether households became owners or leaseholders was often a quirk of fate: for instance, whether one's workplace had a microbrigade or whether sufficient materials or land were available locally for self–building. Furthermore, income–based rents, at first glance apparently equitable, began to be perceived as unjust. Many families paid relatively high rents for small or poorly located housing, and others spent little for large, centrally located units.

In response to these objections, the 1984 law established a totally different payment system principally based on the 'value' of the unit, including its size, construction quality, location, and depreciation. Under the new system, housing built or distributed by the government is amortized over a fifteen–year period (twenty years for high–rise buildings). Personal loans (not mortgages) are provided to purchase new units and for self–building and repairs by the People's Savings Bank, Cuba's only institutional source of consumer loans. However, credit is not available to buy existing units or privately owned land or to finance housing exchanges.

Households unable to afford these payments could automatically have the term of the loan extended and their monthly payments reduced to 20–25 percent of income, and in some cases further reductions were possible. The 1988 law lowered the maximum proportion of income paid by low–income families to 20 percent (for owners) and 10 percent (for renters). In 1988 loan payments averaged 16 percent of income. The relatively short repayment periods – and hence higher monthly payments – were deliberately set to absorb excess spending power in the economy. Agricultural co–operatives, however, have longer repayment periods (20 years, with 25 in mountainous areas).

In keeping with economic reforms of the mid–1970s, differential interest rates and pricing policies were instituted. Purchasers of new state–built housing pay about 85 percent of production costs at 3 percent interest. Microbrigade members receive a further 10 percent discount on the purchase price and interest reduced to 2 percent. Agricultural cooperatives receive building materials at wholesale prices and pay 2 percent interest in mountainous areas and 3 percent elsewhere. Households purchasing materials for repairs or construction are charged relatively high materials prices, required to make a 15–25 percent down payment, and charged 3 percent (new construction) to 4 percent (repairs) interest. Residents of buildings repaired or rehabilitated by government agencies (including the social microbrigades) are given discounts on costs. Furthermore, the government pays for major repairs over a certain maximum as well as the share owed by low–income residents who cannot afford to pay (BNC–BPA–INV 1989).

Property and personal income taxes were abolished in the early 1960s. Therefore, disposable income is the same as actual income (except for the self–employed who pay a monthly business tax), unlike many industrialized countries where income taxes often represent 20–50 percent of personal income. Ongoing operating costs are relatively low, with no real estate taxes, heating bills, or liability insurance (although optional fire and disaster insurance is now available).

Tenure Security and Housing Market Flexibility

The Urban Reform Law abolished private renting and subletting, with the exception of hotels, vacation homes, and 'guest houses.' But there was no forced 'rationing' of living space, as occurred in the wake of wartime destruction in parts of socialist Europe. Small families in large houses were not forced to move to smaller units or share their homes with others.

This situation has made it extremely difficult to accommodate the changes in household composition and internal migration. Families generously take in visiting friends and relatives but often find it impossible to get them to leave. Many divorced couples continue living together or with their former in-laws, sometimes along with their new spouses. People accepting jobs in distant provinces often live in hotels or worker hostels for extended periods, making it difficult to bring their families with them.

To deal with this situation, the 1984 housing law permitted residents to rent out rooms on a short-term basis at free-market prices to no more than two households. It was seen as a transitional measure to provide more dwelling options for recently divorced people, married couples living apart, people doubling up with friends and relatives, and employees temporarily transferred to other parts of the country. Setting maximum rents was considered in the course of drafting the 1984 law but was rejected as an administrative nightmare to enforce. Cuban officials have stated they expect complaints about exorbitant rent levels and some redistribution of income toward 'landlords' but that in the long run the only way to overcome this situation is to build more housing. The fact that renters usually share the same dwellings with their landlords tempers some of the worst potential abuses.

A potential landlord's greatest fear is that he or she will not be able to evict lease violators, and for that reason relatively few homeowners have agreed to rent out rooms, despite the enticement of free-market rents. Tenure security has constituted such an absolute right – nonpayment is dealt with by attachment of wages and unneighbourly behaviour usually through social workers or the criminal justice system – that the police are loath to carry out the few evictions that are ordered.

An issue producing greater controversy is the conflict between two rights: the right of residents to determine who lives in their homes and the right of tenure security. The 1984 law and previous regulations prohibited homeowners from evicting immediate family members. To discourage other unwanted household members from staying, owners could get a court order to withhold up to 50 percent of their income for six months. If they still refused to leave, an eviction could be ordered but was unlikely to be executed. Based on this experience, the 1988 law retained the government's role in arbitrating between household members and withholding wages, but ended police responsibility for physically removing unwanted inhabitants except in cases of clearly antisocial behaviour. At the same time, additional household members were protected from eviction – regardless of their relationship to the owner – such as mothers with children, the elderly, those who contributed to acquiring or renovating the house, and others.

Achieving housing market flexibility may conflict with other goals as well. Cuban policymakers seek to prevent housing from becoming a source of unearned enrichment. Hence they restrict home sales and sometimes take a dim view of house exchange brokers. At the same time, they would like to encourage people to move to homes more appropriate for their family size and health needs, nearby their current workplaces, or in underpopulated areas. But intra-, not to mention inter-, provincial swaps are difficult to arrange without intermediaries. Moreover, when the government cracked down on private free-market sales, it found people unwilling to sell because 'legal' prices were so low, not only compared with free-market prices but also with those of new government units. Steep depreciation formulas left homes built more than twenty-five years ago worth only 30–40 percent of comparable new housing. The government responded by adopting a dual pricing structure: it buys dwellings at higher prices but sells at lower ones.

Popular Participation

Massive public participation in a vast array of civic and economic activities has consistently been a hallmark of the Cuban revolution. Yet at the same time, there has been a pervasive notion that in a socialist society the state can and should ensure that all citizens have the basic necessities of life. The evolution in policy regarding the microbrigades, self-built housing, and other forms of voluntary construction labour reflects both of these tendencies.

Self-building[12]

In the absence of clear national policy regarding self-built housing before the 1984 law, local governments, publicly owned enterprises, and assorted private individuals stepped in to fill the void. A 1985 study revealed that, aside from items foraged from the natural environment such as wood and thatch, self-builders obtained most of their construction materials from local agencies and workplaces and to a small extent from small-scale illegal private manufacturers. Indeed, even dwellings of wood and thatch had at least cement floors (CEE 1984a), and quality has steadily improved ever since materials (and limited credit to buy them) became increasing available in the late 1970s.

Many self-builders obtained land from local government or through legal private sales. But others bought sites illegally or squatted on public or private land (sometimes with local government complicity or acquiescence). Some peasants owning land on the outskirts of cities and towns sold illegally subdivided lots. Infrastructure provision was minimal or absent. For instance, there were 300,000 illegal electrical hookups as of 1979 (one-sixth of all dwellings receiving electricity), which had been reduced by 1987 to 85,000 (half of them in the eastern provinces).

A special census of self-built housing conducted in 1983 (CEE 1983) revealed that 180,000 units had been completed between January 1981 and September 1983, and another 90,000 were under construction (including *bohíos* and other poor-quality units not included in other official statistics). Two-thirds of them were new units, and the rest were replacement housing. Of the 45,000 better quality units officially reported in 1986, one-fifth were replacement housing, one-quarter were additions to existing dwellings (usually on the second floor), and the rest constituted completely new houses.

---

12) For further information on self-building, see CEE 1983, CTVU 1984, Gomila 1988, INV 1988, Mathéy 1989, Rodríguez Bello 1985, and Zschaebitz and Lesta 1988.

The 1984 housing law declared a crackdown on uncontrolled construction. Until then, building and land use regulations were either nonexistent or only half-heartedly enforced. But since the mid-1980s, local authorities have more actively policed private (and public) construction and even demolished some illegal dwellings in their early stages of construction (León Candelario 1986). Moreover, bank loans are conditioned on obtaining a building permit.

National recognition has stimulated more self-building but has also produced a new set of problems. By early 1989, more than 135,000 units were under construction, creating a nearly insatiable demand for materials. Similarly, demand for state-owned sites greatly exceeded supply. Studies showed that the expense and difficulties of self-building tended to favour the more affluent, and self-building was associated with several well-publicized cases of black-marketeering, speculation, and cronyism. All these factors led to measures in 1988 designed to give priority to completing units rather than new starts and to allocate materials, land, and other building assistance to workers based on need, job performance, and social behaviour. At the same time, municipal agencies, with the assistance of the block-level CDRs, are attempting to catch up with badly needed infrastructure. But the number of officially recognized self-built completions actually declined from over 45,000 in 1986 to less than 33,000 in 1988, primarily as a result of the crackdown on illegal building, growing demand for materials by microbrigade projects, and greater control of materials on building sites, which in turn made a dent in the black market supply.

The 1984 law, recognizing the need to foster higher densities, promoted the creation of temporary building co-operatives to provide a way for self-builders to work together to build multifamily housing. Building cooperatives organized through workplaces were to receive priority for state land. But initial experiences with cooperatives proved problematic. Moreover, the microbrigade revival in all its forms seemed to obviate the need for such entities. Therefore, the 1988 housing law dropped provisions for cooperatives, but explicitly permitted 'groups' of people to voluntarily build together – e.g., two- to four-family structures.

Microbrigades[13]

The reasons the microbrigades were created in the early 1970s, and revived in the mid-1980s, were essentially similar: pent-up housing demand in urban areas (especially Havana), labour shortage in construction, plummeting workplace productivity, and greater emphasis on collective allocation policies. Why then were they on the verge of elimination, and what explains their resurrection?

The microbrigades grew rapidly until 1975 and then leveled off when materials shortages prevented further expansion. In 1978 officials proposed phasing out the programme for a number of reasons. First, microbrigade housing was perceived to be of lower quality and higher cost than equivalent buildings erected by state brigades. Microbrigade workers, who continued to receive their regular salaries from their workplaces, earned on average higher wages than unskilled construction

---

13) On microbrigades see Gomila 1988, Mathéy 1988, and Sicilia López 1987.

workers. Productivity was assumed to be lower since microbrigade members worked mostly on labour–intensive traditional and semiprefabricated buildings, and it was believed they lacked the skills to be employed on some of the new large panel and high–rise technologies.

Second, employees in workplaces without microbrigades and most of those living in unsafe and overcrowded dwellings were excluded, since almost all urban housing was distributed through the microbrigades. Third, the microbrigade system appeared to conflict with enterprise self–financing established by the new Economic Management and Planning System. Fourth, by the late 1970s overall productivity in the economy was increasing at a healthy rate, making it more difficult to remove workers without affecting production.

Despite trade union opposition, the slow phaseout began. In this 'twilight' period, the microbrigades were paid through the Ministry of Construction, rather than their workplaces; some 20 percent of the units were allocated for relocation housing for those in dangerous situations or whose homes were cleared for public works; and working in a microbrigade increasingly became seen as an activity just for people needing housing.

Meanwhile, the expected benefits of state–brigade construction failed to materialize. The rate of new housing construction dropped; both quality and productivity declined; and infrastructure and related community and commercial facilities largely ignored. Equipment, materials, and labour were often shifted to higher–priority projects. High turnover produced a less skilled and motivated building work force. Despite some degree of youth unemployment, construction jobs remained unattractive. Labour shortages proved so acute that Havana started temporarily 'borrowing' construction workers from the eastern provinces, where higher birth rates had led to a slight labour surplus.

The factors leading to the 1986 revival of the microbrigades involved not only the construction ministry's evident failure to improve production of housing and other projects but also the array of events provoking or coinciding with Cuba's 'rectification' process. They included wage inflation and overstaffing in many workplaces; the accumulation of vast sums of money – licitly and illicitly – by some selfemployed and other individuals (and related corruption and speculation scandals); a decline in voluntary work; concern with juvenile delinquency and other social problems and the apparent association of some of these problems with slum housing; and severe contraction in imports purchased with hard currency, provoking temporary layoffs.

The microbrigades, in their revived forms, seemed to offer something for everyone. Prior objections evaporated: microbrigades were now seen as reducing costs and promoting higher quality, productivity, and efficiency. Employees in overstaffed workplaces maintain their ties and seniority while temporarily transferring to the microbrigade – a politically more palatable solution than massive layoffs – and their salaries are reimbursed to the workplace by the central government. 'Social microbrigades' have provided neighbourhood–based jobs for unemployed youth and housewives and involved local residents in repairing and rehabilitating their own buildings.

Ill. 6: The 'Social Microbrigades' specialize in renovation and rehabilitation of existing neigh-bourhoods.   (Foto: K. Mathéy)

Ill. 7: Women's participation ranges around 20% in the regular, and around 50% in the 'social' microbrigades.   (Foto: K. Mathéy)

Costs are reduced by producing more with no increase in total salaries (except for those members of 'social microbrigades' not previously employed). Higher productivity and quality in construction can be achieved by a more motivated labour force, which can also call upon its own workplace to help resolve equipment and transportation bottlenecks. By developing their own productive infrastructure, microbrigades' resources are less vulnerable to being shifted to other projects. Moreover, microbrigades have been assigned to work on high–rise and other prefabricated buildings.

Unlike the 1970s microbrigades, which primarily concentrated on a few large–scale housing developments on the outskirts of major cities, the 1980s microbrigades are decentralized to each municipality. Hence the microbrigades have been in the forefront of seeking new designs for 'in–fill' and contextual building. There is even talk of establishing 'neighbourhood architects,' the design equivalent of the newly instituted local 'family doctor.'

The resurrected microbrigades affected women in a number of ways. In 1988 women represented 22 percent of the workers in regular microbrigades and had an even more prominent role in the social microbrigades devoted to new construction. Moreover, the initial emphasis on community facilities resulted in more than 100 child care centres for 20,000 children completed in two years in Havana alone, roughly 20 times the number originally planned for that period.

Several of the themes of rectification appear in connection with the microbrigades, although not without some resistance. One is an emphasis on combining self–interest with unselfish assistance to others. This is manifested in the microbrigades by allocating 40 percent of units to others, by devoting nearly half of their efforts to building community facilities, and by ensuring that all employees in need in the workplace are equally eligible to receive housing, whether or not they participated in construction. In addition, voluntary work is an integral part of the microbrigade concept: brigade members themselves work longer hours than normal; others from the workplace help out evenings and weekends; other citizens contribute labour through their CDRs or their workplaces. Some microbrigades function only after regular working hours (usually residents of slums and shantytowns who have not been able to get paid leave from work or from workplaces that cannot spare workers). A few microbrigades building community facilities by day have formed nighttime microbrigades to erect housing.

Some of these themes have occasionally met with incomprehension or outright resentment, which illustrates some of the dilemmas inherent in the microbrigade system. When the microbrigades were first revived, the proportion of units turned over for assignment to others was 50 percent. Pressure from the microbrigades – including informal slowdowns – pushed the percentage down to 40 percent. The enormous demand for housing has led some microbrigades to favour buildings with as many as units as possible, at times resulting in structures larger than appropriate for the site.

Although many microbrigade members are not motivated by their own need for housing, most are – and they sometimes become resentful if passed over when units are allocated. Brigade members have no objection to building community facilities and understand the need to construct day care centres, clinics, hospitals, schools, and family doctors' offices. But they prefer building facilities directly serving the housing they are erecting rather than working on unrelated projects.

Initial results have been impressive, but transitional and ongoing difficulties remain. Within eighteen months, Havana alone had more people incorporated in microbrigades than existed in the entire country in 1975. Inevitably, such rapid growth has created an array of problems: organizational difficulties; shortages of tools, machinery, and safety gear; large numbers of inexperienced workers requiring training; repetitive use of hastily – and often poorly – designed buildings; and delays in completing detailed blueprints, leading to premature building starts and subsequent problems in quality. Materials shortages, especially for finishing work, have meant that once again new projects are started before others are completed. Although productivity gains through better management have been remarkable in a number of workplaces, in others, attempting to maintain production has meant putting in overtime. Workplaces, schools, and neighbourhood organizations compete for voluntary workers, and it remains to be seen how long people can continue working such long hours without affecting their health, family lives, studies, and other commitments as well as the quality of construction.

Future Directions

Self–building and the microbrigades are likely to continue to occupy a prominent role in Cuban housing policy. Cuban officials generally prefer microbrigades over self–building for ideological and practical reasons: higher productivity through the use of more advanced technology and mass production, construction of community facilities and units for others in need, democratic allocation of units, contribution to controlling inflation and increasing productivity in the economy as a whole, and avoiding urban sprawl by promoting higher residential densities (BNC–BPA–INV 1989, Gomila 1988).

Nevertheless, state brigade–built housing is favoured in regions with greater labour reserves and where needed to ensure a stable labour force for economic development. But self–building is encouraged for additions, most in–fill housing, as well as in rural areas, small towns and cities, and the outskirts of larger urban areas. Indeed, self–building will probably continue to represent as least half of new construction. The main concern will be to improve quality, channel growth, assure affordability, and prevent illegal building and other illicit activities.

Until now 'popular participation' in housing issues has primarily consisted of taking part in actual construction – whether as self–builders, microbrigade members, or through other voluntary work – and attending block–level meetings called periodically by elected delegates to discuss local problems. But local planning departments have been urged to tap opinion in a variety of other ways (León Candelario 1986, Medina 1988). One is by fostering greater participation by the population in the discussion and approval of local land use, zoning, and master plans. Another is to survey residents' opinions about their experiences living in new planned developments to provide information for improving building and site designs.

Comprehensive and decentralized planning was inadvertently given a boost by the post–1986 building boom. The sudden plethora of disjointed and poorly planned projects made policy makers realize that greater coordination was necessary. In Havana the Group for the Comprehensive Development of the Capital was formed to promote neighbourhood and city–wide long–term and short–term coordination and to foster better urban design (Coyula 1989, Rey 1989). A similar group was soon created in the city of Santiago de Cuba.

Havana's Comprehensive Development Group soon saw the need to promote interdisciplinary neighbourhood–level planning and coordination. They established a pilot programme – called 'Workshops for Comprehensive Change' – in three areas: two inner–city slum neighbourhoods and one suburban shantytown that pioneered the social microbrigade concept. Project staff consists of architects, engineers, sociologists, and social workers who usually are residents of neighbourhoods. Project directors are respected community leaders rather than centrally appointed professionals or administrators. The Comprehensive Development Group envisions such neighbourhood programmes as incipient forms of urban neighbourhood government similar to the 'People's Councils' established to coordinate local activities in small towns in the mid–1980s.

Conclusions

Housing is widely acknowledged by Cuban leaders to be one of the country's most pressing problems. The 1984 and 1988 housing laws, the 1980s construction upsurge, and the revival of the microbrigades attest to their commitment to correct past mistakes, to seek new solutions in creative and flexible ways, and to devote more attention and resources to this issue.

But the importance of Cuba's housing problem reflects not only past neglect, errors, and the legacy of underdevelopment; it is, ironically, also the product of success in other areas. Other major problems have receded into the background in comparison to housing. Unlike the vast majority of developing nations – including many socialist ones to some degree – Cuba is no longer plagued by mass unemployment, low wages, malnutrition, poor health care, illiteracy, and low educational levels, in part because resources were primarily devoted during the revolution's first two decades to stimulating economic development and providing educational and health facilities rather than housing.

Housing is now accorded greater attention because of popular pressure and wider recognition of its role in promoting economic development, regional balance, orderly urban growth, and labour force and family stability. This makes it more likely that Cuba will attain its goal of producing 9.5 units per 1,000 inhabitants by the year 2000. The main challenge will be to use its resources effectively and efficiently to achieve that objective. But public and private production is not expected to increase appreciably at least until the early 1990s. More materials will be available and the current wave of community facility construction will be largely completed. However, other major construction projects – such as roads, dams, urban infrastructure, hotels, agricultural and industrial projects and a new major school–building programme – may still absorb much of the new resources. More importantly, Cuba's problems in earning hard currency and changes in Eastern Europe may have a significant impact on Cuba's economy and on the pace of building.

To what extent are Cuba's housing policies and their outcomes different than those found in capitalist Third World countries? Or, a related question, what features of Cuba's housing policies can be considered socialist?

At a time of major upheaval and change in both developed and developing socialist countries, attempting to define what constitutes socialism in general and socialist housing policies in particular is somewhat risky. This is complicated by a number of other factors. Specific housing policies may not appear particularly 'socialist' in themselves, but they function within the context of an overall social, economic, and political system that differs from capitalism. Moreover, most socialist Third World countries have mixed economies and are in the early stages of their transition to socialism. Cuba is of particular interest since it is one of the socialist Third World countries with greatest state involvement in the economy and longest experience of transition.

Despite the low priority accorded housing and the persistence of deterioration and overcrowding, Cuba's record stands in sharp contrast to the rest of the nations of Latin America (and other capitalist Third World countries), where one–third to one–

half of the urban population subsists in miserable slums and shantytowns and the rural population is even more poorly housed. Cuban families enjoy security of tenure and relatively low shelter costs, protections that would be the envy of even many U.S. and Western European households. Neighbourhoods are socially and racially integrated. There are no private banks, large–scale housing developers, land speculators, or construction companies.

The notion of what constitutes 'socialist' housing policy has been undergoing a considerable metamorphose in both developed and developing socialist countries. The image derived from Eastern European socialist countries was of housing owned, managed, and built (industrially) by the state and rented out at low cost as a social service (rather than as a commodity) to those in need.

Most of these features have been challenged or modified in Cuba over the last 30 years. This process illustrates some of the dilemmas and contradictions of the transition to socialism in a Third World country. Take, for instance, the issues of tenure and responsibility for construction and maintenance. Cuba's initial Urban Reform law combined home ownership for existing tenants and state construction and ownership for new housing. But after experimenting with public rental housing, Cuba opted again for home ownership. The overriding need to devote resources for economic development and other social programmes in Cuba and in other poor countries means that relatively little can be destined to housing. Hence, a considerable proportion of units is likely to be self–built for a relatively long period of time. Moreover, most of the improvement in the existing housing stock will come from maintenance, repair, and rehabilitation by residents (Medina 1984, 1988). Therefore, it was concluded that the tenure status most conducive to fostering such activities would be home ownership (Vega Vega 1986).

Virtually no country – socialist or otherwise – allocates housing based solely on need. Indeed, most socialist Third World nations usually give priority for what little state–built housing exists to workers in government agencies and key industries. The evolution of housing distribution policy in Cuba reflects this dilemma of balancing the needs and merits of the population, and the needs of economic development.

Similarly, the policy of providing dwellings free or at low cost as a social service meant that few units could be built and adequately maintained, while contributing to excess cash in the economy and consequent black marketeering and inflation. Housing is more like food or clothing than education or health care in that its occupancy or value can be readily transferred. Therefore, it functions more like a commodity than a social service, but within the context of a socialist economy. The pursuit of profit is not the driving force in the economy as a whole or in the housing sector.

Deregulation of renting and housing exchanges has provided greater flexibility to the housing market but at the cost of free market–prices. The about–face on deregulation of buying and selling, and the subsequent system of dual pricing, illustrates the difficulties even socialist economies have in suppressing unearned income from housing without draconian administrative measures, many of which have proved unworkable.

Can Cuba's experience be applied elsewhere? Many of Cuba's housing policies, such as the microbrigades, would be virtually impossible to implement in capitalist countries, given private control of workplaces and unemployment. Cuba's experience, however, may be of greater relevance to socialist developed countries, many of which have experienced low productivity coupled with labour shortages – but this will depend in part on future directions after the 1989 upheavals in Eastern Europe. It also may be applicable some socialist developing countries, if their level of development is taken into account.[14]

References

Acosta, Maruja, and Jorge E. Hardoy. 1971. *Reforma Urbana en Cuba Revolucionaria*. Caracas: Síntesis Dosmil. English Translation: *Urban Reform in Revolutionary Cuba*. Occasional Papers 1. New Haven: Antilles Research Program, Yale University, 1973.

Agüero, Nisia. 1980. 'La vivienda: experiencia de la revolución cubana.' *Revista Interamericana de Planificación* 14 (June): 160–173.

BNC = Banco Nacional de Cuba. 1975. *Desarrollo y perspectivas de la economía cubana*. Havana: Banco Nacional de Cuba.

BNC–BPA–INV = Banco Nacional de Cuba, Banco Popular de Ahorro, and Instituto Nacional de la Vivienda. 1989. *Cuba: Política habitacional y su financiamiento*. Paper presented at the VI Reunión del Comité Técnico de ALIDE (Asociación Latinoamericana de Instituciones Financieras de Desarrollo) para la Vivienda. Havana, October.

BPA = Banco Popular de Ahorro. 1988. Población y fondo de viviendas, 1971–1985. *Economía y Desarrollo* 88, no 2: 118–123.

Barkin, David. 1978. 'Confronting the Separation of Town and Country in Cuba.' In *Marxism and the Metropolis*, edited by W. K. Tabb and L. Sawers, 317–37. New York: Oxford University Press. Similar versions published in *Antipode* (1980) 12 (3): 31–40 (in English); and in *Boletín de Estudios Latinoamericanos y del Caribe* (Amsterdam), No. 27 (December 1979): 77–95 (in Spanish).

Björklund, Eva. 1989. *Good Housing for Everybody: An Original and Promising Approach to a Difficult Problem*. Paper presented at the International Conference 'Thirty Years of the Cuban Revolution: An Assessment,' Halifax, Canada, November.

Butterworth, Douglas. 1980. *The People of Buena Ventura: Relocation of Slum Dwellers in Post–revolutionary Cuba*. Urbana: University of Illinois Press.

Castex, Patrick. 1986. *La politique de production–distribution du logement à Cuba. Paris:* Groupe de Recherche et D'Echanges Tecnologiques.

CEE, Comité Estatal de Estadísticas. 1980. *Anuario Estadístico de Cuba: 1980*. Havana: CEE.

CEE, Comité Estatal de Estadísticas. 1983. *Censo de Viviendas Construídas por la Población 1981–1983*. Havana: CEE.

CEE, Comité Estatal de Estadísticas. 1984a. *Censo de Población y Viviendas: 1981. República de Cuba*. Vol. 16. Havana: CEE.

CEE, Comité Estatal de Estadísticas. 1984b. *La población cubana en 1953 y 1981*. Havana: CEE.

CEE, Comité Estatal de Estadísticas. 1986. *Anuario Estadístico de Cuba: 1986*. Havana: CEE.

Coyula, Mario. 1985. 'Vivienda, renovación urbana y poder popular: Algunas consideraciones sobre La Habana.' *Arquitectura y Urbanismo* 2: 12–17. English versions: 'Housing, Urban Renewal and Popular Power: Some Reflections on Havana.' *Berkeley Planning Journal* 2 (Spring–Fall 1985): 41–52; 'Housing, Urban Renovation and Popular Power.' *TRIALOG* (Darmstadt, West Germany) 6 (1985): 35–40.

---

14) See Mathéy 1988 for a discussion of the possibilities of transferring the microbrigade concept to other contexts; the Summer 1985 issue of *TRIALOG* (Darmstadt, West Germany) devoted to shelter policies in socialist Third World nations; and Wells's (1986) description of the problems of transferring Cuban construction methods to other developing nations.

Coyula, Mario. 1989. *Al reencuentro de la ciudad perdida.* Havana: Grupo para el Desarrollo Integral de la Capital.

CTVU, Centro Técnico de la Vivienda y el Urbanismo. 1984. *XI Seminario de la Vivienda y el Urbanismo: La construcción de viviendas por esfuerzo propio.* Memoria. Havana: Editorial del Centro de Información de la Construcción.

DCE, Dirección Central de Estadística. 1976. *La situación de la vivienda en Cuba y su evolución perspectiva.* Havana: Editorial Orbe.

Díaz–Briquets, Sergio. 1988. 'Regional Differences in Development and Living Standards in Revolutionary Cuba'. *Cuban Studies* 18: 45–63.

Deas Martínez, Mirta and Luis Roberto Ginarte. 1988. *Proceso de desarrollo del territorio de montaña de la provincia Santiago de Cuba.* Paper presented in the II Jornada Científica Internacional sobre Planificación Regional y Urbana. November. Havana: Instituto de Planificación Física.

Eckstein, Susan. 1977. 'The Debourgeoisement of Cuban Cities.' In *Cuban Communism* (3rd Edition), edited by I.L. Horowitz, 443–474. New Brunswick, N.J: Transaction Books. Spanish translation: 'Las ciudades en Cuba socialista'. *Revista Mexicana de Sociologia 40* (1, 1978).

Estévez, Reynaldo. 1984. 'Análisis de las realizaciones de viviendas en Cuba y en otros países socialistas. Recomendaciones.' Paper presented at the XI Seminario Nacional de Viviendas y Urbanismo sobre 'La construcción de viviendas por esfuerzo propio,' Havana, March. Havana: Centro Técnico de la Vivienda y el Urbanismo, MICONS (mimeo).

Fernández Núñez, José Manuel. 1976. *La vivienda en Cuba.* Havana: Editorial Arte y Literatura.

Fields, Gary. 1985. 'Economic Development and Housing Policy in Cuba.' *Berkeley Planning Journal 2 (1–2):* 53–80.

Glazer, Howard. 1989. 'Architecture and the Building Industry in Contemporary Cuba.' In *Cuba: A Different America,* edited by W.A. Chaffee Jr. and G. Prevost, 76–101. Totowa, N.J.: Rowman & Littlefield.

Gomila, Salvador. 1988. 'Participación popular en la solución de los problemas habitacionales. La experiencia cubana.' Paper presented in the Seminario Internacional sobre Autoconstrucción, Construcción por Esfuerzo Propio y Autogestión en la Producción de Viviendas en América Latina, University of Kassel. West Germany. April 23–24.

Gugler, Josef. 1980. 'A Minimum of Urbanism and a Maximum of Ruralism: The Cuban Experience.' *International Journal of Urban and Regional Research 4* (4): 516–34. Also published in *Comparative Studies in International Development 15* (Summer 1980); and *Revista Mexicana de Sociología* 43 (October–December 1981): 1465–86.

Hamberg, Jill. 1986. 'The Dynamics of Cuban Housing Policy.' In *Critical Perspectives on Housing,* edited by R. Bratt, C. Hartman, and A. Meyerson, 586–624. Philadelphia: Temple University Press. Reprinted as *Under Construction: Housing Policy in Revolutionary Cuba.* New York: Center for Cuban Studies, 1986.

INV, Instituto Nacional de la Vivienda. 1988. *Resumen Anual.* Havana: Instituto Nacional de la Vivienda, Dirección de la Economía.

IPF, Instituto de Planificación Física. 1985. *25 años de planificación física.* Havana: Editorial Científico–Técnico.

IUA, International Union of Architects, Cuban Chapter. 1963. *Architecture in Countries in the Process of Development.* Cuban delegation's presentation to the Seventh Congress of the International Union of Architects, Havana, Cuba. 1963. Havana: n.p.

Landstreet, Barent. 1981. 'Urbanization and Ruralism in Cuba.' In *Dependent Agricultural Development and Agrarian Reform in Latin America,* edited by L. R. Alschuler, 147–68. Ottawa: University of Ottawa Press.

León Candelario, Isabel. 1986. *Las Direcciones Municipales de Arquitectura y Urbanismo (DAU).* Havana: Instituto de Planificación Física, Departamento de Inversiones.

Lewis, Oscar, Ruth M. Lewis, and Susan M. Rigdon. 1977; 1978. *Living the Revolution.* Vol. 1: *Four Men;* Vol. 2: *Four Women;* Vol. 3: *Neighbors.* Urbana: University of Illinois Press.

'Ley 48. Ley General de la Vivienda.' 1984. *Gaceta Oficial de la República de Cuba 22:* 101–22.

'Ley 65. Ley General de la Vivienda.' 1989. *Gaceta Oficial de la República de Cuba 3:* 5–32.

Luzón, José, 1988. 'Housing in Socialist Cuba: An Analysis Using Cuban Censuses of Population and Housing.' In *Cuban Studies* 18: 65–83.

Mace, Rodney. 1979. 'Housing.' In *Cuba: The Second Decade,* edited by J. Griffiths and P. Griffiths, 121–30. London: Writers and Readers Publishing Cooperative.

Mathéy, Kosta. 1988. 'Microbrigades: A Cuban Interpretation of Self-Help Housing.' *TRIALOG* (Darmstadt, West Germany) No. 18: 24–30. Updated and expanded versions in: *Bulletin of Latin American Research* 8 (Spring 1989); *Habitat International 12* (4, 1988): 55–62; *Netherlands Journal of Housing and Environmental Research 4* (1, 1989): 67–83.

Mathéy, Kosta. 1989. *Appraisal of Self-Help Housing Policies and Practices in a Socialist Third World State: The Case of Cuba.* Paper presented at the International Conference 'Thirty Years of the Cuban Revolution: An Assessment,' Halifax, Canada.

Medina, Norman. 1984. *Control Urbano y las futuras Direcciones de Arquitectura y Urbanismo.* Havana: Instituto de Planificación Física.

Medina, Norman. 1988. *Experiencias en la formación e implementación de políticas locales de renovación urbana.* Paper presented in the II Jornada Científica Internacional sobre Planificación Regional y Urbana. November. Havana: Instituto de Planificación Física.

Morejón Seijas, Blanca, Margarita Rodríguez Cervantes, Beatriz Erviti Díaz, and Mayda Sotto Roque. 1988. 'Patrones de migración interna, distribución espacial de la población y condiciones de vida en Cuba,' Chapter IV of *Cuba: Interrelación entre desarrollo económico y población.* Havana: Centro de Estudios Demográficos, Universidad de La Habana, 317–406.

Ortega Morales, Lourdes, Alfonso Alfonso González, Angela Rojas Avalos, Gilberto Hernández Garmendía, and Obdulio Coca Rodríguez. 1987. *Nuevas tendencias en la política habitacional y la producción de viviendas en Cuba. Panorama de su desarrollo,* Hamburg: Technical University Hamburg–Harburg, FSP 6. Vol. 27.

Perdomo, José, and Norma Montes. 1980. 'Las proporciones económicas territoriales en la República de Cuba.' *Cuestiones de la Economía Planificada 3* (March–April): 103–21.

Rey, Gina. 1989. *Vivienda y desarrollo integral en Cuba: La Habana, por una ciudad más humana, bella y funcional.* Paper presented at the International Conference 'Thirty Years of the Cuban Revolution: An Assessment,' Halifax, Canada. November.

Roca, Sergio, 1979. 'Housing in Socialist Cuba'. Miami: Florida International University, International Conference on Housing Problems, 1979. Published in *Housing, Planning, Financing, Construction,* edited by O. Ural, 62–74. New York: Pergamon Press, 1979.

Rodríguez Bello, Ricardo. 1985. *La construcción de viviendas por esfuerzo propio en la provincia de Matanzas.* Paper presented in the I Jornada Científica Internacional sobre Planificación Regional y Urbano. November. Havana: Instituto de Planificación Física.

Sección Cubana FPAA. 1979. *Transferencia de tecnologías en la vivienda y sus condicionantes en Cuba.* Havana: Departamento Editorial del Centro de Información de la Construcción.

Segre, Roberto. 1980. *La vivienda en Cuba en el Siglo XX: República y Revolución.* Mexico: Editorial Concepto. Also published as *La vivienda en Cuba: República y Revolución.* Havana: Universidad de La Habana, 1985.

Sicilia López, Arnaldo. 1987. 'Las microbrigadas: Una manifestación popular en el campo de las construcciones,' paper presented in the Conferencia Internacional sobre la Vivienda y el Urbanismo. February 19–21, Havana. Published in *Información–a–Dirigentes* No. 7–8 (1987): 43–62.

Slater, David. 1982. 'State and Territory in Postrevolutionary Cuba: Some Critical Reflections on the Development of Spatial Policy.' *International Journal of Urban and Regional Research 6* (March): 1–33.

Susman, Paul. 1987. 'Spatial Equality in Cuba.' *International Journal of Urban and Regional Research* 2 (June): 218–42. Similar version published as 'Spatial Equality and Socialist Transformation in Cuba.' In *The Socialist Third World: Urban Development and Territorial Planning,* edited by D. Forbes and N. Thrift, 250–81. Oxford: Basil Blackwell.

Vega Vega, Juan. [1962]. *La reforma urbana de Cuba y otras leyes en relación con la vivienda.* Havana: n.p.

Vega Vega, Juan. 1986. *Comentarios a la Ley General de la Vivienda.* Havana: Editorial de Ciencias Sociales.

Wells, Jill. 1986. *The Construction Industry in Developing Countries: Alternative Strategies for Development.* London: Croom Helm.

Zschaebitz, Ulrike and Francisco Lesta. 1988. *Construcción por esfuerzo propio en la Ciudad de La Habana hasta 1985: Algunos alcances para su estudio tipológico.* Hamburg: Technical University Hamburg–Harburg, FSP 6, Vol. 36.

Nicaragua

Kosta Mathéy

Introduction

In the Third World, as elsewhere, housing is only a secondary problem, and can hardly be solved without a wider and simultaneous redistribution policy on the national, if not the international, level. Therefore, when after the Nicaraguan Revolution of July 1979 the Sandinistas started to convert the capitalist economy of the previous Somoza regime into a mixed economy with a strong social bias, it became of interest what could be achieved with mutual support between the government and the popular classes. If the Nicaraguan model were successful, it might give hope to the millions of homeless people in many parts of the world and encourage other governments to adopt at least some elements of its policy.

The Prerevolution and Early Postrevolution Situation

Nicaragua is a small country with a surface area of 129,541 square kilometres and a population of 3.5 million in 1987 (MINVAH, 1987). Housing has been a problem for a long time. In 1972 a severe earthquake hit the capital, Managua, killing 10,000 people and destroying 50,000 houses. In the following years little was invested in housing, and none of it benefited the poor. Further losses were suffered during the battles which preceded the liberation and by a flood in 1982.

When the Sandinista government gained power it inherited a housing deficit of 250,000 units which meant that two–thirds of the population were in need of decent housing. The 1971 census recorded that less than 61 per cent of dwellings had only dirt floors, 46 per cent were without sanitary facilities, 36 per cent had no access to water, and 59 per cent lacked electricity. In 1979 the population was 2,700,000 or 439,026 families. The housing stock consisted of 376,973 houses, which left 62,053 (14 per cent) families without homes. Of the existing houses, 187,890 were substandard (only one room or structurally dangerous), an overall housing deficit of

71

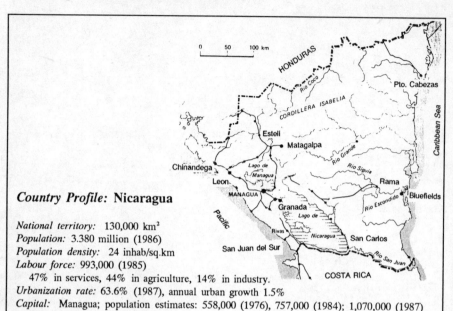

Country Profile: Nicaragua

National territory: 130,000 km²
Population: 3.380 million (1986)
Population density: 24 inhab/sq.km
Labour force: 993,000 (1985)
   47% in services, 44% in agriculture, 14% in industry.
Urbanization rate: 63.6% (1987), annual urban growth 1.5%
Capital: Managua; population estimates: 558,000 (1976), 757,000 (1984); 1,070,000 (1987) inh.
Average natural growth rate: 3% (1973–1984)
Life expectancy: 58.1 years for men; 62 years for women
Infant mortality: 7.4% (1983)
Illiteracy rate: 50% (1978), 13% (1984), 22% (1989), primary school enrolment 99%
Religion: Catholic
Language: Spanish
Educational expenditure: 10% of budget
Military expenditure: 20.4% (1980); 23% (1984); 50% (1988) of budget
Major export products: coffee 31%, cotton 29%, sugar 7%, meat 6%, fresh fruit 5%.
Major markets: US 39%, FRG 13%, Costa Rica 9%, France 6%, Netherlands 5%.
Foreign assistance: $ 6,200 million (1987);
   sources: 64% CMEA, 23% OECD countries, 12.7% EEC

Some important dates:
1502	First landing by Christopher Columbus in Nicaragua
1838	Liberation from Spanish occupation, proclaimed independent republic
1912–1933	Repeated occupation by US troups
1926–1933	Liberation struggle against US occupation led by Augusto César Sandino
1934	Assassination of Augusto César Sandino
1937	Beginning of dictatorship by Somoza family
1961	Foundation of FSLN
1972	Earthquake completely destroys the city of Managua
1979	July: Victory of popular uprising against dictatorship, Somoza flees to the USA
1979	(20. July) Revolutionary Sandinista government takes office
1984	First democratic elections, Sandinistas re–elected (65%)
1985	Trade embargo imposed by the US
1990	(Feb.) Second democratic elections, Sandinistas (41%) fail to gain the mayority

Sources: Die Länder der Erde, Köln: Pahl–Rugenstein, 1982. Third World Guide, Montevideo: Third World Editors, 1988. J– Collins (Ed.), NICARAGUA, San Francisco: Institute for Food and Development Policy, 1985. B. Higgins, A Revolution in Development Theory. In: TRIALOG (forthcoming). Meyer, W., 1990, 'Die Rache der Unentschlossenen', in ILA No 134 (April), Bonn: Informationsstelle Lateinamerika.

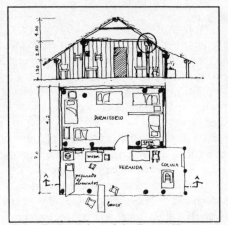

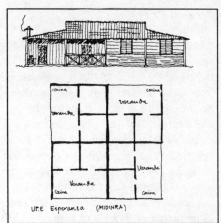

Ill. 1: Traditional rural dwelling in Nicaragua
(drawing by M. Curutchet)

Ill. 2: New rural housing provided by MIDINRA,
the Ministry of Agriculture   (M. Curutchet)

249,943 units (Curutchet, 1987:19). It was calculated that this deficit would increase at a rate of 40,000 units per year, of which 25,000 could be attributed to decay of existing housing, plus an additional demand of 15,000 would arise from the natural population growth (MINVAH, 1984a).

It would have been unrealistic to expect an instant solution from the new government. Apart from the fact that housing was only one among many pressing needs, the Sandinistas needed time, peace, and expertise to develop housing policies for their future society. Hence, the most urgent difficulties had to be solved on an ad hoc basis and some early decisions would need to be revised at later stages. One might compare their situation with that of a non–swimmer who finds himself thrown into the water: the need is merely to swim, not perfection of style. Many observers and revolutionary tourists were disappointed when they discovered problems with scarcity, incompetence, and bureaucracy, with which most societies have to struggle because these problems may stem from psychological and sociological roots, as well as political roots. In addition to these typical constraints the war with the Contras (US–financed counter–revolutionaries) caused a death toll of not less than 43,000 and displaced more than 150,000 people (Curutchet, 1987:135, Vance, 1987:170–71). In September 1988, the country was severely hit by a hurricane which erased whole settlements on the Atlantic coast and in the interior lowlands. In Managua alone, several hundred kilometres from the coast, more than 1000 houses were completely destroyed, and another 30,000 heavily damaged.

Is Housing a Priority in Development?

By definition the financial investment capacity of developing countries is very limited. Thus any state resources will be carefully compared with investments in other sectors. Once a decision is made in favour of housing, there is competition for funds between different regions and between urban and rural areas.

Sectoral Priorities

Given the backlog in fixed industrial investment in all developing countries and the heavy burden of foreign debt, investment in the productive sector is normally granted priority over housing. There is a tendency to treat housing as a consumption item or as a social service. Only under the threat of political uprising will most governments be inclined to allocate resources to the housing and consumption sector in order to maintain the stability of the political system.

In Nicaragua, which inherited an extremely high foreign debt from the prerevolutionary government, the prime development objective was to strengthen economic capacity of the nation and to achieve a positive balance of payments. This meant that 'productive investment' was perceived as the most important requirement for reaching self-sufficiency in food production and for expanding exports by means of improved cultivation of cash crops, particularly coffee, sugar and cotton. Expenditures on education and health were given next priority. It was thought they would have a greater and more direct effect on the economy, and that they would reach a greater number of people with the same limited resources: it has been argued, for example, that the literacy campaign, which benefited almost two million Nicaraguans, was less costly than providing 2,000 families with houses (Argüello, 1985). However, even the social programmes in health and education had to be curbed, together with most housing programmes because the imposed war absorbed an ever-increasing share of the economy. Eventually that share reached 60 per cent of all government expenditure. The budget earmarked for housing, which represented almost 3 per cent of the GNP in 1982–1983, was cut back to 0.5 per cent in 1986, 0.4 per cent in 1987, and even less in the years thereafter, but it remained a constant share of about 10 per cent among all social sector investments (Alcaldía de Managua, 1989:8; MINVAH, 1987; Reyes, 1988). In line with this decision the Nicaraguan state has refused to assume sole responsibility to provide direct financing for housing. Instead, foreign aid has been explicitly declared a key source of funding for shelter projects (MINVAH, 1987:5).

However, housing is not always considered a social expenditure or a consumption item in Nicaragua. The Ministry of Agriculture, for example, emphasizes that adequate accommodation counts as a productive factor in agriculture (MINVAH, 1981:42), and it provides houses as an integral part of many of its own development schemes. In this sense, the now dissolved Ministerio de la Vivienda y Asentamientos Humanos, or MINVAH (Ministry of Housing and Human Settlements) gave priority to those housing schemes linked to forestry, fishing, mining and similar projects before trying to satisfy the general need (Tapia, 1984:98).

Regional Priorities

The economic model pursued under the prerevolutionary Somoza regime had caused extreme regional imbalances in the pattern of fixed capital investment, provision of services, and the distribution of wealth. The urbanization process proceeded in an uncontrolled manner, following the requirements of transnational capitalism, and turned the capital, Managua, into a typical *primate city* (cf. Linsky, 1969/72). Although only 22 per cent of the nation's population lived in the city, 93 per cent of all sewage installations, 85 per cent of all construction investment, and 80 per cent of all other investments were concentrated in Managua (Tapia, 1984:91; Curutchet, 1987:95). The strategy of the Sandinistas was intended to counterbalance this pattern and to decentralize productive investment and political responsibilities. For example, the share of all investments made in the Managua region was reduced to 66 per cent in 1981, and to 42 per cent in 1983 (Curutchet, 1987:95). The long term spatial distribution of the population was planned to correspond with the economic development potential of the regions. Assuming an overall population of 5 million in the year 2000, a hierarchical but balanced system of towns and smaller population centres was foreseen with an even distribution of services throughout the country. This plan, the Sistema Urbana Nacional (SUN), envisaged the following:

Managua would remain the *capital* and the most important administrative centre where most key services would be concentrated, such as the seat of government, national broadcasting and specialized hospitals.

Nine *centros regionales* (regional centres) would contain a population of 20,000 to 100,000 each, and serve surrounding areas of an additional 50,000 to 500,000 inhabitants.

Nineteen *centros secundarios* (secondary centres) would contain a population of 10,000 to 20,000 each, and serve a catchment area of 25,000 inhabitants.

Fifty–five new or existing settlements with populations of 2,000 to 10,000 inhabitants would become *centros de servicio* (service centres) and provide centralized services for an additional 5,000 to 25,000 persons living in dispersed villages.

The plan assumes 70 per cent of the nation's population living in towns of more than 1,000 inhabitants and 30 per cent *dispersed* rural population. If rural population currently constitutes 43 per cent of the total population in Nicaragua (Third World Guide, 1989/90:422), we can see that further urbanization of the population is intended and that Managua will be permitted to grow much faster (140 per cent) than the nation as a whole (66 per cent). It may be disputed whether such a development is desirable and unavoidable, but the recent influx of refugees from rural areas into the cities (as a consequence of the war) may justify such a pessimistic prognosis. However, little thought seems to have been given to how the negative social, ecological, and macroeconomic effects of such a fast urbanization, which we have observed elsewhere in the world, can be avoided. The primacy of Managua in this century has been valued positive for its ethnic connotation in so far as it mirrors the distribution of indigenous population before the arrival of the Spaniards in Nicaragua (Higgins, 1990:16).

The war has forced the government to devote a higher proportion of spending than planned for the two most backward Special Development Zones in the eastern

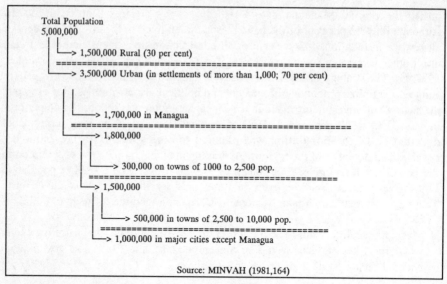

Ill. 3: Proposed Distribution of the Population in the Year 2000

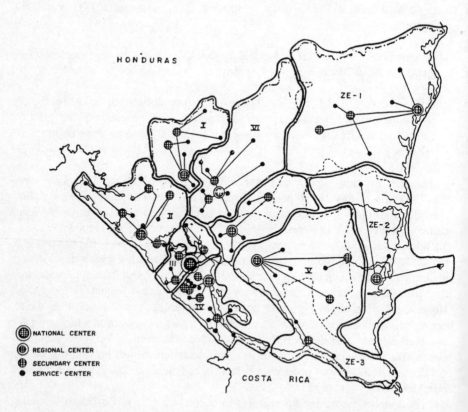

Ill. 4: The National Urban System applied to the Nicaraguan territory (adapted from Velarde 85)

parts of the country, which coincide with those areas affected most directly by war damages. More than 250,000 peasants have lost their homes and productive bases and needed to be rehoused as '*desplazados'*. In 1986 the share of government–provided housing for the rural population reached 60 per cent (MINVAH, 87:8). Several new settlements have been built near the frontier, offering better protection than isolated hamlets, and a minimal infrastructure (like roads) has been provided. In spite of additional investments pumped into the area for strategic installations and other military reasons, the intended decentralization policies have been hindered by the war.

The Institutional Framework

The State Apparatus

One of the first undertakings of the revolutionary government in 1979 was the creation of the *Ministerio de la Vivienda y Asentamientos Humanos,* MINVAH (Ministry of Housing and Human Settlements), a fusion of the previous *Viceministerio de Planificación Urbana* (Town Planning Vice Ministry), the *Oficina de Inquilinato* (Rent Office), and the *Banco de la Vivienda de Nicaragua* (Housing Bank). The ministry had two main departments with distinct responsibilities:

The *Dirección de Desarrollo Urbano* (Physical Planning Office), in charge of town and regional planning, including the preparation of *Planes de Desarrollo* and *Planes Reguladores* (master and development plans) in line with the *Ley de Uso del Suelo* (land use law) of 1980, but not implementation of own investments.

The *Dirección General de Vivienda* (Housing Department), responsible for planning, programming, supervising, and implementing all investments made by the ministry. Its functions included the building and management of state housing projects, the redistribution of land, and the co–ordination of infrastructure and services, including those to be provided by other agencies, like service departments or ministries.

The provision of technical services belongs to the activities of specialized enterprises, such as: the *Instituto Nicaraguense de Acueductos y Alcantarillas* (responsible for supply of drinking water, sewers); the *Instituto Nicaragüense de Energía* (responsible for electricity, street lights), *Juntas Municipales* (responsible for garbage collection, road surfacing, etc.).

Although MINVAH had a great variety of responsibilities and employed more staff than most other ministries, it depended on the (Economy) Planning Ministry, which decides on the allocation of state monetary resources. Finance for housing projects is provided by the *Banco Inmobiliario de Nicaragua, S.A.,* BIN (National Mortgage Bank) and foreign agencies (MINVAH, 1987:6). MINVAH also had dependent subsidiaries of its own, such as the *Empresa de Construcción de Viviendas Nacional, COVIN* (State Building Companies). Other state bodies, such as the municipalities or the *Ministerio del Desarrollo Agropecuario y de la Reforma Agraria, MIDINRA* (Ministry of Agriculture) might have their own planning boards, may develop land or build houses themselves, but they had to obtain approval of MINVAH before they could execute their schemes.

Over the years the MINVAH grew into a superministry while its budget declined because of the war. Therefore in February 1988, the decision was made to dissolve the MINVAH and to distribute its responsibilities among a number of independent institutions. (The process was labelled 'compactación'). Most tasks, like all aspects of urban and regional planning, were passed to the local governments *(alcaldías municipales)*, emphasizing the idea of decentralization and greater popular participation. Managua as a special case has maintained an independent office of urban development, infrastructure, and housing. MINVAH's former legislative responsibilities have been taken over by *INITER,* the Nicaraguan Institute for Territorial Structure at the central level. The construction of houses and infrastructure is now handled independently by *COVIN,* the state construction enterprise. Co-ordination and research on a national level will be the responsibility of a new housing department established within the Ministry of Construction in 1989. This unit was also preparing a new housing bill expected to be passed in 1989/90.

Popular Participation

Without the support of large sectors of the population the Sandinista revolution could never have succeeded in overthrowing the Somoza regime. After the victory, the reconstruction had to rely on intense co-operation with the local population since a functioning state apparatus was yet to be built. Therefore, since the beginning, popular participation was seen as an integral ingredient of national housing policy:

> *Through their mass organizations the population actively participated in the elaboration and application both of the provisions laid down in the plan, and in other political decisions with a direct impact on the people's future* (MINVAH, 1983:24; translation by the author).

Formal instruments of popular participation have been introduced in political control and execution of policy. Many local communities successfully negotiated with authorities in cases where the bureaucracy failed to adequately satisfy their demands. One of the first instances of such a negotiation process in the field of housing was reported from the barrio *San Judas* in Managua (Vance 1987).

The main instruments of popular participation are the *organizaciones de masa* (mass organizations), and among these in particular the former *Comités de Defensa Sandinista,* CDS (Sandinista Neighbourhood Committees), the *Milicias Populares Sandinistas,* MPS (Militia), the *Asociaciónes de la Mujer Nicaragüense Luisa Amanda Espinosa*, AMLAEs (women's organizations), the *Juventud Sandinista 19 de Julio* (Sandinista Youth Clubs), and the labour unions (Ruchwarger, 1987). At least initially, most of these mass organizations constituted a formal part of the Sandinista Party System *FSLN (Frente Sandinista de Liberación Nacional)*. But since these organizations are locally based and primarily concerned with solving day-to-day problems, many citizens joined these groups without being a member of the party or even belonged to a different political party.[1] Reflecting this variety of political viewpoints, and the necessity of grass root activities for the reconstruction after the war, the formal link with the party was given up for the neighbourhood committees in 1988 after intense and frank public discussions. The women's organization followed this example soon after and changed its name to *Movimiento Luisa Amanda Espinoza (MOLAE)*. The reorganized neighbourhood committees are now called 'community development committees' and are given important responsibilities in local self–government and administration (Light, 1988).

Already before their recent transformation the neighbourhood committees play a key role in popular participation. In many ways they are similar to Cuba's *Comités de Defensa de la Revolución (CDRs)*, except in Nicaragua they already existed before the revolution, when they worked underground. They operate on several levels, the block and street level, the neighbourhood level where they were named *Comité de Barrio Sandinista (CBS)*, at the municipal (zona), the regional, and at the national level. At the local level, special interest committees exist everywhere to take care of specific tasks, such as vaccination campaigns and preventive medicine, sanitation awareness, co–operation with solidarity groups abroad, cultivation of communal gardens to grow basic crops, improvement of infrastructure, reforestation, etc. (Mathéy, 1984:117). Sometimes the local CDS also organizes or co–ordinates voluntary house building and infrastructure improvement activities (Curutchet, 1987:69, Darke, 1987:110). These voluntary work campaigns have become known under the name *rojo y negro* (red and black) for the colours of the Sandinista movement.

At the central level representatives of the CDSs are installed in all ministries where they function as members of the programme co–ordination commissions (CPCs). However, because there is no direct linkage between the local CDS representation and the decentralized executive branches of the authorities, grass–roots control is often thwarted, such as in the case of the allocating vacant sites, or the repair of deficient services (Mathéy, 1984:113).

An example of popular participation in housing can be seen in the prescribed distribution procedure for sites and building materials within housing projects, which belongs to the responsibilities of the *Comité Regional de Asignación de Lotes y Módulos Básicos* (CRALOMBA),[2] a local committee. It consists of one representative from the ministry (MINVAH, until 1988), one from the regional government, one each from the *Frente Sandinista de Liberación Nacional, FSLN* (the Sandinista party), the *Central Sandinista de Trabajadores, CST* (trade unions), and the CDS (neigh–bourhood committee) (MINVAH, 1984:13).

When any *new houses* have to be allocated, the selection of applicants is normally left to the local CDS which has the most intimate knowledge about the applicants'

---

1) Nicaragua is a multiparty state. Within parliament there are parties in coalition with the FSLN and parties in the opposition, e.g., the Liberals and the extreme left. The right wing parties, which co–operate with the US–financed contras, refused to take part in the 1984 elections.

2) The committees were created as an outcome of a co–operation agreement between the MINVAH and the CDS in September 1983 (Ruchwarger, 1987:170).

housing needs and social merits in terms of contributing to the solution of neighbour-hood problems (as a way to determine priorities among several applicants with similar housing needs). A certain share of houses and building sites may also be distributed through the labour unions (Morales, 1989:18). Any disputes or subsequent tenancy conflicts are referred to one of the *Comités Regionales de Asuntos Habitacionales, CRAHs* (regional committees), which, having been established in February 1984, are composed of one MINVAH official and two representatives from the mass organizations (MINVAH, 1984a:18). In both cases the ultimate power lies with the delegates of the mass organizations because decisions are made by simple majority vote.

Improvements in the Housing System

Land Policy

In a mixed economy the questions of land ownership and privately rented housing tend to be conflicting because vested interests of private capital rarely harmonize with the requirements of a socially oriented housing policy. Before the revolution, Nicaragua experienced excesses of land speculation, particularly by the Somoza family: there was consensus that their land should be expropriated once the Sandinistas had taken power. However, *no* attempt was made to nationalize all land since many smaller landowners had been supporters of the Sandinistas and real estate had been one of the few means for middle class people to invest savings in a time of steep inflation. Therefore, the main interest of the revolutionary government was to rectify injustice from past land speculation and to prevent speculation in the future. This was to be achieved primarily through a series of new laws generally referred to under the name 'Reforma Urbana' (Urban Reform) (Alcaldía de Managua,1989:4).

Only a few weeks after the Sandinistas had taken power in 1979, they prohibited the sale of deeds for unserviced land in and around the cities (*Ley de Intervención de Repartos Ilegales, 1979*). Thereby they stopped the previous practice of speculative land subdivisions which forced the poor to pay exorbitant sums for small plots in neighbourhoods which were no better than slums, i.e, no water, no sewage, no paved streets, etc. By a subsequent law, the land of all existing 420 shanty towns (with 84,000 lots) was expropriated, and the ownership transferred to the state (Oficina Nacional de Repartos Intervenidos). Any rents or leases which the occupants of the land continued to pay, were to be reinvested in urgently needed services and infrastructure as part of a housing improvement programme *(mejoramiento habitacional)*. However, inflation soon reduced the purchase power of the rents collected, and left the programme without funds.[3]

Thirteen thousand of the expropriated sites were immediately passed on to the

---

3) For example, while 20 million córdobas were collected from the residents in all substandard neighbourhoods (MINVAH, 1984b:19) and an additional 68.5 million córdobas derived from 35,000 dwellings and 50,000 plots under its management in 1982, only 8.85 million córdobas were invested in the improvement of not more than 353 dwellings (Tapia, 1984:98).

occupants because their accumulated payments over twenty or more years were estimated equal or superior to the value of the land (*Ley de Titulación de Lotes...*, *1982*), and the ownership of the remainder would be transferred to the occupants once their monthly payments had added up to pay for the land.

The private ownership rights over land that was not used to satisfy the housing needs of its owner were further restricted in 1981 (*Ley de Expropriación...*, *1981*). Any vacant urban land which had been zoned for residential use, could be expropriated under the condition that it was needed for a public interest development, including housing (*Ley de Bonos de Expropriación ...*, 1983). The previous owners were entitled to compensation which, since 1983, has been in the form of certificates that will only be exchanged for money after twenty years. These provisions were intended to curtail the speculation of urban land, not to nationalize land in general. In the countryside, for example, some 30 per cent of the 377 hectares of expropriated land had already been reprivatized by 1984 (MINVAH, 1984b).

As a further provision to keep speculation under control any transfer of land ownership was regulated and all property changes required clearance by MINVAH up to 1988. At the present there is no restriction on the transfer of building sites between individuals. This way, access to land and houses is easier than before, but at the same time the market is tightening up as institutions increasingly buy dwellings to convert them in offices, and better houses are sold to foreigners who are in possession of dollars (Morales, 1989:36).

To summarize the land policy in Nicaragua, private ownership of land was maintained, and even sanctioned, provided that the land was to be used by the owner. In fact, the number of private landowners increased significantly as a result of the rural and urban land reform laws. Except for the cases of expropriation, there was no monetary value set on the land, and small farmers or residents of *urbanizaciones progresivas* do not have to pay for land for the time being. However, a revision of this practice has been on the agenda for a number of years, but was deferred due to the chaotic economic situation caused by the war (inflation amounting to several hundred per cent a year). The idea is that people will have to pay for the urbanization cost of vacant land, but not to charge a commercial price ruled by supply and demand.

Tenure Groups and Housing Rights

Different forms of housing tenure are sometimes promoted or attacked for ideological grounds. For example, owner occupation is often understood to reinforce capitalist relations. Private renting is perceived as an instrument for exploitation because a landlord renting rooms or part of a house derives income by taking advantage of his capital, rather than from a productive activity.

In fact, in prerevolutionary Nicaragua more than 30 per cent of the population (54 per cent in Managua) paid rent, and the majority of the renters were the poor, who, as in most other countries, had little opportunity of defending themselves against unscrupulous landlords (Alcaldía de Managua, 1989:10; Ruchwarger, 1987:171). So it came as a great relief to them when early in 1980, one-half year after the victory of the revolution, all rents were reduced to 40 to 50 per cent of their previous value (*Ley de inquilininato,* 1980). It was claimed by the government that this measure benefited more than 75,000 families (Alcaldía de Managua, 1989:5). Similar to the provisions made in relation to the illegal subdivisions, it was further foreseen that in cases where a landlord did not provide appropriate maintenance and repairs of the property, the state could intervene on behalf of the tenant and carry out the necessary repairs with the rent paid by the tenant. This legislation for the protection of tenants and leaseholders is extremely favourable on paper, but not always practical. Cases have been reported (Sánchez, 1984) where the new reduced rent was below the mandatory rates and taxes, which made it financially impossible for a landlord to pay for necessary repairs and maintenance out of the rents he receives.

In 1982 a more radical bill recommended the outlawing of private rental housing altogether, on the principle that a tenant would have paid off the cost of a house after twenty years of rent payments. After having been extensively discussed by the public at all levels, this bill was substantially modified and tempered before its eventual approval in 1983:

> *Before the government presented the law to the Council of State, CDSs in all major cities organized neighbourhood assemblies to promote mass discussion and debate on its provisions. The country's newspapers published the complete text of the bill. The Council of State received the final proposal only after public input substantially altered the bill. Some CDS members argued that although the law would weaken the power of the big landlords, it could also indiscriminately affect poor and working–class families who rent a wing of their homes or own some extra small property to augment their modest income. Others felt that inheritance restrictions might hurt poor families. The government took these criticisms into account and added special clauses and exceptions to avoid adverse affects among the popular classes* (Robinson, 1984, 3:13).

The same provisions which had been proposed for private renters also apply to the housing stock owned or managed by the government. The ownership of these dwellings will automatically be transferred to the tenants after a maximum period of twenty years. The exact length of the rental period depends on the income of the tenant since the rent paid is calculated not to exceed 15 per cent of family income. The amount is revalued periodically to stay in line with inflation (MINVAH, 1987:5). On the other hand, severe sanctions are foreseen in cases of rent arrears, including forcible removal from the dwelling (Sánchez, 1984).

The principle of private home ownership was never challenged in Nicaragua. On the contrary, owners can obtain credits for building houses,[4] and many dwellings from the state housing stock have been sold to their occupants over the last years. For example, 82.6 percent of families are owner occupiers today, and among low income families the share is as high as 89.8 per cent (Alcaldía de Managua, 1989:10); in rural areas it practically reaches 100 per cent.

---

4) Créditos Hipotecarios from the Banco Hipotecario for periods between 1 and 20 years, at an interest rate of 14–20%. If the credit is intended for purchase of a house, the applicant must provide securities; for repairs there is no such requirement (MINVAH, 1987:6).

Housing Production

The State Sector

We are used to measure the success of a nation's housing policy by the number of units completed within a certain time span. However, for the majority of the population nonmaterial elements of housing policy, such as the introduction of rent control or land reforms can have a much more significant impact than the construction of a limited number of houses which are then allocated to a lucky few. We should keep this in mind when we look at the figures of new housing provided by the Nicaraguan state. These figures favourably compare with housing production performance under the Somoza regime, amounting to no more than 1,617 houses between 1966 and 1970 (Vigil, 1983:2). Nevertheless, also after 1970, construction was unable to catch up with the need generated by natural population growth, not to speak of alleviating the deficiencies of the housing stock inherited by the revolution from earlier periods.

In terms of physical housing production, Nicaraguan policy operates five distinct house building programmes: mass housing projects, self–help or building materials banks, peasants' villages, the progressive development programme, and settlement upgrading.

Housing Complexes (Complejos Habitacionales): This mass housing programme supplies finished houses and apartments (*complejos habitacionales*) of a relatively high standard. It was the favoured approach of the Ministry of Housing in the first years after 1979. The houses are built by direct labour through the state construction company COVIN. Each development comprises 150 or more units and is frequently linked to a new production enterprise, i.e., mining or agriculture (42.5 per cent).[5] The rent for a dwelling is related to the building cost which makes it too expensive for the average population. In the first ten years of the revolution, 1980 to 1989, a total of 12,094 dwellings have been completed under this scheme, representing 47 per cent of all houses built by the government, but the programme was discontinued because of the financial constraints of the war economy (Alcaldía de Managua, 1989:6): whereas a peak of 3,098 units had been completed in 1982, the figure has dropped to a mere 370 in 1987 (Morales, 1989:26).

Self–Help Programmes and Building Materials Banks (Proyectos de Autocon–strucción, Mejoramiento Habitacional, Bancos de Materiales): Even before the victory of the revolution, several self–help core housing projects had been launched with World Bank funding in Nicaragua. After 1979 these projects were completed in line with initial plans, except for a change in the selection criteria for participants: For the last 700 units, spread over thirteen project areas (MINVAH, 1984b), the applicant's participation in communal activities was also taken into consideration,

---

5) Mining settlements: Roita, Siuna, Bonanza, Mina el Limón; Sugar production complexes: Ingenios Benjamín Zeledón, Javier Guerra, Germán Pomares, Julio Buitrago, Camillo Ortega; banana plantations: El Viejo, Tonalá; rice farm: Rigoberto Lopez (Alcaldía de Managua, 1989:8)

Ill. 5:   *The 'Módulo Básico' is a prefabricated timber house and distributed through the building*
material deposits ('Banco de Materiales')   *(Drawing: M. Curutchet; Foto: K. Mathéy)*

apart from financial acceptability. However, further sites–and–services projects, which continued to be popular in other Latin American countries, were rejected in Nicaragua on the grounds that they would reinforce individualism as opposed to collectivism (Vance, 1987:172).

Formal *proyectos de autoconstrucción* (self-help projects) were replaced by the programme of the *bancos de materiales* (building materials banks), and initially targeted at those applicants who were in possession of a building site or who lived in a house in urgent need of repair. These people could purchase loose building materials or complete kits for a standard house at favourable, controlled prices. In

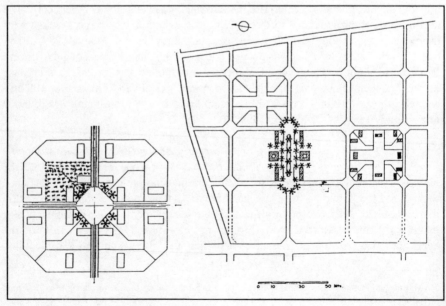

Ill. 6:   *Tisma, a new rural settlement.*   *(Source: Velarde, 1985)*

1983, prefabricated timber houses of 36 square metres were introduced as an alternative. The so-called *módulos básicos* made extensive use of indigenous building materials and could be assembled by the users within a few hours. The production capacity for these units was drastically reduced when the sawmill of Ocota was destroyed by the Contras in 1984 (Curutchet, 1987:67). Allocation of units and provision of manpower for collective facilities were the responsibility of neighbourhood organizations. Altogether 6,951 módulos básicos have been distributed — 60 per cent of them in Managua alone (Alcaldía de Managua, 1989:7).

Peasants' Villages: From 1982 onward, a large number of peasants became homeless through the war. To accommodate them, and to resettle others living in areas where attacks by counterrevolutionary guerrillas (the 'contras') were rampant, new villages housing between 30 and 160 families were built by the government. The location of such villages was chosen to comply with three requirements:

1. The site should offer good possibilities for self–defence.
2. The soil in the surroundings should be suitable for farming.
3. Provision of basic infrastructure (water, transport, etc.) must be relatively easy.

Like in urban areas the villages were supplied with 'módulos básicos' in the beginning, but as the programme expanded and resources became extremely scarce, a more modest solution was introduced with only a roof where the occupants could fill in the walls little–by–little (plan techo).

Until 1989, approximately 300 new villages were built, with a total of 10,017 dwellings (Alcaldía de Managua, 1989:7). In addition, another 3,419 units were provided directly by the MIDINRA (Ministry of Agriculture) or by other institutions (MINVAH, 1987:10 and table 4). Most of the villages were built in zones most affected by the war: Region I (Las Segovias), Region IV (Matagalpa and Jinotega along the northern border to Honduras) and Special Development Zone III (Rio San Juan, on the border with Costa Rica) (Curutchet, 1987:135).

Progressive Urbanization (Urbanizaciones Progresivas): In the main cities, the housing problem was too big to be dealt with through the programmes of the *complejos habitacionales* or the *módulos básicos* alone. Therefore, as a complementary measure, an ad hoc response introduced in 1982 became the main instrument to rehouse the victims of that year's flood (caused by the hurricane 'Aleta') in Managua. Alternative sites in so–called *urbanizaciones progresivas* with basic infrastructure (communal water taps, electricity, public transport) were given to those people who had become homeless, and free transport was offered to move all reusable building materials from their previous sites. In 1984, in an attempt to gain control over the growing problem with squatters, the progressive urbanization programme was extended to general need applicants and benefited particularly those who had settled on geologically unsafe land (earthquake and flood hazards) or on sites earmarked for uses other than residential. In this second stage, infrastructure had to be provided by the residents themselves due to the economic constraints, and technical assistance was lacking to draw up a comprehensive and long term development concept.

The concept of the *urbanizaciones progresivas* appears similar to the sites–and–services projects of other countries, at least in the initial period. However, there are several important differences. First, in Nicaragua the land was given to settlers free of charge with full security of tenure making it possible to reach that part of the population in greatest need of housing. Second, almost all Urbanizaciones Progresivas are located within the city near the main bus lines, not far out in the periphery. Only very recently have sites been distributed further away from the urban centres. Thus men and women can follow their usual work patterns, which often involve part–time and occasional jobs. Third, the principles of collective organization, political neighbourhood representation and communal work are fostered among dwellers of these settlements — mainly by delegating important responsibilities to the CDS of the neighbourhood.

Up to 1989 some 33,985 plots had been allocated as part of the programme, and more than half of them (57.2 per cent) were located in Managua (MINVAH, 1984b:34; Alcaldía de Managua, 1989:6). In the following two years more emphasis was given to other cities, reducing the share of Managua to 55.7 per cent (MINVAH, 1987). In quantitative as well as in qualitative terms the progressive urbanization programme became the most significant contribution among the various 'physical elements' of Nicaraguan housing policy until very recently.

Settlement Upgrading (Mejoramiento de Urbanizaciones): Most urban houses, particularly in earthquake–ravaged Managua, are located in unplanned neighbourhoods and lack some or all basic infrastructure and services. During the revolution, many of these places supported the Sandinistas and the population now expected fast and visible improvements in their living conditions. Therefore, upgrading these settlements was assigned high priority within housing policy. However, long term investments could only be made after land use plans were defined for each settlement. The methodology for upgrading popular settlements in Managua was elaborated in co–operation with foreign experts.[6] As land use plans proceeded, most of the 420 informal settlements were included in the *programa de mejoramiento de urbanizaciones,* and approximately 50,000 families have benefited in one way or another from the programme (MINVAH, 1987), by receiving better services such as rain water drainage, a paved road, a day clinic etc. The concept implies that the government

Ill. 7: Informal settlement in urban Nicaragua, part of the upgrading programme. (R. Vallebuona)

6) Technical assistance was given, in particular, by the city of Amsterdam, the Universities of Delft in the Netherlands and Darmstadt in Germany, the Instituto de Pesquisas Tecnológicas in São Paulo in Brazil.

provides the necessary building materials, and the people contribute their own labour force (Reyes, 1988). Given actual economic constraints, upgrading has become the most important physical element of urban policies in the very recent past.

The Impact of State Housing Programmes

Together, the various housing programmes (but excluding the sites distributed in the progressive developments and neighbourhood upgrading where the impact is difficult to quantify), provided almost 28,000 dwellings in seven years: an average of 4,000 per year (or 1.14 units per 1,000 inhabitants). Assuming an occupancy rate of six persons per dwelling, we arrive at 6.85 houses completed for every 1,000 families, i.e., every house would have to last for 146 years; or given a housing deficit of 377,000 units in 1981, the last person in need of a house today would have to wait ninety–four years to receive a government dwelling. This calculation includes neither the additional demand of an estimated 15,000 units yearly arising from the normal population growth, nor extra housing needed to absorb internal migration flows.[7]

At first sight, the housing output by the state in Nicaragua is not particularly impressive, either on its own, or when compared with state housing programmes in other countries. However, this relatively modest figure becomes more meaningful when the composition of the target group is reviewed. In Nicaragua by 1984 figures, 17.8 per cent of the housing output reached the absolute poor earning less than one minimum wage; another 78.1 per cent went to the next income bracket of one to three times the minimum wage. This meant that only 4.1 per cent benefited middle and upper income groups. For comparison, in typical low–income housing programmes of other Latin American states, such as those sponsored by the World Bank, the bottom 30 to 60 per cent of the population tend to be excluded because they are too poor to meet the financial obligations set by the programme (cf. Peattie, 1987: 69–76).

The Contribution of Nongovernmental Organizations

Since 1979, a substantial number of foreign based nongovernmental agencies and solidarity groups have supported various kinds of development projects in Nicaragua, many of them also improving local housing situations. For some time this kind of co–operation was a potential source of conflict between the local community and central state institutions (Curutchet, 1987:97): On the one hand, the organizations abroad often had established partnerships with specific neighbourhoods in Nicaragua. Personal relations evolved and helped to mobilize foreign funds to support a particular development project tailored to suit this specific community. On the other hand, such projects did not necessarily conform with the priorities set by the central planning authorities who tried to achieve a balanced and rational distribution of limited

---

7) The figures were derived from the tables reproduced in MINVAH, 1984a.

resources. Furthermore, the state tried to control and co–ordinate all help offered by foreign nongovernmental organizations through a central office in order to guarantee that all financial transactions connected with it were handled by the National Bank and exchanged at the official 'commercial' rate.

From 1986 onward, as the spending capacity of the ministry of housing dried up because of the war economy NGOs were given more freedom to invest according to their own priorities. This is particularly true for the period from 1986 onward. Since these organizations tend to work directly with the local communities, it is difficult to obtain a clear picture about the overall impact of their support, but my impression is that since 1986 more houses were built with NGO finance than with government funding.

Private and Informal Sector Housing

Although the Nicaraguan state acknowledges the right of each of its citizens to a decent house, this does not imply that the house has to be provided by the state or voluntary sector. After all, Nicaragua is a mixed economy and mortgages are available to owner occupiers, but until recently they have had to compete with MINVAH for the very limited funds of the *Banco Inmobiliario de Nicaragua S.A.* (BIN). In the first years the share of the private sector loans was negligible, but according to more recent sources this share reached 55 per cent in 1986 (MINVAH, 1987:8).

A problem in the private sector entails the supply of building materials, which are extremely scarce — particularly since 1984. In an attempt to guarantee access for low income families, the sale of particular products, like cement or lumber, was under state control, but this produced a black market where prices were several times higher than at official outlets. After liberalization of the market all prices increased notably, and a perceivable acceleration of building activity concentrated on a smaller section of the society.

However, there are no indications that private housing is being built for sale or for lease on a commercial basis, a positive indication of effective legislation against property speculation and protecting tenants rights. On the other hand, the sharing of one dwelling by two or more families, or subletting without financial interest to friends or distant relatives — known as *inquilenatos* in many Latin American countries — is on the increase in Nicaragua.

The last resort for the urban homeless is the squatter settlements, and Nicaragua has experienced distinct periods when the homeless relied on these. One of these periods was immediately after the revolution when squatters took advantage of the disappearance of the oppressive police apparatus maintained by the Somoza regime. Expropriation of speculative subdivisions soon thereafter permitted the government to offer better alternatives to squatting (Morales, 1989:34). However, when the supply of such land was used up in 1981, some 4,400 new squatter plots, involving more than 25,000 people, were reported for the capital Managua (Curutchet, 1987:61). This activity could be brought under control through the programme of the progressive settlements with relative success. However, a new wave of squatting occurred shortly

Ill. 8: Squatters in Managua immediately before the elections in 1984.   *(Foto: Kosta Mathéy)*

before the elections in 1984 when it was unlikely that the governing Sandinistas would risk confrontation with squatters, and can be attributed to the increasing number of refugees fleeing from the countryside where the conditions of the war inhibit a productive and peaceful life. Most recently, the damage caused by the 1988 hurricane has forced many additional families into makeshift dwellings in the cities. There were attempts to relocate these squatters in new progressive settlements again, but since these were now situated more in the periphery, many of the moved families have been reported to come back and settle illegally in more central locations (INIES, n.d.; Morales, 1989:34). Instituting a prohibitive public position in regard to squatting in Managua proper has been estimated to because of the high growth of several satellite cities in the region over the last years, in particular San Marcos, Masatepe, Tipitapa, and Diriomo (Higgins, 1990:20)

However, in contrast to the neighbouring nations, squatters in Nicaragua do not risk forcible eviction by the police: therefore there are no mass invasions or overnight building sites. Instead, an early process of grassroots organization and participation is typical, and the established CDS structure facilitates negotiation with the authorities for an early provision of communal services and infrastructure.

The Choice of Technology

Options differ considerably for the best choice of technology to satisfy the housing needs of a Third World revolutionary society. Some people think that the use of so-called 'appropriate technologies' would help to serve a maximum number of people in a short time and would save foreign exchange by relying on local building materials. Other experts argue that in the aftermath of a revolution the people expect better quality housing for everyone and that traditional building methods lack the necessary productivity to satisfy the increased demand.

In Nicaragua the policy concerning the question of housing technology evolved through different phases. In the first two years after the revolution, there was a relatively open approach, and the construction of uniform concrete block houses, including those belonging to the World Bank's self–help programme, went on simultaneously with experiments in rammed–earth and bamboo construction, or similar appropriate technologies. There was an experimental farm for bamboo at Rama, several adobe experiments in Managua, and a Centre for Appropriate Technology (CITA) run by MIDINRA near Esteli. Later on, these ventures were discontinued, albeit not for ideological reasons alone. The Rama farm was in the war zone and stopped operating about 1983. MINVAH gave up its adobe experimentation site in Managua in 1982, which may have been a direct consequence of the fluctuation of staff in that office in that period. The CITA/MIDINRA centre was closed in 1986 after internal management problems (Curutchet, 1987:81–87).

By 1983, preference had shifted toward prefabrication and cement–based construction, and this tendency appears to be reinforced through the advice of the state construction enterprise, COVIN and, indirectly as well, by co–operation with Cuban institutions. It was hoped that the cost of high quality developments (*Complejos*) could be lowered in the long run, and that the durability of the houses could be increased at the same time, as expressed in a publication of the MINVAH:

> '*As a priority the housing demand created by rural and urban productive units will be satisfied by these housing development schemes (complejos habitacionales). In order to maximize the advantages of prefabrication and standardization in the production process these programmes are being carried out with heavy construction methods*' (MINVAH, 1984b:8; translation by the author).

However, built results from heavy construction and industrialized building methods were often disappointing. The approach was criticized on several grounds. It was reasoned, for example, that heavy construction would cause too heavy a drain on foreign exchange since 55 per cent of the cost of cement was on imported energy (Tapia, 1984:101); other high quality building materials and components (electric installations, metal fittings, ceramics), which are typical requirements of the housing complexes, had to be imported and were difficult to obtain, thus delaying the completion of the units (MINVAH, 1984b:45). Also poor architectural design and the incompatibility with Nicaragua's socio–cultural context have been raised in the discussion (MINVAH, 1981:84). Even official publications admit that the expected higher productivity could not be achieved: MINVAH (1984b) calculated a productivity rate of 3.3 (highest) for timber houses, 2.92 for conventional solid construction, and 2.3 (lowest) for the prefabricated small panel system known under the name Sandino, introduced in 1982.

Criticism of prefabrication, financial difficulties, and an explicit preference for less ambitious technologies by international and foreign nongovernmental agencies helped in the acceptance of wider use of local materials and small–scale production from about 1985 onwards. For example, several municipalities purchased low–cost machinery for the production of fibre cement roofing tiles to substitute for corrugated iron and asbestos cement sheets. In 1988, the Technical University in Managua (UNI) joined these efforts and also started research into alternative building materials, including adobe, and methods.

Conclusion

The absolute number of houses built by MINVAH since 1979, and the problems of increased squatter settlements in Managua over the last years, do not suggest a great achievement for Nicaraguan housing policies. However, we must bear in mind that the Nicaraguans chose to put the main emphasis on nonphysical improvements in housing provision and on social services in general, in order to benefit the largest number of people with the limited resources available. Within all items of social expenditure, housing was assigned the third priority after health and education (Vance, 1987:171), and being rated a social service there was little attempt to recover the investments made (Alcaldía de Managua, 1989:9).

Since 1981, the housing deficit has grown by 17,000 units annually (Ruchwarger, 1987:170). The declining output in government shelter projects and the overall worsening of housing situation in Nicaragua must be attributed to the war economy. which has drastically curbed the disposable budget for housing construction. The influx of refugees has also frustrated the decentralization policy and produced a chaotic situation in the cities where many people have sought new homes.

Not all problems in Nicaraguan housing can be explained by the war alone. Due to the poor teaching facilities prevalent in the prerevolutionary period, and to the brain drain responding to meagre income opportunities within Nicaragua today, the level of available professional and academic skills has been severely restricted. This condition affects public authorities in particular, and is aggravated by problems of co-ordination and competition between different ministries and other state institutions. Certainly these restrictions are endemic in most parts of the developing world, but they tend to be even more severe in periods following a political overthrow.

However, the popular character of the Nicaraguan revolution prepared the path for well-organized grassroots participation, and the local community has been able to offset many of the constraints rooted in the central economic or administrative level on many occasions. This learning experience, which might not have been necessary under more peaceful conditions, will certainly help to build up a real grassroots democracy once the war has been overcome in Central America.

In spite of the many problems discussed, the housing policy implemented by the revolutionary government in Nicaragua contrasts favourably with that typical in other Latin American or Third World countries: A much greater share of all houses built were in small towns and villages, which reduced the proportion for the capital from 83.5 per cent before the revolution to 18.8 per cent today (Alcaldía de Managua, 1989:9). Ninety per cent of all state housing investment directly favours low income groups (Tapia, 1984:101), a figure which would be difficult to encounter in any truly capitalist country, including the industrialized world. A comparison with socialist countries, such as Cuba or China, is more difficult since a key question might be how effectively income differentials were reduced in the first place.

However, an even more remarkable and genuinely revolutionary achievement is the free access to land and basic services for the majority of the population, as provided within the *urbanizaciones progresivas* programme in urban areas. In rural areas agrarian reform represents a similar approach since land titles are also distributed to small farmers free of charge, and housing is explicitly considered a productive (and not consumption) investment. By adopting these two principles, other Third World countries should be able to solve at least part of their housing problems, but this would also imply sacrificing certain 'freedoms' currently enjoyed by landed and finance capital and represent a step toward a mixed economy.

Acknowledgments

I wish to thank the many colleagues who discussed earlier versions of this chapter with me and thereby helped to clarify several of its ambiguities, and to update the information. I owe particular thanks to Mirina Curutchet and Jill Hamberg who commented extensively on the manuscript, to Auxiliadora Reyes who informed me about the most recent policy changes, and to staff of Mansell Publishing, the Journal of Urban Affairs and Latin American perspectives for stylistic corrections.

Appendix: Housing Legislation 1979 – 1983

Ley de (intervención de) repartos ilegales (26th September, 1979).
 Prohibits the sale of plots in illegal subdivisions.
Ley de inquilinato (2nd January, 1980).
 Reduction of all housing rents to 40–50 per cent of their previous value, except for high quality housing for which 5 per cent of its assessed value is the permitted maximum rent per year. In cases where the landlord fails to carry through the necessary repairs, the government may intervene on behalf of the tenants and take over the management of these dwellings.
Ley de donaciones del casco urbano (4th January, 1980, amended 8th April, 1980 and 5th May, 1980).
 Municipalization of all unused sites in the centre of Managua, for which a general development ban had been issued after the earthquake of 1972. Compensation is to be paid to the previous owners after deduction of all tax debts.
Ley de regulación de las cuotas de amortisación de viviendas del sistema financiero nacional y del MINVAH (1980).
 Reduction of mortgage payments to correspond with the average income situation of the population affected. All mortgage payments done within the past 20 years will be counted as downpayments toward the transfer of ownership to the occupants.
Ley creadora de la corporación nicaraguense de bienes raices (CONIBIR) (4th April, 1980).
 Creation of a subsidiary of MINVAH to handle the administration of the housing stock in MINVAH's care.
Ley sobre el uso del suelo en las areas de desarrollo de los asentamientos humanos (30th August/Sept., 1980, amended 12th May, 1983).
 Transference of planning authority to MINVAH, today executed through the *Alcaldías* (townships). Establishment of Planes de Desarrollo (Development plans) and Planes Reguladores (Zoning Plans) as legally binding documents.

Ley procesal de inquilinato (17th February, 1981, amended 21st December, 1981, annulled 6th July, 1983).
Procedural instructions related to the Ley de Inquilinato.
Ley organica de la corporación constructora de viviendas (31st August, 1981).
Creation of the state-owned direct labour and planning enterprise COVIN.
Reglamento de la ley organica de COVIN (11th December, 1981).
Procedural instructions related to the ley organica de la corporación constructora de viviendas.
Ley de expropriación de tierras urbanas baldias (14th December, 1981).
Provisions to enable the expropriation of any unused urban sites if needed for the public interest. Compensation to be paid in form of investment certificates at an annual interest rate of 2 per cent over a period of twenty years after which the value is due for cash payment (by 1985 some 377 hectares had been expropriated according to this law, and slightly more than 30 per cent of this land had been reprivatized (MINVAH, 1984b).
Ley de expropriación de predios baldios en el casco urbano del centro de la ciudad de Managua (16th December, 1981).
Provisions for the expropriation of sites in central Managua.
Ley de titulación de lotes en repartos intervenidos (2nd January, 1982, amended 9th April, 1982 and 7th October, 1982).
Provision of ownership titles to the owners or occupants of private sites under government administration.
Reglamento de la ley de titulación de lotes en repartos intervenidos (12th October, 1982).
Procedure instructions related to the 'Ley de titulación...'
Ley de bonos de expropriación de tierras urbanas baldias (6th June, 1983).
Compensation for expropriated urban sites in the form of certificates.

References and further reading

(The titles marked with an asterisk* have been cited in the text)

Alcaldía de Managua (1989)*, *Politicas de Vivienda. Informe del Periodo 1979–1989.* Managua: Dirección de Desarrollo Municipal, Dapartamento de Vivienda; April.

Argüello Hüper, Alejandro (1985)*, La vivienda urbana dentro de las prioridades del desarrollo nacional. In: *International Conference Hamburg 1985: Urban Renewal and Housing for Low Income Groups in Metropolitan Areas of Latin America,* Hamburg: TUHH / FSP 6, Pages: 25–34.

Chávez, Roberto (1985), Urban Planning in Nicaragua. In: Carmona, Marisa & Tummers, Lidewij. *Contribución al Estudio de Saneamiento Integral en Managua,* Delft TH, Afdeling der Bowkunde, Pages: 37–48. Reprint 1987 in: *Latin American Perspectives 53 (14):* 226–236.

Curutchet, Mirina et al. (1983), *Jose Benito Escobar – Un Asentamiento Rural en Nicaragua.* Nicaragua Projektet, Lund: Universidad Téchnica.

Curutchet, Mirina (1987)*, *Vivienda y participación en Nicaragua sandinista.* Cordoba/Argentina: Fac. de Arquitectura, Universidad Nacional.

Darke, Roy (1987)*, Housing in Nicaragua. In: *International Journal of Urban and Regional Research,* vol. 11, no. 1, London, Pages: 100–114.

Downs, C. & Kusnetzoff, F. (1982), The Changing Role of Local Government in the Nicaraguan Revolution. In: *International Journal of Urban and Regional Research,* No 6, Pages: 533–548.

Higgins, Bryan R. (1990): *Space and Place in the Urbanization of Nicaragua.* Paper presented at the international conference 'Sustainable Habitat on an Urbanized Planet?', Berlin 19.–25. March, 1990.

INEC (Instituto Nacional de Estadísticas y Censos) (1982), *Anuario Estadistico de Nicaragua,* Managua.

INIES, n.d.*. Los asentamientos espontáneos en Managua. In: *Revista Nicaragüense de Ciencias Sociales.* Managua.

Ley de Bonos de Expropriación de Tierras Urbanas Baldias* of June 6th, 1983.

Ley de Expropriación de Tierras Urbanas Baldias (1981),* published in *La Gaceta* 14.12.1981.

Ley de inquilininato (1980),* published in *La Gaceta* 2.1.1980.

Ley de Repartos Ilegales (1979),* published as 'Decreto 97' in *La Gaceta, Año LXXXIII, No 18,* Managua Sept. 1979:137–139.

Ley de Titulación de Lotes en Repartos Intervenidos (1982),* published as decreto 923 in *La Gaceta, año LXXXVI, no. 16,* Managua 1982: 169–171.

Light, Julie (1988)*. Article in: *The Guardian* of August 31, 1988:18.

Linsky (1969/72),* Some Generalizations Concerning Primate Cities. In: Breese, G. *The City in Newly Developing Countries,* London 1969/72.

López, Francisco (1987), La Problematica Urbana en Managua. In: *Cuadernos de Sociología,* Managua: UCA: 11–16.

MINVAH (1980a) (Informe sin titulo). Managua: mimeo.

MINVAH (1980b) Programa Bancos de Materiales y Apoyo a la Autoconstrucción. In: *Taller Internacional sobre Mejoramiento Barrial en América Latina, 5.–23.11.84 México, D.F.,* Managua/Mexico: MINVAH/INDECO, mimeo, 9 pages.

MINVAH (1981) Seminario sobre Planificación de los Asentamientos Humanos y la Vivienda Rural en Nicaragua (23.3.–10.4.1981)*. In: *SIAP Documento No 31,* Managua: mimeo, 207 pages.

MINVAH (1982) La Tierra en el Desarrollo Urbano. Caso de Nicaragua. In: *XIV Congreso Interamericano de Planificación de la Sociedad Interamericana de Planificación, Mex,* Managua: MINVAH – mimeo, 12 pages.

MINVAH (1983), Urbanizaciones Progresivas. Alternativa para el Desarrollo de Asentamientos Humanos*. In: *Seminario Internacional en Berlin (Oeste) y Vienna (Sept. 83),* Managua: MINVAH – mimeo, 38 pages.

MINVAH (1984a)*, *El Deficit de Viviendas.* Managua: mimeo, 10 pages.

MINVAH (1984b),* Los Asentamientos Humanos en Centroamerica y Panama. In: *IX Conferencia Centroamericana Permanente de Vivienda y Desarrollo Urbano,* Managua: mimeo, 46 pages.

MINVAH (1984c), Die Beteiligung des Volkes bei der Bereitstellung von Wohnungen (Seminar paper, Santo Domingo 1982). In: Müller–Plantenberg, C. & Rempel, R. *Soziale Bewegungen und Räumliche Strukturen in Lateinamerika,* Kassel: GHK: 265–309.

MINVAH (1984d), Mejoramiento Urbano para Grupos de Bajos Ingresos. In: *Taller Internacional sobre Mejoramiento Barrial en América Latina, 5.–23.11.84 México, D. F.,* Managua: MINVAH, 16 pages.

MINVAH (1984e), *El MINVAH – Organización y gestión.* Managua: mimeo, 18 pages.

MINVAH (1985), Informe sobre Aspectos de Vivienda y Desarrollo Urbano / Nicaragua. In: XII COPVIDU. Conferencia Centroamericana Permanente de Vivienda y Desarrollo Urbano: *Vivienda Progresiva y Desarrollo,* San José: Inst. Tecnico de Costa Rica, 10 pages.

MINVAH (1987),* La Vivienda en Nicaragua. In: Unión Internacional de los Sindicatos de la Construcción, *Simposio Internacional Sindical sobre la Vivienda,* Sofia, Bulgaria: mimeo, 14 pages.

MINVAH – Dirección de Sistemas Urbanos (1983), *Politica de Ordenamiento y Desarrollo de los Asentamientos Intermedios y Rurales en Nicaragua.* Managua: mimeo, 28 pages.

Martínez, Jorge (1986), El Proceso de Conformacion de un Sistema de Asentamientos Humanos y el Desarrollo de la Hegemonia Popular: El caso de Nicaragua. In: Carrión, Diego et al. *Ciudades en Conflicto: Poder local, participación y planificación en las ciudades intermedias,* Quito: Editorial El Conejo – Ciudad: 333–354.

Mathéy, Kosta, (1984)*, Basis and Methodology for the Design of an Integrated Development Project in Ciudad Sandino, Nicaragua. In: Bruno et al., *Development of Urban Low Income Neighbourhoods in the Developing World,* Darmstadt: 105–132.

Mathéy, Kosta (1985), Housing Policies in the Sandinista Nicaragua. In: *Trialog no 6,* Darmstadt (BRD): 42–48.

Mathéy, Kosta (1986), Schwerpunkte aktueller Wohnungspolitik in Nicaragua. In: Augel, Joh. et al. *Die verplante Wohnmisere,* Saarbrücken: Breitenbach, pages: 281–204.

Morales, Ninette & Torres, Olimpia (1989)*: *Elementos Base para la Formulación de una Politica Nacional de Vivienda.* Documento Interno. Managua: Secretaria de Planificación y Presupuesto, Dirección de Planificación Física; May.

Peattie, Lisa (1987), Affordability. In *Habitat International vol. 11, No 4,* pages 69–76.

Ramírez Velarde, Luis F. (1985), An Answer to Spontaneous Rural Settlements: Nicaragua – A case study. In: *UNCHS-Seminar on planning for settlements in rural regions*, Nairobi & Managua: mimeo, 36 pages.

Reyes, Auxiliadora (MINVAH) (1985), El Problema de la Vivienda Popular Urbana en Nicaragua. Políticas, Programas y Instrumentos. In: *International Conference Hamburg 1985 Urban Renewal and Housing for Low-Income Groups in Metropolitan Areas in Latin America*, Hamburg: TUHH: 36–56.

Reyes, Auxiliadora (1988 – November)*. Personal interview at the Meeting of the City Architects of Socialist Capitals (in La Habana). Taped but unpublished.

Robinson, William (1984)*, Zur neuen Wohngesetzgebung in Nicaragua. In: Müller-Plantenberg, C. & Rempel, R. *Soziale Bewegungen und Räumliche Strukturen in Lateinamerika*, Kassel: GHK, pages: 311–314.

Ruchwarger, Gary (1987)*, *People in Power,* South Hadley (Mass.): Bergin & Garvey.

Sánchez, Domingo (1984)*. Personal interview with Domingo Sanchez, member of the National Council for the *Partido Socialista Nicaragüense,* now congress delegate for the 'Frente Sandinista'.

Schuman, Tony (1986), Urban Housing Policy in Nicaragua. A comparative view (Addendum to Hamberg: The Dynamics of Cuban Housing Policy. In: Bratt, Rachel et al., *Critical Perspectives on Housing*, Philadelphia: Temple University Press: 625–633.

Tapia, Octavio (1984)*, Die Tendenzen der Wohnungspolitik im Nicaragua von heute. In: Bruno, Eugen, Mathéy, Kosta; Körte, Arnold, *Umgang mit Wohnquartieren unterer Einkommensgruppen in Entwicklungsländern.* Darmstadt: Archimed: 87–103.

Third World Guide 1989/90, Montevideo.

Vance, Irene (1987),* The Community as Evaluaters: Experience with Community Participation in Self-Build Projects in Managua. Skinner, Reinhard et al. *Slum Upgrading for the Urban Poor,* Manila: Island: 169–196.

Vigil, Miguel Ernesto (1983), Ministerio de Vivienda y Asentamientos Humanos. *Antecedentes y Gestión.* Exposición ante la Junta del Gobierno de Reconstrucción Nacional y el Gabinete de Gobierno, Managua: MINVAH – mimeo, 12 pages.

Villeda, Angeles de (1983), Urbanizaciones Progresivas: Alternativa para el desarrollo de asentamientos humanos. Deutsche Stiftung für Entwicklung, ZS Wirtschafts– und Soziales, *Financiamiento del Habitat para Sectores de Bajos Ingresos,* Berlin: DSE: 125–152.

Williams, Harvey (1982), Housing Policy in Revolutionary Nicaragua. In: Walker, Thomas, (Ed.), *Nicaragua in Revolution,* New York: Praeger.

Williams, Harvey (1984), Sandinista Housing Policy after Five Years. *25th annual Convention of the International Studies Association* (Conference paper), Atlanta, Georgia, USA.

Guinea Bissau

Julio D. Dávila

With an area of 36,125 square kilometres (slightly less than Switzerland) and a population of under one million, Guinea Bissau is one of the smallest countries in Africa. In September 1974, the African Party for the independence of Guinea Bissau and Cape Verde Islands (PAIGC), founded by the legendary Amilcar Cabral, took over the government of this Portuguese colony in West Africa which until then was known by its colonial name of Portuguese Guinea. The PAIGC Government inherited one of Portugal's least–productive colonies, with an export economy weakened by an eleven–year liberation struggle and an estimated quarter of its largely rural population dispersed in neighbouring countries as a result of the war. Despite a heavy toll in human lives and a crippled economy, the long war would eventually bring the people of this small West African nation political independence and with it, tangible improvements in living standards (Rudebeck, 1982).

Fifteen years after gaining independence, however, Guinea Bissau remains among the thirty–eight poorest countries in the world, with a *per capita* income of US$195 in 1984 and an economy dependent largely on small–scale, mostly subsistence, agriculture (World Bank, 1987a). The once generous flow of foreign aid that allowed the PAIGC to provide health and education to the native African population has been dwindling dramatically. Faced with intense external pressure, the Government has recently adopted a World Bank structural adjustment programme aimed at promoting exports, reducing imports and cutting Government expenditure even at the expense of the social services sector. Some of the recent measures include laying–off a fifth of the (urban–based) state employees and helping half of them resettle in rural areas.

This chapter examines late colonial and post–independence policies in the fields of urban and regional planning, land, housing and provision of urban infrastructure in Guinea Bissau. While many PAIGC policies may be seen as 'proto–socialist', international pressures on an economy that never quite 'took off' made pragmatism

97

Country Profile: Guinea Bissau

National territory: 36,125 km²
Population: 910,000 (1986)
Population density: 24 inhab/sq.km
Labour force: 427,000 (1985), 81% in agriculture
Urbanization rate: 27%
Capital: Bissau; 120,000 inhabitants
Natural growth rate: 1.7% (1975–1982)
Estimated urban growth rate:
Life expectancy: 44.4 years for men; 47.6 years for women
Infant mortality: 15.4%
Illiteracy rate: 81.1%
Religions: Two-thirds profess traditional African beliefs; nearly one-third are Muslim
Language: Portuguese (official), spoken is mostly the 'crioulo' dialect, a mixture between
    Portuguese and African languages.
Educational expenditure: 15.3% of budget (1983)
Military expenditure: 8% of budget
Major export products: oil seeds (dates and peanuts) 42%, fish 34%, wood 7%, fresh fruit
    4%.
Major markets: France (99%)
Foreign assistance: $ 66.4 million (1985);
    sources: OECD 46%, IDA 14%, OPEC 6%, CMEA 2%

Some important dates:

15th century: first Portuguese trade settlements
1956   Foundation of *PAIGC* (independence party)
1959   Begin of armed guerilla struggle against Portuguese occupation
1972   First free elections in liberated areas
1973   Resistance leader Amilcar Cabral assassinated by Portuguese agents
1973   Definitive liberation of Portuguese domination, declaration of independent republic
1980   Military coup led by João Bernadino, government bodies were centralized. Former
       president Louis Chabral sought exile in Cuba after spending a term in prison.
1984   Attempted *coup d'état*, its leader Paulo Correira was executed in 1986.

Sources: Die Länder der Erde, Köln: Pahl–Rugenstein, 1982. Third World Guide, Montevideo: Third World Editors, 1988. Politisches Lexikon Afrika. München: C.H. Beck, 1985. J. Dávila: Shelter, Poverty and African Revolutionary Socialism, London: IIED, 1987. Map indicating urban centres with more than 3,000 inhabitants or more (in 1979) from Dávila, op.cit.

an habitual type of policy among its political leaders.[1] Shelter policies and territorial planning must be seen in the context of development strategies and the economic realities faced by a Government agenda too burdened with the urgency of political and economic survival. It may be ironic that in a climate of shrinking international (and national) safety nets, a stagnant economy and a set of neo–liberal economic policies will work in the direction of containing the size of the urban sector, an ideal so often espoused by socialist planners.

From Forsaken Colony to Forsaken Nation

The Colonial Legacy

Guinea Bissau's history has been marked by frequent and often massive population movements. One of the earliest on record is the Mandinga invasion in the thirteenth century following the annexation of a large area of present–day Guinea Bissau into the dominion of the Emperor of Mali. The Mandinga conquest pushed the tribes of the mainland towards the coast. Some were integrated in the Muslim Mandinga culture while others, like the Papel and the Manjacos, formed small independent kingdoms. Several foreign invasions had profound effects upon the spatial distribution of population within present–day Guinea Bissau, an example of which is that of the Fulas in the nineteenth century which also drove some of the population in the interior plains closer to the coast. Today's rural and urban settlement pattern is as much a result of these large migratory movements as of the regime imposed upon the territory's inhabitants by the Portuguese colonizers, particularly in its last and most suffocating phase – the war of Independence (1963–1974).

Exploration of the West coast of Africa to set up trading posts led the Portuguese to settle in the Cape Verde islands in 1445 and a year later in present–day Guinea Bissau. The first European settlers in the islands soon engaged in trade with the continent. Guinea Bissau depended administratively on Cape Verde and was little more than a hunting ground for slave traders until the abolition of slavery in the second half of the nineteenth century. As early as the seventeenth century a string of fortified towns along the coast suggested not only that the European presence was not always welcome by local tribes but also that there was strong competition among European powers for these territories and its ports. Disputes over the 'ownership' of African territories were to be settled in the Berlin Congress of 1885.

Not long after the Paris Treaty of 1886 (which delineated Portuguese Guinea's boundaries with the two neighbouring French colonies of Senegal and Guinea Conakry), growing demand in Europe for products such as groundnuts and palm oil led to an intensification of the direct exploitation of the colony by the Portuguese and by other European traders. This was accompanied by violent pacification campaigns

---

1) These are societies which "could be said to be engaged in the 'transition to socialism' to the extent that efforts are made and institutions designed in such a way as to pre–figure or increasingly to embody the eventual forms of 'full socialism'" (White, 1983).

against the most troublesome local ethnic groups who up to then had been left virtually undisturbed given the absence of European settlers.

This period set the essential pattern of colonial exploitation, an economy based upon the export of agricultural products cheaply produced by peasants who, in addition to producing food crops for their own consumption, would grow groundnuts and palm kernels for sale to the Europeans. Unlike in Angola and Mozambique, the Portuguese did not impose a policy of forced labour upon the Guinean peasantry (Wield, 1983). However, some monetarization of the peasant economy was assured by the imposition of a hut tax in 1903, which forced farmers to grow crops for sale. This led to uprisings that were not totally quelled until the 1930s under Portugal's Salazarist regime (1926–1974). In the first decades of the century trade was largely dominated by French companies with Portugal merely charging export duties. Under Salazar, virtually all export–import trade in the African colonies was left to the network of outlets of the privately–owned Companhia União Fabril, whose operations also covered other Portuguese colonies.

Local hostility against the Portuguese was expressed in various forms at different times but systematic and politically organized opposition only started in the 1950s with the appearance of several nationalist movements. The strongest – and most successful – of these was the PAIGC, founded in 1956 by a group of Guinean and Cape Verdean intellectuals under the leadership of the now legendary Amilcar Cabral (cf. Davidson, 1981). Cabral came from a Cape Verdean family and through his work as an agronomist for the colonial government had gained a solid knowledge of Guinea Bissau and its people. In 1963, after a fruitless political campaign to persuade the Salazarist regime to grant independence to Guinea Bissau and the Cape Verde Islands, the PAIGC undertook armed revolt. Through internationally backed guerrilla warfare the rebels gradually managed to control an expanding area in the mainland territory.

Portuguese territorial planning, housing provision other than for civil servants and the supply of basic infrastructure (such as sanitation, potable water and electricity) outside a restricted European core in key administrative towns had been negligible until the start of the war. Although the colonial administration never devised a policy of forcefully controlling the inflow of African labour force to urban areas (as in Britain's African colonies or indeed in South Africa until very recently) views were often expressed about the convenience of keeping farmers in their villages 'where their presence is so necessary as the cornerstones of agricultural development' (Vega, 1949).

Nationalist denunciations of Portuguese colonial practices led to an international outcry in the early 1960s (conveniently voiced after other European powers had relinquished most of their colonies). Portugal's colonial authorities found themselves at pains to improve their tarnished international image. These efforts included producing a book both in Portuguese and English which, in addition to pictures showing children of different races happily sitting next to each other in Bissau's schools, among other things carried plans for a low–income neighbourhood in the outskirts of Bissau (the Bairro de Ajuda). The alleged aim of this housing scheme was to provide each African family in the city with a dwelling (Vega, 1949). The project was built a few years later but the design and construction specifications were so high that even in the unlikely event of its being allocated to Africans as claimed by the colonial authorities the cost of the houses was far beyond the reach of the African poor. The scheme would prove very useful during the war for accommodating some of the 30,000 Portuguese troops hastily brought in by General Antonio de Spínola to quell the nationalist revolt.

The Liberation Struggle

By the late 1960s, the PAIGC guerrillas had managed not only to reorganize agricultural production but also effectively to improve living conditions among the peasant population in the liberated areas. They had done so by laying the first stones in the construction of a new independent society in these areas (Davidson, 1981). The foundations for such a project included an independent health system, schools and technical assistance to the farmers, a judiciary system (the People's Courts) and even a chain of People's Stores where producers could exchange their crops for such basic goods as soap, oil and salt. In sharp contrast to the Portuguese–held territories where agricultural production had gradually declined almost to a halt, in 1973 the liberated zones were producing a food surplus. Added pressure was put on the colonial authorities through PAIGC's policy of providing no incentives to cash crops, which were seen as prolonging the life of the colonial export economy.

In September 1973, several months after Cabral's assassination by Portuguese agents at his home in exile in Conakry, PAIGC's Popular Assembly meeting in the southeast of the country unilaterally proclaimed national independence. Portugal's formal recognition and withdrawal from the territory did not take place until one year later, after the April 1974 coup had in turn ousted Portugal's four–decade long dictatorship to open the way to a new European democracy.

During the war, strategic territorial planning became a high priority for the Portuguese. More infrastructure was built in the span of a few years than in five centuries of domination. These were busy years for Portuguese contractors, paving roads (including the country's main thoroughfare from Bissau to Gabu) and building bridges, military barracks (some of which now house schools and ministries) and hospitals. It is ironic that the best examples of public works left to the revolutionary government were built to fight it.

Less permanent efforts were geared towards the construction of strategic hamlets (*aldeamentos*) where the rural population was to be concentrated and controlled during the war. Some of these were actually built at great expense and included a military administrative core, residential areas in easy–to–survey gridiron layouts, ring roads surrounding the settlement to move military equipment quickly around the hamlet in the event of an uprising and some buildings which show the hamlets' martial character, such as health posts, barracks and landing fields[2]. There are accounts of the great difficulties faced by the peasants when constrained to live in

---

2) To our knowledge there is no assessment of this first example of 'social military engineering' in Guinea Bissau. Plans for the new 'aldeamentos' and master plans for the existing towns where the peasant population was to be concentrated are collected in: Portugal 1973.

these hamlets. Apart from frequent human rights violations and the obvious cultural incongruities of accommodating extended families in a layout designed for a nuclear family set–up, the hamlets rarely provided enough land nearby for the farmers to cultivate for their own needs. Family members were often forced to seek work in the cities or in neighbouring countries to buy foodstuffs.

The First PAIGC Government, 1974–1980

The first Government of the PAIGC, led by Amilcar Cabral's half brother Luiz, received financial and political support from international donors such as Sweden, the USSR, Algeria, Cuba and the United Nations to launch a Programme of National Reconstruction. Inspired by Amilcar Cabral, PAIGC's philosophy was essentially one of putting an end to the exploitation of the people of Guinea Bissau by whatever group or class of people. Although explicitly advocating socialist principles of economic and social organization, the policies of the new Government would prove essentially pragmatic from the start (Hochet, 1983).

The long war had considerably weakened the country's economy: the area of cultivated land decreased from 410,000 hectares in 1953 to 125,000 in 1972. Attacks on villages and air raids had forced an estimated 150,000 peasants out of their land to neighbouring countries and to the cities (particularly Bissau whose 1970 population was an estimated 70,000). No estimates exist as to the numbers killed. Dykes, irrigation canals and entire fields were devastated by bombing. Apart from a brewery in Bissau and a few sawmills, the Portuguese left little in the way of manufacturing industry.

The agricultural surplus produced with PAIGC support in the liberated areas proved insufficient also to cover the needs of the regions maintained artificially by the Portuguese during the war (including the largest urban centres of Bissau and Bafata). The new Government's view was that at least while production returned to normal levels, the shortfall had to be met through imports (Davidson, 1981). External aid played and would continue to play for several years a decisive role in covering what would eventually become an almost perennial food deficit, one which has been particularly acute in the urban areas. Between 1979 and 1982 food aid covered over 80 per cent of total food imports for household consumption and almost half the national deficit.

Under PAIGC's Reconstruction Programme, agriculture was to be accorded highest priority, with heavy industry acting as a 'dynamic force' behind it. The tasks of organizing and mobilizing the labour force were entrusted to the PAIGC, the 'liberation movement in power'. Although a few farmer co–operatives and state farms were organized, the bulk of agricultural production would continue coming from traditional farming. Development strategies followed the framework drawn in the liberated areas, with an initial emphasis on food crops rather than cash crops for export. The network of People's Stores (now extended to cover the whole country) and SOCOMIN (a joint venture between the state and private enterprise) took over the monopoly on export–import trade previously held by Companhia União Fabril. Implictly acknowledging the lack of skilled workers in its own ranks, the PAIGC did not opt for large–scale nationalization of the economy. Thus, for instance, some 270 private traders were authorized to operate as agents of the state in rural areas (Galli, 1987).

Internal political efforts were geared towards gaining the backing of those who had held posts during Portuguese rule, most of whom were concentrated in the larger urban centres. This proved a very difficult task and the ensuing years were not altogether free of threats to PAIGC's stability in power and of tensions between PAIGC members and former colonial personnel (Galli, 1987). An increasing depend–ence upon foreign aid to support a Soviet–style industrialization while supporting a growing urban–based bureaucracy gradually alienated Cabral's Government from the rural population that had given PAIGC crucial support during the war.

Although the Party's prevailing ideological principles remained unchanged in their stress of agriculture as the basis of Guinean development, in practice the Government failed to mobilize the peasants to generate a surplus which would sustain the urban population, and more specifically the growing state apparatus. A lack of incentives for agricultural production (in the way of higher prices, for instance) was compounded by the almost negligible volume of investments in infrastructure to support agricultural trade. This meant that it would usually be cheaper to import rice from as far away as Pakistan than to transport it from surplus–producing areas in the south of the country.

Farmers' political alienation combined with the Government's inability to cope with severe economic problems to produce a mounting tension among factions within the party. In November 1980, a coup ousted Luiz Cabral's Government. Control of the state was assumed by a new Council of the Revolution led by one of the main guerrilla leaders in the liberation war, Bernardo 'Nino' Vieira. The first PAIGC Government had failed to put forward a 'national project' that would help unite Guineans behind common development objectives.

The Second PAIGC Government, 1980 –

Except for a coup attempt in 1985, which led to the execution of six plotters and to international protests including the suspension of some aid funds[3], Vieira's Govern–ment has enjoyed stability. Upon taking power, Vieira proclaimed its commitment to rectifying the previous Government's mistakes and wrongdoings. As Rudebeck has pointed out, the political programme remained unchanged as did "the structural conditions which determine the country's developmental context" (Rudebeck, 1982). In 1981, the Government launched its economic stabilization programme for 1982–83, which was soon followed by the sectorially–oriented First Four Year Develop–ment Plan 1983–86 (FFYDP), outlining development priorities (Guinea Bissau 1982a; Dowbor, 1983). Yearly updates of the plan sought to correct it during its course and,

---

3) The Portugal–based Gulbenkian Foundation allegedly withdrew all aid to the country in protest for such dictatorial excesses. See 'Guinea Bissau: Post Revolution Politics', *West Africa* magazine, July 26, 1987.

following an agreement with the International Monetary Fund in 1983, these were to be progressively reinforced with more austere measures (Lima Handem, 1987).

The FFYDP set out a strategy to achieve national self–sufficiency in food production and an increase in exports through limited state intervention in the economy while creating incentives for the private sector (including farmers). In order to meet these goals, several imbalances and policy failures had to be redressed, including, among others, a deficit in the balance of payments (exports barely covered a fifth of imports), a fiscal deficit (state expenditure was covered only in half by revenue), a poor rate of project completion, a deficient agricultural trade and a poor support to agricultural production. Under the new plan, state investment in agriculture was to increase from an average of 11.1 per cent of total investment in 1978–81 to 15.4 per cent in 1982 and 30.1 per cent in 1983. Industry's share was to be gradually reduced from 23.2 per cent in 1978–81 to 10.0 and 4.0 per cent, respectively[4]. Housing received an explicit mention in the FFYDP and so did the spatial dimension, expressed in the official aim to "correct regional imbalances".

The liberalization measures of the stabilization programme and the FFYDP had a positive impact upon agricultural production but lost momentum in 1985 and 1986. The economic slowdown was partly due to a seemingly ineluctable fall in the international prices of most of the country's main exports (groundnuts, cashewnuts, fish, palm kernels and forestry products). For a World Bank mission which visited the country in February 1986, though, most of the blame lay with "implementation delays and inadequate measures on the part of the Government" (World Bank, 1987:2). Economic liberalization was not taking place fast enough. Producers still found smuggling their surplus to neighbouring countries more profitable than selling it to the Government. The Government not only was spending too much but was doing so with too many employees. By late 1985 the fiscal deficit amounted to 36 per cent of GDP while the balance of payments deficit was around 30 per cent of GDP. Moreover, international aid still represented roughly half the GDP of some $170 million.

The Bank outlined a stabilization programme aimed at breathing new life into the liberalization measures (World Bank, 1987). The programme (to whose adherence all future aid has been conditioned) follows the general lines of structural adjustment packages: a devaluation of the Guinean peso, rises in agricultural producer prices and a reduction of consumption levels particularly in the form of Government expenditures and staff (by 30 per cent by 1990) with the aim of balancing its budget and allowing it to concentrate on much needed investments in infrastructure. The World Bank programme received further official backing when the Fourth PAIGC Congress, held in November 1987, endorsed a partial retreat of state intervention and the transition to private enterprise, particularly in the commercial sector (*West Africa* magazine, 1987).

---

4) Other sectors given priority in the FFYDP were fisheries, forestry and mining, each of which received 7.5, 2.8 and 2.0 per cent of the total state investments planned for 1983–1986; Government of Guinea Bissau, 1982a.

Urban and Regional Development: Policies or Contingencies?

At the time of the 1979 census, the national population numbered 767,731, of which 73 per cent lived in 3,600 rural villages (locally known as *tabancas*) of less than 2,000 inhabitants. Bissau, the capital city, at 105,273 had the largest urban population, followed by Bafatá and Gabú, with populations of 13,429 and 7,803, respectively. No reliable statistics exist for any other year except 1950, when the census put national population at 517,290, Bissau's at 17,255, Bafatá's at 3,570 and Bolama's (then the third largest settlement) at 3,075. Most of the country's largest urban centres and settlements are located on the banks of the main rivers which drain the country, the Geba and the Cacheu[5].

PAIGC's urban and regional policies may be said to have originated at the time of the war of independence against the Portuguese. Party leaders and particularly Amilcar Cabral believed that a clear–cut rural–urban dichotomy had developed within Guinea Bissau: while the Portuguese colonial army had gradually narrowed down their control to the urban areas, the rebels had gained territory in the countryside (CIDAC, 1983). Cabral repeatedly expressed worries about the dangers involved in taking over a state apparatus previously run by Africans under colonialist control. He advocated the need to create a new and decentralized administration after indepen–dence: "all structural decisions are to be based on the needs and and condition of the peasantry, who are the vast majority of our people" (quoted in Davidson, 1981:101–102). He even spoke of discarding altogether the idea of a capital city for the new free nation[6].

Some of Cabral's hopes nearly materialized shortly after his death. Not long after the declaration of independence in September 1973, the rebels anounced that Madina de Boé, a small and remote hamlet in one of the poorest regions of the country, near the border with Guinea Conakry, would become the nation's new capital. Behind such decision was a desire "to avoid urban concentrations in a country dominated by a rural economy" (CIDAC, 1983). This was soon reversed, however, due to practical reasons, not least the fact that Bissau, the capital under the colonial administration already had the necessary infrastructure to serve such a purpose. Given the enormous constraints faced by the new Government, one cannot but conclude that no more realistic decision could have been reached.

The first PAIGC Government inherited a state administration, administrative personnel and an infrastructure largely geared to war requirements. One of PAIGC's first tasks was to adapt all these elements to the exigencies of the new, independent Government. This ranged from creating new laws and eliminating old ones, to turning

---

5) There is no official definition of 'urban centre' in Guinea Bissau, but for the purposes of this paper it is taken to include those settlements with a population of over 2,000 inhabitants (Guinea Bissau, 1979).

6) "In fact we are against the whole idea of a capital. Why shouldn't ministries be dispersed? After all, our country is a small one with passable roads, at least in the central areas. Why should we saddle ourselves with the paraphernalia of a presidential palace, a concentration of ministries, the clear signs of an emergent elite which can be soon become a privileged group?" (cf. Davidson, 1981).

large army barracks into Government offices.[7] In the field of human settlements these included nationalizing all land, the division of public investment by sectors and regions, unprecedented public investments in public services and even in housing the active promotion of popular mobilization.

Bissau's economy contracted sharply after Portugal's withdrawal. Ninety per cent of the country's few industries (which included car and ship maintenance installations as well as food and beverage production plants) were concentrated in the capital and in the second largest city, Bafatá (Adreini & Lambert, 1978). The capital city's economic base lay in trade and in the services it provided to the colony's administration. Most of the goods consumed there were imported from Portugal. Without the large amounts of capital poured in by the colonialists, and without the consumer market provided by the war economy (especially the 30,000 troops and some of their families), a substantial part of the city's enterprises lost their sources of demand.

In the space of a year and with U.N. assistance the PAIGC encouraged the resettlement in productive agricultural areas of 35,000 war refugees returning from neighbouring countries as well as 40,000 peasants who had either fled to the cities or who had been resettled by the Portuguese in the *aldeamentos*. This helped to mitigate the impact of the collapse of the urban economy, which for many years had been subsidised by Portugal's central bank, and thereby reduced unemployment rates in the larger urban areas.

The first PAIGC Government was characterized by an increasing concentration of capital and activities in Bissau: with 14 per cent of the national population, Bissau received 39.1 per cent of total state investments between 1978 and 1980 (Guinea Bissau, 1982b). Although in theory agriculture was to be first in the list of Government priorities (Goulet, 1978), state resources went largely towards boosting the export sector and more specifically to the development of industrial projects in and around Bissau: industry received 23.2 per cent of all state investments between 1978 and 1981, while agriculture was left with a mere 11.1 per cent (Dos Santos, 1984). This followed a model of development geared not only towards catering for internal consumption needs but also towards diversifying exports in the hope of improving foreign exchange reserves.

The Vieira Government's First Four–Year Development Plan sought to incorporate the notions of spatial planning into national development planning. The Plan's section on urban and regional planning states that priority must be given to defining and implementing a territorial policy geared towards "preventing or eliminating regional imbalances" (Guinea Bissau, 1982a). It also notes that up to the early 1980s, a shortage of human and financial resources had allowed only a few projects aimed at attaining a more balanced distribution between urban and rural areas to materialize. Until that point, the impact of such limited actions had therefore been minimal. Despite this and although it fails to spell out the means through which correction to

---

7) Nevertheless, some old colonial laws have been preserved, such as the 'Regulamento Geral das Edificações Urbanas', dating from 1960 and the 'Regulamento da Ocupação e Concessão de Terrenos', from 1961.

this imbalance could be achieved, this Plan represents the first attempt to introduce the notion of territorial planning into the overall development planning process.

There are no data available on the regional distribution of investments for the first three years of implementation of this Plan. Yet, according to the investment schedule for the period of the Plan, Bissau is supposed to have received 25 per cent of all the state investments, while the remaining eight administrative regions were expected to receive shares of total investment "more commensurate with their share of national population".

Finally, structural adjustment policies may have brought a paradoxical return to Cabral's views and to ideals so often espoused in Third World socialism: the battle to turn 'consumer cities' into 'producer cities'[8]. An initial phase of cutting back in public sector expenditures has led to the laying off of some 3,000 state workers. As part of an ILO scheme to help the private sector absorb them, some 1,500 workers (and presumably their families too) have been resettled in rural co-operatives away from the capital to work as farmers, mainly producing food. The $2.4 million project is being funded by international donors like UNDP and the EEC and includes land reclamation and construction of housing. This project is highly controversial, to say the least, as any attempt to resettle people necessarily is. However, the fact that recruitment to the scheme has been oversubscribed endorses the disturbing view that Bissau's largely state–supported economy has failed to provide many of its poorer inhabitants with the means of fulfilling even the most basic needs (Addison & Demery, 1986).

Land Policies

Land nationalization (National Laws numbers 4 and 5, 1975), although a necessary move given the PAIGC Government's political priorities, in practice did not bring about a dramatic change in tenure patterns. Except for the devastation and massive population displacements brought about by the eleven–year liberation war, tribal land ownership in the rural areas[9] had been left almost untouched by four centuries of colonial rule[10]. With the possible exception of the largest urban centres, where the more important Portuguese assets were concentrated, the significance of nationaliz-ation lay largely in its symbolic re–affirmation of the new Government's intentions to control the country's resources rather than in its political or economic value in re-allocating land tenure. These laws transferred all private land–ownership to the state, which in theory allocates it to whomever needs it, thereby following traditional land allocation mechanisms. In Bissau, the local state committee is responsible for

---

8) For a discussion and examples of these views see the Introduction in Forbes & Thrift, 1987.

9) For a description of traditional land tenure patterns and the laws governing them in Guinea Bissau, see Hochet, 1983: 31–32.

10) The country's unhealthy climate and lack of mineral resources and the much better prospects offered by the other two Portuguese colonies in mainland Africa contributed little towards turning Guinea Bissau into an attractive place for European settlers and investors.

establishing land–use patterns, assessing individual demands for land and allocating plots on the basis of such assessments.

In urban areas two types of plots are allocated upon payment of a yearly lease, the distinction between them being the durability of the materials used in the construction of the planned building (these may be either 'permanent' or 'precarious'). The lease may be inherited by the heirs of the original lessee but it may in theory be withdrawn if the lessee fails to build within one year of the original allocation. The state has the right to revoke the lease 'in the public interest', upon what an indemnity must be paid. However, in practice enforcement of the law is rendered difficult by the lack of cadastral surveys and trained personnel to prepare (let alone update) a cadastre at a city– or a regional–level. New constructions in Bissau may take years before they are registered and the relevant tax levied. It has been estimated that about two–thirds of the city's housing units have been built without a building permit from the planning authorities. Dième reports that there have been cases where houses built without a permit have been demolished although he fails to mention any specific examples (Dième, 1981).

For several years now, attempts have been made to reform or replace the remaining colonial laws and procedures which regulate the use of urban land and the granting of building permits. These were preserved after independence, on the grounds that they did not collide with the Government's political and development priorities. However, whether due to pressures from some tribal groups whose traditional tenure patterns could potentially enter into conflict with stricter laws or due to a lack of personnel to prepare and ensure that the law is properly enforced, no new laws have been issued since 1975.

Shelter and PAIGC's Development Strategies

The Housing Crisis

Despite the total lack of reliable, regularly–produced statistics, available evidence points to a growing urban housing crisis. Increasing overcrowding, low–coverage and deficient public utilities and the near stagnation of both the formal and informal housing construction sectors have been almost permanent urban features of the country's life as an independent nation. This is not to say that under Portuguese rule conditions were any better among the African population. A substantial number of Guineans have benefited from improvements in their living standards in the period after 1974. But despite such real improvements, the housing crisis remains a further manifestation of the economic, technical and political factors that still hinder development in this small economy.

Census statistics are of limited value in judging this, but they are of some help in describing housing conditions. Data collected during the 1950 census of the native population show a count of 125,085 traditionally–built huts in the country, with a total of 226,671 rooms ('divisões'). Each hut housed an average of four persons. The

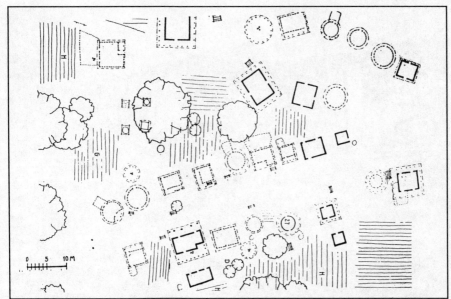

Ill. 1: Traditional Beafada hamlet in the 'tabanca' of Binhalom in the Quínara region, east of Bissau.
(Source: Blazejewicz et al., 1981)

census also collected information on traditional construction methods[11]. Around 70 per cent of the huts had mud walls and the remaining had bamboo walls. No figures were collected on the African population's access to safe water supply, sanitation or other social services. Some sources suggest that these were limited exclusively to the European quarters of the most important colonial administrative centres such as Bissau, Bolama, Bafatá and Gabú. During the war, such services were increased on a par with other basic infrastructure such as bridges, roads and barracks at points of strategic importance for counter–insurgence actions.

Indeed, a short walk around the centre of these towns today helps corroborate this. Virtually all of these settlements consist of a central core where shops, Government buildings and the residences of the colonial administrative personnel and traders were located, with paved roads and services such as electricity (generated locally), and water and sanitation networks. Nowadays, these old colonial cores are largely inhabited by diplomats, expatriates and civil servants. The low–income African population typically occupies the surrounding urban and peri–urban areas which, except for higher densities and the beginnings of some building lines, bear little physical difference from traditional villages nearby.

Data gathered by the 1979 national population census also has some, albeit limited, use for an assessment of housing conditions. Unfortunately, the census questionnaire

---

11) For a detailed discussion of traditional construction methods in the different regions of Guinea Bissau see Blazejewicz et al. 1981.

Ill. 2: A well in a low–income 'bairro' of Bissau.   *(Foto: J. Dávila)*

made no distinction between a 'house' and a 'household'[12]. This has little or no implication in a study of conditions in rural areas where each household is usually allocated one dwelling. In urban areas, however, where dwellings usually, and increasingly, accommodate more than one household, this hinders a more systematic study of changes in housing and living conditions. In the early 1980s each dwelling in Bissau housed an average of 1.6 families, or 9.1 persons (Pfister, 1981).

The 1979 census also showed that, counting Bissau out, 31.7 per cent of the country's households lived in dwellings with one or two rooms and 81.8 per cent lived in dwellings with five rooms or fewer rooms. The study quoted above, on the other hand, showed that in Bissau 47.6 per cent of all households lived in dwellings with one or two rooms and 76.0 per cent lived in dwellings with fewer than five rooms. The housing shortage clearly weighs down on all social groups. But with recorded cases of eighteen persons living in dwellings of 100 square metres in Bissau's poorer quarters, there remains little doubt that Bissau's poorer inhabitants are worse off in terms of living space at their disposal than the country's rural majority.

The 1979 census suggests that traditional construction remains an important form of shelter, even in urban areas. In that year 87.7 per cent of Bissau's houses had mud or adobe walls, compared to 75.7 per cent for the rest of the country. Another material widely used on walls was bamboo. In contrast – and not surprisingly, given the high cost of imported materials – only 0.3 per cent of all of Bissau's houses had walls built with reinforced concrete, while in 9.6 per cent of all dwellings some

---

12) The term used in the census document is 'agregado' implying an extended family. No mention is made of the concept of 'household' as opposed to that of 'family' (Pfister, 1981).

cement had been used. Taken as a whole, the country revealed a much lower use of such 'Western' materials, with 0.1 per cent of all dwellings using reinforced concrete and 2.0 per cent using some cement on their walls.

The large majority of buildings and houses reported by the census as built with non–traditional materials existed before independence, but these are generally located in the old colonial quarters of administrative centres. A small number of such buildings, however, include a few that were constructed after independence, either as residences for senior Government officials and expatriates, or for Government offices.

A study commissioned by the Government in 1981 with funding from the United Nations remains the most detailed analysis of the housing sector in Guinea Bissau. Already in 1981 the roots of a severe housing crisis were clearly visible. For F. Pfister, author of the study, the main problem associated with housing production in urban areas was the virtual lack of building materials. Not without alarm he noted that as a consequence "with the possible exception of traditional huts in the villages which are still entirely built using traditional methods and materials, the entire sector is paralysed" (Pfister, 1981).

The harsh reality brought home by such words raises the question of the adequacy of different 'solutions' to the housing problem *vis–à–vis* others. According to the study, construction activities, including housing production, are undertaken by several agents. These include foreign enterprises (which generated 73.9 per cent of the sector's registered value added in 1981), national enterprises (14.7 per cent), including two co–operatives, the Ministry of Public Works (11.4 per cent) and lastly, the 'informal sector' whose output has been estimated at 2,300 to 2,500 units a year for the whole country (and whose contribution to the sector's value added is, by definition, unrecorded)[13]. Informal housing includes all forms of traditional construction and accounts for a substantial part of the housing stock in the urban areas and virtually all in the rural areas (Pfister, 1981).

Contrary to what staunch defenders of indigenous architecture might argue, traditional construction methods are of limited use in urban centres with a population the size of Bissau's and perhaps even Bafatá's. The labour–intensive constructions found in the country's *tabancas* (villages) is made possible not only through collective efforts but also by the availability of time and materials left at the end of each harvesting cycle. In urban areas, on the other hand, a population largely employed (or even under–employed) in the service or petty–trading sectors will not have enough time at their disposal for building or even maintaining traditionally–built housing. Moreover, although no data are available it is not inconceivable that the situation in Bissau may not be unlike that noted by Pinsky for Maputo, where transport of traditional materials to construction sites in the city is as costly in foreign currency terms as importing non–traditional construction materials (Pinsky, 1985), due to the unavoidable use of imported fuel in transport.

The few construction materials that are imported into Guinea Bissau are either allocated to national construction companies or else are reserved for Government

---

13) 'Formal' and 'informal' sector activities in this paper are taken to mean simply officially registered or unregistered productive activities, respectively.

projects financed with hard currency. This undermines the development of both the formal and informal construction sectors. For Pfister, the limited availability of such materials was not only rapidly leading to critical housing shortages in urban areas but was actually restricting the creation of new jobs for craftsmen and construction workers in urban areas (Pinsky, 1985).

Little of the Government housing built in the post–independence period has escaped the problems affecting other state investments: several projects have been initiated, particularly in Bissau, which have suffered from similar problems as the industrial enterprises set up by the first PAIGC Government, ones such as lack of finance and shortage of skilled manpower and inputs. Many have been left unfinished (Forster & Lopes, 1984). In a context of acute housing shortages affecting all social layers, most of the new housing units finished after 1974 whether by national or foreign enterprises have been allocated to groups who are either implicitly or explicitly perceived as playing a key role in supporting the economy (such as members of agricultural co–operatives, the staff of some ministries and expatriates working for foreign aid donors) or else to those who occupy key political positions in the national Government (such as high Government officials and the old freedom fighters).

Public utility services such as water supply, sanitation and electricity are largely limited to the larger urban centres (defined here as those with over 2,000 inhabitants in 1979). And among these, the capitals of the nine regional districts have slightly better conditions[14]. A foreign–backed programme to improve water supply in the countryside has been underway since the early 1980s. It envisages the construction, by 1990, of 5,500 wells in villages around the country. By the end of 1984, 1,600 wells had been built, and it was estimated that as a result of this effort around 220,000 rural inhabitants already had access to safe sources of water[15].

On average, Bissau's residents enjoy slightly better services than the rest of the country. But even there, access to electricity, water and sanitation is notoriously low by any standards. Only slightly over a tenth of Bissau's population had access to electricity and piped water. Twelve per cent had no sanitary means of disposing of excreta at all and among those who did there was a high use of pit latrines, usually a short–term solution. If one were to exclude Bissau from the first column, figures for the rest of the country would be even lower, as the population of the capital city boosts averages up slightly. It is highly likely though, that efforts like the rural water supply project mentioned earlier may have helped raise the percentage of population with access to water supply.

---

14) For administrative purposes the country is divided in 9 Regions (including Bissau's Autonomous Sector) and these further into 34 Sectors, each one of which has its own administrative capital.

15) Data obtained from the National Directorate of Water Resources and from Krishna et al., 1983.

Shelter and the PAIGC Agenda

For half a dozen years after Independence, activities in the fields of housing, construction and urban and regional planning were not much more than a reflection of the Government's 'fire–brigade' approach in confronting the country's economic and political difficulties and in co–ordinating external donations. Despite a shortage of funds the volume and allocation of state investments in construction were essentially determined on the basis of the demands coming from whatever ministry or department was in need of new premises or installations and happened to have access to external aid. During such a period "despite some attempts at establishing a programme and a set of controls to guide it, the construction sector . . . was wide open to the influence of all sorts of (conflicting) conceptions and technologies" (Forster & Lopes, 1984). It would not be until the end of the decade that planning could be used to allocate scarce state funds somewhat more efficiently. Nonetheless, planning efforts remain seriously hampered by a notorious lack of reliable statistics and a shortage of trained personnel[16].

The Third PAIGC Congress (1977) stated that the housing problem merited 'particular attention' in a national development plan. The Congress advocated the promotion of traditional building materials as opposed to costly imported ones. The Congress also stated – albeit somewhat vaguely – that "any effort aimed at improving living standards demands coordination between different Government institutions and the active and conscious participation of the country's communities" (cf. Forster & Lopes, 1984). As these statements suggest, the urgency of fostering popular participation and reinforcing a process of institution–building was still clearly present in the country's leading political minds. But not so the specific ways in which these were to be put into practice, as the notorious absence of a more determined form of planning would suggest in the ensuing five years.

Between 1978 and 1980, the Government undertook the first–ever studies on the living conditions of Bissau's poor. There was a growing preoccupation among high–ranking officials and politicians about the appalling conditions of many of the city's largest low–income *bairros*. This was a sore to PAIGC's main goal of ensuring the wellbeing and prosperity of the people of Guinea Bissau (PAIGC, 1979:3). On the other hand, the search for solutions to the problems faced by the urban poor also squared well with the first PAIGC Government's policy of wooing a growing urban population, even at the expense of the larger rural population.

The First Four–Year Development Plan (1983–86), the first planning instrument in the young nation's history, described housing as a human basic need only second to food. The FFYDP stated that the satisfaction of such need "is an absolute priority and an indispensable foundation to start off the development process". Housing was also "a powerful instrument for mobilizing national economic resources". The importance of self–help was emphasized "as the starting point for future (Govern-ment) policies and intervention, whether in the area of housing or in sanitation

---

16) A highly desirable outcome of the recent World Bank adjustment programme for the country would certainly be a strengthening of planning mechanisms.

projects. . .". Consistent with its economic liberalization principles, the FFYDP favoured an institutional support for the construction process rather than the supply of finished products.

The gradual process of withdrawal of any form of direct state intervention in housing finally reached completion with the comprehensive adjustment programme supported by the World Bank. This states that the Government lacks the resources "to meet out of the budget the pressing housing needs of the population". Thus "the most effective policy for the Government is to support popular construction with education programs and with whatever aid is needed to remove administrative barriers, such as unclear land titles". More encouragingly though, it also admonishes the Government not to spend scarce resources on housing foreign technicians and instructs it to cancel a 642–dwelling project for housing foreign consultants planned for the late 1980s (World Bank, 1987:51).

Industrialized Construction versus Self-Help Housing

The first PAIGC Government's idea that rapid industrialization was to provide the basis of sustained growth permeated many areas of state action, including state construction and housing. Some of the construction projects launched before 1980 that would help to the demise of the first Government included an expansion of the highway linking Bissau with its nearby airport, an extension of the airport's main building, two presidential palaces in regional capitals and a 96–flat complex on the outskirts of Bissau (to be built using Cuban pre–fabrication technology).

Not long after several of these were already under way it became apparent to Government officials that local expertise could not cope either with the large size of the projects or with the sophisticated technology they required. This, coupled with the realization that their high cost risked using up an inordinately large share of very scarce state financial and human resources, led the Government to abandon the projects long before they were completed (Rudebeck, 1982; Forster & Lopes, 1984). Other, including less sophisticated projects, have not been under operation on a continuous basis largely due to lack of replacement parts or of skilled personnel to run them[17]. Needless to say these initial industrialization efforts contributed little to solving the housing crisis.

A growing difficulty in importing construction materials was also leading Government officials to look for effective ways out of the constraints imposed by the dependence on imported materials and technologies. A growing consensus seemed to be emerging among Government planners that pre–fabricated and five–storey buildings could not and would not provide an effective solution to urban housing problems. It was in this context that the use of local materials and popular participation in self–help projects emerged as a serious viable alternative to Government–backed Western–style construction. Self–help housing was seen by the Government as the only solution capable of effectively tackling all these issues at the

---

17) Dos Santos noted that "the productive sector of the urban–industrial economy operates at below 25 per cent of its built capacity" (Dos Santos, 1984:51).

Ill. 3: Use of Cuban pre-fabrication technology in a now-paralyzed state housing project in Bissau. (*Foto: J. Dávila*)

same time. A self-help housing programme was drawn up which included a pilot project in a remote rural area.

After a promising start, however, the self-help programme did not fulfil its goals: due to insufficient organization and institutional support, the housing units in the first self-help project that was undertaken (Antula) had to be finished by conventional construction systems (Forster & Lopes, 1984). It was not until two years later that proper self-help projects would be under way[18]. Here too the programme's coverage is very limited and only a few housing units have been finished. Though some of the obstacles encountered in these projects are common to all construction projects, a more detailed assessment of these projects is certainly needed to draw some lessons of use for future projects. Particular emphasis should be placed on such aspects as the logistics of financing and implementing projects and assessing the participation of users. This in itself is an area that merits some attention, as the next section will show.

State Institutions and Popular Participation

Soon after independence responsibility for state construction activities was concentrated in the State Commissariat for Public Works (CEOPCU). Towards the

---

18) Two examples of this are a project for housing the families of workers in the Ministry of Public Works in Brá, and housing for a cooperative of agricultural workers in Caboxanque (both initially launched in 1980 but still unfinished by the mid-1980s).

end of the 1970s new departments were created in CEOPCU to include other tasks, such as planning urban and regional development. In 1980, a special department was added to co–ordinate state actions in the area of housing. The problems faced by the staff of the Commissariat and the Ministry of which it is a part have been and remain not unlike those faced by other Government departments: lack of resources to invest, let alone to produce long–term plans or assessments of the sectors they are to help guide.

The search for alternative forms of tackling the growing problem of inadequate housing and infrastructure led to an encouragement of popular participation and mobilization. The roots of this date back to the war years when the PAIGC established a system of village and neighbourhood committees elected locally (*comités de base*), "to act as organs of grass–roots political direction and to manage new social institutions emerging in the liberated zones" (Goulet, 1978). Furthermore, three types of 'mass organizations' were set up (i.e. for youth, women, and workers), with representation in the local committees. In theory "it is through the mass organizations that the Party establishes and develops its links with the popular masses . . ." (PAIGC, 1979).

Despite being one of the cornerstones of the post–independence policies pursued by the PAIGC, community participation has not proven a good vehicle for state–promoted housing or infrastructure projects. The examples mentioned earlier of attempts to incorporate users in state directed self–help projects did not meet with success. On the other hand, the few settlement upgrading projects that got off the ground in Bissau's low–income neighbourhoods were designed to follow what was essentially a top–down approach (Goulet, 1978). And yet the survival of traditional patterns of community organization in village work (in which housing construction plays an important role) and the experience of political organization in the areas liberated by the PAIGC during the war would seem to offer a large potential for successful community involvement in such projects, particularly at a pre–liberaliz-ation phase, when the political context seemed more appropriate.

Although in theory the Party and the state are parallel structures which comple-ment one another in their political and executive functions, the function of Party–related structures (such as the *comités* or the mass organizations) is one of communi-cating top–level decisions down rather than providing effective channels of communication for expressing popular needs[19]. In searching for explanations for the apparent failure of state–promoted efforts, some authors have argued that the main obstacle remains peasant mistrust of the state (i.e. Galli, 1987). For others, part of the problem lies in the Government's inability to tap other effective means of collective participation, such as the country's seventy co–operatives (with a membership of some 11,000) (Avena, 1988). Finally Lopes (1982) and Rudebeck (1982) expressed doubts about the country's political institutions as providing an effective framework for mass

---

19)   In the course of my interviews with the leaders of the Zone Committee in Bissau's Zone II (which incorporates 45 *comités de base* in the city's poorest and most densely populated settlements) they appeared to perceive the function of the committees as being more one of disseminating Party guidelines and decisions and increasing the degree of political awareness of the people, rather than as channels for effective settlement demand–making.

political participation; they saw post–independence developments as a drift away from active political work and close collaboration between the Party and the population (as was the case in the liberated areas during the war) towards a more technocratic, non–ideological state apparatus in the hands of the group of 'non–revolutionary petty bourgeois' so feared by Cabral. The recent economic reforms may have confirmed their views.

Shelter and the Financial System

The few available studies of the housing sector have placed an emphasis on the need to strengthen the financial sector. But despite past good intentions, the country still lacks a housing finance system. Most of the capital invested in construction is either foreign or is made available to the national Government by foreign donors for specific projects. None of the main domestic financial institutions (the Central Bank, the Cassa Econômica Postal, the Cassa de Crédito da Guiné–Bissau and the Fundo Nacional de Desenvolvimento) has a specific credit line for housing projects. Indeed, all public investment (including the few housing projects mentioned earlier) has been funded by external financing (World Bank, 1987). Other non–Government large–scale housing projects have also been funded through external assistance funds, as all of these are aimed at housing expatriates. Smaller scale private construction, including the urban informal sector, is generally funded by the users themselves, through savings or ad hoc loans.

Independence and Social Development

Although it is difficult to assess the extent of changes in living standards before and after independence most available evidence points to unequivocal improvements after 1974. In the 1950s Castro estimated the country's birth rate somewhat vaguely at between 40 and 60 per 1,000 inhabitants, the death rate at 20–35 per 1,000 and the infant mortality rate at 180–200 per 1,000 (Castro, 1980). However, even if one takes the upper limit in the last two figures and compares them with recent data it would appear that not much improvement has taken place: the World Bank and FAO have estimated that in 1982 the the country's birth rate was 40.6 per 1,000, the death rate was 29 per 1,000 and the infant mortality at an even higher figure of 250 per 1,000.

Figures on health services, on the other hand, do suggest some progress since independence. Portuguese Government statistics must be taken with some care, however, largely because in the 1950s and early 1960s these were used to show the adequacy of colonial rule at the time of Portugal's entry in the United Nations while during the war they were used as political propaganda against nationalist fighters. In 1960 the Portuguese claimed to have four hospitals and six rural health centres, seventeen rural maternity posts and fifty–one first–aid posts, as well as one doctor per 23,240 inhabitants and one nurse per 22,346 (Chabal, 1983). Statistics for the late 1970s put the figures at 14 hospitals (of which 10 are in settlements of under 5,500 inhabitants), 130 rural health centres, one doctor per 13,700 inhabitants and one nurse per 1,257 (FAO, 1982), considerable improvements even if accounting for the colonial administration's profligacy.

Education is another area where post–independence progress is palpable. State education under colonial rule was reserved exclusively for whites and *assimilados*[20] while the Catholic Church was left in charge of the education of African children. Chabal notes the inadequacy of religious schools in providing children even with a minimum level of literacy to become *assimilados* (Chabal, 1983). In 1964–65, official statistics showed that there was a total of 132 primary schools, with 12,173 students (of which approximately 80 per cent were in missionary schools) as well as two secondary schools with 843 students.

Many authors agree that until the start of the war, over 99 per cent of the local population had no access whatsoever to formal education. By the time of independence there were only fourteen native university graduates. By contrast, towards the late 1970s there were over 79,000 students enrolled in 698 primary schools, 16,355 in twenty–eight secondary centres and 509 in six technical training centres. In 1981 there were 1,041 students on scholarships abroad. Adult literacy, although still low by international standards, had risen to 9 per cent.

Conclusion

For nearly a decade the 'safety net' of international assistance provided two successive Governments the necessary support to reconstruct an economy ravaged by four centuries of neglectful colonial rule and ten years of fierce fighting. Unquestionable improvements in living standards were achieved. And yet the challenge seems to have proven gargantuan.

Preoccupied first with launching an ill–fated industrialization programme and then with its own political survival, the first PAIGC Government effectively failed to address the question of a growing urban housing crisis. The Government that succeeded it in 1980 and has governed the country ever since preferred a path of reduced state intervention and found in self–help schemes a convenient ally. But the real problems remained an all too real lack of state financial and human resources to tackle problems that were secondary in the political agenda.

Two quite distinct development strategies and several policy mistakes later, the country is now being forced to taste the bitter medicine of structural adjustment. This may prove beneficial in some respects. The new measures will hopefully help strengthen the state planning system. Higher prices for agricultural products may encourage farmers to export more of their produce through official channels. The balance of payments may be redressed again (although today's commodity prices are lower in real terms than they were some thirty years ago, when the country last had a surplus).

---

20)   According to Amilcar Cabral, before the start of the war, only fourteen Africans had ever had access to university education. (Chabal, 1983).

But the massive cutbacks in state staffing levels and in social expenditure normally associated with such packages are likely to be particularly harmful for the country's urban poor: a large proportion of Bissau's low–income households depend directly or indirectly upon the state for their survival, either through direct employment or subsidized foodstuffs. A failure of the schemes to generate employment outside the state could prove disastrous for many families already facing hardship (as the readiness of thousands of people to take up resettlement to rural areas has demonstrated). They must be helped either to find adequate employment in productive activities, even if this means resettlement in farming co–operatives, or to be provided with enough subsidies to pay the higher prices granted to farmers. The irony is that although structural adjustment is in theory designed to strengthen the country's position in the global economy in order to qualify for more aid, in fact the Government may be in more need than ever of an external hand. The first PAIGC Government was brought down partly because it left far–away farmers to their own devices. The urban poor are much closer.

Note

This article is based on research carried out in 1984–1985 with funding from the Canadian International Development Agency (CIDA). A full report was published by the London office of the International Institute for Environment and Development (IIED) in 1987.

References

Addison, Tony and Demery, Lionel, 1986, 'Poverty Alleviation and Structural Adjustment', Overseas Development Insitute, London (mimeo).

Andreini, J.C. and Lambert, M.L., 1978, *La Guinée Bissau: D'Amilcar Cabral à la reconstruction nationale, Harmattan,* Paris.

Avena, Yvan, 1988, 'Da experiência cooperativista na Guiné–Bissau', *Soronda: Revista de Estudos Guineenses,* No. 5, January.

Blazejewicz, D., Lund, R., Schoning, K. and Steincke, S., 1981, *Arquitectura Tradicional: Guiné–Bissau, SIDA,* Stockholm.

Castro, A., 1980, *O sistema colonial português em Africa,* 2nd edition (first published in 1962), Caminho, Lisboa.

Chabal, P., 1983, *Amilcar Cabral,* Cambridge University Press, UK

CIDAC, 1983, 'A relação campo–cidade desde a luta de libertação até a independência', *Cadernos CIDAC, Questões Internacionáis,* Series Estudos, No. 6, Lisbon.

Davidson, Basil, 1981, *No Fist is Big Enough to Hide the Sky,* Zed Press, London.

Dième, I., 1981, 'La crise du logement en Guinée Bissau. Etude de cas: la ville de Bissau', unpublished dissertation, Institut des Techniques de Planification de l'Economie Appliquée, Algiers.

Dos Santos, A.R., 1984, 'Estabilização e subdesenvolvimento: lições da Guiné Bissau', in *Economia e Socialismo,* No. 60, Lisbon.

Dowbor, Ladislau, 1983, *Guiné–Bissau: a Busca da Independência Econômica,* Brasiliense, Sao Paulo.

FAO, 1982, 'Guinée–Bissau: stratégie de développement agricole', Mission Report, Rome (mimeo).

Forbes, Dean and Thrift, Nigel (editors), 1987, *The Socialist Third World: Urban Development and Territorial Planning,* Blackwell, UK.

Forster, Marco and Lopes, Carlos, 1984, 'Etude sur politique, planification urbaine et habitat en Guinée Bissau après l'indépendence', report commissioned by the Groupe de Recherche et d'Echanges Technologiques (GRET), Paris (mimeo),

Galli, Rosemary, 1987, 'On Peasant Productivity: The Case of Guinea Bissau', *Development and Change,* Vol. 18, No. 1, January.

Goulet, D., 1978, *Looking at Guinea Bissau: A New Nation's Development Strategy, Overseas Development Council,* USA.

Guinea Bissau, Government of, 1979, National Population Census, Ministerio da Coordenação Econômica e do Plano, Bissau (mimeo).

Guinea Bissau, Government of, 1982a, *Primeiro Plano Quadrienal de Desenvolvimento Econômico e Social, 1983–1986,* (three volumes), Secretaria de Estado do Plano e de Cooperação Internacional, Bissau (mimeo);

Guinea Bissau, Government of, 1982b, 'Diagnòstico regional do Comité de Estado da Cidade de Bissau', SEPCI, mimeo.

Hochet, Anne Marie, 1983, 'Paysanneries en attente: Guinée Bissau', *Série Etudes et Recherches* Nos 79–80, ENDA, Dakar.

Krishna, Chauhan S. et al., 1983, *Who Puts the Water in the Taps?,* Earthscan, London.

Lima Handem, Diana, 1987, 'A Guiné–Bissau: adaptarse a crise', *Soronda: Revista de Estudos Guineenses, No. 3,* January.

Lopes, Carlos, 1982, 'Ethnie, état et rapports de pouvoir', in Institut Universitaire d'Etudes de Développement, *Itinéraires: notes et travaux,* No. 22, Geneva.

PAIGC, 1979, *Programa do Partido,* INACEP, Bissau.

PAIGC, 1979a, Memòria do Primeiro Congresso Extraordinário, Bolama.

Pfister, F., 1981, 'L'habitat en Guinée Bissau', unpublished report for UNDP–UNCHS–Government of Guinea Bissau (mimeo).

Pinsky, Barry, 1985, 'Territorial dilemmas: urban planning and housing in Mozambique', paper presented at the seminar *Shelter Policies in Third World Nations,* Kleve, Germany, May (mimeo).

Portugal, Government of, 1973, *Ordenamento rural e urbano na Guiné Portuguesa,* Overseas Ministry, Lisbon.

Rudebeck, Lars, 1972, 'Political mobilisation for development strategy in Guinea Bissau', in *Journal of Modern African Studies,* Vol. 10, No. 1, pp.1–18.

Rudebeck, Lars, 1982, 'Problèmes de pouvoir populaire et de développement: transition difficile en Guinée–Bissau', in Scandinavian Institute of African Studies, *Research Report No* 63, Motala, Sweden.

Rudebeck, Lars, 1988, 'Observações sobre a economia política do desenvolvimento de uma aldeia africana', *Soronda: Revista de Estudos Guineenses,* No. 5, January.

Vega, A., 1949, 'Algúns aspectos da estrutura economica da Guiné Portuguesa', in *Boletim Cultural da Guiné Portuguesa,* No. 14.

West Africa magazine, July 26, 1987, and November 1987.

White, Gordon, 1983, "Revolutionary Socialist Development in the Third World: An Overview", in White, G., Murray, R. and White, C. (editors) *Revolutionary Socialist Development in the Third World,* Wheatsheaf, UK, p.3.

Wield, David, 1983, 'Mozambique – Late Colonialism and Early Problems of Transition', in White, G., Murray, R. and White, C. (editors), *Revolutionary Socialist Development in the Third World,* Wheatsheaf, UK.

World Bank, *World Development Report 1987,* The World Bank, Washington.

World Bank, 1987a, *Guinea–Bissau: A Prescription for Comprehensive Adjustment* (A World Bank country study), The World Bank, Washington.

Cape Verde

Christina von Schweinichen

The Political and Historical Setting

The islands of Cape Verde lie nearly five hundred miles off the coast of West Africa, an archipelago of nine inhabited islands and several smaller, deserted ones. They are divided into two administrative regions: *Barlavento* and *Sotavento,* their main towns being, respectively, *Mindelo* and *Praia.* The latter is also the capital town of the country.

Historically, Cape Verde was an important port serving the triangular trade (particularly slaves) between Africa, America and Europe. Deforestation and monoculture led to serious soil erosion, the main cause for recurrent and long famines, which in modern times have been so severe that 30,000 to 40,000 people died of starvation during 1942–47 and a further 10,000 in 1958–59.

High unemployment has always accompanied the recurrent agricultural crises, pushing farmers, who are the vast majority of the population, into migration to Africa and the USA. The estimated 600,000 Cape Verdeans living abroad are more than those living in their home country. The majority live in the USA, with other minorities in Senegal, Brazil, Portugal, France, Holland and Italy, and currently about 6,000 leave the country every year.

There are strong historical ties between the Cape Verde Islands and Guinea Bissau on the African continent. Before 1879 the two colonies were administered as a single territory, and for several centuries there has been migration between them. These ties have also bound together the respective liberation movements in the two countries.

In the period immediately after the Second World War, various attempts were made in Guinea and Cape Verde to establish trade unions along with social and recreational clubs. Although anything but radical, these organizations had a nationalist orientation and were soon outlawed by the colonial authorities. In 1956, the *Partido Africano da Independencia da Guiné e Cabo Verde* (PAIGC) was founded as a clandestine political party. Although only one among several nationalist movements struggling for independence at that time, PAIGC was the most unified and was most

121

successful in the long run. In the first elections for a National Assembly in 1975, the PAIGC gained 92 per cent of the votes and two weeks later, upon the fall of the Salazar regime in the motherland, declared independence from Portugal.

The party was working towards reunification of the two countries until the coup in Guinea Bissau in 1981, when PAIGC departed from this goal and simultaneously changed its name to *Partido Africano da Independencia de Cabo Verde* (PAICV). On the same occasion the constitution was amended to a one–party system and declared

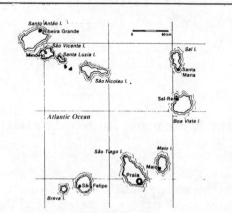

Country Profile: **Cape Verde**

National territory: 4,033 km²
Population: 333,000 (1986), plus more than 400,000 living abroad.
Population density: 77 inhab/sq.km (1978)
Labour force: 121,000, 45% in agriculture (75% according to other sources)
Urbanization rate: 35%
Capital: Praia; 47,627 inhabitants (1979)
Estimated natural growth rate: 1.7% (1975–82)
Life expectancy: 62.3 years for men; 66.0 years for women
Infant mortality: 8.7%
Illiteracy rate: 63.1%
Religion: More than 90% Catholic
Language: Portuguese is official language, Creole is spoken.
Educational expenditure: 10.6% of budget
Military expenditure: 4% of budget
Major export products: fresh fish 78%, fruit 8%, crude minerals 4%, hides and skins 2%, salt.
Imports: more than 90% of food must be imported.

Some important dates:
1445 First landing of a Portuguese sailor.
1503 Portuguese colony
1956 Foundation of PAIGC (liberation party)
1975 Peaceful liberation from Portuguese domination. First free elections accumulate 92% of
      votes for PAIGC, declaration of independent republic.
1979 Decentralization of political structure

Sources: Die Länder der Erde, Köln: Pahl–Rugenstein, 1982. Third World Guide, Montevideo: Third World Editors, 1988. Politisches Lexikon Afrika. München: C.H. Beck, 1985.

the PAICV the 'leading force of society' in Cape Verde. In line with the theories of its founder Amilcar Cabral, who had been murdered by the Portuguese in 1973, the PAICV is a mass party, standing for a society free from exploitation, and a 'revolutionary democracy based upon national unity and popular participation'. However, the PAICV was cautious to avoid orthodox Marxist rhetoric. When Cabral, who had spent a year in Cuban exile, was asked in an interview whether PAIGC was Leninist, he answered that 'although in Guinea the concept of the political party, like that of European parties, grew from the class struggle, the outlook of the PAIGC was above all grounded in the needs and experiences of the people of Guinea and Cape Verde'. Therefore, they differ from European parties because their primary goal is the overthrowing of colonial rule and the building of a new and independent nation. In its second party congress in 1983, the PAICV confirmed its ideological position by defining itself as the 'people's avantgarde'. The president of the republic is also the secretary general of the party. The constitution defines Cape Verde as a sovereign democratic republic, with an anti-colonial and anti-imperialistic policy, directed by the party.

Cape Verde has maintained strong commercial links with Portugal, but pursued the principle of non-alignment politically which helped to secure foreign aid from many different countries. In spite of its valuable strategic location in the middle of the Atlantic it has never allowed the installation of foreign military bases; however, it supported Angola in its second liberation war by allowing Cuban airplanes to land on the islands during the airlift that helped to defeat the South African invasion. Furthermore, Cape Verde maintains close relations with Mozambique, Guinea Bissau and Angola for the support granted by their respective governing parties in the resistance against the former Portuguese colonial power.

Land Policy

The Cape Verdean system of land ownership has evolved over centuries and is marked by a confusing mixture of rights, involving leases, crop sharing, water allocation, and sale of inheritance, and by a very small but powerful class of outright land owners. In 1974 there were spontaneous land occupations by landless farmers who endorsed the political demands put forward by the PAIGC. Subsequently, all land owned by foreigners and large landholdings were nationalized after PAIGC's victory in the elections the following year. After long discussions in 1982 an agrarian reform law was eventually passed, outlawing all forms of crop sharing but remaining much less radical in regard to other issues. Given that a Marxist-Leninist guerrilla movement had taken Cape Verde into independence, many land owners feared that more severe measures would be enacted against their privileges, including expropriation. However, since many land owners live abroad and by sending money home contribute to the nation's balance of payments with more than 50 per cent of the GNP, mass confiscation of their property would admittedly have had a devastating effect on the national economy and was not being considered a useful measure by the party.

Urbanization and Housing Supply

Cape Verde has suffered from the same urbanization phenomenon as most other Third World regions, particularly Praia and Mindelo. A large number of peasants had moved to these towns to escape the severe droughts and to be where foreign aid reached first. Thus the urbanization rate rose from 22 per cent in 1975 to 34 per cent in 1980, and continues to increase. For lack of serviced land, the migrants have concentrated in informal and unstructured settlements without water and electricity in the urban periphery. The town centres, however, which still have a number of colonial buildings, are being developed in the international fashion with concrete structures accommodating administrative, commercial and social activities.

Although a relatively large proportion of the rural–urban migrants join the building sector as unskilled labour (18,000 or 28 per cent of the resident and economically active population in 1985, and 24,400 in 1985), the productivity of the construction enterprises remains too low to catch up with the increasing housing demand. In 1985 the housing deficit was calculated as 19,155 units and is expected to reach 31,000 by 1990, or 25 per cent above the existing housing stock. To satisfy the demand the annual production rate should be multiplied six fold compared to the period 1980–85.

Housing Policy

As in most Third World countries, investments in the housing sector have been considered of secondary importance in the state budget until very recently. Government spending gave priority to other investments in the productive or social sector. However, international assistance allowed the state to adopt a public housing programme of limited scale and mainly served a new class of bureaucrats and civil servants which emerged in spite – or because – of an elaborated system of decentralized political representation and popular participation in the decision–making process. The private sector, dominated by foreign enterprises, was hesitant to invest in the building industry because of the limited paying capacity of potential buyers, and undefined future policy perspectives. In addition, the availability of an abundant and cheap labour force would not have justified significant capital investment in labour saving machinery.

Thus independence did not bring about new and better housing opportunities for the whole of the population. Furthermore, housing production in the public sector was hindered by overlapping or badly defined responsibilities between the *Ministério de Obras Públicas* (Ministry of Public Works), state enterprises such as the *Empresa Estadal de Construção* (EMEC, a building company) and the *Empresa Pública de Materiais de Construção* (MAC, a building materials company), and other authorities. Imported building materials are being centrally administered and distributed through the *Empresa Pública de Abastecimento* (EMPA), which also supplies spare parts for foreign–made machinery.

Ill. 1: Fogo, Cha de Caldeiras: In the countryside people build with the available natural materials.
(Foto: C. von Schweinichen)

Not until 1982 were the institutional conditions to deal more efficiently with housing and urbanization improved as a consequence of decentralization in the administrative structure. Then the municipalities were granted a certain autonomy, allowing them to work closer with the local artisans, labourers (*pedreros*), and small builders. Some local authorities were also able to secure technical assistance from foreign non-governmental agencies: in 1982 São Tiago received aid from the Italian agency *Africa '70* and from 1987 onwards Sal received Italian aid.

Since initially only the two towns of Praia and Mindelo had their own planning and project offices with some technicians and equipment, activities and resources of the new local *Secretariados Administrativos* were co-ordinated centrally through the *Administração Interna*. However, certain infrastructure works, such as the main road net, remained the responsibility of the *Ministério de Obras Públicas*. Typical activities of the *Secretariados Administrativos* include:

- Planning and execution of municipal buildings.
- Technical advice and supervision of private house-building activities. For example, in various places different types of houses and settlement layouts have been developed on the basis of the typical Cape Verdean 'basic house', consisting of two rooms, kitchen, bathroom, and an internal patio. (These houses based on a module of 3.3 x 3.3 metres fit into the most economical standard site of 9.5 x 12 metres.)
- Setting up and improving small-scale enterprises.
- Development of local building-materials production.
- Training of technicians and artisans.
- Issue of building permits.

However, since these local agencies tend to lack sufficient qualified staff, so far they have felt themselves unable to respond efficiently to the demand of the public and fulfil all their responsibilities.

In 1986, the Second Development Plan was put into practice, giving top priority to private enterprise, including the informal sector. In the housing field more attention was given to the needs of low income families, and co-operation with non-governmental and voluntary agencies was intensified at the project level. The most successful projects started with this kind of assistance include:

- The self-help upgrading project 'PACIM' in some blighted neighbourhoods *Campinho* and *Ilha d'Madeira* of the town *Mindelo* at *São Vicente*. The project involves 380 families and is under the direction of the *Ministério da Administração Local e Urbanismo* (MALU) in co-operation with the Swedish non-governmental agency (NGO) 'ARO' (Rathsman; 1987; PACIM, 1986).
- An upgrading project in Praia involving 1,700 families. Also this project is administered by MALU (*Ministério da Administração Local e Urbanismo*) with United Nations assistance (UNDP and UNCHS).
- A community development project at *Ponte d' Agua*, also in Praia. It is directed by the local municipality in co-operation with a Belgian NGO.

Special support is also given to smaller self-help housing groups of twenty to fifty families through the *Cooperativa de Apoio a Autoconstrução Popular* (COOAP). Examples for projects assisted by COOAP are:

- *Associação de entre-ayuda ny construção de habitaçãoes* (AECH), a group of thirty members having built twenty-one houses in Mindelo on the Island *Sao Vincente*.
- The *Cooperativa de Autoconstrução da Cidade Velha* (COOPAC-CV), a self-help group in Praia with twenty-five members and thirteen houses completed.
- The *Grupo de Tahiti*, a self-help group comprising thirty-six families of the barrio Tahiti in Praia (eighteen houses built).

Ill. 2: Houses built of local materials serve a tailors' co-operative in São Tiago, Pedra Badejo. Design and technical assistance by GAT, Assomada.
(Foto: Christina von Schweinichen)

Ill. 3: New high standard houses in Sal, Zona Centro, using imported materials and imported design elements.
(Foto: Christina von Schweinichen)

Most of these groups receive external funding on the understanding that they will be operating a revolving fund scheme – but it is still too early to evaluate the viability of the concept in the Cape Verdean context. The building loans cover material, not labour, and the repayment of the loan is calculated according to family income. Typical problems include training of the participants, self–administration of the groups, job organization, and regular supply of building materials. Cement particularly, which is the most commonly but not always correctly used binder, is in short supply. Local materials such as basalt, lime, gypsum, pozzolana and clay are available and could substitute for most building material imports, but so far only the PACIM project successfully tried to link house construction with local building materials production. More recent projects aim at developing alternative building technologies and are linked to German aid at São Vicente and to Italian assistance in São Tiago. In the latter case the objective is the building of a production line for small scale prefabricated building elements, such as pillars, lintels, floor tiles, or hollow blocks (Africa '70, 1985 and 1986).

Conclusion

After an initial emphasis on productive investment and (quantitatively neglectable) direct housing provision by the state the Second Development Plan marked a policy shift towards a more pragmatic approach in the 1980s, which acknowledges the traditional self–help input by the population in the solution of shelter needs. This trend was endorsed by the First National Civil Construction Congress in 1987. Further needs are being seen in the strengthening of the local building materials industry, professional training, in improving physical planning and land use control.

Bibliography

Alves, F.E.S. (1985). Apoio estadal e financiamiento ao associativismo no sector da habitação: situação actual e perspectivas. Ministerio de Urbanismo, Praia. Mimeograph.

Alves, F.E.S. (1986). Co–operativa de apoio a autoconstrução popular, COOAP. Termos de Referencia de um projecto piloto de apoio a autoconstrucao am Cabo Verde. Ministério de Urbanismo, Praia. Mimeograph.

Africa '70 (1985). Construire e progettare a Cabo Verde. Milano (Internal publication, distributed at G.A.T./ Gabinete de Apoio Tecnico, Sao Tiago).

Africa '70 (1986). Produçao dos elementos prefabricados, GAT, Gabinete Apoio Tecnico. Assomada: mimeo. (Internal publication, distributed at G.A.T./ Gabinete de Apoio Tecnico, Sao Tiago).

Le Courrier (1988), no. 107, Cap Vert, report ges. Pp. 15–31. Paris: UNESCO.

McCulloch, J. (1983). *In the twilight of revolution. The political theory of Amilcar Cabral.* London: Routledge & Kegan Paul.

Ministério do Plano e da Cooperação, Direcção Geral de Planemiento (1987). IIo Plano Nacional de Desenvolvimiento 1986–1990. Vol III. Praia.

PACIM (1986), Projecto de autoconstrucao assistida, Campinho e Ilha d'Madeira. Vol. II: dossier para procura de financiamento. Mindelo (São Vicente): Gabinete de Apoio Técnico.

Primer Encontro Nacional sobre a Construção (1987). Constroi-se Cabo Verde, construindo. Conference papers. Praia: Ministério de Obras Públicas (MOP).

Rathsman, Per (1987). The Pacim Project, Mindelo, Cape Verde Islands. *TRIALOG* no. 13/14. P. 48–51.

Angola

Otto Greger

Starting Point

Independence Day was 11 November 1975. With a land area of 1,247,000 square kilometres and now 9.5 million inhabitants, Angola stands at the beginning of a new chapter of its history. Almost 500 years of Portuguese colonialism; more than fourteen years of armed liberation war of the People's *Movement for the Liberation of Angola* (MPLA); violent conditions amounting to civil war with the rival movements, the *National Front for the Liberation of Angola* (FNLA) and the *National Union for the Total Independence of Angola* (UNITA) struggling for supremacy; and, finally, the bloody so-called second liberation war against the regular South African and Zairian invasion forces fighting alongside these groups, took their toll of the young People's Republic. Few African countries acceded to independence in such painful and inauspicious circumstances as Angola.

Nationwide destruction, demolition and removal of transportation, industrial equipment and agricultural machinery, electrical installations, sanitary and other facilities from public buildings and private houses by their former owners, and the sinking of loading and unloading facilities in the ports by the colonial army during its dispersion and the advance of South African troops: all this was followed by a brain drain almost unrivalled in history.[1] Seized by panic, more than 450,000 Portuguese and other expatriates, previously in leading and key positions in Angola, as well as 60,000 Angolan specialists fled a country marked by:

1. An extreme structural heterogeneity in terms of economic geography (i.e., population distribution, transport development, availability of resources, dominating production methods and structures).

---

1) Colombian author Gabriel García Márquez, after his visit to Angola in 1976, estimated the material losses at, among others, 28,000 vans (i.e. more than 80 per cent of the total number of vehicles), 3,000 cars, 144 bridges, 1,531,000 head of cattle.

Country Profile: Angola

National territory: 1,250,000 km²
Population: 9.5 million (1988)
Sex ratio: 97 male per 100 female (1988)
Population density: 7.6 inhab/sq.km
Labour force: 25% in industry, 33% in agri–
culture, 42% in services (1988)
Urbanization rate: 25% (1988)
Capital: Luanda; 1,200,000 inhabitants (1982)
Natural growth rate: 2.8% (1988)
Estimated urban growth rate: 5.8% (1988)
Life expectancy: 45 years both sexes (1988)
Crude birth rate: 47 per 1,000 (1988)
Crude death rate: 20 per 1,000 (1988)
Infant mortality: 13.7% (1988)
Religion: majority profess traditional African religions. 4% are Catholic.
Language: Portuguese is official language, eight main Bantu dialects. *Illiteracy rate:* 97%
Educational expenditure: 11.5% of budget (1982)
Military expenditure: 21% of budget (1983)
Major export products: crude oil 72%, diamonds 13%, petroleum products 10%, coffee 5%
Major markets: France 81%, Netherlands 6%, Switzerland 5%, UK 4%
Foreign assistance: $ 101.5 million (1985); (OECD countries 50%, CMEA 10%, EEC 7.2%)

Some important dates:
1482 First landing of a Portuguese sailor
1575 Foundation of Luanda
1836 Ban on slavery
1884 Portuguese colonial powers are confirmed at the 'Berlin Conference'
1951 Portuguese constitutional reform turns Angola from a colony into an overseas province.
1956 Foundation of the MPLA (liberation movement) led by Dr. Agostinho Neto and
developing a Marxist ideology. Subsequently support from Cuba, the USSR, and
socialist African states.
1961 Foundation of FNLA, a countryside–based liberation movement, which subsequently
operated with the support of the CIA (1962...), the Zairean (1965) and Chinese (1973)
governments, and eventually adopted pro–imperialist interests.
1961 Popular uprising against Portuguese domination and beginning of armed liberation
struggle. More than 50,000 Africans killed by Portuguese army.
1962–72 Strong foreign investments to exploit Angola's crude oil resources, economic boom.
1966 Foundation of UNITA, a split–off of FNLA, with an opportunistic orientation.
1974 Military coup by part of the Portuguese army displaces the Portuguese–Angolan
government under Caetano
1975 January: Provisional government formed incorporating 3 ministers each of MPLA,
FNLA, UNITA and the Portuguese administration. General elections planned for Nov.
1975 June: Armed conflict breaks out between FNLA, UNITA, and MPLA, fuelled by foreign
finance (USA, USSR, China, South Africa, Cuba). Declaration of the independent
People's Republic of Angola through MPLA
1975 August: Partial occupation of Angolan territory through South African troops.
1976 12,000 Cuban soldiers arrive to support the MPLA. Military defeat of FNLA and
UNITA. South Africa withdraws its army, but continues to supply and finance UNITA.
Exodus of Portuguese and other foreign experts, industrial production declines by 75%.
1976 MPLA adopts doctrine of 'scientific Socialism', implying partisan rather than grass roots
democracy ('poder popular'). The conflict between the two lines provokes a (defeated)
coup.
1980 Establishment of decentralized regional governments and (indirect) general elections
1989 Withdrawal of Cuban troops after peace talks and treaties involving Angola, South
Africa, Namibia, USA

*Sources: Information provided by the author. Die Länder der Erde, Köln: Pahl–Rugenstein, 1982. Third World Guide,
Montevideo: Third World Editors, 1988. Politisches Lexikon Afrika. München: C.H. Beck, 1985.*

2. A mortality rate of 30 per cent of one–year–old babies.
3. Almost one million people suffering from malaria, tuberculosis and leprosy.
4. An adult illiteracy rate of nearly 90 per cent.
5. A pronounced divergence between urban and rural sectors with practical halt of the exchange of goods.
6. A collapsing infrastructure with consequent breakdown of distribution and marketing systems, increasing gravity of the food supply situation, and slump of productivity in conjunction with blooming speculation and black market.
7. A manufacturing output of only 28 per cent of its 1973 level.
8. Attempts to exert pressure as well as open and covert political influence on the part of Anglo–American, French–Belgian and South African capital, as a consequence of the wide–reaching economic intertwining of the country with the world market which Portugal had pursued after the beginning of the armed liberation struggle in 1961 in order to defend her colony.
9. Enormous numbers of refugees and migration movements to the cities, especially to 'safe' Luanda, caused by military invasion in the South and North. Continuing economic sabotage on the part of 'old' and new privileged groups in the public administration, as well as escalating outflow of foreign exchange from the private sector of the economy.

Such starting conditions hindering the social transformation process were consequently the basis for the MPLA government's intervention.

Immediate Action

In addition to material and political incentives to mobilize the population within the framework of mass organizations and basic institutions of the *poder popular* (people's power), the takeover of farms and businesses is initially an improvised response to the settlers' abandoning of thousands of farms, factories and other enterprises. State intervention is seen as unavoidable to stop production grinding to a standstill. Furthermore, provision is made for the formal nationalization in non–punitive or confiscatory form of private companies and key industries, such as mining and medium to large–scale enterprises of the processing, bank trade and insurance sector, transport and large–scale landholding. First public planning aimed at the coexistence of public and co–operative sectors as well as mixed enterprises, joint ventures and private companies (Neto, 1976).

One measure to improve the desolate situation in the rural sector is the expropriation of abandoned commercial farms, the largest of which are run under the aegis of the Ministry of Agriculture (among them the world's largest coffee plantation). Within the framework of the collectivization of agriculture and the building up of co–operatives, farmers are not forced into the co–operative movement, regarded as a step which would be counter–productive. There have rather been attempts to convince them on a long–term basis of the benefits of collective agricultural production. Land is distributed among the landless, light industry has begun to be restructured to meet the demands of farming according to the MPLA's slogan "Agriculture is the basis of economic development, industry is the deciding factor".

This package is meant to remove internal economic asymmetry by territorial planning. The development of rural areas – in 1979, 58.3 per cent of Angolan employees were still working in the agricultural sector, and 80 per cent of the entire population depended on it – is to help achieve a more even distribution of production capacities throughout the national territory. This, however, has remained a largely political aspiration. Massive, continued logistical as well as financial support by South Africa, Zaire, Morocco and the U.S.A., along with most of its Western allies, for UNITA, in conjunction with an escalating undeclared war (pursued by South African invasion forces with the objective to create a permanent *cordon sanitaire* along the Angolan–Namibian border and the strategic aim to push northwards to the Benguela railway) block not only the intended balanced overall development. They also have a devastating impact on agriculture and food production, road and rail transport, rural–urban trade and the rest of the hinterland economy, and virtually deepen regional disparities stemming from colonial times, in that public investment focuses on politically and strategically consolidated areas. Continuing rural–urban migration of peasants who flee their farms and villages to seek refuge in towns and settlements along the main roads or railways – and who depend on government assistance and international food aid for survival – causes further disparity to the disadvantage of contested rural areas. The number of these refugees, primarily coming from the Central Highlands, has been estimated at about 600,000 by the International Committee of the Red Cross (ICRC).

Disastrous consequences for the country's economic, social and cultural (re)– construction are also caused by human and material losses due to South African intervention, as well as to the fact that since the early 1980s Angola has been forced to spend almost 45 per cent of its budget on defence and security.

During 1980–85, at least 100,000 deaths among adults occurred through fighting, sabotage and military raids, untreated injury or disease and war–related famine, while almost 45 per cent of overall under–five child deaths – a death toll which means that every four minutes a small Angolan child is lost – are attributable to the impact of agonizing war and economic destabilization (UN, 1985). An estimate of physical damage, based on totalling economic costs of destabilization and warfare and the economic growth losses resulting from reduced investment amounts to U.S.$17 billion over 1975–85.

All this is set against the background of a committed austerity policy which government, party leadership and leading cadres of the industry have adopted in order to keep Angola independent from such Western creditors as the *World Bank* (IBRD) and the *International Monetary Fund* (IMF).

The Construction and Housing Sector:

Starting Point and Emergency Measures

Because of bottlenecks on all sectors immediately after independence, urban structural problems and the desperate housing situation had to be given low priority. Preference was given to the restructuring and reconstruction of the agricultural, industrial and transport sectors. Until 1977, the construction industry, which was particularly affected by the mass exodus of Portuguese specialists, clearly focused on planning and construction to repair roads, bridges, railway lines and airports, *conditio sine qua non* for the quickest possible restitution of internal transport for the establishment of balanced exchange conditions between all regions of the country. In addition, the revolutionary government considers mass literacy and the expansion of elementary schooling, as well as the gradual replacement of private medicine by an extension of preventive health care, to be fundamentals of further development. They are emphasizing universal primary education, massive adult literacy programmes, primary health care, access to safe water, immunization, mother and child–care clinics and improved nutrition. Accordingly, reorganization and construction of facilities for state–run, free educational and primary health services were given further high priority. First successes in these areas cannot be denied: in less than two years, more than one–half million Angolans took part in literacy courses (Conchiglia,1978); the total number of students almost doubled in comparison with 1972–73 (Angola, 1976). A nationwide polio vaccination campaign and other vaccination programmes (TB, diphtheria, measles) have been launched in co–operation with foreign – mainly Cuban – specialists to treat 1.5 million children (Decke, 1978), and mortality of one–year-old children fell from 30 to 10 per cent (Márquez, 1977:20). Since mid–1981, the infant mortality rate began to rise again due to the escalating effects of war.

Given the necessary concentration of the remaining resources of the building sector on the above–mentioned areas and the fact that the 407 private civil engineering companies existing before independence had dropped to fifty–three by September 1976 (in fact, only seven or eight were active (Resende de Oliveira, 1976:2476) and further that of the 700 (mostly Portuguese) managers, only sixty (among them only four architects) remained in the country (Conchiglia, 1978:9), the paralysis was evident, particularly in civil engineering and housing. In addition to the abrupt loss of practically the total management and skilled labour force, this sector was also faced with an acute shortage of qualified construction workers, as well as a general shortage of raw and building materials, machinery, tools and means of transport. Nationalization of all private civil engineering and building companies which was vital under these conditions was followed by first measures for its complete restructuring and reorganization within the state sector. This sector now assumed, in addition to its traditional control function, an increasing range of planning functions, especially the crucial task of implementation which had been left to the private sector before independence. In the face of the available, strongly planning–oriented specialized labour force structure, this proposed change must be mainly confined to a declaration of intent. This is shown (despite the insufficient degree of availability of reliable planning data and the lack of binding administrative, legal and procedural basics) by the relative 'surplus production' in the planning area without the consequent project realization at this stage – so to speak 'bottom–drawer planning'. At the same time a constant flow of migrants spills over the urban fringes, especially Luanda, as a result of the continuing unstable military–political situation in large areas of the country, with fatal consequences – interrupted transport and communications, shortages, starvation, etc.

In consequence, the functionaries in charge of planning and planning–related work are unreliable, the founding of state and mixed civil engineering and supplier companies is slow and there is no impetus for stimulating local production of construction materials, such as cement. On the other hand, ". . . the need for immediate action to improve the living conditions of the population calls for the adoption of methods which have recourse to a far–reaching participation of those involved . . . which must be effectively supported by the responsible structures . . ." (Angola, 1978:11).

Self–help housing is intended to be "one of the most effective approaches for an *immediate* solution both to the workers' housing problems in the cities as well as the reorganization of the farmers' lives in general . . .", and ". . . the building of collective facilities which are indispensable for the social and economic development of the population, such as kindergartens, schools, health centres, community shops, etc., should be brought in. . . ." (Angola, 1978:11). The local labour force demands simple, functional types of construction in conjunction with the adoption of uncomplicated building methods with as small a percentage of prefabricated components as possible. This concept of 'state–guided and/or state–organized construction on the self–help principle', primarily aimed at the rural sector, signals intent and requirement at the same time. It reflects MPLA's pragmatic attitude towards the population's existing habits, such as their own construction of the necessary dwellings, whereby traditional rural house construction has remained largely unaffected by advanced technology because formerly there had not been any formal public intervention, nor had any non-traditional building material been available. In this area, public intervention to stimulate collective basic construction initiatives remains confined to the supply of the most necessary tools and equipment to simplify and improve traditional building methods, such as wooden moulds for a more efficient manual production of clay bricks.

This concept, however, is equally an indication of the deficient manpower resources and the limited efficiency of planning authorities and building contractors, with the consequence of a further concentration of planning and building activities on cities in the coastal area, especially the traditional MPLA stronghold of Luanda. The concentration of control functions in the centre stands in an inverse relationship to the absence of effective structures of the construction sector in the periphery. Despite regular decentralization attempts and repeated campaigns to this effect, the tendency has been even stronger since the failed *coup d'état* in May 1977 of the 'Faction Nito

Alves'.[2] The FNA's previous instituting of basic initiatives – *poder popular* and local as well as corporate self–administration – was countered by the MPLA leadership temporarily with strengthened emphasis on control and discipline, or in more general terms, with state intervention.

The relationship between basis and superstructure at that time is characterized by the tendency of the state leaders to direct, or at least control, every form of the people's involvement, whereas economic difficulties, emergencies and urgent decisions too often have the effect that bureaucratic decisions take the place of (joint) decisions by the people involved. This means de–facto stagnation, since the public bodies involved are often less able than the people involved to implement the underlying plans. One of the best ways to implement the first housing programmes within the framework of organized self–help construction is to encourage the few remaining specialists in the production of light prefabricated parts which can be easily assembled by the dweller himself. At the same time, the Ministry of Construction and Housing states that the establishment of a heavy prefab–component industry for housing construction was not desirable at that time because of the actual Angolan conditions – enormous territorial expansion with a small total population, extremely heterogeneous population distribution and correspondingly dispersed settlement structure – and because of primarily economic/political considerations; building on traditional principles would retain its full importance for a long time (Angola, 1978:10). To some extent, this already shows the 'two lines' of future Angolan housing policies, although such first attempt with light, prefabricated building elements of a system which was imported from Cuba without any modifications at first was a fiasco. The extremely simple modular system, type *'Sandino'* which could be set up without special equipment, comprising non–insulated, prefabricated concrete slabs which are inserted into the vertical grooves of equally prefabricated concrete supports spaced 1.04 metres apart, failed to take account of special socio–cultural patterns of the Angolan people, and of differing climates of the Angolan highlands and coastal areas. In both areas, it was (or was intended to be) used primarily by farmers and urban or fringe migrants. Adapted neither to cultural or climatic demands, simply technically adapted, such a system could not gain acceptance in Angola. Evidence of this is still seen today in some provinces of the country: wall and support elements piled up as well as houses that have never been occupied or that have been abandoned.

Urban Policies

Much more difficult and complex than in the countryside and in the intermediate urban centres is the housing situation in Luanda, one of the oldest European colonial cities (dating from 1576) and today one of Africa's ten largest cities. The parasitic capital with its colonial character, the country's most important industrial city, centre

---

2) Group around former Minister of the Interior Nito Alves who, in radical – and often racist – rhetoric, called for a rapid nationalization.

of administration, consumption and services, accounts for 70 per cent of the national industrial production. 16.8 per cent of the total and around 70 per cent of the urban population of Angola live in Luanda, marked by a regular population increase. Between 1940 and independence the population increased (despite the exodus of 300,000 Portuguese from its greater region) to more than 700,000 and is today – without the equivalent economic growth – estimated at 1.6 million.[3] The conse-quences are severe:

> The social and economic segregation of its inhabitants is reflected by the asymmetry of Luanda's urban organization and the dual character of its physical appearance. The absolute majority, almost 80 per cent, of its population is pressed into mediocre (8 per cent) or inferior (67 per cent) dwellings, although the percentage of the latter is only 60 per cent of the total urban area (Schümer, 1977:212). An average occupancy rate of seven persons per housing unit in the central districts, and nine persons in the urban shanty towns (in 1981), indicates an increasing deterioration of the substance of dwelling units whose number totaled around 120,000 in 1979, with the occupancy trend continuously increasing.

The public utility services would satisfy the demands of a city of 250,000 inhabit-ants: for example, there is a shortfall in school facilities for approximately 35,000 students; urban infrastructure networks, notably the sewerage and water supply systems, cover only 60 per cent of the city's area (Angola 1979:13).

The first political measure taken by the Revolutionary Council for improving the tense situation was the nationalization of abandoned flats forty–five days after the absence of the (mostly Portuguese) dwellers, as well as the expropriation of all condominiums and rental houses not used by the owners. Their distribution among the people hit hardest by the housing shortage, assistance from the housing committees and basic organs of the *poder popular,* and spontaneous squatting brought temporary relief to the housing market until June 1980. These measures helped even more after South Africa's military operations in July 1981 and December 1983 caused further floods of rural migrants into Luanda.

The new housing legislation is also intended as a way to overcome the (urban) colonial society. Under the slogan "The flat for the dweller", it secures the right of occupancy without permitting its rental to a third party, prohibits trade flats and regulates rent levels on a uniform basis. Not all these measures can be oriented to the maxim "Nationalization following politically, economically and technically sustainable principles". Shortage of resources controlled by the communal bodies, especially the lack of trained personnel, did not permit continual maintenance of urban high–rise buildings. The result was accelerated wear due to excessive occupancy rates and, despite campaigns to awaken the people's awareness, to improper use of the new architecture which failed to meet the social and cultural habits of its new dwellers. But, what could have been the alternative to improvisation at this stage?

---

3) Based on a government census in Luanda and its satellite town Viana, 1987, and on CIPRO, 1982: Section 4.2.

Further priority was given to the gradual improvement of the 'musseques', Luanda's squatter settlements spread over the entire city, interrupted by concrete residential quarters, where over 60 per cent of the city's population live in precarious and unstable conditions (CIPRO, 1981: Section 4.2). The largest, Cazenga, covers twenty-five square kilometres. Although first construction programmes have been launched in some of these shanty towns to provide a basic technical infrastructure and to build small communal facilities, their implementation is slow despite the fact that preparatory planning work has been completed. At the same time, the urban fringes continue to move outward. New *musseques* emerge, grow unplanned and steadily, with state intervention confining itself to minimal regulation of the process. Compared with their predecessors from the colonial period, building density is lower, spatial distribution is more even, and more resistant building materials are used.

In regard to urban condominium building, houses damaged during the war are in the process of being repaired and completion of the buildings left unfinished by the Portuguese is under way. Out of 130 rough constructions in Luanda alone with a total area of one million square metres (living space for about 2,500 families plus office and business areas), twenty buildings were given priority for completion (CIPRO: 1981: Sections 4.7.1; 4.9.1; 4.9.2.1). On these so-called pilot construction sites, a novel training programme developed in close co-operation between the *Ministries of Construction* and *of Education* is being implemented for the training of foremen and specialized workers. Unskilled workers attend literacy courses on construction sites and are simultaneously given the necessary vocational qualification through their practical work. Such a demand-oriented, 'combined' training is also available to secondary-school students, who are trained as senior construction engineer cadres in conjunction with practical work on site. Construction progress is therefore slow, not only because of the lack of building plans, spare parts or permanent lack of materials. This is another reason why international co-operation has been sought, especially from Cuba, since mid-1976. The Angolan construction sector employs, apart from some 2,000 skilled workers, middle-level technicians and Cuban managers, more than 40,000 Angolan workers of whom 5,438 have completed their training as construction workers to form the 'backbone' of the first construction brigades.

Standing on Two Feet:
Public Housing Construction and Organized User Participation[4]

After the first three years of development of public housing construction marked by stagnation and improvisation, forecasts were made concerning Angola's overall population growth, its urbanization, Luanda's growth rate, and demand for dwelling space calculated until 2010 on the basis of a first-dwelling-space census, up-dated population statistics and projections of the socio-economic development of the country (Decke, 1981:87ff). These projections show the total demand for the period

---

4) This paragraph is based in parts on an unpublished article by Allan Cain, Development Workshop, entitled *'Building Participation in Angola'*.

1980–90 amounting to more than 15,000 housing units per annum on the basis of an average family size of 5.3. For the two decades following, the dwelling space requirements have been projected as follows:

1990–2000   56,000 housing units per year (5.3 persons per unit)
75,000 housing units per year (4 persons per unit)

2000–2010   122,000 housing units per year (5.3 persons per unit)
162,000 housing units per year (4 persons per unit)

It is evident that the young People's Republic will not have the material or manpower resources even to come close to covering this demand within the foreseeable future. One strategy for the long–term solution to these problems is:

• Creation of the material preconditions for the building up of modern urban mass housing facilities, making use of technical and technological progress to develop the construction sector and to increase productivity.
• Introduction of technological approaches in terms of partial prefabrication, with the aim of simplified housing construction and the development of methods for the production of heavy prefabricated elements, for the construction of public buildings (Schümer, 1977:210).
• Planning and preparation of urbanization projects to materialize such housing construction.

The other strategy provides for the stimulation of 'state–organized self–help building' and collective user participation through technical orientation and organizational support by the central and local bodies of the Ministry of Construction and Housing, above all in the initial phase and in the rural sector.

The first stage of public high–rise construction involves a five–storey Cuban building type consisting of light, partially prefabricated elements of simple construction standards, with a degree of prefabrication. From this so–called E–14, as well as its successor model E–15 which is better adapted to local conditions, 3,000 flats were built with the initial co–operation of Cuban construction brigades. Most of the flats are temporarily used to accommodate foreign experts and *Internacionalistas* from Cuba, other COMECON countries, Portugal, Brazil, Sweden and Italy. The ground plans are sufficiently adapted to the climatic situation through cross-ventilation and effectively shaded façades; the area of the flats varies from 55 to 80 square metres and from three to five rooms, with one household balcony provided for the sitting room and kitchen. On the basis of these two 'prototypes' of semi-industrialized building with partial prefabrication in Angola, local architects of the National Directorate of Town Planning and Housing developed a multistory block of flats using light prefabricated elements, which takes more account of the requirements and living habits of Angolan dwellers. Today, it is known as *'Luanda–1'*, although recently another type of building of Yugoslavian origin is found in newly developing housing areas in Luanda. This *'Sistema Tunel'* is a four–storey dwelling complex based on a partition system whose ceilings and partitioning walls are concreted storey–by–storey in one action using reusable sliding casting scaffolding. Non–load-bearing walls (both longitudinal and partitioning) are made of brickwork. This

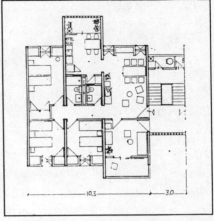

Ill. 1: Early post-revolutionary housing scheme ('Luanda-1') — an adaptation of the Cuban model 'E-14'. (Foto: Otto Greger)

Ill. 2: Plan of the same project. The internal layout is identical with the Cuban model despite the cultural and climatic differences.

building system presently constitutes the most recent part in the development of public Angolan housing construction.

Popular Participation and Self-Help

Community participation in Angola can be divided into three basic categories:

1. Traditional village self-help in the sector of non-market oriented rural subsistence economy.
2. Political mobilization in order to materialize particular goals, a way to promote participation that has its roots in the resistance and liberation struggle against Portuguese colonialism.
3. Mechanisms set up by the state to encourage community participation in order to realize long-term development aims, such as institutionalization of participation.

This chapter focuses on the third category, above all on the housing sector.

Probably one of the Angolan revolution's most promising attempts to use the country's own resources is the national programme for *autoconstrução*, housing construction by self-help based on the principle of learning by doing. A special law enacted in December 1980 explicitly emphasizes the social character of planning and building activities as reflected, for instance, in collective or individual participation. Collective consciousness-building is an inherent part of joint construction efforts and eventually results in the use value of completed buildings for the community. According to the slogan that building is more important than architecture, the form of the completed works is less emphasized than the social and psychological effects this activity induces on the individual participant and the community on the whole.

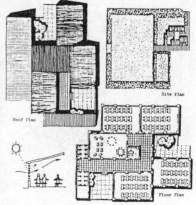

Ill. 3: 'Autoconstruç ão orientada' – a low-income housing scheme being built in collective and assisted self-help. *(Foto: O. Greger)*

Ill. 4: Prototype of a primary school for urban squatter areas to be built by the local community with local materials.

The Ministry of Provincial Co-ordination is responsible for all self-help projects. The Ministry of Planning defines priority zones for participation projects, while the Ministry of Construction and Housing is responsible for the complex task of co-ordinating the input of all public organizations involved, of elaborating urbanization plans, evaluating possible benefits of different building types and construction methods including those based on traditional architecture, of developing prototypes of new housing and community buildings, and of planning and carrying out upgrading projects. Regional offices have been set up in eighteen provinces of the country working closely together with local administrations. In co-operation with the National Directorate of Urbanization and Housing (responsible for housing construction by self-help with the technical direction of the state), also non-governmental organizations such as the Canadian Development Workshop initiate popular housing programmes.

Architectural Aspects

The *Development Workshop* was also engaged in a nationwide survey to analyze past projects with an emphasis on:

● Identification of problems and potentials in the realization of local participation projects.
● Analysis of traditional and new organizational networks which could be used in granting technical and organizational assistance.
● Evaluation and assessment of locally available building materials, appropriate technologies and technical skills that can be recommended and further improved for self-help construction projects.

Not all results from this report have been as encouraging as hoped. To overcome recurrent problems future projects should put a stronger emphasis on:

1. *The further development of appropriate production techniques for self–help construction using locally available building materials.*

It was found that there is a permanent undersupply of modern building materials; particularly in rural areas the present demand for materials to build housing and community facilities can only be satisfied after long delays. It is expected, however, that a policy of smaller, decentralized building production units relying on locally available resources will remedy the situation. As a first measure, a new hand–press has been developed featuring considerable improvements over the established CINVA–RAM press or similar models. Its advantage lies in its product diversity ranging from solid blocks to semi–hollow blocks, floor and interlocking roof tiles. Other small–scale equipment for on–site production of building components are presently under development.

2. *Preparation of technical documents and information manuals for unskilled construction workers, particularly for the so–called 'energizers' (social workers).*

The newly established regional planning offices which were set up in order to promote and support various basic activities in the construction sector through their 'energizers' are desperately understaffed and lack basic technical and information material. In order to increase their efficiency a number of studies, working materials and manuals have been commissioned to facilitate communi-cation between self–help builders, 'energizers' and administrative staff in the regional offices. The first new handbooks are already available and comprise, among other things, guidelines for the design of appropriate, climatically suitable buildings for all of the fifteen environmental zones of the country, a manual describing the production of cement–stabilized soil blocks using the newly conceived hand–press, planning guides for urban sites–and–services and upgrading projects, a handbook for the planning and collective construction of elementary schools; and didactic material to be used in communal education.

3. *Fast provision of public facilities and basic infrastructure under the premise that national resources, both personnel and material, shall be used extensively.*

Owing to the country's educational boom – the total number of Angola's elemen-tary–school pupils will quadruple in nine years – existing schools are overbur-dened (up to three teaching shifts per day) and deteriorate fast, so that all available rooms, whether dwellings, storehouses or factory floors, need to be converted into provisional classrooms. However, only about 15 per cent of the total area presently used for teaching can be classified as suitable for this purpose. As there is still no exact survey of the total teaching area presently used more accurate information is needed to guarantee the most rational distribution of new premises which will be built through collective self–help. Therefore, the Education Delegate of Luanda province has launched an initiative to offer advanced training courses for communal planning cadres. Participants are instructed in simple polling and surveying techniques, in reading of city maps, preparation of simple sketches, and the use of a new surveying and polling form.

The importance of such measures can be shown, for example, in Sambizanga – a *musseque* with a population density of more than 1,000 inhabitants per hectare and which is extremely short of classrooms. An elementary school is being constructed by the squatters as part of a pilot project, using locally produced, cement–stabilized soil blocks. In an exemplary way, these measures demonstrate the principles of state–organized, participatory building in Angola, which can be characterized by:

- Integration in an overall development programme in order to avoid competition with other projects for scarce resources.
- Conception as part of an integrated project to address the population's basic needs in the most efficient manner possible.
- The application of the most simple, application–oriented instruction of the participants to maximize effects of professional training and learning of general knowledge matters.
- Relying on the trial and error method in the implementation and further improvement of housing and infrastructure projects and programmes. Pilot projects shall help to achieve an optimum compromise between technical and administrative requirements and user demands (Angola, 1978:6ff).

Recent policy trends and future perspectives

Severe shortages of housing and structural problems still mark the situation in the cities at the end of the first decade of independence, especially because war provokes an almost continual migration into the cities. The revolutionary government has therefore attempted in recent years to find a far–reaching solution to these problems through an improvement of the institutional framework. Since mid–1983, an increasing number of local district committees, decentralized government offices and dwellers' committees have been set up and have been allocated powers for local administrative functions, including also the organization and implementation of aided self–help housing projects.

By channelling such activities through new sectoral and decentralized institutions it is hoped that the bureaucracy of the established central offices can be bypassed and efficiency enhanced. Implementation of projects shall be made easier for both applicants and assistance staff through the introduction of a simplified one–page application form serving to obtain building approval, planning advice, surveying services, technical assistance, allocation of building materials and rental of building tools and other equipment. It must be admitted, however, that the notorious shortage of qualified staff (aggravated by the absence of many professionals serving in the armed forces) tends to limit technical advice, in practice, to the distribution of standard type drawings.

Considering this shortage of qualified staff, and conceived as part of an energetic anti–bureaucracy campaign, the prohibition on private house construction was lifted again. Moreover, it is hoped that this measure will release additional investment capacities by the petty bourgeoisie, and channel them into socially productive use.

The risk of unlawful gains by the private sector is considered smaller than the potential damage caused by the growing bureaucratic encrustation in the state sector.

Progressive structural improvement and integration of suburban squatter settlements within the formal city are being continued. In addition to the inhabitants, representation and participation through the local organs of the *poder popular* (people's power), more emphasis is put on voluntary work of industrial collectives or by employees in the public sector on so called 'red Saturdays'.[5] Innovative approaches are often the outcome of practical ad–hoc solutions. For example, sponsorships have emerged between the staff of industrial or administrative work centres on the one side, and schools or health care centres in the *musseques* on the other, by which the employees have initially built such social facilities and agreed to ensure their further maintenance.

Once the initial attempts to stop the concentration of investments in the capital by town planning and inter–regional development measures had failed, a new strategy aims at overcoming the contradiction between town and the countryside by a combination of different instruments. In particular, the role of Luanda as the capital city is meant to be redefined, and *urban* growth rates shall be slowed down through improvements in the *rural* sector – including better employment opportunities, wage increases, free social security, and the construction of new village community centres. This policy of 'urbanization of the rural population' (villagization) will be complemented by a process of 'ruralization of the urban population' (deurbanization) – including, for example, campaigns to recruit volunteers for cultivating agricultural land in the urban periphery. The urban farming approach particularly, ideologically integrated in the process of social, political and economic transformation, was a practical necessity to counter the disastrous consequences of the escalating war and its subsequent interruption in the cities' food supply: it is a declared aim to achieve self–sufficiency of urban and rural consumer centres in the quickest possible manner, and to eradicate urban parasitism and regional disparities at the same time.

The *Projecto Cinturão Verde,* the planning of a green belt around Luanda, is linked to an irrigation project of the nearby reservoir of Kikuchi and to the establishment of small, integrated settlement satellites where some of the capital's co–operatively based undertakings will be relocated. A medium–term aim is the diversification of agricultural production in addition to the most basic crops, to supply the regional population by almost 100 per cent.

In accordance with the slogan of MPLA–PT (Labour Party) – the land belongs to its cultivator – land of this future agricultural zone will be distributed among those inhabitants of Luanda's city region who are interested in agricultural production and who have the necessary education and/or experience (Angola, 1978: 7ff). Also in other provinces, similar measures are envisaged and will absorb and retain rural–urban migrants within their area of origin away from the capital.

Complementary to this concept of urban ruralization stands a rural settlement policy of establishing decentralized *núcleos,* defined as an integral form of

---

5) Compare the organization of voluntary work in *domingos rojos* in Cuba, and *rojo y negro* work in Nicaragua (remark by the editor).

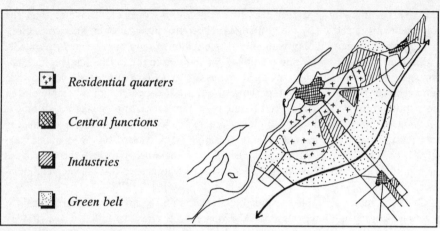

Residential quarters

Central functions

Industries

Green belt

Ill. 5: The city is surrounded by farm land: Luanda is supposed to be self-sufficient in food.

agricultural settlements. Comparable with Mozambique's *aldeias comunais*, such settlement units are designed as gradually growing villages with a maximum population of 250 families, offering various facilities adapted to its particular development stage and the inhabitants' demands. However, due to ongoing military operations during the war, this programme had to limited to a few restricted areas of Angola so far.

In spite of the recent peace treaty, the restrictive situation is still felt everywhere and thwarts many development attempts: bad roads in conjunction with technical transport problems aggravate the handicap of the country's long distances and represent a bottleneck in the balanced distribution and supply of goods and services. Several development projects have failed due to the lack of skilled technicians and trained workers, the absence of a conclusive administrative and planning framework, deficient co-ordination and co-operation among the many ministries involved, and still underdeveloped monitoring and evaluation procedures.

Another impediment to successful planning and building policies after 1975 is the *Angola's é grande* (Angola is great) syndrome. This irrational but desperate endeavour for large-scale investments has produced many white elephants such as the *Cidade Desportiva* (sports city) or Luanda's 'Square of the Revolution'. At least in the very recent situation marked by economic difficulties, emergencies and a continuing war it may be questionable whether the costs of building such monuments are really indispensable for developing self-confidence of a still young, newly independent state, or whether they can rather be interpreted in terms of exaggerated representation ventures by a young and still unconsolidated political system ". . . still marked with the birth-marks of the old society" (Marx, vol. 20). Although such conservative tendencies are certainly too weak to take control of the whole country, they nevertheless demand their budgetary and social toll, and defer the achievement of political and economic independence.

A Luta Continua, a Vitória é Certa (Struggle goes on, victory is certain), MPLA's well-known slogan from the days of armed liberation, has been changed by the people in the streets and squares, in villages and cities, to "victory goes on, struggle is certain". Lúcio Lara, Organization Secretary of the MPLA–PT, says: "The process is dialectic: Angolan people are conscious that the alternative to MPLA is colonialism".

References

Angola, 1976: *Jornal de Angola*, Luanda, 11 November 1976.
Angola, 1978: *Auto Construção*. Luanda: Ministério da Construção e Habitação.
Angola, 1979: *Esquema Preliminar do Plano Director da Cidade de Luanda*. Luanda: Ministério da Construção e Habitação / DNPF.
Bissio, B., 1983: A experiencia do Poder Popular. In *Cuandernos do Tercer Mundo* No. 61, Rio de Janeiro, December, pp. 63–8.
CIPRO, 1981: *Plano Director da Citade de Luanda. Proposta Téchnica*, Lisboa/Luanda 1982.
Conchiglia, A., 1978: 'Die Brücke kubanischer Freundschaft'. In *Informationsdienst südliches Afrika*, No. 2, Bonn, February, pp. 9–10.
Decke, B. A. 1978: 'Angola'. In P. Ripken (ed.), *Südliches Afrika: Geschichte, Befreiungskampf und politische Zukunft*, Berlin, pp. 43–82.
Decke, B. A. 1981: *Terra é Nossa. Koloniale Gesellschaft und Befreiungsbewegung in Angola*, Bonn.
Neto, A., 1976: 'O trabalho é a base de toda a construção socialista'. Speech delivered at the People's Palace on 17 July 1976. *Jornal de Angola*, Luanda, 18 July 1976.
Resende de Oliveira, M. (Minister for Public Works, Housing Construction and Transport), 1976: In *Marchés Tropicaux*, No. 1611, 24 September 1976, p. 2,476.
Schümer, M., 1977: Die Wirtschaft Angolas 1973–1976. *Ansätze einer Entwicklungsstrategie der MPLA–Regierung*, Hamburg.
UN, 1985: Security Council, S/17648, 22–XI–85, United Nations, New York.

Further Reading

Cain, Alan, 1985: Building Participation in Angola. In Mathéy, K. (ed.), *Socialist Housing, TRIALOG 6* (Special Issue), Darmstadt: Vereinigung zur wissenschaftlichen Erforschung des Planens und Bauens in Entwicklungsländern, pp. 30–2.
Kress, Albin, 1985: Volksrepublik Angola. Aufbruch in eine neue Zeit. Berlin: Staatsverlag der DDR.

Mozambique

Paul Jenkins

Introduction

No study of any aspect of Mozambique since independence can be undertaken without reference to the prevailing political and socio–economic situation. Although an in–depth study is outside the scope of this chapter, a summary of basic information is prefaced and some suggestions for further general reading are included in the bibliography. Nevertheless, it is important to understand that at independence in 1975, Mozambique was particularly underdeveloped even in comparison to other countries in the sub–region, which generally had achieved independence a decade earlier without protracted military struggle. In economic terms this underdevelopment was evidenced in the low levels of investment by Portugal and the development of a service economy with a high dependence on markets outside the country (principally Portugal, Rhodesia and South Africa) primarily for transport and large–scale migrant labour. By 1974, the trade deficit had risen to $200 million, with exports covering only half of imports. Portugal also exported surplus population to its colonies, the number of settlers in Mozambique rising to more than 200,000 before independence. In social terms a dualistic system developed, which, although not institutionalized like apartheid in South Africa, ensured preferential access to social benefits of work, housing, education and health for the colonial population and a small indigenous assimilated class, while effectively denying this access to the vast majority of the indigenous population. One example of this is that 93 per cent of the total population was illiterate in 1975, which still has far reaching consequences for Mozambique in the second decade after independence, in terms of the severe shortage of skilled personnel.

At independence the vast majority of the Portuguese settler population fled, often creating economic sabotage, obliging the new government to undertake emergency measures to ensure a continuation of public and economic life, despite acute limitations. Almost simultaneously South Africa began an economic boycott by

Country Profile: Mozambique

National territory: 799,380 km², Coastal length: 2470 km
Population: 11,673,725 million (Census 1980), 14,170,000 (1986)
Population density: 14.6 inhab/sq.km (1980), 16.6 Inhab./sq.km (1984)
Population density – arable land: 154 inhab./sq.km (1985)
Labour force: 7,671,000 (1985); 83% in agriculture, 18% industry, 16% in services.
Urbanization rate: 13.2% (1980)
Capital: Maputo; 900,000 inhabitants (1980)
Estimated natural growth rate: 2.6%/annum (1975–80)
Estimated urban growth rate: 7.6%/annum (1970–80)
Life expectancy: 44 years (1980)
Infant mortality: 12.5%
Illiteracy rate: 93% (1975), 72% (1980), 59% men & 85% women (1985)
Religion: Traditional religions in rural areas. Christian and Muslim in towns.
Language: Portuguese (official). Bantu dialects mostly spoken, including Swahili and Macao
Military expenditure: 43% of budget
Major export products: fish 26%, fruit 16%, petroleum products 12%, tea 11%, cotton 11%
Major markets: US 27%, Portugal 16%, South Africa 7%, UK 7%, Netherlands 6%
Foreign assistance: $ 355.6 million in 1985;
    sources: OECD 62%, EEC 25%, CMEA 15%, OPEC 2%,

Some important dates:
1498 Landing by Vasco da Gama
1505 Establishment of Portuguese trade post, becomes important centre for slave trade
1752 Mozambique becomes Portuguese colony
1960 National resistance against foreign occupation, defeated in massacre of Mueda
1962 Founding of FRELIMO liberation front in exile (Dar es Salaam) (unification of three existing liberation movements: UDENAMO, MANU, UNAMI)
1964 Beginning of armed liberation struggle by FRELIMO
1971 Legal status modified into a Portuguese overseas province
1974 Coup in Portugal, new government starts negotiations with FRELIMO
1975 Declaration of independence
1977 The 3rd FRELIMO congress decides on the transformation of the liberation front into a Marxist–Leninist elite party
1982 Cooperation agreement with former enemy Portugal
1983 The 4th FRELIMO congress declares Mozambique a socialist state
1984 Non-aggression treaty with South Africa

Sources: Die Länder der Erde, Köln: Pahl–Rugenstein, 1982. Third World Guide, Montevideo: Third World Editors, 1986, 1988. Politisches Lexikon Afrika. München: C.H. Beck, 1985. Atlas Geográfico Volume 1, República Popular de Moçambique (Ministério de Educação), Stockholm: Esselte Map Service, 1986. Mozambique: An Introductory Economic Survey, Washington: World Bank, 1985. Mozambique: Country Profile, London: Economist Intelligence Unit, 1987.

Housing data:

Average housing density (persons/house unit): 4.7 (1970), 4.3 (1980)
Housing stock in permanent materials: 6% (1970); 8% (1980)
Access to internal piped water supply: 3% housing stock (1970), 4% housing stock (1980)
Access to external piped water supply: 0% housing stock (1970), 9% housing stock (1980)
Access to domestic electricity supply: . . 3% housing stock (1970), 4% housing stock (1980)
Sanitation by latrine: . . . . 47% housing stock (1980)

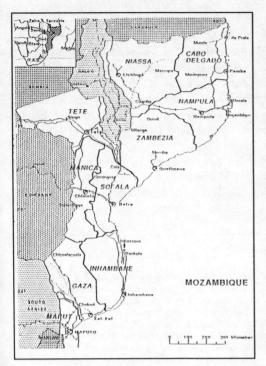

Physical characteristics

Approximately half of the territorial area is made up of coastal plain, maximum altitude above sea level less than 200m, the rest being part of the Central African Plateau and escarpment, primarily in the north and west, where over one eighth of the area is made up of land at altitudes of over 1000m above sea level.

Mozambique is traversed by many rivers, principally running West–East, five of which constitute major river basin complexes, the largest being the Zambezi River Basin with an extension of 14,000 km², and the coastline is characterized by many small to medium size islands and small inland lagoons.

The climate is tropical – the north, centre and southern coast being characterized as warm–humid; the upper Zambezi valley and southern interior of the coastal plain as hot–dry, and the higher altitude areas in the centre and north–west as tropical upland. The flora is of three principal types: savanna and open forest occupying two–thirds of the territory; and the rest dense forest, in upland areas in the centre–north.

reduction of its use of Mozambican transport facilities, migrant labour recruitment levels and a unilateral alteration of the system of payment in gold equivalent for this labour – the main sources of foreign exchange. During the late 1970s Mozambique in support of the struggle for independence, applied the international boycott to Rhodesia at enormous economic cost. Rhodesia in reply directly invaded Mozambique, causing severe human and economic losses, and initiated a policy of destabilization via support to armed bandits in Mozambican territory. After liberation of Zimbabwe, South Africa directly assumed the role of destabilization, through military attacks and support to armed banditry (principally via the so-called Mozambican National Resistance – Renamo), which has brought country-wide disruption, destruction and atrocities without any political or social objectives. This was accompanied by a series of natural disasters such as cyclone damage, flooding and especially drought, which affected all of southern Africa intensely in the period 1982–84.

As a result of these factors and compounded by the deepening world economic crisis which especially raised import costs at the same time as lowering export prices, the country experienced severe economic decline from 1981 to 1987, with the economy contracting by 33 per cent and export earnings falling to 35 per cent of 1981 levels. The resulting lack of foreign exchange has affected all sectors of the economy, including the family agricultural sector (where the majority of the population exert their economic activity), due principally to the breakdown of the commercial system. The social costs are almost impossible to estimate, but as an indicator 31 per cent of all rural health posts and 36 per cent of all primary schools functioning in 1981 were no longer functioning in 1987. This has counteracted the initial rapid progress in provision of social benefits achieved immediately after independence. A systematic programme to arrest economic decline and simultaneously alleviate the emergency situation was initiated by the government in 1987 through the Economic Recovery Programme and National Emergency Programme, with considerable initial success. However, the process of socio–economic recovery has not yet reached many people due to the continuing security situation, and the long term development effects of many of the macro–economic interventions initiated.

The general situation in Mozambique is described as critical in the recent United Nations report *The Emergency Situation in Mozambique: priority requirements for the period 1988–89*, with over 1.1 million displaced persons, who have lost virtually all their possessions, apart from an estimated 2.2 million affected by severe shortages of

---

Socio–demographic Characteristics

The Mozambican population is made up of a great number of ethnic groups, of which the principal are: Makonde, Makua–Lomwe (representing over one third of all the population) and Yao in the north; Maravi and Ngune in the north–west; Shona–Karanga in the centre; and Tsonga, Chopi, Tonga and Ngune in the south. Asian and European minorities are also present.

Principal languages are Bantu: Makonde and Swahili in the north; Shona in the centre; and Ronga–Changane in the south, all of which exhibit numerous regional dialects. The official national language is Portuguese. The majority of the population are animist, Christianity being found primarily in urban areas and Islam predominant in the north, especially the coastal area. Cultural groups north of the Zambezi generally practice matrilinear succession while those in the south, patrilinear succession.

Mozambique can be characterized as a relatively large and sparsely populated country both in global and regional terms, but with a relatively high population growth rate. In 1980 45% of the population was under 15 years of age. The eleven provinces, including the capital city Maputo, display considerable differences in population levels, family size and settlement patterns, the most populous being the two central coastal provinces of Zambezia and Nampula, which between them include about 40% of the total population and which have a relatively long history of settlement. A large proportion of the population lives within 50km of the coast.

The country displays a very low level of urbanization, with only 13% of the population living in the principal urban centres, and follows urbanization patterns similar to those in other under– developed countries in possessing a primate city, Maputo (755,300), several times larger than the next largest settlements, Beira (228,783 inhabitants) and Nampula (158,099), and with other principal urban areas distributed throughout the country, mostly administrative/market centres (1980 census figures).

Social Characteristics

Mozambique initially achieved considerable success in development of the social sectors as evidenced in the statistics available up to 1985. The effects of the high priority given to education can be seen in the 40–50% literacy rate of the 15–24 age group compared to the 8% of the over 60 age group.

Health services also were given high priority, receiving a regionally above average of 7% of central government expenditure, mostly invested in para–medical training and development of a broad based primary health care system, and restricted list of essential drugs. By mid–1980, an estimated half of the Mozambican population had access to preventive health care, and about one third to curative care.

The housing sector received considerably less priority, but considerable development of communal supply of services was achieved, especially access to safe water supply and basic sanitation by latrine.

food and other essential items, and the 2.6 million people who are affected by commercial food shortages. As these figures do not include the estimated 700,000 persons displaced in neighbouring countries, an estimated 7.5 per cent of the total population is displaced internally and 12.3 per cent both internally and externally.

It is against this background that the development of housing policy in post–independence Mozambique is reviewed and analyzed. The structure of the review is partly chronological, dividing the post–independence period into five principal periods which have similar characteristics, State and non–governmental interventions are evaluated separately. Subsequently several key issues are individually examined to highlight specific problems, although this at times has meant a recapitulation of aspects touched on in the chronological analysis.

Shelter Programmes and Periodization: State Interventions

Pre–Independence Period

The role of the state in housing before independence was primarily regulatory, with only 1 per cent of the housing stock in state possession. The responsibility for housing supply for the colonial population was principally in the hands of the private commercial sector, which experienced an extremely rapid expansion during the latter part of the decade 1960–70 and up to 1973–74. General economic expansion was due to the war effort and increased immigration, tourism and trade, principally evidenced in the many speculatively built high–rise apartment buildings in the southern European–style urban centres.

The local population was mainly left to fend for itself with limited individual resources. In both rural and periurban areas they squatted on or rented land without secure tenure; hence, the majority of house construction was of a temporary nature. Despite attempts to control emigration from rural areas, the economic development inevitably attracted urban immigration, which to a great extent was ignored by the colonial authorities. This *laissez faire* attitude encouraged the early development of large spontaneous settlements around the 'cement' cities of the colonial *élite* and near to major workplaces, such as industrial sites and the port–railway complexes of the principal urban areas. In these unplanned and largely unserviced *suburbios* speculators rented land or low–grade house units while awaiting the slow expansion of the 'cement' city, at which point tenants were generally summarily evicted.

Three state interventions in the area of housing before independence are exceptions to the above, principally in Maputo City (then Lourenço Marques) and after 1970:

- The state–sponsored *Junta dos Bairros e Casas Populares*;
- The state–sponsored *Gabinete de Urbanização e Habitação da Região de Lourenço Marques* (GUHRLM), which initiated sites and services schemes with limited support to self–help house construction in periurban areas outside the city limits.

- The six-year plan by the Lourenço Marques City Municipality to lay out 1,600 hectares with 45,000 house plots in sites and services areas in periurban areas within the city limits.

The Immediate Post-Independence Period: 1975-76

Immediately after independence in the initial review of activities undertaken by the Council of Ministers, the need for a housing policy which redressed the balance between urban and rural areas was stressed. Even before independence, during the transitional-government period, private commercial house building activities, which were predominantly in the main urban centres, had started to come to a halt and an exodus of the colonial population had begun. An estimated 200,000 people left the country, including the vast majority of skilled technical and administrative personnel.

In February 1976, the nationalization of all dwellings not used by the owner as a family residence was announced by the government. In addition, the dwellings of individuals who left Mozambique were guaranteed for three months, after which they were also nationalized. The immediate effect of the nationalization programme was to make some 50,000 house units available. By July 1977, many had been allocated to families previously residing in the periurban squatter areas, which were affected by floods in February of that year. Rents were fixed by the newly created *Administração de Parque Imobilario do Estado* (APIE – State Housing Agency), and were calculated on the basis of income, family size and house type, averaging between 10 and 20 per cent of family income.

The *Ministry of Public Works and Housing*, which had been created by the transitional government, was given the responsibility for completion of apartment buildings which were abandoned in various stages of construction, and reorganization of the private building and building material industry, much of which was also abandoned by the owners. With respect to the former a *Co-ordinating Commission for Unfinished Buildings* was created, and simultaneously administrative commissions were nominated for most of the abandoned construction firms, mainly concentrated in the two principal cities. The intention was to redistribute this capacity on a national level, through state construction firms in each province, accompanied by a decentralized system of provincial directorates of the ministry. This reorganization involved a total of sixty construction units, eighty construction material production units, two units for preparation of construction projects, one unit for supply and maintenance of construction equipment, and one wholesale construction material supply unit – an estimated total of 22,000 workers.

Initially the existing pre-independence state interventions in housing in the periurban areas were continued, despite increased financial restrictions. The interventions were primarily undertaken through expanding the activities of the *Gabinete de Urbanização e Habitação da Região de Maputo,* although at times joint activities were undertaken with the City Municipalities. These interventions included residential plot demarcation and provision of basic infrastructures in periurban areas, provision of low-cost house designs and construction of prototype houses, provision of technical and skilled labour assistance for self-help construction, construction of

Ill. 1: A typical Mozambican house in the peripheral Maputo area. Reeds are the principal walling material, supplemented by old roof sheets. *(Foto: P. Jenkins)*

central workshops as bases for the interventions and prefabrication of certain components; and social surveys and mobilization.

With the entry of Mozambique to the United Nations, assistance was requested to support these interventions. A project was formulated which initially proposed various schemes to start in 1977. The finance included technical assistance and equipment provision to support the various existing interventions in Maputo and Beira (flood resettlement programmes, prefabricated techniques); the Machava self–help house programme (conventional techniques); and the training of topographers at the school in Maputo.

For rural areas in 1975 the government announced a programme of establishing communal villages as the means to improve rural housing, provide access to social benefits such as education and health care and develop collective agricultural production. This programme, together with the establishment of state farms on the basis of abandoned farms and plantations, was to be the major attempt to redress the vast urban–rural disparities. Support for this programme in the form of house typology and model village layouts was provided initially by the *Gabinete de Urbanização e Habitação da Região de Maputo*, the executive responsibility being initially divided between various ministries, and later with the *National Commission for Communal Villages*. Approximately 1,000 communal villages were formed within the first few years of the programme. About half were based on the strategic settlements established by the Portuguese army to counteract the popular support for Frelimo in the liberation war, and most of the rest were based on settlements being established after the severe floods in Gaza and Inhambane Provinces in 1976–77, and some created to accommodate returning refugees.

New Post–Independence Directions: 1977–80

Direct state intervention in the field of housing two years after independence continued to be mainly concentrated in the programme to finish off apartment blocks, mostly in Maputo. However, the construction of small numbers of new house units began in 1977, initially mostly in provincial capitals, which had a certain autonomy of decision in this respect – workshops for the production of light prefabricated housing being set up for this purpose in each province. Increasingly, however, new house construction was related to new economic development projects, such as the construction of textile plants, expansion of coal extraction and the construction of north–south road links. Indirect state intervention continued principally through the United Nations Assistance Programme to the *Gabinete de Urbanização e Habitação da Região de Maputo*, because the City Municipalities' capacity to carry out programmes continued to be limited by lack of both technical and financial resources.

The necessary political orientation for development of activities in the field of human settlements was provided in the Directives of the Third Frelimo Party Congress, which took place in 1977. With reference to social policy the following observations were made: in rural areas the communal villages will create conditions for the progressive improvement of housing conditions and the provision of infrastructure and social amenities, as prerequisites for construction and improvement of housing, will be a basic state responsibility. However, the principle of people relying on their own efforts must be established for the improvement of housing conditions in the current period of shortage of resources and capacity.

The directives formulated during the congress indicated that a state department should be created to enable the definition of guidelines and strategy for planning urban centres:

- the drawing up of urban plans and projects for social equipment and infrastructure,
- the organization of people into self–help construction programmes and housing construction cooperatives,
- support for the development of credit and savings schemes linked to housing,
- definition of responsibilities of workplaces in housing personnel,
- development of regulations for private house construction and transmission,
- study of standardization of elements for civil construction of housing at commercially accessible prices,
- study of improvement of traditional housing,
- support for the people in appreciation of the nationalized housing stock and its correct use,
- and training programmes for planning, housing and development of communal villages.

The directives specifically made it clear that the provision of housing was not regarded as a priority for the state, but was to be subordinated to the socialization and increase in productive capacity of the agricultural sector as the base, and of the industrial sector as the "dynamic and decisive factor" in the economy. This position was reflected in the major tasks outlined for the construction industry, where housing and infrastructure were subordinated to agriculture and transportation, and where specific tasks for housing were mentioned only in the context of completion of approximately 1,100 unfinished apartments by 1980.

As a result of these directives, the *Direção Nacional de Habitação* (DNH – National Housing Directorate) was established in April 1977 within the *Ministry of Public Works and Housing* (MOPH), based on the existing *Gabinete de Urbanização e Habitação da Região de Maputo*. A project revision was proposed for UN assistance to the new National Housing Directorate, providing for increased technical assistance in order to develop the existing project to include four new pilot projects in infrastructure construction, sites and services, and improvement of traditional construction in Maputo, Angoche (Nampula Province), and Pemba (Cabo Delgado Province). It also included assistance in building up management and technical capacity within the directorate, and assistance in implementation of a research programme to define priorities, build up a data base for physical planning and establish a housing finance institution.

Other tasks initially undertaken by the National Housing Directorate included development of physical planning standards and house typologies, assistance to the communal village creation programme, preparation of regional development schemes, development of specific housing and urban planning projects and development of a strategy to house contracted foreign technicians.

Although projects in the smaller towns of Pemba and Angoche were initiated with varying success, the major interventions of the National Housing Directorate were concentrated in Maputo in order to test options more rapidly. Based on an analysis of the existing self–help house construction programme, which stressed the need for less input of skilled assistance, these interventions laid more emphasis on physical planning, provision of basic infrastructure, and support for self–help house construction through creation and equipping of community workshops, training in simple construction techniques, investigation of housing credit and regulations for housing co–operatives, social surveys and mobilization. The major new initiative was to develop a strategy for gradual upgrading of spontaneously occupied periurban areas through a pilot project in Bairro Maxaquene in Maputo.

This project was initiated in 1977, based on survey work undertaken in late 1976. It included a strong element of community involvement and despite limited funds and organizational problems, by the end of 1979 had implemented an urban plan involving approximately 45,000 residents, and initiated planning of an expansion area to include another 26,000. Land was redistributed, street networks and land reserves for social equipment created, and provisional lot subdivision initiated. However, the provision of infrastructures and social equipment lagged somewhat behind the land–use reorganization, because of restrictions of financial and executive capacity in the various implementing agencies, although a successful basic sanitation pilot project was initiated. Also, despite land redistribution, secure land titles were not allocated, with the result that housing improvement with permanent materials continued to be discouraged.

With the extinguishing of the existing city municipalities and creation in 1978 of new City Executive Councils subordinate to City Assemblies, detailed proposals for

Ill. 2: A tree–room model type house belonging to the member of a 1979 formed housing co–operative in a Maputo peri–urban Sites–and–Services site.   *(Foto: P. Jenkins)*

the functions and organization of the City Councils were developed in the First National Meeting of Cities and Communal Bairros in February 1979. These involved proposals for the territorial limits of the twelve major urban areas and their subdivision into communal *bairros* (neighbourhoods), as a preparation for the first national elections and census since independence (planned to commence mid 1980), and many other aspects of city administration.

Specifically included were a series of resolutions on urbanism, which more clearly defined the responsibilities for, and typology of, urban interventions. Most of the resolutions on urbanism were based on the recent experiences in upgrading in Maxaquene, and include, in summarized form; the need for popular participation in urban planning; balanced regional and urban development; planned provision of sites and services; use of appropriate technology; development of appropriate house typologies, norms for plot layouts, co–operative forms for building material production, distribution and house construction; creation of financial support mechanisms for urban development; and the need for correct relationships for implementation of urban interventions between the local *Grupos Dinamizadores* (Dynamizing Groups – popular mobilization) and the City Councils (management and technical support).

Some of these resolutions were already being put into practice – the statutes of the newly created Popular Development Bank included proposals for credit for house construction. Another major factor affecting housing was the publication of the Land Law (6/79 of 3–7–79), based on article 8 of the Constitution which nationalized all land under state control. One of the major objectives of this law was to prohibit real-estate speculation, and land for residential use is specifically free from any payment.

The responsibility for land use control was defined as the City and District Executive Councils, which at the time were still in creation.

Given the basis of the new administrative structure, the Land Law and the policies defined in the First National Meeting of Cities and Communal Bairros, the basis for physical planning had been created, with the responsibility for executive interventions being attributed to the Executive Councils. However these were in the process of creation and partial transformation from what remained of the previous city municipalities, and had virtually no trained personnel. The National Housing Directorate as a result changed its emphasis from experimental pilot projects, to concentrate on developing planning standards and training basic level planning technicians, to be distributed throughout the country in provincial planning offices, to provide a minimum of support for the planning of rural and urban communities. A new United Nations assistance project was formulated to assist in this transform- ation. This change of emphasis of the National Housing Directorate, however, left a vacuum in terms of indirect state interventions in the field of housing. The Executive Councils had no existing capacity, and as the UN project support for existing pilot housing projects was terminating, this meant that even these limited interventions were interrupted.

Planning to Overcome Under-Development: 1981–84

At the beginning of the 1980s, direct state intervention in the field of housing continued both in the form of completion of apartments and new construction, although the balance of output was now in the latter. In general the productivity of the building sector grew during the period 1977–81. Most of the new house construction was linked to economic development projects, and projections for these were included in the preparation of the first central economic development plan, the *Plano Prospectivo Indicativo (PPI) 1981–90*.

The *Plano Prospectivo Indicativo* indicated that in 1980 the total number of house units in permanent material nationwide was 147,150 (data from the First National Population Census of 1980), and that this number should increase during the decade to more than 280,000, an increase of (90 per cent), of which more than a third should be built by direct state intervention. The proposal for state construction of these units was divided into 45 per cent in urban areas or industrial complexes, and 55 per cent in agro–industrial complexes. Of the total, the construction of nearly 20,000 units was to be linked to projects financed with external assistance. Taking into consideration the above figures, approximately three million house units would still be constructed of precarious materials by 1990, and of these about 30 per cent would be divided between large agricultural projects and communal villages, the rest being in urban areas or dispersed rural situations. An estimated 330,000 of these precarious house units would need renewal during the decade, given that the average life span of reed house was four years and of a mud and wattle house, ten years. The vast majority of this construction would be by self–build methods.

The plan stressed the need to give the Executive Councils directives for urban development, and to equip them with house projects and the ability to financially and technically control the execution of projects and land use. Emphasis was laid on the need for provision of both physical and support resources to assist self-help house construction, including transport, credit, and free technical assistance, and on collective group organization as a means to channel this assistance. No financial or material means, however, were projected in the plan to provide this.

The permanent house units proposed for direct state intervention during the decade were planned on the basis of planned availability of construction material, and to achieve the desired speed of construction, the majority were projected to include a high degree of prefabrication. One large single project was planned to include construction of 12,000 of these units, to provide housing for technical and management staff for large industrial projects in four locations; Maputo 4,800 house units; Matundo (coal mining), 2,400 units; Mocuba (textile mill), 2,400 units; and Dondo (iron and steel plant) 2,400 units.

This project was planned by the National Housing Directorate, and in December 1981 contracts for assistance for importation of equipment and material and technical assistance were signed with the Democratic Republic of Germany. A special department for this project – *Gabinete de Assistência ao Director Nacional de Habitação para o Projecto das 12,000 Habitações* – was created within the National Housing Directorate to execute the detailed design and construction control of the project. After initial logistical and organizational difficulties, this department proposed several alterations to the original proposals, including low cost non–prefabricated construction techniques as part of the technical solution. The first construction started on 300 house units in Maputo (Bairro de Universidade) in early 1983.

Although the National Housing Directorate included a Housing Studies and Development Department, the major emphasis of activities was increasingly in the area of physical planning and training. In 1982, the Directorate organized the First National Meeting on Urban Planning, with participation from the provincial directorates for public works and housing, and the recently formed provincial planning delegations and city executive councils. The reports to this meeting underlined the extreme practical difficulties being encountered by all of these institutions, the executive councils in particular being unable in many cases to create construction and planning departments. Only one city – *Maputo* – had a minimum of technical staff and had initiated urban studies and basic sites, and services and assistance to self–help house construction programmes for periurban areas, although being completely unable to continue the previous interventions in upgrading which had been initiated by the National Housing Directorate with UN support.

The meeting traced guidelines for the priority development of basic sites–and–services schemes *(malhas de ordenamento urbano)* to be undertaken at a city level primarily by the executive councils, with assistance from the provincial planning delegations. The National Housing Directorate undertook to develop directly City Structure Plans, planning norms for the main urban areas, and continued development of regional development plans. It concentrated its resources, which were becoming scarcer due to the overall economic difficulties the country was experiencing, on training.

The Fourth Congress of the Frelimo Party, which was held in 1983, reviewed development since the Third Congress in 1977. It was reported that from 1977 to

Ill. 3: The '300 house Project' is the only built part of the ambitious early 1980 plan for 12,000 houses to be built by East German prefabricated techniques. (Foto: P. Jenkins)

1982, the state building sector made available nearly 3,500 new conventional housing units, apart from improved water supplies and sanitation, especially in urban areas and communal villages. State intervention also included subsidies estimated at about 50 per cent of total depreciation costs of the state housing sector. Indirect state intervention in upgrading periurban areas had affected approximately 50,000 people. It observed however that problems still existed in the planning and control of construction investment and supply of technical equipment and building materials. The need for decentralizing building and building capacity was stressed, including programmes to encourage small–scale and self–help building. It was emphasized that despite the above developments, simple mechanisms to involve people in the solution of their own housing problems still had to be found, and that the relevant institutions must, through improved co–ordination, establish a housing and house–building policy with clearly defined mechanisms to assist people to build houses with their own resources.

The institutional nature of the emphasis of the National Housing Directorate on physical planning and training was subsequently reinforced when, in December 1983, there was a general government restructuring. As part of this restructuring, the *Ministry of Public Works and Housing* was transformed into the *Ministry of Construction and Water Affairs* (MCA), reflecting the fact that the major tasks in public works were civil engineering infrastructure projects. At the same time the *National Housing Directorate* was transformed into the *National Institute for Physical Planning* (INPF), under a newly created *Secretariat of State for Physical Planning*, located within the *National Planning Commission*, thus reflecting the need to link physical and economic planning. Although the *National Institute for Physical*

Planning maintained in principle a normative role in housing through the *Department of Housing Studies and Development,* its major activities continued to be in physical planning and training.

In late 1983 the *Gabinete de Assistência ao Director Nacional de Habitação para o Projecto das 12,000 Habitações* transferred to the *Ministry of Construction and Water Affairs* within the *National Directorate for Economy of Construction* and was renamed the *Gabinete de Programas de Habitação* (PROHABITA) – Housing Programmes Office – reflecting its emphasis in technical and executive aspects of house construction. The office initiated a series of studies and pilot projects to assist in the definition of terms of reference for housing programmes, with particular emphasis on appropriate technological solutions. It maintained responsibility for overall supervision of the 12,000–house project, although actual construction of housing in this was restricted almost entirely to the university *bairro* in Maputo.

Within the *Ministry of Construction and Water Affairs,* however, other direct interventions in the area of housing had begun to cease, since both national production and importation of building material were drastically reduced with the severe deterioration of the general economic situation since 1982. In 1983, the *Co-ordinating Commission for Unfinished Buildings* was extinguished, having made available approximately 1,000 house units. With the restructuring in 1984, responsibility for direct intervention in housing was defined to be with the executive councils, and the *Ministry of Construction and Water Affairs* initiated the handing–over of responsibility for on–going house construction projects.

The executive councils, however, were still poorly equipped, with low level trained personnel, and totally dependent on central government funds – thus with the general economic difficulties they were also inadequately financed. As a result, the only interventions possible were residential plot layouts, usually with only the most rudimentary of services – sand roads, public water sources and basic sanitation via dry pit–latrines. The lack of infrastructure and building material, and in most cases peripheral locations of sites, however, meant slow plot occupation.

The most successful city programme was in Maputo, which was the only city to have a minimally equipped technical staff; there in a Basic Urbanization Programme over 10,500 plots were laid out between 1981 and 1985. By 1985, 66 per cent were allocated and 43 per cent occupied. Of these house units, 83 per cent were of precarious material, as opposed to 60 per cent in general in the city, despite a co-ordinated Programme of Support to Self–help House Construction, mainly due to the severe shortages of conventional building material. The relative success of these programmes was in the fact that the house units built in these sites–and–services areas, despite their peripheral locations and lack of infrastructure, represented 22 per cent of the overall increase in housing stock in the city. However, Maputo was the exception, and in general the provision of house plots was totally inadequate in relation to demand.

Redefinition of Objectives: 1985–88

Despite the directives of the Fourth Congress of the need for co–ordinated action to define a housing policy, after the government restructuring in 1984 no one institution was responsible for housing, and various related functions were dispersed:

- Project development was divided between the National Institute for Physical Planning – regional and urban planning and residential standards, and *Ministry of Construction and Water Affairs* – technical and executive construction projects.
- The production of industrial and semi–industrial building material and state house construction projects involving foreign finance were generally the direct responsibility of the *Ministry of Construction and Water Affairs.*
- State house construction projects and the administration, maintenance and rehabilitation of state housing stock was the responsibility of the provincial governments and City or District Executive Councils, which were insufficiently equipped.
- Self–help house construction (and maintenance) was assisted by specific departments in various ministries and executive councils, although it was generally of individual responsibility and depended on the general variable *Market Fund* of building material produced for, but not consumed by, state construction projects.

This diversity of responsibility of interventions was partly responsible for wide discrepancies in levels of housing investment and house typology, especially between state and individual house construction. In general the difficulties of building material supply and finance restricted most forms of house construction, but virtually no technical or statistical studies were available to determine the existing situation. In 1986 the Housing Programmes Office within the *Ministry of Construction and Water Affairs* initiated various studies to attempt to provide a partial data base (see the bibliography).

One of these studies (Analysis of State Construction Data 1975–86) indicates that during this period 5,141 house units were constructed in 131 different projects, representing about 13 per cent of the overall total of state construction projects. In general, approximately 50 per cent of the total number of house units constructed were in the two major cities of Maputo and Beira, and 30 per cent were linked to economic development projects outside of major urban areas, reflecting principally the directives of the Third Frelimo Party Congress. In fact, the majority (77 per cent) of the house units were constructed in the years 1975–83, before the Fourth Congress. Most of the new constructions were of conventional construction with reinforced concrete (58 per cent), or prefabricated (33 per cent), very few being of mixed construction and only forty units being of improved traditional construction.

Another study of the variation in the housing stock in Maputo, however, showed a situation that was somewhat different. Despite being the major focus for state house construction since independence (41 per cent), this study indicated that state house construction in the period 1980–85 in Maputo only represented 3.6 per cent of the global increase in housing stock, with approx. 19 per cent of this stock in state control in 1985. Although state construction and housing units were generally of a high standard, almost half (49 per cent) of the total housing stock remained localized in spontaneous settlements, without secure tenure, adequate infrastructure and often in high density, unsanitary conditions, and more than half of the total (56 per cent) were of precarious materials. The study estimated that the housing deficit rose on average 4.45 per cent per year.

However, a significant proportion of new construction was in the new sites and services areas, and a more detailed study of these areas showed the relatively rapid improvement in standards associated with security of tenure, despite difficulties of access to permanent building material, reinforcing the potential efficiency of a strategy of state support through indirect rather than direct interventions in the field of housing. The major proposal of the report thus focused on the need for the state to prepare residential areas with a minimum of infrastructure, stimulate increase in industrial, or semi–industrial building material production, and distribute this material in such a way as to stimulate individual investment in housing; and the need to create specific institutions at a national level to support the Executive Councils in development of these indirect interventions.

Based on the Presidential Decree 73/83 of 29–12–83, the Ministerial Diploma N⁰ 73/83 of 21–1–87 established the principal objectives and functions of the Ministry of Construction and Water Affairs, among which the following were specified for the *Housing Programmes Office*:

a. Promote the development of construction projects for housing and infrastructure, defining appropriate technologies, necessary resources and costs.
b. Stimulate the construction of housing, and in particular assist the Executive Councils, Provincial Governments and construction firms in realization of house construction programmes.
c. Create a data base relevant to housing programmes.
d. Participate in the definition of a national housing policy, with particular reference to construction aspects.

However, at the time of writing no professionally qualified personnel are presently employed by this office, and the existing intermediate and basic trained personnel are inadequate even to control the present low level of state investment, let alone develop housing programmes and policy.

Based on the Presidential Decree 18/83 of 28–5–83, the Ministerial Diploma 61/88 of 11–5–88 established the principal objectives and functions of the *Housing Studies and Development Department* of the *National Physical Planning Institute:*

a. Participate in studies which allow a clearer definition of a national housing policy to ensure a harmonious development between housing and the Mozambican human *habitat*.
b. Analyze housing need in conjunction with other relevant institutions.
c. Study and propose criteria to normalize and regulate the process of planning and executing housing programmes, with reference to urban structures, materials and technology, and socio–cultural and economic aspects of *habitat* and its role in the development process.
d. Evaluate house construction programmes, plans and projects when necessary.

e. Participate with the relevant institutions in the definition of a credit policy which facilitates the access of Mozambican workers to obtain individually owned housing.

f. Contribute to the study and realization of programmes which study workers' housing problems, with specific attention to supporting self–build construction."

The personnel situation presently in this department is even less adequately equipped than the above, and hence the major activity of the department is predominantly preparation of ad hoc construction projects.

In practice, since 1985, the growing economic crisis severely affected building material production and increasing proportions of material had to be imported, which with heavy import restrictions reduced direct state investment in house construction drastically, paralysing most projects in course and postponing initiation of new projects indefinitely. Likewise, indirect interventions were affected because the Executive Councils were totally dependent on state finance for residential plot development, and the 'Market Fund' for building material for distribution to the population. Their technical capacity was further reduced with the restrictions on direct recruitment of foreign technicians, and slow (or non–existent) provision of national technicians. The only interventions which continued were those with a foreign aid input, and in the field of housing these were primarily restricted to specific small scale non–governmental initiatives which had little general impact.

In late 1987, however, within the context of the Government Programme for Economic Recovery, two interventions were initiated:

1. The creation of an autonomous *Fund for the Development of Individual Housing*, under the supervision of Ministry of Construction and Water Affairs, and financed from central government funds, to build housing for sale as a means to mobilize individual finance, initially mainly directed at social groups with access to foreign currency.

2. The preparation of a project for rehabilitation of infrastructure and generation of employment presently agreed with the World Bank for financing through the International Development Agency, and including both a 'sites and services and upgrading' component (involving residential plot layout, construction of infrastruc– ture and core houses, and material and financial support to self–help construction); and a 'rehabilitation and completion of buildings' component (involving rehabilita– tion of degraded state housing units and completion of still unfinished apartments and office buildings). This project is currently being developed as a pilot project with interventions in the two major cities of Maputo and Beira.

In parallel with the development of these projects, two projects were proposed by the government for assistance in the area of human settlements, to be included in the *United Nations Development Programme*, 1987–92. Both of these were initiated as *Preparatory Assistance Projects* in 1987 with technical support from the *United Nations Centre for Human Settlements (UNCHS–Habitat)*, one in regional planning in the *National Physical Planning Institute* and one in national housing policy development in the *Ministry of Construction and Water Affairs, Housing Programmes Office*. The latter project has to date begun to develop baseline studies to prepare an analysis of actual and projected housing supply and demand in Mozambique, on the basis of which recommendations on housing policy and strategies will be proposed, and subsequent pilot projects developed. Concurrently being studied is the necessary reinforcement of the Mozambican institutions involved in the housing sector, specifically those involved in the above initiatives.

Non-Governmental Interventions

The only recorded non-governmental intervention in the housing sector before independence is the creation of the *COOP* housing co-operative, which in Maputo in 1970 included 544 housing units situated in the central city area predominantly for the colonial population. The COOP housing co-operative retained its autonomy after independence, although abandoned housing units were nationalized as well as individual residences.

During the immediate post-independence period (1975–76), there is no record of non-governmental intervention, apart from occasional, and more or less spontaneous, collective participation in construction of infrastructures, organized by Dynamizing Groups. In general, few non-governmental organizations had existed before independence, probably due to the low general level of education, widespread disruption of family life caused by migrant and forced labour, and colonial repression of any organization which could be a nucleus for resistance. This situation continued to be the case after independence also, when most voluntary forms of association were those instituted by the state, principally the Organizations of Mozambican Women, Youth and Workers.

Specifically within the housing sector, little governmental attention was focused on the creation of collective, non-governmental forms of organization, except to some extent in the communal village programme. However one housing co-operative formed itself independently in a periurban sites and services area of Maputo in 1979, when its members began a mutual savings scheme. In 1980, an agricultural co-operative movement was initiated with state support in Maputo City *Green Zones* – agricultural areas within the city limits.

During the early 1980s the general growth of Mozambican non-governmental organizations remained slow, despite increasing governmental support, which was concentrated on agricultural production and marketing. Specific support was also given to the *bairro* based pilot housing co-operative in Maputo by the *Construction and Urbanization Directorate* (DCU) through the *Self–Help House Construction Support Programme*, and an attempt was also made, with assistance from the *Ministry of Construction and Water Affairs Housing Programmes Office and the National Institute for Physical Planning*, to develop another pilot housing co-operative based on a large industrial enterprise. Neither of these experiments were successful due principally to the shortage of building material and high levels of organizational and technical support necessary.

However, the Maputo Construction and Urbanization Directorate also pioneered construction co-operatives, which were used as the basis for the recent basic sanitation programme in the city, producing prefabricated latrine slabs as developed in the Maxaquene upgrading project. These co-operatives were relatively successful, as they produced a low cost product much in demand by the local population. However, once again a high level of technical and organizational input was necessary, and after supplies of nationally produced cement (the basic building material necessary for the slab construction) became unavailable, the programme came to rely almost exclusively on foreign financial assistance, and thus on state support, through which this support was channelled.

This technical, organizational and financial support for both housing and construction co-operatives came principally from foreign non-governmental organizations acting in Mozambique. Some of these organizations had been active since even before independence as political solidarity organizations for Frelimo, and others were international non-governmental organizations which had initiated activities more recently. Initially the activities of these organizations were in supply of skilled foreign technicians called *co-operantes*, but as Mozambique's economic difficulties deepened, they became more involved in developing and channelling funds for small-scale projects, including co-operative development and production of improved traditional building materials in provincial centres.

In recent years non-governmental interventions in the field of housing have continued to be principally initiated and supported by non-Mozambican organizations. One exception has been the initiation of a house building programme for agricultural co-operative members in Maputo, which is currently constructing a one-hundred house pilot project. This also is totally dependent on foreign financial assistance however. Another exception is the formation in 1985 of a Construction Co-operative out of the Popular Housing Brigade which had been used to build the workers' housing at the IFLOMA sawmill and particle board factory in Messica in Manica Province, and which was principally involved in small scale local production of hand burnt bricks and roof tiles. This initiative stimulated the creation of several small production co-operatives in the surrounding villages, some of which formed a common association which received support from the *International Year for Shelter of the Homeless* trust of the United Kingdom to assist their consolidation during 1987.

A recent survey of non-governmental organizations active in the field of human settlements in Mozambique by the *Mazingira Institute* of Kenya lists nine international organizations, mostly dealing with general rural development and relief work, of which shelter activities are a part. The only Mozambican non-governmental organizations which are mentioned as active in this field are the agricultural, housing and construction co-operatives in Maputo and Messica, which are continuing to expand slowly with a fairly high level of international assistance.

Useful experience has been gained, however, both in the application of simple criteria for urban planning and land-use control, and also in the mechanisms for support to self-help house construction, use of building brigades and appropriate low cost technological solutions. Although these interventions are limited in scale – in the order of hundreds of housing units constructed – their innovative use of appropriate technologies and organizational forms is of considerable importance to housing provision in general.

Popular Mobilization, Participation and Self-help

After independence Frelimo organized the establishment of a series of *Dynamizing Groups* in neighbourhoods, workplaces and institutions as a form of social mobilization and organization to replace the defunct local administrations and guard against sabotage, in the often chaotic conditions during and immediately after the Transition Period. These Dynamizing Groups were modelled on local committees formed in the areas liberated and administered by Frelimo in the northern parts of Mozambique during the liberation struggle, members being elected in public meetings. No general plan of activities for these Dynamizing Groups were established, and the development and scope of their activities depended to a great extent on the personal qualities of the elected members. The Dynamizing Groups continued to develop their role in community organization during the latter part of the 1970s and the early 1980s, but increasingly became responsible for a myriad of basic local administrative controls, ranging from registry of residency, permission to travel, to ration card distribution. Although they played a key role in the organization of community participation in the important pilot project in upgrading in Bairro Maxaquene, Maputo, their role generally during this period became less that of popular mobilization and more of administrative control.

The involvement of the Dynamizing Groups in shelter–related activities was generally limited because central, and to a lesser extent local, government controlled most construction–material production and distribution, with precedence to the centrally planned construction projects. As a result there was little material with which to develop local shelter–improvement activities. The few local activities that were possible were generally initiated by the City Councils and/or non–governmental organizations, and these attempted to work in close co–ordination with the Dynamizing Groups. This was especially so with respect to the development of local control of land use and construction in residential areas. However, in many cases the continuing high rate of urban influx and slow rate of supply of house sites put intolerable pressures on the Dynamizing Groups, and these soon became involved in unofficially allocating land and authorizing construction, despite their lack of capacity to control these activities and the clearly defined responsibility for this area of the City Councils.

This primary role of administrative control of the Dynamizing Groups was particularly reinforced by their key role during the *Operation Production* in 1984, which attempted to round up all unofficially employed adults and oblige them to enter agricultural productive activities, usually state farms in northern provinces with shortages of labour. This operation was soon abandoned after much public criticism, but the ability of the Dynamizing Groups to mobilize was severely affected. This situation had been compounded at times by the abuse of power by the members of the Groups, who although elected, worked voluntarily in their free time. Subsequently the secretary of the groups and a permanent administrative assistant were financed from central government funds for each *bairro*, mainly to deal with the growing administrative workload, although the secretary had still to be approved in a public meeting. Attempts were made to set up *Frelimo Party* cells at neighbourhood level to continue the parallel party/state apparatus existing at national and local government level, but very few of these cells were in place towards the end of the decade. The Dynamizing Groups also became subordinate to an intermediate level of district administrations in the major urban areas, and thus had no direct link to local government structures. As a result the popular influence of the Dynamizing Groups waned and as clear directives as to the limits of their administrative role were not issued, the level and type of activity continued to differ considerably from *bairro* to *bairro*, depending on the initiative of the members.

With the deteriorating security situation around the principal and secondary urban centres in the latter part of the 1980s, and the subsequent rapid increase in urban influx, the problems facing all forms of local administrative control became severe. The Dynamizing Groups' capacity to respond to this situation was limited, and increasingly their role was reduced to a few key administrative controls, and local initiatives at communal self–help became increasingly rare. Their existence, however, is potentially still an important asset for shelter–improvement programmes.

Individual self–help has continued to be the major force in house construction and improvement, which is severely limited in the periurban areas due to shortages of both conventional and traditional construction material, and the vast majority of urban households in all the urban centres now occupy land spontaneously, the greater part with only the minimum of over–utilized services.

Nationalization of Land

The Land Law (6/79 of 3–7–79), which came into effect on 25–9–79, based on article 8 of the Constitution, nationalized all land under state control. One of the major objectives of this law was to prohibit real estate speculation, and land for residential use is specifically free from any payment. The responsibility for land–use control was defined in the law as the City and District Executive Councils, which at the time were still in creation.

The law itself was couched in general terms, and only in 1987 were the interpretive Regulations published, being more or less exclusively produced by the Ministry of Agriculture, and hence concentrating on agricultural land–use and rural areas. As a result, despite ad hoc attempts by various City Councils to develop internal norms, and the initiation of codification of residential land–use regulations by the National Institute for Physical Planning based on the experiences thus gained both in the application of simple criteria for urban planning and land use control, no legal process for physical planning has been established. No specific institutions are presently responsible, or minimally equipped, for this area of activity at either a national or local government level, and the existing institutions are involved in ad hoc and often conflicting interventions.

The procedures for land concession have consequently become labyrinthine and irrational – the only entities which are capable of resolving individual cases are those with considerable socio–political or economic influence, whether government, private or individual – and the vast majority of land occupations are made spontaneously, whether for residential or other purposes. Although in principal only residential and family–sector agriculture land use is exempt from land taxation, in practice the institutions involved have no capacity to up date their outdated cadastre systems (which in the pre–independence period only covered the immediate urban areas), and no administrative capacity to control actual land use or collect taxes. These factors have led to increasingly chaotic situations, such as land banking by powerful institutions in the more developed urban areas and unofficial speculation in land principally in the periurban areas. Urgent attention needs to be focused on this area of activity, whether from the point of view of the necessity of creation of planned residential areas, or from the need efficiently to administer land as a basic productive resource.

Nationalization of Rented Accommodation

The legal Decree 5/76 of February 1976 nationalized all dwellings not used by owners as family residences, as well as abandoned dwellings, reserving for the state the sole right to rent housing. As part of the nationalization declaration the government indicated that it would not honour the substantial national debt which this represented, estimated at about $125 million, which was primarily owed to bankers and land speculators. The immediate effect of the nationalization programme was to make 50,000 house units available. Rents were fixed by the newly created *Administração de Parque Imobilario do Estado* (APIE – State Housing Agency), and were calculated on the basis of income, family size and house type, averaging 10–20 per cent of family income.

In 1979 the Law 8/79 established the regulations for rented accommodation, but without establishing the State Housing Agency as a legal entity. For this reason no legal process of alteration of ownership was effected. With the nationalization of the banks, the national Banco Popular de Desenvolvimento, therefore, inherited the majority of the mortgages. No clear mechanisms for allocation of housing were established either and the State Housing Agency continued for many years to be the focus of much public criticism of irregularities committed by its staff. The available stock was quickly distributed, and already in the 1980s severe housing shortages for transferred government employees and for foreign workers began to be felt.

As the State Housing Agency was not established legally, it retained a national level directorate subordinate to the Ministry of Public Works and Housing, later Ministry of Construction and Water Affairs, and in each major city a municipal level directorate subordinate to the Executive City Council. In practice these had no financial or administrative autonomy, and as rents were set far below economic levels, not even adequate to cover administrative costs, finance for functioning came from central government funds via annual grants for current and capital expenditure to the Executive City Councils. The vast majority of the nationalized housing stock was in the principal urban areas, probably at least 50 per cent in Maputo alone, however until 1986 no full register was attempted. Most of the stock was in the central 'cement' city areas, including nearly all the existing walk–up and high rise apartments, but all rented housing units in the surrounding *suburbios* were also nationalized, and thus the stock included a proportion of precarious house units also.

As the general economic situation weakened, central government grants were inadequate to cover routine maintenance, which, allied to the fact that many of the new tenants were unaccustomed to apartment–living, brought about rapid deterioration of the stock. Campaigns were mounted by central and local governments through the Dynamizing Groups and *Mozambican Woman's Organization* to help people adapt to inner urban life, but with the shortages of physically and economically available alternatives, many people continued to cook on open solid–fuel stoves, grind corn–meal with heavy pestles and mortars and keep small livestock in their houses. Many of the units were overcrowded, and soon many of the building services, such as lifts, waste disposal, water supply and sewage systems, were no longer functioning. By the mid 1980s much of the stock needed major rehabilitation, and as pointed out in the Fourth Frelimo Party Congress, a great part of the state's economic capacity for intervention in the housing sector was taken up in subsidies estimated at about 50 per cent of total depreciation costs of the state housing sector.

In the light of this situation, in September 1987, Law 8/87 altered the basis of calculation of rents to 'link the rent more directly to the costs and characteristics of the building and not the characteristics and income of the tenants', as an integral part of the nationwide economic recovery programme. Factors taken into account are size of plot and covered area, quality, age and localization of the house unit and any special installations. Around this time it was estimated that for the city of Maputo, for example, where the majority of these units are concentrated, the state rental housing stock, excluding the house units in precarious material in the *suburbios*, was approximately 35,000 units, only representing nineteen per cent of the city total. To give some perspective, in 1980 the total Maputo city housing stock only represented six per cent of the total national stock, and forty–four per cent of the total urban stock. Thus state rental housing represents a relatively small proportion of the national housing stock – probably less than one per cent of national stock, or less than five per cent of the housing stock in the twelve principal urban areas.

In the absence of accurate data from the State Housing Rental Administration, APIE, it is estimated that rents rose approximately 100 to 150 per cent overall, while basic minimum wages rose approximately three times during the same period. In fact, rental increases are proportionately less than increases in utility costs, and represent proportionately less of household expenses. State rents are still heavily indirectly subsidized – the new level of income probably not covering new administration costs let alone maintenance, rehabilitation or amortization costs. The recent initiative of the *Ministry of Construction and Water Affairs* – the *Urban Rehabilitation Project* – includes a housing sub–component which projects the rehabilitation of a selected number of residential apartment blocks in both Maputo and Beira. Estimates for this project indicate that even after recalculation of increased rents for a three bedroom flat (100m^2) after rehabilitation, according to the existing table, these will not be sufficient even to repay the rehabilitation costs, and in fact will be several times less than the alternative of a 25–year mortgage for construction of basically finished first phase (three rooms, 33m^2) core house on a periurban house plot, even with a reduced interest rate.

This means that although a large proportion of tenants might favour relocation to self–owned or house plot situations for social reasons, the majority cannot afford this alternative without a considerable drop in housing standards, as well as more unfavourable location. The conclusion is that many will remain as tenants, covering increased rents through illegal sub–letting and/or overcrowding. What is more worrying is that they may decide not to pay high utility costs, and hence accelerate the degradation of the housing stock through use of unsuitable alternatives such as solid fuel for cooking and poor sanitary conditions without direct water supplies.

In the light of these facts, alternative methods of administration of the state housing stock are presently being studied, including the possibility of creating state firms at provincial level with administrative and financial autonomy to this effect. In practice, illegal subletting of state house units is becoming more widespread, especially to supply the demand for accommodation of foreign personnel who can pay in convertible currency. However, indirect forms of rental have existed for some time in the *suburbios* where the majority of house units are individually owned, and there is presently some evidence of new house construction specifically for illegal rental in these areas.

House Construction Standards and Technology

The widespread abandonment of the construction and construction material industry by the predominantly private sector owners and their skilled personnel immediately before and after independence led to the initiative of the *Ministry of Public Works and Housing* to redistribute the remaining installed construction capacity through creation of state construction firms in each province. This in itself was a massive undertaking, given that previously most of the construction activity had been concentrated primarily in the two major cities, Beira and Maputo.

Direct state intervention after independence continued to be mainly concentrated in the programme to finish off apartment blocks, mostly in Maputo, which were mostly high–rise reinforced concrete structures planned for a high level of infrastructure and services. In the other provincial capitals, and in principal economic development projects from 1977 onwards, workshops for the production of light prefabricated housing were set up by the newly created state construction firms as the system of attaining the projected targets for the construction of new house units. By the beginning of the 1980s this represented the preferred state house construction technology outside the two major cities. The systems used were generally based on the Cuban *Sandino* light prefabricated post and panel system, with local adaptations. Standards of construction, whether in finishing apartment blocks or new construction, were continued at a high level of finish – for instance, three bedroom apartments often had two or three complete bathrooms.

In general the productivity of the building sector grew during 1977–81, and projections for the sector included in the preparation of the first central economic development plan, the *Plano Prospectivo Indicativo (PPI) 1981–90*, were optimistically based on this expansion, projecting a 90 per cent increase in permanent house units throughout the decade. Over a third would be built by direct state intervention, primarily in urban areas and industrial and agro–industrial complexes, relying to a great extent on externally funded support. In addition, another three million house units were projected to be constructed of precarious materials by self–build methods; about 30 per cent would divided between large agricultural projects and communal villages, the rest being in urban areas or dispersed rural situations. No conventional building materials, however, were projected to be made available for this sector.

To achieve the desired speed of construction, the majority of house units to be constructed by direct state intervention were to include a high degree of prefabrication. One large single project was planned by the National Housing Directorate to include construction of 12,000 of these units, and contracts for assistance for importation of equipment, material and technical assistance were signed with the Democratic Republic of Germany. Initially projected to include importation of complete heavy panel prefabricated unit fabrication plants, after initial logistical and organizational difficulties, the special department created to manage the project – *Gabinete de Assistência ao Director Nacional de Habitação para o Projecto das 12,000 Habitações* – proposed several alterations to the original proposals, including low cost non–prefabricated construction techniques as part of the technical solution. The first construction started on 300 house units in Maputo (Bairro de Universidade) in early 1983. This construction project, still in process, represents virtually the only product of this large scale project.

The need to develop appropriate technical solutions – often referred to as *improved traditional technologies* – had been stressed as far back as the Third Frelimo Party Congress and First National Meeting on Cities and Communal Bairros in 1979, but little had been done in practice except on a small scale in pilot projects to develop these techniques. At the time of the Fourth Frelimo Party Congress it was reported that from 1977 to 1982 the state building sector had made available nearly 3,500 new conventional housing units; however, it was observed that problems still existed in the planning and control of construction investment and supply of technical equipment and building materials. The need for decentralizing building and building capacity was stressed, including programmes to encourage small–scale and self–help building. It was emphasized that despite the above developments, simple mechanisms to involve people in the solution of their own housing problems still had to be found, and that the relevant institutions must, through improved co–ordination, establish a housing and house–building policy with clearly defined mechanisms to assist people to build houses with their own resources.

After 1984, the Housing Programmes Office initiated a series of studies and pilot projects to assist in the definition of terms of reference for housing programmes, one of these indicating that up to 1986, 58 per cent of direct state house construction was of conventional masonry construction using the reinforced concrete frame system inherited from Portugal (an earthquake–prone area); a further 33 per cent used prefabricated techniques (principally the light panel systems); the remaining were of mixed construction with only 40 units being of improved traditional construction. Standards were uniformly high, and consequently material utilization; for example, the amount of cement to build a typical unit of average 100m² covered area was over 14 tons, compared to the model self–help house type (33m²) of the Maputo City Council which required under 7 tons, or 3 tons for the three room first phase.

Other studies focused on appropriate technological solutions including a study: *Strategy for the Development of Basic Construction Material Production in Mozambique*, which researched natural sources of building materials and proposed simple means of transformation, including the use of such alternatives as pozzolanas. The Department of Building Materials within the Ministry of Construction and Water Affairs also initiated a programme in certain rural areas of support to the local production of hand made clay bricks and use of lime and adobe; improved traditional building materials and techniques were used also in the house construction programme in communal villages of the Secretary of State for Cotton. Experience with building brigades and appropriate low cost technological solutions were also gained in the support programme for workers housing at the IFLOMA complex in Manica province, and in the support to pilot housing and construction co–operatives in Maputo.

These interventions were, however, limited in scale – in the order of hundreds of housing units constructed – although if supported adequately their innovative use of appropriate technologies and organizational forms could be of considerable importance to housing provision in general. The vast majority of house construction in Mozambique uses traditional materials and techniques. Many of these could be improved with the application of quite simple technologies, which is becoming increasingly important given the widespread urban influx accelerated by the war situation. Many previously small secondary urban centres have multiplied several times in size during the last few years, and the availability of local sources of collected building materials is usually limited and quickly becomes inadequate for a larger community, necessitating exploitation of other potential resources requiring more sophisticated transformation techniques. For the principal urban areas access to industrially produced construction material such as cement is essential, although there is much scope for local small–scale fabrication of components. However, during the last five years the quantities of basic construction material reaching the public through official channels have been minimal. Assistance with more efficient use of material and more appropriate technologies and house typologies has already been developed in many of the above pilot projects; however, its widespread dissemination requires considerably more government support.

Government Structure Related to Housing

Administrative and Financial Structure

The first specific institution responsible for national housing policy and programmes was created in 1979, with the creation of the National Housing Directorate within the Ministry of Public Works and Housing. This entity, however, did not have control over all aspects of housing provision, because administration of state–owned rented accommodation remained the direct responsibility of the *City Executive Councils* under general supervision of the ministry itself. Provincial governments had considerable autonomy with respect to local house construction programmes and a specific commission was created at a national level for creation of communal villages in rural areas.

Despite concentrated efforts by the National Housing Directorate in development of pilot projects, increasing limitation of resources and political decision to transfer direct responsibility for development of local housing programmes to provincial governments (which proved impossible to implement because of the general economic situation and shortage of trained personnel), signified a weakening of the base for provision of housing and support for individual house construction.

The government reorganization of 1983 consolidated the emphasis of previous National Housing Directorates on physical planning through creation of the Secretariat of State for Physical Planning within the National Planning Commission, and the emphasis of the *Ministry of Construction and Water Affairs* on civil engineering infrastructure projects. Housing was defined as a responsibility of provincial and municipal governments, but no specific administrative apparatus was created to respond to this decision. The responsibility for national policy development became ill-defined.

As a result, the existing local government institutions were unable to undertake this added responsibility; few housing interventions were undertaken at a local government level, apart from the continued administration of state owned rented accommodation and the distribution of land for residential purposes. The *Ministry of Construction and Water Affairs* thus continued to be responsible for direct state interventions in house construction, which due to the prevailing economic situation became almost totally reliant on foreign finance. This ministry also continued to control all production of industrial and semi-industrial building material.

Given the growing economic and security problems, and consequent difficulty in manufacture and provision of construction materials, the vast majority of house construction continued to be based on individual initiative and resources, which were generally limited. As a result housing deficits increased at all levels, generally evidenced in growing occupancy rates of existing housing stock, at the same time that this stock deteriorated rapidly in quality. In the light of this situation, several other state and para-statal institutions began to develop interventions in the area of housing directly linked to economic development projects, and non-governmental organizations began to assist in shelter related activities linked to rural development and emergency relief work without clear administrative incorporation.

Recently there has been an attempt to redefine the institutional responsibility for housing at a national level, but the detailed responsibilities and relationship between the two national entities thus proposed and the provincial governments is as yet unclear, and neither the national or local institutions have as yet been minimally equipped with adequate resources, especially trained manpower. The recent initiatives taken by the Ministry of Construction and Water Affairs demonstrate this situation clearly, and the UNDP/UNCHS Technical Assistance Project is currently assisting in defining necessary institutional development.

Financial mechanisms for housing investment also remain in an embryonic stage, despite the early definition of responsibilities of the *Popular Development Bank* and a subsequent detailed study undertaken by the *National Housing Directorate*. This has been principally due to the general shortage of construction material, and the priority distribution of this material to direct state investment projects. No mechanisms for generation of finance for housing projects have been created at a local government level (provincial or metropolitan), and state investment in housing remains reliant on provision of central government funds. Even in cases of nongovernmental interventions where supply of adequate material has been guaranteed, generally through foreign aid, no access to credit has been obtained. This position was reinforced due to the relatively high interest rates, and the complete absence of housing finance structures within the bank.

In this respect two recent initiatives of the Ministry of Construction and Water Affairs are innovative: one in the proposal to create a special fund for development of individual housing, outside the existing financial institutions, and the other in the proposal of on–lending of World Bank–supplied finance through the existing financial institutions to individual house builders, on a cost–recovery basis to create revolving funds for housing related investment. These innovations are, however, still in very initial phases of development, and it is too early to assess their possible impact.

Technical and Executive Structure

The responsibility for technical support for housing related activities was originally invested in the *National Housing Directorate*, and after the dissolution of this institution passed to the *Executive City Councils*. As indicated above these local government entities were generally unable to create the necessary administrative structures to support housing activities; this is true of their technical capacity, which remains extremely weak. As noted above the two national level institutions currently with housing support functions have specific tasks defined with relation to technical support for housing, with slightly different emphases. Neither, however, is even minimally adequately staffed for this activity.

The responsibility for executive housing activities continues without adequate definition, being in principle the responsibility of local government structures at both, a provincial and metropolitan level, with support from the *Housing Programmes Office* in the *Ministry of Construction and Water Affairs* and the *Housing Studies and Development Department* of the *National Physical Planning Institute*. However, the relationship between these two national and various local government institutions with respect to responsibility for development of housing programmes is unclear, and this is an area which is currently being studied within the overall context of development of housing policy.

Appraisal

Housing Policy Development

The principal policy statements of the Frelimo Party have delineated the general context for a national housing policy; these are most developed in the directives of the Third Party Congress of 1977 with specific reference to housing. These general policy statements are consistent on the necessity of development of a basis for self-help housing as a general policy, the state supplying an enabling role in provision of land, social services and amenities, and reorganization of the construction sector. Specific effort was also to be concentrated in combating urban/rural imbalance through socialization of the rural areas, based on communal villages and regional development projects.

No specific definition of housing policy has been undertaken, however, on the basis of these general directives, and the majority of both state and non-governmental interventions since independence have been developed ad hoc in response to specific situations. This is true of major policy-affecting decisions, such as nationalization of rented accommodation and rental policy; preparation of the *Plano Prospectivo Indicativo* (Ten-Year Development Plan) and redistribution of construction capacity; as well as of particular interventions, such as specific pilot projects including *Maxaquene, Messica* and others.

More specific definition of policy-developing strategies was subsequently undertaken in the First National Meeting on Cities and Communal Bairros, and the First National Meeting on Urban Planning, but the resolutions formulated in these National Meetings do not constitute housing policy as such. In fact, they have not been particularly influential in even defining types of specific interventions.

The need for development of a national housing policy is clearly recognized by the government, and in recent years has been defined as part of the responsibilities of both the *Housing Programmes Office* in the *Ministry of Construction and Water Affairs*, and the *Housing Studies and Development Department* of the *National Physical Planning Institute*. In this context the *Ministry of Construction* requested technical assistance from the United Nations specifically to assist development of national housing policy, which resulted in the constitution of the current UNDP/-UNCHS Technical Assistance Project mentioned above.

Legislation has generally followed the general policy formulations with respect to housing in defining the structure and competence of institutions responsible for construction, housing, planning, finance and creation of communal villages, and specific laws regulating land use, rented accommodation, territorial organization and creation of co-operatives.

A more specific study of the legal-institutional framework has highlighted in detail difficulties created by the lack of, or conflicting, legislation. Specific action needs to be taken to clarify conflicting legal aspects and propose adequate legislation for housing and planning to overcome the present situation of impasse with respect to definition of processes for physical planning and land use control, management of the state housing stock, and mechanisms for development of state, non-governmental and individual initiatives in house production, including financial credit mechanisms.

The lack of definition of these mechanisms at both national and local government level currently severely restricts the co–ordinated development of housing projects and programmes, as does the lack of adequate technical and executive capacity.

Most of the above aspects are presently part of the current study of housing policy development. However, considerable investigative work still remains necessary to develop a database for housing at a national level, subsequently to analyze actual and projected housing supply and demand patterns, and to propose the alternatives for housing policy and strategies for housing programmes and pilot projects to be developed. In the meantime the country is rapidly changing as effects of the economic structural readjustment programme take effect. This is particularly so in the area of housing with the advent of the relatively large–scale World Bank–financed investment project. Whether Mozambique will be able, given its acute difficulties of shortage of managerial and technical personnel, to benefit positively from this assistance in terms of self–determination of housing policy remains to be seen.

Conclusions

The principal intention in this chapter has been to analyze housing policy develop– ment through a review of existing data on state and non–governmental intervention in the area of housing in Mozambique since independence. It is proposed that evaluation of developmental performance of Mozambique with respect to housing policy be undertaken in terms of the Mozambican government's own stated intentions, and also in the light of experience of other countries in similar situations such as described elsewhere in this book. It is stressed that this report represents work in progress, and it is hoped that it contributes to the better understanding of shelter policies in socialist Third World countries.

Assessment of the developmental performance with respect to these policies will inevitably involve debate on the nature of 'socialist societies'. This issue has been analyzed by Gordon White (1983) with reference to six countries, including Mozambique. His proposal that these societies should be designated as 'proto– socialist', implying that only certain initial steps towards socialism have been taken, or 'state socialist', indicating that these societies are characterized by highly statist forms, certainly applies in the case of Mozambique.

Equally applicable, despite the fact that Mozambique has developed within a specific historical and political perspective considerably different from many other such countries, is the thesis put forward by White that revolutionary socialist development in Third World countries has generally undergone three characteristic transitions and stages of development, defined by him as *revolutionary voluntarism* (the application, in a chaotic and rapidly changing post–revolutionary socio–economic situation, of methods developed during the revolutionary period of politico–military struggle, especially with respect to mass mobilization, and restriction of market– based economic activity) *bureaucratic voluntarism* (state consolidation and direction of the social economy through the wide application of administrative controls, with the aim of rapid economic development), and *reformism and market socialism* (with the development of a more complex economic structure and diversification of social demands, policies focus on the need for economic efficiency, with acceptance of market forces, and the tendency for greater political pluralism and cultural diversity is reflected in the renewed definition of 'socialist development' in the context of national economic potential and socio–political needs and demands).

These stages are reflected in the state interventions in the area of housing in Mozambique, with reference to the nationalization of rented accommodation and land, intervention by the state in construction activities and development of the socio-economic role of *grupos dinamizadores* in the *initial phase of transition* up to 1977; the directives of the Third Frelimo Party Congress, development of the Plano Prospectivo Indicativo 1980–90, and subsequent concentration of resources in state house construction programmes, despite recommendations of the Fourth Party Congress, in the *intermediate phase of transition* from 1977 continuing through the period of economic decline and growing war situation during 1982–86; and the relatively recent internationally supported initiatives in the general context of the Economic Recovery Programme – alterations to the state rental structure, the creation of the *Fund for the Development of Individual Housing*, and the World Bank-sponsored Urban Rehabilitation Project – in the *third phase of transition* as of 1987.

As far as non–governmental interventions are concerned, despite being consistently referred to as important elements in development of housing policy, these have developed mostly without, and even despite, state intervention. As mentioned in the text, the vast majority of housing in Mozambique is financed, constructed and maintained by individual initiative, although of an extremely low quality, and mostly lacking any form of communal infrastructure. The strategic involvement in key pilot projects by international non–government organizations has also indicated important alternatives for more effective state intervention in an 'enabling role'. However, due mainly to the fact that the state still predominantly defines housing in terms of its economic use value, ignoring almost completely its importance as an element of economic exchange and accumulation in national development, the economic importance of these options has not been realized. They have not as yet had any determining effect on policy development.

In July 1989 the Frelimo Party will hold its fifth congress. It remains to be seen what political direction for the state will be defined by the party in this congress, in the light of the current rapid social and economic changes, and what possible effects this will have on housing and housing policy development in Mozambique.

Appendix: Selection of Legislative Documents

Instituto Nacional de Livros e Discos, 1980: *Constituição da República Popular de Moçambique*, Maputo, September

Instituto Nacional de Livros e Discos, 1980: *Lei de Terras* 4º Sessão da Assembleia Nacional, Maputo, May.

Instituto Nacional de Livros e Discos,1980: *Lei do Arrendamento* 4º Sessão da Assembleia Nacional, Maputo, September

Boletim da República 21–1–1987, I Serie/Nº 3 *Ministerio da Construção e Aguas*, Diploma Ministerial Nº 25/87.

Boletim da República 23–12–87, I Serie/N⁰ 51 *Conselo de Ministros* – Decreto N⁰ 37/87.
Boletim da República 11–5–88, I Serie/N⁰ 19, *Comissão Nacional do Plano* – Diploma Ministerial N⁰ 61/88.

References and Further Reading

Candeias L., 1988, *Enquadramento Jurídico-Institucional do Sector da Habitação na República Popular de Moçambique*, Nairobi: UNCHS (Habitat) November.
Candeias L. and Jenkins P., 1988: *Política de Habitação*, Nairobi: UNCHS (Habitat) September.
Chalmers University of Technology, 1977: *The Malhangalene Survey* Gothenburg, Sweden.
Forjaz J., 1984: *Research Needs and Priorities in Housing Construction Activities in Mozambique*. Maputo: Instituto Nacional de Planeamento Físico.
Forjaz J., 1985: *Housing and Planning Issues in Independent Mozambique*. International seminar on shelter policies in socialist Third World nations, Kleve (Germany).
Frelimo, 1977: *Documentos da 3⁰ Congresso – Directivas Económicas e Sociais* Maputo: Dept⁰ de Trabalho Ideológico da Frelimo.
Frelimo, 1983: Report of the Central Committee, 4⁰ Congress, *Mozambique – Out of Underdevelopment to Socialism*, Maputo.
Garcia M.L., 1989: *Aspectos Gerais da Problemática Jurídica do Uso e Ocupação do Solo Urbano na República Popular de Moçambique*, Nairobi: UNCHS (Habitat), March.
Gibbs L., 1984: *Iniciativas Habitacionais*, Maputo: Instituto Nacional de Planeamento Físico, May.
Hanlon J., 1984: *Mozambique: The Revolution under Fire*, London: Zed Books.
Hanlon J., 1986: *Apartheid's Second Front: South Africa's war against its neighbours*, Harmondsworth: Penguin.
Iwansson P., 1984: *Messica – Planificação e Uso de Solo*, Lund: Dept⁰ of Building Function Analysis, School of Architecture, University of Lund. October.
Iwansson P., 1985: *Housing Policy in Mozambique*, International seminar on shelter policies in socialist Third World nations, Kleve (Germany), May.
Jenkins P., 1982: *Considerações sobre a Problemática de Habitação na Cidade de Maputo*. Maputo: Direcção de Construção e Urbanização, Conselho Executivo da Cidade de Maputo, June.
Jenkins P., 1986: *Estudio da Situação Habitacional da Cidade de Maputo – Variação do Stock Habitacional nos Anos 1980–85*. Maputo: Gabinete de Programas de Habitação, Ministério de Construção e Aguas, August.
Jenkins P., 1987a: *Project 100 Houses – Pilot Housing Project for Agricultural Co-operatives in Maputo City*. Maputo: Gabinete de Programas de Habitação, Ministério de Construção e Aguas, May.
Jenkins P., 1987b: *Estudo de Construção Habitacional Estatal 1975–86*. Maputo: Gabinete de Programas de Habitação, Ministério de Construção, July.
Jenkins P., 1988a: *Principal Legislation Relevant to Planning and Housing in Mozambique since the Colonial Period – a Bibliography*, Nairobi: UNCHS (Habitat), July.
Jenkins P., 1988b: *Interventions in the Area of Housing since Independence – Review and Analysis*. Nairobi: UNCHS (Habitat) July.
Jenkins P., 1988c: *Analysis of Housing Characteristics: Comparison of Census Information 1970–1980*, Nairobi: UNCHS (Habitat) September.
Jenkins P., 1988d: *Residential Area Characteristics in Mozambique*, Nairobi: UNCHS (Habitat) December.
Kossick D., 1983: *The Role of Co-operatives in Basic Urbanization Programs in Maputo, Mozambique*. Maputo: Direcção de Construção e Urbanização, Conselho Executivo da Cidade de Maputo, November.
Loxley J., 1978: *Housing Finance in Mozambique*, UNOTC Project MOZ/75/021/ Maputo: Direcção Nacional de Habitação, August.
Mozambique, 1974: *1⁰ Recenseamento da Habitação*. Lourenço Marques: Instituto Nacional de Estatística, April.

Mozambique, 1979a: *Resolução sobre o Urbanismo*, 1º Reunião Nacional sobre Cidades a e Bairros Comunais, Documento Nº 5, Maputo.

Mozambique, 1979b: *Informação sobre o Projecto de Assistência Técnica das Nações Unidas para o Sector Habitacional*, Maputo: Direcção Nacional de Habitação, July.

Mozambique, 1980: *Habitação e condições de vida da população*, Maputo: Conselho Coordenadore do Recenseamento.

Mozambique, 1981: *Approach to a Physical Planning Institution in a Socialist African Country*, Maputo: Direcção Nacional de Habitação, August.

Mozambique, 1982: *Relatorio do 1º Reunião Nacional de Planeamento Urbano*, Maputo: Direcção Nacional de Habitação.

Mozambique, 1983: *Contribuição para o Estudo do Habitat Moçambicano*, Maputo: Direcção Nacional de Habitação, May.

Mozambique, 1986: *Síntese do Programa das Actividades do Deptº de Estudos e Desenvolvimento de Habitação 1986*, Maputo: Instituto Nacional de Planeamento Físico, July.

Newitt M., 1981: *Portugal in Africa: the last hundred years*, C. Hurst.

Pinsky B., 1982: *The Urban Problematic in Mozambique: Initial Post–Independence Responses 1975–80*. Toronto: Centre for Urban and Community Studies, September.

Pinsky B., 1985: *Territorial Dilemmas: Urban Planning and Housing in Mozambique*, International seminar on shelter policies in socialist Third World nations, Kleve (Germany) May. (See also similar contribution in *A Difficult Road*).

Raynauld R., 1984: *Problemas Habitacionais na Cidade de Maputo – O Fornecimento de Materiais de Construção*. Maputo: Direcção de Construção e Urbanização, Conselho Executivo da Cidade de Maputo, January.

Rosario M., 1986: *Resumo das Actividades Realizadas no Periodo Fev. 82 a Junho*. Maputo: Gabinete de Programas de Habitação, Ministério de Construção e Aguas.

Rosario M., 1984: *Aspectos Tecnicos da Construção de Conjuntos Habitacionais na República Popular de Mozambique*, Iº Jornadas de Engenharia e Ciências Naturais. Maputo: Gabinete de Programas de Habitação, Ministério de Construção e Aguas, May.

Rosario M., (no date, 1985?): *Que Programas de Habitação?* Maputo: Gabinete de Programas de Habitação, Ministério de Construção e Aguas.

Rosario M., 1986: *Estratégia para o Desenvolvimento da Produção de Materiais de Construção Basicos na República Popular de Mozambique*. Maputo: Gabinete de Programas de Habitação, Ministério de Construção e Aguas, July 1986.

Saevfors I., 1986: *Maxaquene: A Comprehensive Account of the First Urban Upgrading Experience in the New Mozambique*. Paris: UNESCO, March.

Saul J. (ed.), 1985: *A Difficult Road: The Transition to Socialism in Moçambique*, Monthly Review Press.

Settlements Information Network Africa – IYSH, 1986: *NGO Shelter Activities in Mozambique*; *Case Study on Latrine Construction Co–ops in Moçambique*; *Case Study on Messica Construction Co-operative, Moçambique*, Nairobi: Mazingira Institute, December.

White G. (ed.), 1983: *Revolutionary Socialist Development in the Third World*, Wheatsheaf Books 1983.

Yachan A., Carvalho P., Robinson V., 1982: *Manual para a Construção de Moradias nas Aldeias Comunais*. Maputo: Deptº de Habitação, Secretária de Estado de Algodão, Maputo.

Tanzania

Karin Nuru

Background[1]

Located on the east coast of Africa, the Republic of Tanzania (constituting the union between mainland Tanganyika and Zanzibar Islands since 1964) has a population of about 18.5 million and covers a territory of 981,082 square kilometres. Seventy-five per cent of the land is either uninhabited or difficult to cultivate because of the ravages of tsetse fly or unreliable rainfall. Thus the majority of human settlements in Tanzania are confined to about 25 per cent of the total land area. A significant feature of the country is, however, the very uneven distribution of the population even within this limited area of habitable land. Thus population density varies from about 170 persons per square kilometre in the Lake Victoria and Dar es Salaam[2] regions, to 2 persons per square kilometre in the drier western and central regions.

Tanzania is an agricultural country where 90 per cent of the population are engaged in the peasant form of agricultural production. Only 13 per cent of the population live in urban areas. There are nineteen major regional towns including Dar es Salaam which has, until now, been the capital of the country.[3] It is also a primate city, so that, in 1981, its population was estimated to be 911,600, whereas that of Mwanza, the second largest urban centre, was just 110,000 inhabitants.

After seventy years of (German and later British) colonial rule, Tanzania became independent in 1961. The struggle for independence was peacefully conducted by the petty bourgeois leadership of the Tanganyika African National Union (TANU), led by Julius Nyerere, and supported by the peasantry. As of 1965, Tanzania became a

---

1) The introductory section was taken from F. Sheriff (1985) with kind permission of TRIALOG, and inserted here in a shortened and edited version.

2) Population density in Dar es Salaam city, however, is 610 persons per square kilometre.

3) The new capital Dodoma is being built in the centre of the territory since the mid-seventies, but many important capital functions still remain with Dar-es-Salaam on the coast.

---- Railway
—— Asphalt road
- - - National boundary
● Factual capital city
○ Growth poles

Country Profile: Tanzania

National territory: 945,087 km^2
Population: 22.46 million (1986)
Population density: 22 inhab/sq.km
Labour force: 10,913,000 (1985),
   83% in agriculture, 11% in services, 6% in industry.
Urbanization rate: 15%
Capital: Dar es Salaam; 870,000 inhabitants (1978). The capital will be moved to Dodoma.
Average natural growth rate: 3.4% (1973–84)
Life expectancy: 53.7 years for men; 57.3 years for women
Infant mortality: 11.1%
Illiteracy rate: 53.7% (men 37.8, women 68.6%)
Religion: Majority African religions, one–fourth Muslims, one–fourth Christians and Hindu
Language: Swahili (official), English and local African languages also spoken.
Educational expenditure: 15.3% of budget (1983)
Major export products: coffee 39%, cotton 12%, copper 7%, tea 6%, spices 5%
Major markets: Indonesia 70%, FRG 14%, UK 13%, Netherlands 5%, Italy 5%
Foreign assistance: $ 497.7 million (1985);
   sources: OECD 76%, IDA 30.8, 2% OPEC, CMEA 1%

Some important dates:
1498 Arrival of Vasco da Gama. Zanzibar becomes important slave trade centre
1861 Zanzibar liberates itself from Oman domination
1884 Mainland of today's Tanzania (Tanganyika) is colonized by Germans
1980 Zanzibar becomes British protectorate
1905 Mau–Mau uprising against German domination in Tanganyika is brutally suppressed
1919 Tanganyika is being administered by the British after World War I (Treaty of Versailles)
1922 Slavery banned by Britain
1954 Foundation of TANU (African National Union) with leader Julius Nyerere
1958 First elections, TANU gains 28 of 30 seats
1960 New elections, TANU gains 70 of 71 seats, Tanzania becomes de facto one–party state
1961 Tanganyika becomes independent
1962 Julius Nyerere elected President with 98% of votes
1963 Zanzibar becomes independent. ASP becomes (1964) only legitimate party of Zanzibar
1964 Tanganyika and Zanzibar unify into Tanzania
1967 Arusha Declaration. Adoption of 'Ujamaa–Socialism' as leading ideology.
1977 New constitution. ASP and TANU unity into CCM = 'Party of Revolution'
1979 Severe economic crisis and increasing conflict with IMF and World Bank about structural adjustment policies as a precondition for further loans.
1985 Nyerere resigns as president, successor is Ali Hassan Mwini
1986 Mwini signs new agreements with IMF to reschedule Tanzania's foreign debt

Sources: Die Länder der Erde, Köln: Pahl–Rugenstein, 1982. Third World Guide, Montevideo: Third World Editors, 1988. Politisches Lexikon Afrika. München: C.H. Beck, 1985. Map: T. Heinrich, 1987.

one–party state in which the president of the party is automatically the president of the republic.

There is a National Assembly counting 204 members; 107 are elected by universal suffrage for a term of five years; the others are nominated by the president and other authorities of state. The powers of the national assembly are the scrutiny of the budget and formalization of governmental decisions into law. The assembly has no political powers as these are reserved for the party. The structural organization of the party is top–down hierarchical, and the decision–making process is highly centralized. Although the grass–roots structure of the party in 'cells' of ten houses or families was established in 1964, these were obviously organized to extend the influence and control of the party into the remotest rural areas.

Since 1967 all the key sectors of the economy have been owned and controlled by the state. Labour unions, which had existed since colonial times, were brought under state control in 1962, and integrated into the 'National Union of Tanganyika Workers' (NUTA, in 1977 renamed as JUWATA) after a number of disputes. NUTA as a mass organization is integrated in the party system, and the Minister of Labour is its secretary–general automatically. The right to strike was abolished in the mid 1960s.

Colonial Housing and Settlement Structure

Under colonial rule, the country was covered by a network of administration centres in order to protect political and economic imperialist interests. Cities like Kigoma and Dar es Salaam gained in economic importance with the introduction of modern means of transportation. Early housing projects in the cities further contributed to social and racial segregation. In urban areas, Africans were only tolerated as a temporary labour force and had to return to the countryside with the termination of employment. They were assigned special residential quarters in the suburbs, where the settlement pattern was extremely dense, and the mandatory housing standards were low compared to the zones reserved for Asians, Arabs or Europeans (Vorlaufer, 1970). Even today, the urban structure of Dar es Salaam and Tanga exposes the system of spatial segregation of ethnic groups inherited from the colonial period.

The settlement network in the countryside also still reflects the economic interests of the ruling colonial powers. Almost no development took place in zones with an unfavoured climate, specifically the south of the country and the upland plateau. Regions with a temperate climate were the favourable sites for capitalist plantations (e.g. the Usambara mountains and areas around Mbeya and Iringa). The preferential development of only a few fertile regions, e.g. around Mount Kilimanjaro, has created pockets with a dense and well equipped network of settlements, but also land shortage and serious ecological problems. The colonial administration was only interested in the local population as a source of labour force which was brought to work on plantations by various coercive measures such as the tax on huts. Therefore scattered homesteads continued as the predominant settlement pattern during colonial times. In 1965, 86.3 per cent of the rural population still lived in scattered settlements, 4.4

per cent in traditional villages and another 3 per cent in settlements linked to plantations (Georgulas, 1967). Still today, about 95 per cent of all houses in Tanzania are of 'traditional' or 'popular' type (as e.g. the urban Swahili house) and relatively few show influences imported from abroad. The average service life of these houses is seven years, and only 15 per cent of the traditional mud and pole constructions are older than 10 years. The living space reflects the basic needs of family life, and the construction is done by the family itself with help from the neighbours, using mainly traditional methods of construction. Traditionally there was no individual land owner-ship, nor any form of building regulations. Land was allocated according to customary law and varied considerably from one tribe to another. Only with the beginning of German domination was customary land law replaced by private property regulations turning land into a commodity. After World War I British rule modified the law governing land use and property in several ways, but did not establish completely equal rights between Africans and whites or Asians. This is particularly true for urban areas (Vorlaufer, 1970).

Towards the end of their domination, the British started to build workers' housing estates as part of so–called development schemes. In the first place, these programmes served the 'development' of profits and responded to the changed political and economic conditions in the world, but increasingly also to the growing strength of the national liberation movement. For the first time, the interests and needs of the people had to be considered. Cheap housing and credits for Africans were conceived as a strategy against the uncontrolled settling of the growing number of migrants into urban areas. Several credit systems and the introduction of new production methods should create an incentive to cultivate more export crops in the countryside, and to counteract migration into the towns (Herzog, 1986).

Post–Independence Development Strategies

After independence the first priority in social development was the agricultural reform. As early as 1962, the newly elected president Nyerere said:

"We must try and make it possible for groups of farmers to get together...it is essential to begin living in villages, for unless we do, we shall not be able to provide ourselves with the things we need to develop our lands and raise our standards of living...for the next few years, therefore, the government will be doing all it can to enable the farmers to come together in the village com–munities..." (Nyerere, 1963).

The idea of concentrating people in villages was maintained in all four development plans which ruled government investment, namely the:

3 year development plan from 1961 to 1964,
1st 5 year development plan from 1964 to 1969,
2nd 5 year development plan from 1969 to 1974,
and the
3rd 5 year development plan from 1976 to 1981.

Another 'revolutionary' principle was the proposition of 'African Socialism' and self-reliance, which was spelt out most explicitly in the so called Arusha Declaration of 1967, and which became the underlying philosophy to the Tanzanian way of development for many years to come. Important goals laid out in the Declaration include a stable supply of food and drinking water for the entire population, the installation of a health service reaching all parts of the country, equal opportunities in education for everybody, and an improved technical infrastructure in the settlements. In the rural areas the 'Village Settlement Programme' was expected to bring about these goals in a fast and rational manner. The first 'settlement schemes' were set up with international technical and financial assistance at the beginning of the 1960s. The expectation was that modernization of agricultural equipment in selected rural settlements would increase production, and eventually improve living conditions in the countryside through rising incomes. However, the settlers had not been integrated into the decision–making process at any time, and therefore could not identify themselves with the project. Moreover, this programme would have meant a radical and abrupt departure from the traditional principle of tribal settlements based upon family descent (Georgulas, 1967). Eventually, the conclusion was drawn that the project was overcapitalized and depended too much on foreign finance. Rated 'unproductive', the programme was stopped in 1966 without having brought about any perceivable benefits to the rural population.

As a contrasting experience, more and more farmers joined the primary agricultural co–operatives which had already emerged in the last stage of colonial domination. This initially spontaneous movement became the basis of the 'Villagization Programme', with the aim of creating Ujamaa villages (which also implied the collectivization of agricultural production). The underlying assumption was that it was impossible to reach the proclaimed aims of social development with a settlement pattern consisting mainly of individual farms and hamlets. At the beginning, people moved into joint settlements voluntarily. But from 1973 on, participation in the

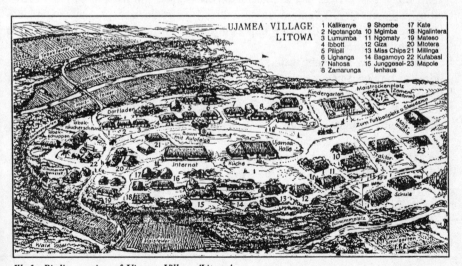

Ill. 1: Bird's eye view of Ujamaa Village 'Litowa'

Table 1: The progress of the villagization programme

Month	Year	Number of villages	Total population in villages	% of total population
February	1967	48	5,000	0.04
December	1968	180	58,000	0.5
December	1969	809	300,000	2.5
	1970	1,956	531,200	4.3
	1971	4,484	1,545,240	12.3
	1972	5,556	1,980,862	15.3
	1973	5,628	2,028,164	15.3
	1974	5,008	2,560,472	17.6
May	1975	6,944	9,140,229	61.6
	1976	7,684	13,061,000	85.0
December	1977	7,373	13,506,044	85.0
July	1978	7,631	13,775,532	87.0
June	1979	8,299	14,874,522	87.0

Source: Prime Minister's Office: various issues 1979–1970. Dar es Salaam.

'Villagization Programme' became compulsory by party decision. In 1979, almost 90 per cent of the country people lived — at least nominally — in 8,300 villages with a population of between 250 and 500 inhabitants each (Table 1 / Maro, 1983).

These villages represent the lowest level in the hierarchy of settlements and were to be provided with basic community facilities (i.e. village health post, primary school, co–operative shop, and safe water supply). This aim has been achieved with a certain success: now more than 40 per cent of the population in the countryside enjoy a regular supply of clean water, considerably more than in most other developing countries. About 90 per cent have a medical post within 10 km distance from home (Hofmeier et al., 1985:181). Other services such as hospitals, banks, commercial post offices and administration are available in the 450 'service centres' all over the country. Twenty of these centres have regional importance with additional services, 111 of them are important on the district level, and the rest serve small urban centres.

There can be no doubt that essential improvements in the social and technical infrastructure became possible through the villagization programme, although neither the economic development nor the upgrading of housing and living conditions has attained the desired level. The reasons for this are, first of all, insufficient logistic preparation and unco–ordinated implementation (selection of wrong sites, lack of qualified advice to the inhabitants and unnecessary bureaucratic obstacles), but also the general economic problems of the country (catastrophic droughts and deteriorating terms of trade).

Land Policies

Prior to independence, Tanzania had a dual land tenure system whereby privatized land ownership in the few townships and some plantation areas was protected by freehold titles, while customary land rights prevailed in the rest of the country. In an important move in 1963, the independent government nationalized all freehold titles and turned them into government leaseholds (Tanzania, 1963). Previous owners were now obliged to pay rent to the government, and development plans were to be laid down for all urban land. This, however, still left the confusion in respect to customary land rights particularly in villages, around the boundaries of old townships, and in certain rural areas where the official encouragement of cash–crop farming was fostering the emergence of a small class of *kulak* farmers. In 1969, therefore, the state introduced the 'Right of Occupancy' system as the only legal land tenure everywhere in Tanzania (Sheriff, 1985:11). The government was obliged to pay compensation for damaged crops, yields, buildings, unconsumed appreciation, etc. on any expropriated land. Every citizen was equally eligible to obtain the right of use for a piece of land, but had no powers to sell it. This provision has helped to do away with excessive land speculation, and has significantly improved conditions for long term town planning and efficient land development.

Housing Policies in the First and Second Development Plan (1961–1969)

Although Tanzania has only a relatively low degree of urbanization amounting to 13 per cent, the most serious housing problems do occur in the towns. At present, the population of Dar es Salaam increases 9 per cent every year, whereas the population growth is merely 4.5 per cent in the regions of Tabora and Rukwa and 1.7 per cent on the coast. The national population increase averages 3.5 per cent per year (Komba, 1980; *Third World Guide 89/90*).

Massive migration from the countryside set in when the restrictions to move into towns were lifted after independence. One characteristic feature of migration in most African countries, including Tanzania, is that only a few of the migrants who have found accommodation in urban slums or squatter areas do want to settle in town permanently, but rather plan to return to their native villages. There are many reasons for this desire, but the traditionally close relationship to the place of birth, the notorious social insecurity in the towns, and better opportunities to survive in the peasant subsistence economy in the countryside do play a role (Elken, 1968; Vogeley, 1988). The effect on the suburbs of Dar es Salaam and other big cities is that a large proportion of its inhabitants neither want, nor can afford, to build a house out of resistant and modern materials to comply with the official 'Building Regulations and Standards' established under European influence.

The first 'Slum Clearance Programme' was started in 1962 with foreign assistance, and was conceived as a measure against the further spread of squatter settlements and unhygienic housing conditions. Dwellings below the established technical standards

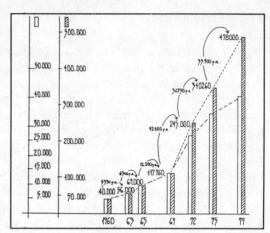

Ill. 2: Hanna Nassif, a typical squatter upgrading area in Dar es Salaam.
(IDA, 1977 / Heinrich, 1987:186)

Ill. 3: Growth of squatter settlements in Dar es Salaam in the period 1960–1979.
(Source: Heinrich, 1987:258)

were to be removed and replaced by standardized low–cost houses. Financial and technical assistance was to be provided by the 'National Housing Corporation' (NHC) which was founded as a non–profit organization with government participation at the same time. NHC's tasks also included the planning and building of community facilities and turn–key projects (Tanzania, 1962). Apart from the slum clearance programme NHC operated a 'roof loans programme' which was its second important objective during the first three year plan. A third, but minor, responsibility was the administration of some 4,350 houses built under various colonial housing schemes.

In line with the initial development goals laid out in the development plans, a housing programme for rural areas was initiated in 1962 for the first time. In all mainland districts 'Rural Constructions and Housing Units' (RCHU) were to be founded in order to support rural house building projects in the co–operatives and villages. The standard composition of a unit included five skilled workers: a joiner, carpenter, bricklayer, blacksmith and plumber. Apart from offering assistance and instruction to village people the units should be in a position to lend out lorries and tools, or draft standard projects acceptable for the provision of credits. As an administrative body the units represented the link between village and district officers.

New Orientation in the Second and Third Five Year Plan (1969–1981)

The government's commitment to provide housing for lower income people remained a valid principle, but it was not presented as the only option any more, and its scale was reduced in the second five year plan. Instead of the 5,000 units included in the previous five year plan only the construction of some 2,000 low–cost houses was projected, but this reduction was to be balanced out by a larger provision of serviced sites. The NHC itself withdrew from low–cost housing, and turned more and more into a contractor for non–residential government construction projects, or built flats to be rented or sold to middle–income people. Although the NHC had a relatively safe income from government subsidies, rent payments and national or international credits it had only been able to make profits up to the beginning of the 1970s. Outstanding rent payments, the continuous rise in construction costs[4], and internal mismanagement accounted for the increasing losses of the Corporation, and no funds remained for the non–profitable low–income housing schemes[5]. According to Kulaba (1981) the public sector has been able to offer housing to only 24.4 per cent of the urban population, and the trend is decreasing. The remaining three quarters of the urban residents have had to rely on their own forces in solving their housing needs.

Realizing the failure of the low–cost housing programme in the first five year plan and faced with dwindling financial means the government now encouraged the people to participate in the provision of housing to a larger extent. In the spirit of the Arusha Declaration 'Building and Loan Associations' were introduced to bring prospective builders together and encourage them to assist each other. The main arenas for this self–directed building activity were core housing and sites–and–services projects, for which the government provided land and installed the basic infrastructure, and which replaced the previous slum clearance programmes. Sites–and–services projects appeared to be easier to organize, met less resistance by the resident population, and responded better to the aspirations of those applicants who qualified for the loans. However, even more important for propagating a self–help approach was the general economic crisis, which made it difficult for the NHC to finance the construction of finished houses. While construction costs rose by up to 10 per cent annually in the 1960s, the rate went up four times that much by the year 1978. Costs almost doubled in the period between planning and implementation of a project. The prices for cement and corrugated iron rose by 100 and 139 per cent respectively in Dar es Salaam in the period between 1974 and 1979 alone.

In 1971, the Mwenge housing construction co–operative was started as a model project with substantial financial and technical assistance from abroad. The project comprised the delivery of a basic house with sleeping room, kitchen, toilet and shower, and the inhabitants could add between 2 and 3 rooms to this core according to their financial means at a later stage (Fig. 1). However, both the design and the technical standard were found unsuitable for replication in a subsequent project, and costs for infrastructure and construction were far too high. The functional setup of the houses with an open living room did not correspond to the traditions of Swahili houses, nor did they provide for renting out individual rooms. Subletting was, however, a financial necessity to most families in order to recover the high construction costs. This was possible in the most commonly built house type developed out

---

4) The average cost for a low–cost unit with three rooms had risen from 23,000 Tsh to 84,000 Tsh. between 1973 and 1981. In 1988, the cost was 60,000 Tsh. *per square metre*.

5) The cost for personnel consumed a considerable share of the NHB budget. At certain periods of time, administration and construction supervision accounted for 25 to 35 per cent of the overall expenditure. Although more than 50 different types of houses were developed for low–income groups by NHC architects only a few of them have ever been built, and even of these types the standard was too expensive in relation to the target group's paying capacity.

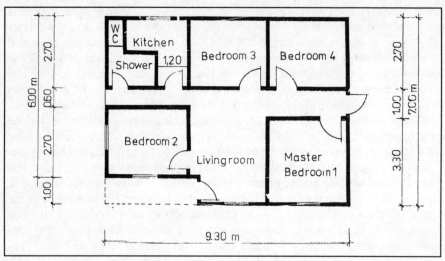

Figure 1: Mwenge Co-operative Housing Society, four-bedroom house

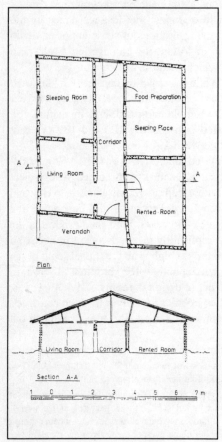

Figure 2: Four-roomed Swahili house

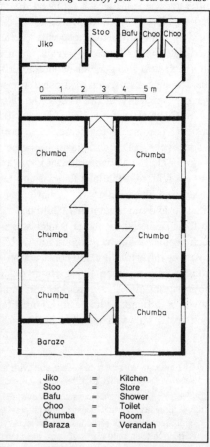

Figure 3: NHC low cost house, type LC 8

of the traditional *Zaramo* house, with influences of the Arab culture predominant in the coastal zone of Tanzania (Figs. 2 and 3).

At the beginning, the pilot project was administered through the NHC. But in 1973 it was handed over to the 'Ministry of Lands, Housing and Urban Development' (MLHUD), and credits were provided by the newly founded 'Tanzania Housing Bank' (THB). These credits required certain securities such as official employment and a minimum income of 1,000 Tsh.[6] — a condition which could not be met by large parts of the Tanzanian population. In fact, only some 540,000 persons (or 3 per cent of the population) in the whole country have a fixed employment. Other applicants who can sometimes meet the bank's security criteria are independent businessmen, but their number is difficult to determine because the formal and informal sectors of the economy overlap. The bank's statistics show that 75 per cent of those who were granted credits from the bank have a monthly income of more than 1,000 Tsh. — which are those belonging to the top 28 per cent of the whole urban, or top 7 per cent of rural population (Table 2 / Kulaba, 1981).

Table 2: Monthly cash income of private households

Monthly income in Tanzanian Shillings	Percentage of households Urban	Rural	Total
0 — 333	20	88	85
334 — 666	37	9	10
667 — 999	15	2	3
1000 — 1999	17	7	
over 2000	11	–	

Source: 1969 Household Budget Survey updated to 1976 values (In: Tanzania, 1978)

The sites–and–services approach was more widely implemented towards the end of the second, and in the beginning of the third five year plan. The 'National Sites and Services Programme' received large–scale international funding (generally 38 per cent of total project costs were covered by foreign finance), but increased political dependence on foreign donor agencies, such as the World Bank.

The first 'National Sites–and–Services Project' was started in Dar es Salaam, Mwanza, and Mbeya in 1974, and 19 other towns were added in a second phase 1976–1981. An integrated approach was sought and comprised, apart from the provision and distribution of surveyed plots, the following elements (Materu, 1986:123):

● squatter upgrading with legalization of land tenure,
● basic infrastructure provision (piped water, drainage, street illumination),
● supply of community facilities (primary school, health centre, market, etc.),
● house improvement and construction loans through the Tanzanian Housing Bank,
● promotion of small scale industries,

6) Calculated on the basis of a 35,000 Tsh. loan and a repayment rate not exceeding 25 per cent of family income.

- provision of equipment and transport,
- training of Tanzanian project staff and management assistance

In order to reach a target group with incomes below 1,000 Tsh. per month, low standards were adopted, and the building regulations amended accordingly. New 'Building Rules for One–Storey Houses on Surveyed Plots' were passed to stipulate the use of local building materials and traditional technologies, such as soil–blocks, bush poles, and thatch in urban areas (BRU, 1977).

Although the aims were clearly defined, the programme did not reach the proper target group since the total costs for the construction of a standard house proved to be beyond the financial means of low–income people. In addition to this, technical and administrative problems caused serious delays in the completion of the various project stages.

However, the provided plot sizes of about 300 square metres in the sites–and–services projects only correspond to the minimum area needed to build an urban Swahili house, or the standard THB type, and are too small to allow the construction of traditional house types known in the country (e.g. Hehe or Gogo houses).

Recent Policy Changes

Up to 1981 Tanzanian Housing Policy was always incorporated in the National Development Plans. But already the two Ardhi Annual Conferences of 1977 (in Mbeya) and 1979 (in Mwanza) endorsed the proposition to pass an independent National Housing Policy document. Such a document was eventually drafted at the Conference of the Ministry of Lands, Housing and Urban Development in Arusha in 1980, and passed in 1982 (Tanzania, 1982). Its main objectives include:

O *the construction of more low cost houses and the rehabilitation of existing ones to improve urban and rural housing conditions in qualitative and quantitative terms,*
O *new housing programmes for income groups below 1,000 Tsh. per month and the promise that these houses will remain affordable to their intended occupiers,*
O *state assistance to individual efforts in building or buying houses, especially through providing easy access to land, loans and building materials,*
O *the promotion of local building materials and the integration of this production in the rural development process to reduce house construction costs and to avoid the use of foreign exchange.*

Additional provisions for the development of the building sector have been laid down in the long–term Development Plan 1981–2000 (Tanzania, 1981), such as

O *expanding the capacity of the construction industry, and the consolidation of the building brigades in the agricultural regions and in the villages,*
O *intensifying research into the production of cheap and durable building materials,*
O *the extension of government assistance in the form of technical advice, site servicing etc., to individuals intending to build or buy good and permanent houses.*

In the subsequent years different administrative measures have been introduced to achieve the goals of the National Housing Policy, including the establishment of a Registrar of Buildings (ROB), or various mechanisms to deliver technical and finan- cial support. The National Housing Corporation (NHC) boosted its house construction activities, and sites–and–services programmes multiplied. Urban self–employed households who cannot afford to buy a house can now opt for a tenant purchase scheme, and public employers are obliged to invest 20 per cent of their net profits into workers' housing, and to offer accommodation to all their employees.

In rural areas local governments are responsible for drawing up annual programmes for the improvement of housing conditions at the village level. Technical support can be obtained from the Rural Housing and Construction Units (RHCU), which already exist in nearly every rural district.

Urban local governments are requested to establish Housing Development Departments (HDD) and a Housing Development Fund (HDF) to encourage and assist low income–people in building houses on a self–help basis, and to offer skilled labour if wanted. The HDF is to provide cheap loans for those not qualifying for a credit from the Tanzania Housing Bank (THB).

The financial resources for the new building programme will come from governmental grants, pension and insurance funds, bank deposits and from public and private employers, e.g. in the form of the 'Workers and Farmers Housing Development Levy' (Tanzania, 1982).

Conclusion

The new Tanzanian Housing Policy is the first coherent legal base for popular housing provision but leaves fundamental problems unresolved at the same time. As Farida Sheriff (1985:14) points out, the current housing policy is a sort of patchwork putting together all the previous policy statements. It continues to emphasize the ideology of 'self–reliance' and of self–help contributions by the villagers, the low–income and poor urban dwellers, and states: "Every man in the village has the primary *responsibility* to build a *permanent* house" and "...the best way to ameliorate

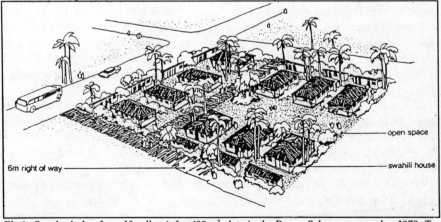

Ill. 4: Standard plan for a 10 cell unit for 400 m² plots in the Dar es Salaam master plan 1979. Ten houses are the smallest administrative unit in Ujamaa –socialism. (Heinrich, 1987:164)

the existing housing shortages (in the urban areas) is to *urge* and assist people to build their own houses" (Tanzania, 1982:29&32; emphasis added). While referring to the massive subsidies enjoyed by the few senior civil servants and bureaucrats, it indicates no intention to redress this imbalance. Instead it obliges the employer to solve the housing problem of his workers: *"From now on every employer has the responsibility to prepare and implement a housing programme for his workers"* (Tanzania, 1982:28). The practicability of this populist proposition is highly questionable, particularly since the government itself is by far the largest employer in Tanzania. (This would again privilege civil servants.) More importantly, however, the number of Tanzanians in regular wage employment is appallingly small. According to the Survey of Employment and Earnings (Tanzania, 1981a), in 1978, the number of total wage earners was only 535,945 (made up of 208,358 in 'Public Services' and 327,587 in 'Enterprises' – largely constituting the parastatels). A crucial gender related dilemma becomes visible when these figures are divided by sex: of the total number in wage employment a mere 11.8 per cent are adult women. The wider and unfair implication of these figures cannot be underestimated in a country which has a majority of 51 per cent woman (Karlsson, 1981) in the total population. Another critical point is the question of unpaid labour of women and men in the self–built housing sector which makes up 93 per cent of the housing stock in Tanzania.

One critical point totally ignored within the current housing policy is the impact of bureaucracy on the housing production and distribution system in Tanzania. Not only do the senior civil servants consume the bulk of the state resources allocated to housing directly and indirectly, but more importantly, complex bureaucratic procedures have greatly hindered a smooth and efficient implementation of even the most elementary housing projects like sites–and–services and squatter upgrading schemes.

The application of a limited number of 'standard designs' in housing projects, as recommended by the Housing Policy, will put an end to the colourful variety in form and function typical for Tanzania's traditional architecture. As experience shows, model house plans developed by NHC, MECCO and NEDCO may comply with building standards, but pay no respect to individual preferences (e.g. ratio between number of rooms and persons per household, possibility of further extension in living area, individual use of outside space). Given the persistently high inflation in con-struction costs (20 to 35 per cent per annum since 1980) it is highly questionable whether low–income groups will have better access to public housing programmes than in the past.

To make implementation of the new Housing Policy successful fundamental changes in the construction industry seem advisable. The long–term Development Plan 1981–2000 suggests a contribution of the construction industry to the GDP of 6 per cent by the year 2000, although, as a matter of fact, it declined from 3.4 per cent to 2.6 per cent over the 1960–62 to 1978 period (Tanzania, 1981; Chadage, 1980). To reach the projected target enormous efforts will be necessary. At present, key building materials industries work at a capacity of 30 per cent (Wazo Cement Factory), or 36 per cent (ALAF galvanized iron sheets). The Dodoma Quarry needs several million Tshs. worth of investment to resume regular production.

On the other hand, traditional building materials become more and more difficult to obtain even in the proximity of the villages, because of deforestation and grazing by large quantities of livestock. Commercialization of traditional building materials, ever increasing prices for manufactured materials, and lack of transport render the construction of a good and permanent house more and more difficult.[7] The government's policy paper does not give any guidance about practical steps to be followed in the use, improvement and marketing of indigenous building materials, or information about the functioning of various governmental, community or non-governmental institutions in the field of housing — a fundamental necessity for self-builders. Therefore the 'household' will remain the most important 'institution' taking care of house planning and construction in Tanzania for a long time to come.

References

Chadage, S.L., 1980: *Housing Problem and the Policy of Socialism. A Case Study of the Housing Problem in Dar es Salaam.* Dar es Salaam: University (Dept. of Sociology).

Edvardsen, K.I. & Hegdal, B., 1972: *Rural Housing in Tanzania.* Dar es Salaam, 101 pp.

Elken, W., 1968: 'Circular Migration'. In: *Ekistics* 4, 149. Athens, pp. 238–241

Georgulas, N., 1967: 'Settlement Patterns and Rural Development in Tanganyika'. In: *Ekistics* 24, 141, Athens, pp. 180–192.

Herzog, J., 1986: *Geschichte Tansanias.* Berlin, 118 pp.

Hofmeier, Rolf & Schönborn, Mathias (Eds.), 1985: *Politisches Lexikon Afrika.* München: C.H. Beck, 510 pp.

Karlsson, R., 1981: 'Housing Conditions in Tanzania 1969–1978'. In: *Bull. Research Information, 1, 4.* Dar es Salaam, pp. 3–7.

Komba, L., 1980: 'The Population of Tanzania'. Paper presented at an International Conference in Arusha, 3rd–8th March 1980. In: Ministry of Lands, Housing and Urban Development: *Towards a National Housing Policy.* Dar es Salaam, 24 pp.

Kulaba, S.M., 1981: *Housing, Socialism and National Development in Tanzania, a Policy Framework.* Dar es Salaam: Centre for Housing Studies.

Maro, P.S., 1983: 'Settlement Policy and Development in Tanzania'. In: *Wissenschaftliche Mitteilungen des Instituts für Geographie und Geoökologie der AdW der DDR,* no. 10. Leipzig, pp. 77–90.

Materu, J., 1986: 'Sites–and–Services Projects in Tanzania'. In: *Third World Planning Review, 8, 2,* Liverpool, pp. 121–138.

Mawenya, A.S., 1988: 'Inflation in the Tanzanian Construction Industry Sector'. In: *The Tanzanian Engineer,* Sept., pp. 26–31.

Nyerere, J.K., 1963: *Speech to the National Assembly on the 10th Dec. 1962.* Dar es Salaam.

Sheriff, Farida, 1985: 'Housing Policies and Strategies in Tanzania'. In: *TRIALOG 6,* Darmstadt, pp. 8–14.

Tanzania, 1962: *National Housing Corporation Act.*

Tanzania, 1963: *The Freehold Titles Conversion and Government Leases Act.* Dar es Salaam.

Tanzania, n.d.: *Prime Minister's Office:* Various issues. Dar es Salaam, 1970–1980.

Tanzania, 1972: *Low–Cost House Types.* Dar es Salaam: National Housing Corporation, 1972.

---

7) The price of mangrove poles had gone up from 7.5 Tsh. in 1977 to 30 Tsh. in 1983, and almost 150 in 1989. Between 600 and 700 poles are needed to built an urban Swahili house. Manufactured materials became 350 to 850 per cent dearer in the period between 1980 and 1987. For example, in 1989, one bag of cement was priced 850 Tsh., while the minimum wage was 2,200 Tsh. (Mawenya, 1988:26).

Tanzania: 1978: *Reducing Housing Costs.* Dar es Salaam: Ministry of Lands, Housing and Urban Development, 9 pp.

Tanzania, 1981: *Long Term Perspective Plan 1981–2000.* Dar es Salaam: Ministry of Planning and Economic Affairs (MPEA), Permanent Planning Commission (PPC), 31 pp.

Tanzania, 1981a: *'Survey of Employment and Earnings 1977–78'.* Dar es Salaam: Bureau of Statistics.

Tanzania, 1982: *The New National Housing Development Policy for Tanzania.* Government Printer, Dar es Salaam 1982, 32 pp. and: Wizara ya Ardhi, Nyumba na Maendeleo Mijini, 1982: *Sera mpya ya Taifa ya Maendeleo ya Nyumba.* Dar es Salaam: (MLHUD), 25 pp.

Third World Guide 89/90. Montevideo: Third World Editors.

Vogeley, D. 1988: 'Verelendung und Urbanisierung in den Entwicklungsländern.' In: *Wirtschaftswissenschaft 36,* 5. Berlin, pp. 726–742.

Vorlaufer, K., 1970: *Koloniale und nachkoloniale Stadtplanung in Dar es Salaam.* Frankfurt, 113 pp.

Further Reading (Compiled by Kosta Mathéy)

Coulson, Andrew (Ed.), 1979: *African Socialism in Practice. The Tanzanian Experience.* Nottingham: Spokesman. 239 pp.

Coulson, Andrew, 1982: *Tanzania. A Political Economy.* Oxford, Oxford University Press, 394 pp.

Doherty, Joe, 1979: 'Ideology and Town Planning – the Tanzanian Experience'. In: *Antipode No. 3,* vol. 11. Worcester, Mass., pp. 12–23.

Freyhold, Michaela, 1979: *Ujamaa Villages in Tanzania. Analysis of a Social Experiment.* London: Heinemann, 201 pp.

Heinrich, Thomas, 1987: *Technologietransfer in der Stadtplanung. Masterplanung in Dar es Salaam durch internationale Consultings.* Darmstadt: Verlag für wissenschaftliche Publikationen, 457 pp.

Hyden, Goran, 1980: *Beyond Ujamaa in Tanzania. Underdevelopment and an Uncaptured Peasantry.* London: Heinemann, 270 pp.

Interdisciplinary Study Group on Planning, 1981: *Bogamoyo Development Proposal.* Delft: University of Technology / Dar es Salaam: Ardhi Institute, 186 pp.

Interdisciplinary Study Group on Planning, 1981: *Mangomeni Squatter Upgrading.* Delft: University of Technology / Dar es Salaam: Ardhi Institute. 115 p.

Rohwedder, J., 1986: *Sozio–kulturelle, ökonomische, und ökologische Determination von angepaßten Bautechnologien in Dar es Salaam, Tanzania.* Dissertation. Stuttgart: Institut für Baustofflehre, Universität, 294 pp.

Salomon, R., 1980: 'Housing Conditions in Tanzania'. Paper presented at an International Conference in Arusha, 3rd–5th March 1980. In: Ministry of Lands, Housing and Urban Development: *Towards a National Housing Policy.* Dar es Salaam, 28 pp.

Shivji, Issa G., 1976: *Class Struggle in Tanzania.* London: Heinemann, 182 pp.

Meyns, Peter, n.d.: *Nationale Unabhängigkeit und ländliche Entwicklung in der 3. Welt. Das Beispiel Tanzania.* Berlin: Oberbaum, 298 pp.

Tanzania (1975): *A Portrait of Dodoma.* Dodoma: Capital Development Authority. 56 pp.

Weaver, James H. & Kronemer, Alexander (1981): 'Tanzanian and African Socialism'. In: *World Development,* No. 9/10, Vol. 9. Oxford: Pergamon, pp. 839–850.

Zimbabwe

Ann Schlyter

Socialist or Social Housing Policies?

The Government of Zimbabwe has declared socialism to be the primary objective, but is there something called a socialist housing policy? In many Third World countries, governments declare their objective to lie in a socialist direction, and inspiration for solving problems related to basic needs is searched for in socialist countries. In Zimbabwe statements have been made that the housing policy should be a mechanism for redressing colonial inequalities and wealth according to socialist goals (Patel, 1985). There is a simplistic but widespread view what elements a socialist housing policy should include. The view of housing as a social right, and the emphasis on governmental responsibility are two such elements that have been mentioned in the formulation of housing policies in Zimbabwe.

The view of housing as a social right was declared by the Minister of Housing in 1981: "The first democratically elected government of the Republic of Zimbabwe has vowed to assure for all its people shelter, food and clothing. These need not be elegant; it is enough that they are of the kind that permit human dignity and human life. Nobody, we say, should be allowed to be so poor as to starve, live in the open field or go naked" (Zvogbo, 1981). The governmental responsibility for housing was also stressed. It must be clear that the society as a whole owes the poor a duty or obligation to live in environments that are not merely dignified but are conducive to better health and a better life.

Putting a stop to speculation in housing and land and emphasis on industrialization to solve housing shortages are two other elements which used to be mentioned as socialist housing policies. These elements have, so far, not been included in the Zimbabwean housing policies for reasons which will be discussed later. Instead of industrialization, building brigades have been presented as the socialist way to increase housing production.

The view of housing as a social right, interpreted as the right for everyone to get a house of at least a very low standard, is hardly an exclusively socialist view, but

197

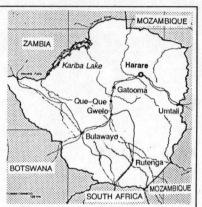

Country Profile: Zimbabwe

National territory: 390,580 km^2
Population: 8.41 million, including some
   170,000 Europeans, 35,000 Asian descendants
Population density: 20 inhab/sq.km
Labour force: 3,410,000; 70% in agriculture,
   25% in services, 15% in industry.
Urbanization rate: 27%
Capital: Harare (ex Salisbury); 656,000 inhabitants (1982)
Natural growth rate: 1.6% (1965–85)
Life expectancy: 56.2 years for men; 59.9 years for women
Infant mortality: 7.7%
Illiteracy rate: 31.2% (men 23.5%, women 38.7%)
Religion: mostly traditional African religions
Languages: English is official language. Most people speak Bantu dialects.
Educational expenditure: 12.8% of budget (1984)
Military expenditure: 13% of budget (1984)
Major export products: Tobacco 22%, pig iron 12%, cotton 8%, nickel 5%, sugar 5%
Major markets: US, South Africa, Australia, FRG, France, UK
Foreign assistance: $ 241 million (1985); sources: OECD countries 89%, IDA 4.2%

Some important dates:
1511 First Portuguese landing
1693 Occupation by African Rozvi–Kingdom, defeat of the Portuguese
1839 Occupation by African Ndebele kingdom, defeat of the Rozvi–domination
1889 Britain claims rights over Ndebele kingdom, and grants trading rights to the millionaire
      Cecil Rhodes, owner of the British South Africa Co. (Therefore the name *Rhodesia)*
1903 Economic crisis, replacement of colonial trading interest through colonial farming
      interest
1923 Self–government through European settlers after termination of Rhodes' rights, status as
      British crown colony
1965 Rhodesia's conservative white government opposes Britain's push to grant civil rights to
      blacks and declares independence. Brutal oppression of African population.
1966 First guerilla activities by national ZAPU and ZANU liberation movements.
1979 First elections following internal and international pressure, blacks gain majority, but no
      effective power
1979 London *Lancaster House Conference* achieves peace in liberation struggle, which had
      caused more than 30,000 dead. New elections with real powers were scheduled for 1980.
1980 Zimbabwe becomes independent with new elected black government under Robert
      Mugabe
1982 Great drought causing food shortage in 1983
1983 Agreement signed with IMF, implying serious cuts in social expenditure
1987 Constitutional reform abolishing 20 parliament seats for whites as contained in the
      Lancaster House agreements. Simultaneously first Five–Year National Development
      Plan.
1985 Parliamentary elections, Mugabe (ZANU) won overwhelming majority.

Sources: Die Länder der Erde, Köln: Pahl–Rugenstein, 1982. Third World Guide, Montevideo: Third World Editors,
1988. Politisches Lexikon Afrika, München: C.H. Beck, 1985.

can be integrated into a humanist–liberal perspective as well. Further, it is not only governments with socialist goals which have increased their interventions into housing: so have states flying all political colours. The labelling of some policies as socialist does influence the debate and formulation of housing policies, but the distinctions seem hardly fruitful to use in an analysis. In countries where a mixed market economy is maintained, as in Zimbabwe, it seems more appropriate to talk about social housing policies.

A social housing policy simply means that the policy is defined in relation to social aims. It does not necessarily include an acceptance of housing as a social right, nor has it to include a redistribution mechanism, though it often does. The social aims of a social housing policy can be more or less explicitly expressed, but it always deals with questions of who in the future will have access to houses of which level of standard.

In this chapter, the preconditions for a social housing policy in the Harare region are briefly outlined. The policy declarations and main housing projects of the new Government are presented. Finally, the social content of the implemented policy is discussed using an analytical model in which three types of social policies are defined: the social right policy, the optimum policy and the avant–garde policy.

Zimbabwe at Independence

In April 1980, Zimbabwe was declared independent under majority rule after sixteen years of struggle. The ZANU–PF (Zimbabwe African National Union – Patriotic Front) party under the leadership of Robert Mugabe had won the first democratic election in Rhodesia in what was announced over the world as a landslide victory. ZANU had been fighting a war for a socialist Zimbabwe. After coming to power the policy developed was pragmatic, emphasizing the reconciliation between blacks and whites. The *Lancaster House Agreement* preserved certain rules for the governing of the country during the first decade of independence.

The policy conducted has been a balance between meeting the great expectations of the African population and mitigating the whites' fear of change. If they lost too many privileges the whites would leave the country, and take much–needed capital and know–how.

In Rhodesia there were about 200,000 whites. In Zimbabwe in 1985, there were about 130,000; and their position is still strong; if not politically, then economically. They own the farms and dominate industry and the banks together with the multi–nationals. In addition to the restrictions laid on space for reforms by this situation, the effects of the vicinity of the powerful neighbour in the south should not be underestimated. With other countries of southern Africa, Zimbabwe is subjected to the destabilization policy of South Africa.

Among several progressive social reforms initiated during the first years were guaranteed minimum wages, free schools, and free health care for the poorest. These reforms addressed the basic needs of food, education and health service. Land for food production and housing for shelter were also considered in these early policy measures, but a land reform did not have any significant impact on the unequal

Figure 1: Living conditions in Chitugwisa suburb outside Harare.   *(Foto: Ann Schlyter)*

distribution of land, and rent restrictions did not increase the number of houses. A recognition by law of women as major persons was a first important step on a way to gender democracy.

Since liberation there has been rapid formation of a new upper or middle class. Refugees returned, now with academic degrees, and moved into the houses earlier inhabited by whites. They obtained posts within national and local governments, posts which they can use to defend their new–won privileges. In the ZANU congress in 1984, this was condemned by the Prime Minister, Robert Mugabe: "We can't have leaders which are preaching socialism in daytime and capitalism at night. To be a party–leader (which certainly is a merit if you are looking for a high post within the government) you have to follow the leadership code, which was adopted by the congress. Leaders may not receive more than one wage, they may not own tenant houses nor more than fifty hectares of land."

Rapid Urbanization

Urban living has always been controlled in Zimbabwe. In 1894, a Town Management Ordinance gave powers to the governing body of an urban area to set up and control native locations (Cormack, 1983:78). From 1945 onwards, local authorities were obliged to set aside land and to provide housing for all Africans working in the towns, except those provided for on approved private premises. The townships being built were technically within the white areas, and thus Africans were living in them not as a right but as a privilege.

The urban Africans were regarded as (temporary) migrant labourers by the settlers, and this view legitimized the poor housing conditions. The policy was to regulate the flow of male migrants according to the availability of employment and prevent the accumulation of unemployed poor people in the city. The men were supposed to work in the town for some years and then go back to their families in the reserves. Still in 1958, fewer than half of all employees in the formal sector were living in houses to which they were allowed to bring their families (Patel, 1984).

Influx control kept the rate of urbanization relatively low and the growth of squatter areas, which accelerated in neighbouring African countries during the 1960s, was prevented. Only with the intensification of the liberation did the implementation of influx control break down. The existing housing areas became heavily overcrowded and some squatter settlements developed. In 1978, 16.8 per cent of the total African population (7 millions) were living in towns. In 1982, the total was about 20 per cent, almost half in Harare. After the war some refugees returned to the rural areas, but the rapid movement into towns has continued. Many women have brought their children and joined their husbands in town.

At independence the urban population was increasing at a rate of about 5.4 per cent each year. Harare was estimated to have about one half million inhabitants. Another 200,000 people were estimated to live outside the city boundary, in the suburb Chitungwisa and in the unplanned area Epworth. Case studies in some townships indicated these figures to be a gross underestimation. As there have been few reliable figures, growth rates are also estimates. It is clear that the Harare region is more rapidly growing than other urban centres. Growth rates have been estimated at between 7.5 and 11.5 per cent.

The Inherited City

Spatial Segregation

Harare has a beautiful city centre, especially in the October spring, when the jacaranda trees are blue with flowers. The vegetation, not the houses or the urban pattern, differs from European cities. Shops, offices, banks, hotels and restaurants are concentrated here. In a continuing grid pattern towards the northeast, 'the Avenues', a residential area is under transition. Old colonial residences are one-by-one replaced by offices, hotels or modern flats in high-rise buildings or exclusive terrace houses.

Harare, or Salisbury as it was formerly called, was planned for segregation. The former white suburban residential areas sprawl around the city, especially in the northeast. There are the bungalows, but at the back of the large gardens there are as many small houses inhabited by the servants.

An area of the type which used to be called a second class commercial area is located in the southwest part of the central grid-patterned city. In this area many of the residents and shopkeepers are of Indian origin. From the central square in this area buses leave for the townships which were built for Africans at quite a distance from the city.

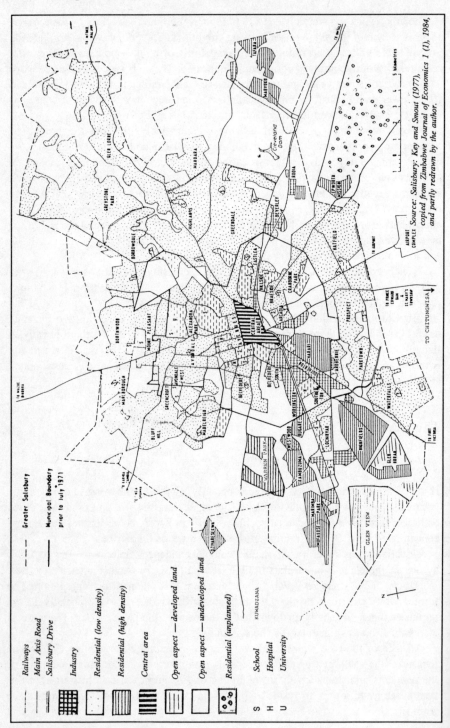

Figure 2: Map of the Harare Region

The oldest African township, *Harare*, was located on the other side of the railway. There is the large African market, and there the buses from the countryside stop. This township, now called *Mbare*, has given its name to the whole city after independence (*Figure 2*). Fifteen townships for Africans were located in the periphery of the city, the largest along the railway close to the industrial area in the southwest: *Highfields*, *Glen Norah* and *Glen View*. In the 1970s, some townships were built outside the city limits in order to provide housing for domestic servants and to reduce their numbers in white areas.

Going south from Harare, passing tobacco farms and a river, one approaches *Chitungwisa* on a stony and infertile ridge. Planned by the previous Government to implement a strict racial segregation of urban space, Chitungwisa was located on so-called tribal land thirty kilometres from Harare.

The Existing Housing Stock

In the townships bachelor hostels were built for migrant workers, who were neither allowed nor given the means to bring their families to the town. Rooms with four to eight stationary beds were lined up along a central corridor. The rooms became black from charcoal fires because no kitchen facilities were provided and the workers had to cook their own food. Berths in hostels provided more than one-fourth of the low-income accommodation units in Harare (Mutizwa-Mangiza 1984).

The hostels were often built as three-storey barracks, but it is the endless lines of *rented* small family-houses which give the character to the townships. The town planning pattern is as inspiring as are the names of areas and streets: 1st stage, 2nd stage, etc., and endless numbers of streets and avenues, just numbered. In huge areas identical small boxes are lined up, and there is little variation between the areas. The size of a dwelling ranges between thirty and sixty square metres, and the space is usually divided into two or three rooms and a kitchen. Sometimes the kitchen is only a roofed area outside. Toilet and shower may either be inside or outside. Electricity is supplied in many areas. *Figures 3 and 4* shows a typical three-bedroom house. If lived in by only one family these older houses provide reasonable space, but the rent was affordable only to a quarter of the income-earners. Harare City Council has always applied the principle of cost recovery.

The poor but rather spacious layout of the townships is derived from the South African miners' housing, inspired by the concept of the garden city but implemented because it fitted into control and order. In his study 'The attitudes of Africans to house and housing', Bettison (1959) noted that the opposition had never addressed bad housing conditions, but centred around the high rents in the housing schemes. Furthermore, he found that the freedom of a slum was often spoken of as a preferable alternative to the order and discipline of municipal housing schemes. Concerning the layout, he noted that urban housing did not encourage men's, women's and children's talk and play so common in the African villages, and that the houses were not designed to fit the living habits.

There were about 70,000 houses under City Council control in Harare and 29,000 in Chitungwisa in 1981. There were about 35,000 units for domestic workers, 5,000

Figure 3: An 'Ultra-low-cost unit'. The owner has dug foundations for a new house.
(Foto: Ann Schlyter)

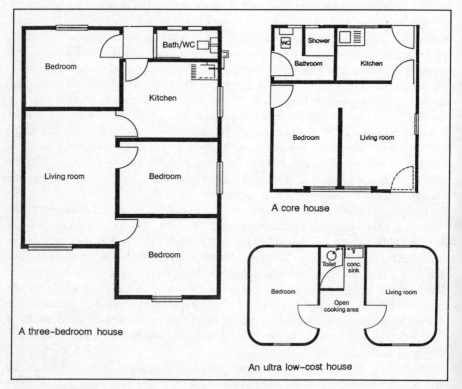

Figure 4: Pre-Independence House Units

units in hostels, 500 squatter houses within the Harare boundary, 2,600 in Epworth and about as many again in transitional camps in Chitungwisa (Hoek–Smith, 1982). All this housing stock was heavily overcrowded due to the large numbers of lodgers in addition to the officially registered tenants.

In the 1960s, *core housing* projects were introduced in order to reduce costs and extend affordability of such units to about half of all income earners. However, self–building, from a core or on a serviced stand, created a dilemma for the racist government, because it was based on the idea of home ownership and Africans were not allowed to own land in urban areas. Eventually home ownership was legalized for Africans, and in Glen View, for example, more than 7,000 plots with a wet core were distributed. Although intended for low–income applicants, seven–roomed houses were mostly built on these plots, to accommodate as many tenants as possible.

In an attempt to meet the emerging squatter problem in late 1970s and provide housing within the system of rented housing, so called ultra–low–cost units were erected on a large scale *(Figure 4)*. The strict control of the urban population made it possible for the previous regime to avoid large *squatter areas,* which sprawl around the cities in so many African cities. To a limited degree, people who earned their living from the urban informal sector could reside within existing settlements outside the city boundary. For example, about two hundred people had since the 1950s lived illegally on European–owned land close to a granite quarry in Derbyshire. But in 1976, due to the war, the population grew dramatically to about 12,000 inhabitants. The population in the squatter areas was poorer and more often unemployed than the average population of the city. Many couples were also living in unregistered marriages, a fact which disqualified them from renting houses from the City Council. In Derbyshire, 18 per cent of the households were headed by women (Patel & Adams, 1981).

During the last years of the war, it was not possible to stop the refugees, and squatter areas began to grow in spite of the government's firm anti–squatter policy. Already in 1976, a squatter settlement in Derbyshire, called *Chirambahuyo*, was destroyed and about 9,000 people were moved to Chitungwisa. Provisions were made for 2,637 plots of 9.5 x 10 metres, with communal water and pit latrines. Chiramba–huyo was declared to be a transitional settlement. People had to build their own mud–brick houses, waiting for an offer of an ultra–low–cost house to rent. However, most of them could not afford even a subsidized ultra–low–cost rent, especially since most were unemployed and had lost their opportunities of finding work within the informal sector. The only large unplanned settlement which remained in the Harare region was *Epworth,* with about 30,000 inhabitants.

Initial Urban Housing Policy after 1980

Far–reaching Objectives but a Slow Start

At independence, the new Government of Zimbabwe had to face an acute and growing shortage of urban housing. Already in March 1981, a five–year development programme for low–income housing was presented. Projections of urban population growth and estimations of the backlog were used to calculate housing demand in the years to come. The Government promised to provide decent houses by increasing construction activities. Exact figures were published for the number of houses to be built, and of what standard. Water, sewerage, drainage and roads were to be provided for each house. The fact that the needs were grossly underestimated is perhaps less serious than the overestimation of the administration's and the building industry's capacity and the availability of resources. Five years later it was apparent that the first plans had been over–optimistic; instead of an increase in building activities, house completion figures had severely decreased.

Initially, housing was under the responsibility of the Ministry of Local Government and Housing. The minister declared housing a social right and governmental responsibility. It seemed that organizational problems delayed the further formulation and development of policies. First there was a change of ministers, then a split of the Ministry, so that a new Ministry of Housing was to be built up. Then again there was an amalgamation of two ministries. So, from January 1984, the responsibility of housing rests with the Ministry of Construction and National Housing.

The responsibility for the implementation of housing policy lies with the local authorities. Compared to other African countries at independence, Zimbabwe had a well established local administration (Jordan 1984), which was an important asset to start with. The administration was, however, divided according to race, although there has been a great effort to bring together the former African areas and the white areas under one administration, the 'one city concept'. Naturally, this has delayed the development of an efficient and creative administration of new housing projects.

In all urban housing the question of land is fundamental, and cannot be separated from the land question in the whole of the country. The Lancaster House agreement stipulated that private ownership of land should be maintained in Zimbabwe. If the Government wanted to gain control of land, the owners have to be compensated at market prices. Urban land has been purchased by the Government, for example, in the low–income areas of Epworth and Kuwadzana; but with the limited resources available, such isolated measures did not permit the build–up of a sufficiently large land reserve for development and thus did not influence market prices. According to World Bank (1985) estimates, Harare would run out of municipally–owned land in little more than two years. The Bank recommended smaller plots and acquisition of additional land. The Government recognizes that land availability is a main issue in housing provision, but so far this has not affected discussions on urban structures or sizes of plots.

Finally, the economic situation constitutes a major constraint for all building activities. Initially, the governmental housing budget was entirely devoted to urban housing. In 1983, the budget was cut by half, and future funding was earmarked for rural areas. Primarily, this decision only affected loans, but then the budget for wages and subsidies had to be reduced as well. The Government was only committed to finish ongoing projects and other spending had to be generated from external donors or from local resources. However, dependency on international funding makes it difficult, if not impossible, to follow an independent housing policy. The number of units built with governmental funding decreased from 12,000 in 1981 to 3,000 in

1984 (Zimbabwe, MPCNH, 1986, Table 2.2). The output was in fact cut only by 50 per cent, taking into account that units were now larger – four rooms instead of two.

Rent Restrictions and Home Ownership

One of the first actions undertaken by the revolutionary regime (Ministry of Local Government and Housing) was the Housing and Building Regulations (Lodger's Rent Restriction) of 1980, intended to prevent exploitation of the poorest members of the society. Thereby rents paid by lodgers in the high density suburbs were limited to a maximum of Z$8 a month. However, the regulation proved impossible to enforce, and it can only be speculated whether it helps to strengthen the position of the lodgers vis–à–vis the landlords. The housing shortage is so desperate that many lodgers are prepared to pay up to five times the maximum rent.

Private property in the form of home ownership is not only tolerated but actively supported and represents the cornerstone of the national housing policy. Among the first policy measures by the new Government was the conversion of rental housing into home ownership, in order to grant greater security to those living in urban areas. This symbolic step was important because before the 1970s Africans were forbidden to own land in urban areas. Under the Smith regime preparations were made to sell some of the old, poorly maintained, City Council houses, but then only in specially designated areas, and at free market prices. After independence, however, when the ownership of the houses was transferred to tenants the purchase price depended on how many years the occupant had previously paid rent for the dwelling. Where the occupancy exceeded thirty years there was no need for payment. The same system of renting with the right later to buy the house at a reduced price is also applied in new housing projects, although only one–tenth of new units are for rent and are usually reserved for governmental staff. Nine–tenths of all new houses are meant to be built by self–help on individual sites which are distributed through the waiting lists in Harare and Chitungwisa.

In the beginning of the 1980s, the waiting list in Harare comprised over 50,000 applicants, and allocations were made according to the date the applicant had entered into continuous employment in Harare. Chitungwisa Town Council has a similar waiting list, priority being given to registered lodgers within Chitungwisa.

High Standard and Cost Recovery

Between 1980 and 1982, the construction of ultra–low–cost units continued in Chitungwisa, but increasingly became the object of strong criticism by inhabitants and politicians. The expectations following independence were high and these housing units symbolized the unequal standards of the colonial society. In October 1982, new minimum standards for plots and houses were laid down by the Minister of Housing. They ruled that

- No plot should be smaller than 300 square metres.
- It was desirable also that bigger plots of 300, 400, 500 and 600 square metres are incorporated in the same project.
- The minimum core house shall consist of two bedrooms, dining–room, kitchen and toilet/shower (*Figure 5*).
- The minimum floor space shall be 50 to 60 square metres.
- Provisions should be made to allow for a further extension by another three rooms.
- No building permits shall be granted for buildings of lower standards (Zimbabwe, 1982).

The abandonment of low–standard housing was certainly met by popular support, though high standards in combination with the principle of cost recovery had conse–quences for the low–income groups which were not always recognized. Nevertheless some local authorities argued for lower standards. The Chitungwisa Town Council, for example, wanted to build two–roomed core houses, in order to increase the total number of new houses and to serve more people on the waiting list. However, this proposition was not approved by the Government; instead three different project alternatives were tabled to bring the high–standard units within the financial means of the population. These programmes were: aided self–help, building brigades and co–operatives.

Three Strategies of Housing Production

The Aided Self–Help Strategy

Aided self–help, building brigades and co–operatives were presented as three strategies of housing production for making houses affordable. The aided self–help strategy is part of the wider housing strategy of home ownership. The pre–revolution–ary *Glen View* experience was regarded as positive.[1] There, many large houses were

---

1)   In the late 1970s, Glen View was the first large area to be self–help built. 7,342 plots for home ownership were provided with a wet core by civil contractors. The invitation to self–builders in 1978 was met with an enormous response: over 17,500 applications were received. The applicants were first expected to have a monthly income of less than Z$100, a limit which was subsequently raised to Z$150. The monthly payment for a plot was about Z$14. Loans in the form of building materials were offered for up to Z$200 to each plot holder, and additional loans on longer terms could be negotiated once the core of the house was constructed. The council offered type plans for houses, but own layouts could also be approved. In addition, 271 plots of 400 square metres for higher class houses were provided. Though Glen View was primarily intended for lower income earners, there was rapid development of big houses on the plots offering rooms for the owner and a number of tenants. A civil servant at the local authority told me: "In the beginning we tried, in our old paternalistic way, to allow only one external door to each house. But we became so unpopular that we could not continue". Lodgers are supposed to register and pay a reduced charge for water and services, but many lodgers do not do so. In the beginning of the 1980s there were on an average 2.5 registered lodging families in each house in addition to the owner's family. In reality, there were more; usually about thirty persons live in each house.

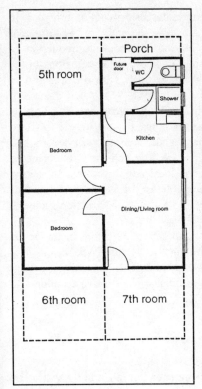

Figure 5:
Post Independence Unit

Figure 6: One of the few building brigades in Kuwad-
zana New Town.   *(Foto: Ann Schlyter)*

built which contained rooms for lodgers catering for the increasing populations
housing demand. Officially, however, the idea of 'one family, one house' was
sustained. The aided self-help housing strategy totally dominated the production of
housing in the Harare region. Experiences from Kuwadzana will be discussed below,
but first it might be interesting to look at the two other, and less successful, strategies.

Building Brigades

The concept of building brigades was presented as an offensive innovation by the new
Government in 1981. After independence, politicians responsible for housing made
a worldwide tour to study different housing strategies. They were startled by the
chaotic urban housing situation of many African countries, did not like the panorama
of the large squatter areas, and were not impressed by the upgraded shanty towns, all
of which represented a standard they did not want to accept for Zimbabwe. They were
impressed, however, by the suburbs of Havana and elsewhere in Cuba, where the
Cubans proudly claimed success in building with brigades (so called 'Microbrigades',
see chapter on Cuba).

Subsequently, the idea of the Cuban building brigades was adapted to Zimbabwean
conditions. Three major categories of brigades were sketched: the construction

brigades, the upgrading brigades, and the building materials production brigades. In Cuba the brigades were first and foremost a way to solve the problem of shortage of labour, which was, at that time, the most serious constraint in housing production. In Zimbabwe, however, there is no shortage of labour, unemployment being one of the largest problems. The Zimbabwean building brigades therefore did not aim to overcome a shortage of labour in the construction industry.

From the beginning it was a bit unclear what a Zimbabwean building brigade really was. In 1981, the Minister wrote: "Any family in need of but unable to afford a house will have to join a brigade. Together the brigade members will donate their labour". But in the end, instead of being units for collective self–help, the brigades turned out to be units of wage workers within the local administration. In theory, through the brigades the state avoids leaving the public to the 'whims and appetites of private enterprise' (Zvogbo, 1981). By competing with the construction industry, the general price level was supposed to be kept down.

In some parts of the country the building brigades became active in the actual construction of housing, such as in Gweru, but not in Harare, where self–help schemes dominated the scene. Even there, however, few of the houseowners built their own houses, for it was cheaper for them to engage small private builders to build in stages.

The Co–operatives

If building brigades had little impact on the housing situation in Harare, the strategy of co–operatives never really got off the ground. In the transitional national development plan for the period 1983 to 1985, published in May 1983, the strategies of aided self–help and brigades were stressed but co–operatives were not even mentioned. Nevertheless, in various contexts politicians continued to talk about the three strategies, including the co–operatives. But interviews with relevant authorities in 1987 gave no evidence of any support to housing co–operatives. Like other entrepreneurs, small builders were free to apply for registration as co–operatives, but few did so because there were almost no direct benefits to be gained.

In 1986 in Chitungwisa, I met groups of residents who had applied for registration as co–operatives. One group wanted to take a loan as a co–operative from a building society in order to improve their individual houses. The other group was originally formed around a housing improvement project, but extended their objectives to include income–generating activities and thereby complied with the requirements for producer co–operatives. They intended to produce building materials both for own needs and for sale, and the profit would then go into housing improvement.

These groups witness the strongly felt need for housing improvement and its capability to organize the community. But in practice they met many hindrances and their initiatives were frustrated by long waiting lists without any advice on how to proceed. Thus some members were demoralized and non–members were discouraged from applying themselves.

Squatters and Upgrading of Sub-Standard Areas

The Demolition Policy

After independence the new Government continued a declared demolition policy against squatters. Almost immediately after taking power, the camp at *Musika* was cleared.[2] Refugees were encouraged to return to their areas of origin. Many, however, had no economically viable alternative where to return, and wanted to stay in Harare. Some of the families staying were then accommodated in former single men's hostels; others became lodgers or squatters elsewhere (Patel, 1984).

Not only squatter areas but also planned areas such as *Chirambahuyo* were demolished, with the only reason given being that they had been temporary or substandard. The area, at that time housing about 30,000 people, was urbanized with well-defined plots, and water and other services installed. The people had built their own houses in mud bricks. In spite of the acute housing shortages these self-built houses were demolished without any compensation to the owners to whom the houses represented quite a substantial investment. Not all of the inhabitants could afford to accept the Government's offer for rental housing, and many went to an unplanned settlement growing in *Chitungwisa, Muyambara*. They had, however, to move again when this area was bulldozed in 1982.

In October 1983, when policy discussions on upgrading and other alternatives to bulldozing had begun, the anti-squatter policy was reconfirmed in statements by the president, followed in action by a nationwide clean-up operation initiated by the central committee of the ZANU (PF) party. Squatters were arrested and taken to prison, their houses demolished. A similar procedure was also aimed against prostitution, and women walking at night in public areas without the company of a man were also arrested, a measure which was met by protests from some women's groups. Shanty towns of about 10,000 people were bulldozed at *Russelldene*, between Harare and Chitungwisa (Butcher, 1987).

Again, the squatters were urged to go back to the rural areas, but many of them did not have access to fertile land, and the drought was severe these years. More than 10 per cent of the squatters were single women, who have more difficulties in getting access to land. Some of the squatters were from neighbouring countries, others lived in unregistered marriages, neither of which was acceptable in the rural villages, nor made them eligible as tenants in City Council houses. Epworth, the largest squatter area in the region, received a substantial share of the families who had been pushed from place to place fleeing from the bulldozers.

---

2)   Musika was initially erected as a 'transit settlement' when the influx of rural population into the city began to grow as a consequence of the war. It was located in the centre of the township of Harare, near to the bus station and the market. Some 700 plastic tents had been erected by the authorities and rented at Z$1 a week. In 1979 the camp was made more permanent by adding 400 shelters of concrete poles and panel.

Upgrading of Epworth

Not all substandard housing areas in the Harare region were demolished during the first years; and one of those that remained was Epworth. In 1983, the Government declared its intention to upgrade the neighbourhood under the premise that the area was not allowed to grow any further, and that the general anti–squatter policy was maintained. In Epworth, however, the original settlers had legally paid rent and lived in the area for such a long time that they could not be treated as squatters. The former land owner, a Methodist mission, had originally allowed settlement and protected the settlers. By 1950, there were approximately 200 agricultural and 300 residential tenants permitted to live there. Most of them had close religious and social ties with the mission. During the liberation war many families found refuge in Epworth, and later on, many families who had been evicted from other squatter areas found a haven here. The density remained low for a low income area.

Most houses in Epworth were built of mud bricks, a few had thatched roofs, but the most common roofing materials were asbestos or iron sheets. Many of the houses were well built and maintained and as good to live in as the low–cost houses provided by the City Council. The area, however, was lacking roads and such services as water, sewerage and electricity.

In 1983, about 28,000 people lived in an area of 3,670 hectares in Epworth and on neighbouring farm land. The state had bought the land and it was administered by the Ministry of Local Government and Town Planning. At the same time it was made clear that progress depended on whether outside funds could be obtained. The *United States Agency for International Affairs*, USAID, was engaged in making a feasibility study, and a programme for upgrading was worked out by the Ministry of Local Government and Town Planning (Zimbabwe, 1984).

Efforts have been made to mobilize the inhabitants in Epworth. Social workers have been acting as liaison between the community and the planners. In June 1983, elections were held for four 'Area Development Committees' of ten members each. Over 10,000 people participated in these elections. The development committees raised and discussed problems faced by the residents, ranging from the need for a clean water supply to high crime rates. The committees have stressed the need for economic activities in the area (unemployment levels were as high as 11 per cent), and proposed development projects in the field of agriculture, tourism and small industries.

The upgrading programme accepts the idea to continue agricultural cultivation in the area. It was probably politically easier to accept the upgrading if the area was not defined as urban. Instead of planning for subdivisions and infill of additional housing (the common practice in urban suburbs), the chosen approach was to grant security of tenure on large plots. However, no agreement was reached with the funding agencies, particularly concerning the terms for the loan, and the project had to be redefined as a cheaper alternative to be exclusively funded by grants from the local Treasury which would be supplemented from revenues raised from residents themselves at a later stage.

In 1985, the implementation of the upgrading was introduced with the demolishing of all houses built in the area since 1983, when aerial photographs had been taken.

In 1986, almost two million dollars were provided by central Government for the first stage of the upgrading (Zimbabwe, n.d.,a). A main road was constructed through the area in order to provide a bus service and delivery link with the city. Three hundred tube wells were drilled by the community and provided with hand pumps (Morgan, n.d.). The building of one upgradable latrine on each of the 3,000 sites began in 1986, after thirty experimental units had been built two years before.[3]

Maintaining the high standard policy, these measures were considered temporary solutions, and planning for piped water, sewerage and electricity was going on. A cadastral survey would permit formal plotting and finalize the process of upgrading of Epworth to the normal standard of Harare housing areas. However, the maintenance of the large plots and the semi-rural character of the area will make the second stage of the upgrading, if it is implemented, an extremely expensive operation.

New Townships: the Kuwadzana Project

The first large new township planned in the Harare region since independence is Kuwadzana. The area is located twenty kilometres west of the city, on virgin farm land. There is no declared policy to support such a location. The policy of the racist Government to locate 'Sowetos' in areas of common land, the former native reserves, has been reversed: Kuwadzana is located on former white land on the periphery, where there was a farm available for purchase and development. The first phase of the project included about 3,750 sites. Eventually the area will provide more than 7,000 sites serviced with roads and public lighting, schools and clinics, a post office and supermarket. The sites are provided with water and sewerage. Electricity can be supplied at a later stage. The plotholders could chose from a series of model plans which were provided but the house type was similar in all models. The size of the core amounted to about 55 square metres, while a complete house measured about 90 square metres. The most popular model plan, chosen by almost half of the beneficiaries, is shown in *Figure 7*.

Politically, the prime objective was to provide housing opportunities for the lower income group in Harare on a fully cost recoverable basis. In line with the home ownership strategy, serviced plots were provided for self-help building. The choice between the three strategies of production – 'self-help', 'building brigades' and 'co-operatives' – was left to the individual household, but the minimum standard of housing, as declared in 1982, remained compulsory. The *United States Agency for International Development* supplied a loan (US$38 million) for finance.

Individual loans for building were offered to the plotholders at sizes proportional to income, with a ceiling of Z$3,230. People with low incomes were expected to build houses of the same size as others, but with a smaller loan. 12 per cent of the borrowers in the first phase, who earned less than Z$130 per month, got an average loan of Z$1,633. On average, these people had raised almost as much themselves

---

3) The upgradable latrine is a type of ventilated pit latrine that can be fitted with conventional flush cisterns and connected to water-borne sanitation at a later stage.

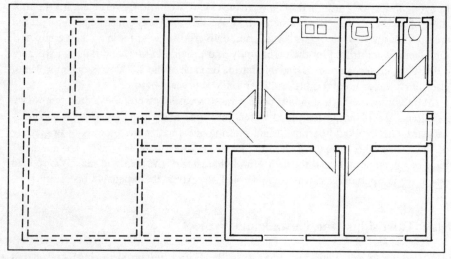

Figure 7: Model Plan, Kuwadzana

during the first six to fourteen months of the building period, which is an impressive achievement. Nevertheless, it was estimated that only a fourth of the low–income earners would be able to build a four–roomed house in eighteen months (Wegge, 1985) and another 50 per cent would manage if they were given time–three to five years–while one–fourth will make no progress.

In theory, plot–holders had the freedom to construct their houses how they wished but in practice the only viable option for almost everyone was to engage a small builder. When five thousand plot–holders had begun, only six had contracted a building brigade while the rest could not afford it. No co–operatives were formed because, according to the City Council, they did not know their neighbours, they were employed, and they were not allowed to live on the site (Harare, 1986). Also, there was no official support for co–operatives either, application procedures were difficult and the waiting list for registration was long. Furthermore only production co-operatives with unemployed people wanting to work were accepted for registration by the Ministry of Co–operatives; there was no possibility of forming home ownership co–operatives.

Given that almost all plot holders were employed, it followed that few, if any, built houses themselves. According to Holin, a great majority of house owners were satisfied with their builders (Holin, 1985). However, in my study of women heads of households, the picture is different (Schlyter, 1987). Almost everyone claimed that she was cheated by the builders, some believed because they were women; others blamed their own lack of supervision over the builder. As they were working to earn an income they could only visit Kuwadzana on Sundays, whereas the wives in households headed by men were able to spend most weekdays on the site.

The building period was difficult, not just for the poorest strata and women headed households. Enormous sacrifices were made in order to raise the money needed in addition to the loan. The fact that the owners were not allowed to live on the site before completion of the house caused economic and practical difficulties. People had to pay rent where they lived and the service charge of Z$22 in Kuwadzana; in addition, they paid bus fares for the women who supervised the builders. Many wives had to give up their own income–generating activities during the period.

As stated before, the objective of the project was to provide serviced land and community facilities to *low–income* households. The houses in Kuwadzana may qualify as low–income housing according to the definition in the development plans and housing programmes, but they are far from affordable for the lowest income quartile. The sites were therefore distributed among people on the waiting list with incomes just below the median income (Zimbabwe, n.d.,b), which was Z$175 for Harare at that time. However, the mean income in the City Council areas was only Z$130, and almost a third of the population earned less than Z$70. It would therefore be more honest to call Kuwadzana a middle–income housing project in which the low–income population comes in as lodgers. Furthermore, there was an inbuilt discrimination against women because among the accepted applicants priority was given according to length of employment in Harare. Although at least 15 per cent of all households in Harare are headed by women, only 2 to 3 percent of beneficiaries are women, reflecting women's weak position on the labour market.

Kuwadzana became a testing ground for the housing policy formulated by the new Government. Through several studies the outcome of the first phase is well documented (Holin, 1985; Patel, 1985; Harare City Council, 1986) and obviously influenced the revision of housing policy in the second phase of Kuwadzana. A list of registered builders was prepared, and the plotholders were advised to sign contracts with builders. However, no lessons were drawn from the observation that low income earners and women had limited access to the project.

Urban Housing Policies after 1985

Policy in Figures

The urban population increased rapidly, but the production of urban housing remained low. It was acknowledged that this trend had to be changed. In 1985, the Ministry presented a long term plan for the construction and housing sectors recommending to allocate more funds to the housing sector and to distribute them over a larger number of households, but also to minimize any subsidies.

In 1985, a housing needs assessment was undertaken to provide a basis for the National Housing Programme 1985–2000 (*Table 1*). A production target of 146,000 houses a year was laid down, whereof 99,000 were meant to be low income houses. The calculations derive from figures of the 1982 Census, which later proved to be unreliable and far too low, at least in the Harare region. In spite of the underestimated need, reported production figures lag behind even more. Although figures like those in Table 1 are only rough estimates they show that at least two million new houses are needed before the year 2000.

According to the National Housing Programme 1985–2000, 61,000 houses shall be built each year in urban areas. The distribution between the different income levels

Table 1. Calculation of Housing Needs for the Years 1985 and 2000

No. of households	1985	1,714,000
No. of houses	1985	749,000
Backlog	1985	965,000
No. of households	2000	2,961,000
New households	2000	1,247,000
Backlog + new households	2000	2,212,000
Rebuilding of old houses	2000	?

Source: Zimbabwe, MPCNH, 1986, extracted from Table 2.1

is equal in the sense that there will be about as many low–income as middle–income houses built in urban areas in Zimbabwe (*Table 2*). But the total cost of middle income housing will represent more than double the cost of low–income housing. Public expenditures will, however, give priority to low–income housing; Z$106m compared to Z$81m on middle–income housing.

In a discussion on social distribution of housing these figures are, of course, meaningless unless they are related to the absolute figure of households belonging to the respective income groups. Unfortunately the National Report (Zimbabwe, MPCNH, 1986) does not provide data on income distribution in the Harare region or other urban areas, but only gives total figures of Zimbabwe (*Table 3*). According to this information, the total investments are ten times larger in middle–income housing (and the public investments three times larger) compared to low–income housing, if calculated per household.

Table 2. Urban Housing in the National Housing Programme

Target income group	No. of units	Total cost (Z$ million)	Public cost (Z$ million)
low	28,000	155	105
middle	27,000	396	81
high	6,000	193	
total	61,000	744	186

Source: Zimbabwe, MPCNH, 1986, extracted from Table 2.4

Policy Debates

The planned bias for middle–income housing in the National Housing Programme has not been publicly exposed or criticized, but housing policy was reviewed more in general in a series of conferences and seminars in the mid–1980s. The leading question was how to increase the housing production. Judged by the numbers of completed dwellings the housing strategies as they were initially formulated had not proved successful. Government representatives argued, however, that the strategies

Table 3. Urban and Rural Housing in the National Housing Programme

Target income group	Total no. of households (million)	No. of Units	Total costs (Z$ million)	Public costs (Z$ million)
low	1,374	99,000	335	239
middle	226	39,000	516	123
high	114	8,000	250	
	1,714	146,000	1,101	362

Source: Zimbabwe, MPCNH, 1986, extracted from Table 2.1 and 2.4

had not been tested long enough, whereas World Bank experts argued for a 'simplification' of policy (World Bank, 1985).

The controversial debate may be interpreted as an ideological struggle, but the actors and the frontlines are not always quite clear. One frontline, at least, can be identified between the market–oriented ideology of the main funding organizations on the one side and the enforcement of state control to guarantee (at least in statements) social distribution of housing on the side of the Zimbabwean Government.

Low–income housing had always been state–controlled in Zimbabwe, as private capital had only invested in upper and middle–income housing. Private rental housing, which was concentrated to the central parts of Harare, was discouraged as an object for investments by the rent restrictions imposed immediately after independence. *The Herald* (30 October 1982) blamed the rent restrictions to be responsible for an almost total stop in private investment in rental housing.

In 1986, in a conference on 'Housing and Urban Development / Public and Private Sector Partnership', the discussion was channelled towards more far–reaching private involvement in housing. The United States Agency for International Development, a co–sponsor of the event, underscored the benefits of the private sector and of market relations in housing provision. The Zimbabwean hosts, however, seemed less convinced about such propositions. In his opening speech the Prime Minister said that wealth was generated through natural resources. In Sub–Saharan Africa these had been exploited by the colonial powers whose economic organization was capitalist. After independence, the private sector continued to dominate these post–independence economies. It therefore follows that the private sector had an inescapable social responsibility to invest in housing and urban development (Mugabe, 1986). In the 'National Report' (Zimbabwe, 1986) to the conference, the private sector was only mentioned in relation to manpower training.

The National Report analyzed many of the constraints to an increase of housing production. For example the low capacity of the construction sector, and the rapid increase in costs of building materials, 15 to 18 per cent each year during the first half of the 1980s, were mentioned. The discussions on social distribution were restricted to the topic of 'urban versus rural'. In the draft summary to the report there was a recommendation, 'that sexual discrimination, with respect to the relevant professional and technical training and to accessibility to housing finance be removed completely'. In the printed version, however, this paragraph was omitted and women as a group are not mentioned. Eventually in 1987, social aspects were specifically discussed in two seminars, one on 'Women and Shelter' and one on 'Housing for All'. In the seminar on Women and Shelter, in her opening address the Minister of Community Development and Women's Affairs stressed housing as a basic human right and reported that women had special difficulties due to lower affordability and lower educational qualifications. The fact that so called low–income housing had building costs beyond the reach of the majority of the low–income people, was admitted by the acting Minister of Public Construction and Housing in his key–note address at the seminar 'Housing for All'.

Policy in Recent Statements

Zimbabwean housing policies have demonstrated a considerable continuity since independence, relying on home ownership, high standard and cost recovery as the marked cornerstones. In policy statements the low–income earners continue to be the target group. The principles are neatly summarized in a recently published document, entitled 'Implementation Manual for Urban Housing Policy', and edited by the *Ministry of Public Construction and National Housing* (Zimbabwe, n.d.,c). The introduction states that housing is a vehicle through which people can improve their material and social conditions, and: 'policies underpinning housing development must induce real redistribution of resources with particular attention to the low income earners'. The manual does not contain the declaration of a new policy, but is a series of previous documents formulating the urban housing policy by central Government now bound into a single volume; implementation procedures are defined for local Governments. The three production strategies are a consistent element. However, *building brigades* are now more clearly defined as units within the work departments of local authorities with the main objectives of promoting small–scale production of building materials and of employment promoting. The manual also lists, for the first time, requirements to be fulfilled by *co–operatives* when applying to the local authorities for sites to build on. But the commitment to this strategy still seems to be weak; there is no requirements listed to be fulfilled by the local authority in order to support the creation of co–operatives.

In analyzing the housing policy of the first five years, the dysfunction between ideological statements and implemented practice in housing policy is evident. In the following period the National Housing Programme intentionally concentrates on housing provision for middle–income groups. Policy statements are now more carefully worded, and the importance to build up competence and capacity at central as well as at local Government level is emphasized, but the gap between statements and implemented policy remains.

Policy Silences

Housing policies must not only be evaluated in relation to statements. As Lebas (1984) has pointed out it can be most useful to analyze the silences in housing policy, too. What problems and whose problems are not addressed in the declarations. For example, there are no statements in Zimbabwe saying that the housing policy is pro-lodging, but in reality it is. The implementation of the three cornerstones makes the renting out of extra rooms to lodgers the only affordable alternative for homeowners, which can be observed in practice in Kuwadzana, and has been proved in theory by Manson & Katsura (1985). This study compares two approaches: to continue to build four-roomed houses and accept lodging, or build two-roomed houses affordable without lodgers. They allege that the second strategy requires three to four times more subsidies and is impossible to be implemented with cost recovery.

Another silence in housing policy addresses the favouring of small private builders. However, like lodging, support of the petty bourgeoisie does not read favourably in policy statements. The building brigades and the co-operatives on the other hand, are repeatedly presented as really socialist elements in the policy and are attractive ingredients in more or less radical political speeches. In practice, however, they are rather marginal phenomena in Zimbabwe daily life although they may still be developed in the future.

A third silence concerns the urban development. Densification of the low-density areas should be a necessary element in a policy for a more equalized urban pattern. In the conventional low-density areas there are already at least two residential houses on each plot: the main house and the servants' quarters. In fact, one-fourth of the African housing in Harare are servants' quarters. It would be a good idea to divide these plots and the 'servants' allowed to buy their houses on the same terms as tenants can buy City Council houses. Further subdivisions of large plots is also conceivable and would permit to build additional small houses which can share existing infrastructure and services. But no such radical propositions were tabled in the first period, and consolidated structures make them less likely to be raised today. A social housing policy in a situation of acute shortage of housing is primarily a question of quantity and social distribution, but spatial distribution and service cannot be neglected.

Conclusion

An Analytical Model

In order to evaluate an implemented housing policy, strategies for social distribution of the housing stock have to be considered together with the production of new units. In line with Gustavsson (1984), I would define three distinctive types of social housing strategies: a social right, an optimum and an avant-garde strategy. Gustavsson, however, is discussing Swedish policy and concentrating on the housing and tenants markets within an existing housing stock. Social housing policies in the Third World have to focus on mass provision of new houses.

To explain the various conceptual backgrounds to these strategies, I will illustrate them in graphs. In *Figure 8*, a curve represents a hypothetical distribution of existing dwellings, according to standard of both the house and the spatial quality. All cities

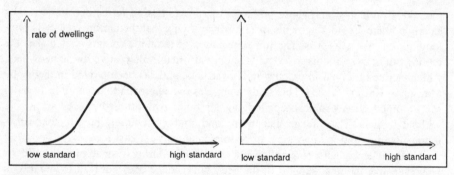

Figure 8: Hypothetical Distribution of Dwellings according to Standard
a) left: in a wealthy, developed city   b) right: in a poor city with a high degree of homelessness

have their own specific curve which differs from the normal distribution shown in *Figure 8,a*. The curve in *Figure 8,b* shows the situation of a city in a developing country with a high rate of homelessness (at point zero) and a large part of the population living in shanty towns.

The Harare housing stock has some special characteristics. The situation is highly polarized with one set of standards in the African areas and another in the former European areas. Because of the low number of middleclass houses a curve describing dwelling standards would almost be divided into two in such a situation (*Figure 9*). Controlled urbanization brought about rather homogeneous housing standards for the African population. The housing stock is of a comparatively high technical standard but severely overcrowded. The curve is therefore high and narrow.

Figure 10 compares the different housing strategies in a schematic way. The *social right strategy* is based on the understanding of housing as a social right, implying that nobody should live beneath a certain set standard. All Government support should be directed to lift as many people as possible above the minimum standard within the shortest period. Therefore houses will have to be built on a mass scale at modest standards in order that everyone can afford it, and those who can't must receive a subsidy. Ultimately the obtainable standard depends on the amount of subsidies that can be made available. The social right strategy will completely shift the curve to the right side of the defined minimum standard (*Figure 10,a*).

In the *optimum strategy*, the minimum standard applies for the majority of the population for quite a long period. The construction of housing of both low and high standard is considered a waste of resources. Instead, houses should be built to a reasonable (medium) standard and fair distribution can be manipulated by subsidizing low–income households directly. Taxes and fees can be used to discourage the production of houses of an excessive standard. The optimum standard strategy aims at reaching equality within a relatively short period.

The *avant–garde strategy* supports the construction of high standard housing. No standard is considered to be too high. Upper and middle income earners are seen as the avant–garde who today can realize the dream of tomorrow. It is generally believed that the lower income groups in some way or another will follow. Thus, the avant–garde strategy attempts to move the whole curve towards the right side in the very long run (*Figure 10,c*). It is, of course, questionable whether the avant–garde strategy can still be considered social housing strategy. Gustavsson argues that it can and compares it to nursery and hospital care in Sweden; no Government service will settle below the highest possible standard, irrespective of waiting–lists.

As an analysing tool these three strategy models will now be applied to the actually implemented housing policy in Zimbabwe for clarification and assessment.

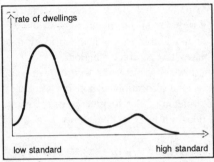

Figure 9:
Hypothetical distribution of dwellings according to standard. The inherited stock of Harare.

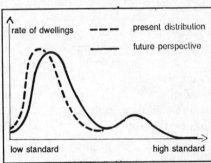

Figure 11: Aim of the avant–garde strategy.

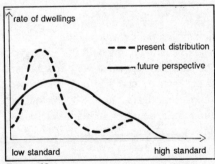

Figure 12:
Possible outcome of the avant–garde strategy.

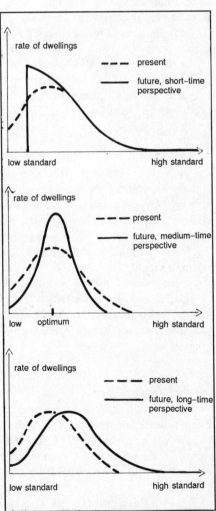

Figure 10: Housing strategies. Distribution of dwellings according to standards
a) Top: The social right strategy
b) Middle: The optimum strategy
c) Bottom: The avant–garde strategy

A Social Right Strategy?

In independent Zimbabwe the first declarations on housing policy stated that every citizen had the right to live in a dignified and healthy environment. This corresponds to the social–right strategy identified above. The bulldozing of squatter areas was motivated in the spirit of this strategy. Inhuman conditions were defined as housing standards lower than the accepted minimum and needed to be destroyed. Unfortunately, the people evicted as a consequence of such action were not provided better accommodation in sufficient numbers, and were left with worse alternatives than before: they had to squat again in areas further out from the city or become lodgers in extremely overcrowded conditions. In spite of the rhetoric of good housing as a social right the squatters were not granted any rights at all. A social–right strategy is hardly compatible with bulldozing, at least if not combined with the provision of better alternatives for all households living below the accepted standard.

It may be true that some of the implemented housing measures would have fitted into a social–right concept, such as the preferential allocation of housing to special needs groups, including, for example, ex–combatants. But to give priority to one group of homeless people on the waiting list does not increase the supply of housing for all.

Public housing subsidies have no tradition in Harare. Under the previous regime the employers of the African were responsible for providing housing for their employees, and the unemployed were not allowed to stay in town. A social–right strategy, however, implies subsidies for those who cannot afford the minimum standard, including the unemployed. This stands in contrast to the principle of cost recovery which has been imposed by certain foreign aid agencies, and which will be the basis of future housing projects. With a fast growing population and rampant unemployment, the cost recovery principle in combination with high housing standards means that the low–income earners are left outside.

Finally, a social–right strategy, if applied in Zimbabwe, should rectify the present split between what is called low–income and middle–income housing. Thus, one can conclude that the Zimbabwean Government has not applied a social right strategy in housing.

An Optimum Strategy

There were certain tendencies in Zimbabwean housing policy which could be referred to as an optimum strategy. For example, the simple core houses built in Chitungwisa can be attributed to an optimum strategy. The standards provided were low but still above what the households in the first income quartile could afford. The poorest tenants or house owners rented one or two rooms to lodgers, and the house thus was shared by at least two families. Owner–occupation encourages individual improvements of the housing stock and gradually raises standards. Also the final phase of upgrading in Epworth can be seen as an optimum strategy. Wells and improvable latrines can be afforded by almost all.

The national policy declarations, however, demanded much higher standards for low–income housing. In Kuwadzana, for example, four roomed, fully serviced houses were prescribed and caused serious problems in terms of affordability. The situation was made worse by the absence of financial assistance (Mutizwa–Mangiza, 1984; Patel, 1984). The upgrading of Epworth as another example also prescribes very high standards. Politicians I interviewed explicitly defended this decision by arguing for an optimum housing policy, defining the high standards as an optimal compromise between various demands. I feel, however, that within an optimum strategy, the promoted standard level should be set closer to the existing reality for the majority and, thereby, able to be implemented on a large scale within a medium–term period. Thus, the high standard level rather corresponds to the avant–garde strategy.

The Avant–Garde Strategy

The dominating tendency in Harare housing policies is the avant–garde approach, although some reservations have to be made due to the dual character of the existing Harare housing stock. Governmental support has been denied to upper–class housing in the former white areas, but it has certainly favoured the emerging middle–class (*Figure 11*).

The identification of the middle–class as an avant–garde in the urban housing strategies has not only occurred in Zimbabwe. Most African nations, regardless of ideological orientation, put emphasis on middle–class housing during their first years of independence. It can be interpreted as optimism and a wish to improve, but it can also be seen as a consequence of the formation and power of the new middle–class. Politicians and civil servants first identify the problems which they meet themselves. But Rakodi (n.d.) who has reviewed research on Zimbabwean housing policy concludes: 'To attribute the absence of socialist housing policies and failure to redistribute housing resources to a state which represents the interests only of capital, the bourgeoisie and peasants is to advance only a partial explanation, and, in particular, to play down the ... room to manoeuvre open to the Mugabe Government'.

Intentionally or not, the building of middle–class housing supports the creation of a middle strata. In the highly polarized former colonial societies such a policy has been recognized as a way to reach greater social stability. Houses for the lower middle–class will be a model for the poor. The workers can aspire to this standard. By giving well–paid employees the possibility to establish themselves in home–ownership areas, and to build rooms for lodgers, they might be able to accumulate capital enough to enter into business as petty–landlords. In inflationary economies, there are few other ways of saving.

According to the avant–garde strategy, it is assumed that somehow low income households will follow suit and move towards better standards. This is, however, an unrealistic assumption. Without special efforts to support the poorest it is much more likely that the curve will take the shape illustrated in *Figure 12*. The rate of households living in good accommodation will certainly increase, but so will the rate of households living in dwellings of poor standard. In other words, the housing conditions will become more unequal.

Note

This paper is a revised version of a paper prepared for the Kleve seminar in 1985 (Schlyter, 1985). Zimbabwe had been independent for five years, a short time for a Government to formulate and implement new policies and my original paper was by necessity limited to a discussion of the strategies adopted by the new Government in relation to the inherited housing situation. Another five years have doubled the age of the independent Zimbabwe. The discussion of housing strategies can be conducted in a less speculative manner. In 1985 and 1987 field work was carried out for a study on housing strategies in relation to women–headed households. This work and more recent information seems to strengthen my arguments, and made me accept the invitation to contribute an updated version of the article to this volume.

Bibliography

Bettison, D.G., 1959: An Attempt to Assess and Evaluate the Attitude of the African to House and Housing. In *Scientific Council for Africa South of Sahara, Housing and Urbanization*, Nairobi, pp. 212–17.

Butcher, Colleen, 1987: *Low Income Housing in Zimbabwe. A Case Study of the Epworth Squatter Upgrading Programme.* Department of Rural and Urban Planning, University of Zimbabwe.

Cormack, I., 1983: *Towards Self–Reliance*. Urban Social Development in Zimbabwe. Mambo Press, Gweru, 1983.

Gustavsson Sverker, 1984. Medelklassen som Avantgarde––Framtidens Bostadspolitik. (The middle class as avant–garde, the housing policy of the future?). In *Arsbok 1984* (Annual Report 1984), The National Swedish Institute for Building Research, Gävle, pp. 7–14.

Harare City Council, 1986: *A Case Study of the Kuwadzana Aided Self–Help Housing Scheme*. Harare: The Department of Housing and Community Services. February.

Hoek–Smith, Marja C., 1982: *Housing Preferences and Potential Housing Demands of Low–Cost Households in Harare, Zimbabwe*. Prepared for the Ministry of Housing, funds provided by USAID.

Holin, M.J., 1985: *Report on a Survey of the Beneficiaries of the Kuwadzana Housing Project, Evaluation of the Kuwadzana (Parkridge–Fontainebleu) Low–Income Shelter Project, Phase I*. (Prepared for submission to the U.S. Agency for International Development), October.

Jordan, J.D., 1984: *Local Government in Zimbabwe*. Mambo Press, Gweru.

Lebas, Elizabeth, 1984: *Re–thinking Social Policies. The Case of Housing Policies in the Inter–War Period. A Comparative Sociological History*. Presentation to the congress of sociologists in Oslo, 17– 19 February.

Manson, Donald and Katsura, Harold, 1985: *Housing Needs Assessment Study: Zimbabwe*. The Urban Institute, Washington.

Morgan, Peter R., n.d.: *Recent Developments in Providing One–Site Sanitation to Peri–Urban Settlements. A Case Study: Epworth Harare*. Blair Research Laboratory, Ministry of Health, Harare.

Mugabe, Robert, 1986: Speech on the Official Opening of the Tenth Conference on Housing and Urban Development in Sub–Saharan Africa. Co–hosted by USAID and the Government of Zimbabwe. Harare.

Mutizwa–Mangiza, Naison D., n.d., possibly 1984: *An Analysis of Low–Income Housing Strategies in Harare*. Harare: Department of Urban and Rural Planning, University of Zimbabwe, Mimeo.

Mutizwa–Mazinga, Naison D., 1985: *A Study of Low–Income Housing Strategies in Harare with special Reference to Affordability*. Discussion Paper No 111. Bradford: University, Project Planning Center.

Mutizwa–Mazinga, Naison D. 1985: Post–Independence Low–Income Shelter Policies in Zimbabwe. In: Romaya, S.M. and Franklin, G.H. (Eds.): *Shelter Services and the Urban Poor*. Cardiff: University of Wales Institute of Science and Technology, pp. 81–98.

Patel, Diana and R.J. Adams, 1981: *Chirambahuyo. A Case Study in Low–Income Housing*. Mambo Press, Gweru.

Patel, Diana, 1984: Housing the Poor in the Socialist Transformation of Zimbabwe. In Michael G. Schatzberg, *The Political Economy of Zimbabwe*, Praeger, New York.

Patel, Diana, 1985. *Evaluation of Secondary Sources of Data: Evaluation of Kuwadzana (Parkridge–Fountainebleu), Low–Income Shelter Project Phase I*. Prepared for submission to the U. S. Agency for International Development, June.

Rakodi, Carole, n.d. probably 1989: *Housing Production and Housing Policy in Harare*. Cardiff: Department of Town Planning, University of Wales, Institute of Science and Technology.

Schlyter, Ann, 1985. Housing Strategies: the Case of Zimbabwe. In *TRIALOG* No 6, pp. 20–29.

Schlyter, Ann, 1987. *Women Householders in Harare*. Paper presented at the seminar on Women and Housing in Harare.

Wegge, Jon, 1985: *Building Progress by Lower–Income Borrowers at Parkridge/Fountainebleu (Kuwadzana)*. Ministry of Public Construction and National Housing, Harare.

World Bank, 1985: *Zimbabwe Urban Sector Review*. Eastern Africa Project Department. Water Supply and Urban Development Division, Washington.

Zimbabwe, 1982: *Remarks by Comrade S. Mumbengegwi* at a Meeting of the Executive Committee of the Local Government Association on Friday, 15 October, Harare: Ministry of Housing.

Zimbabwe, 1983: *Transitional National Development Plan* 1982/83–1984/85. May.

Zimbabwe, 1984: *Epworth Urban Upgrading Programme. Project Report for a Community–based Agricultural Programme*. Harare: Provincial Planning Office. August.

Zimbabwe, 1986: *Report on Housing and Urban Development in Zimbabwe: Public and Private Sector Partnership*. Harare: Ministry of Public Construction and National Housing.

Zimbabwe, 1987: *Housing for All, Report on a one day symposium, held in Harare* 1 October, Harare: Ministry of Public Construction and National Housing.

Zimbabwe, n.d.,a: *Project Profile: Epworth Upgrading*, Harare: Ministry of Public Construction and National Housing.

Zimbabwe, n.d.,b: *Project Brief on Kuwadzana High Density Housing Project*, Harare: Ministry of Public Construction and National Housing.

Zimbabwe, n.d.,c, probably 1979: *Urban Housing Policy. Implementation Manual*. Harare: Ministry of Public Construction and National Housing.

Zvogbo, E.J.M., 1981. (Foreword). In Diana Patel and R.J. Adams, *Chirambahuyo: A Case Study in Low–Income Housing*, Mambo Press, Gweru, 1981, pp. ix–x.

Ethiopia

Sabine Wendt, Sabine Wähning,
Kosta Mathéy and Matteo Scaramella

The Setting

Situated in the Horn of Africa, Ethiopia is one of the most populous countries in Africa. According to the census of May 1984, its population is currently estimated to be around 43 million. About 89 per cent of the population is rural. Addis Ababa, the capital city, is located in the central highlands and has a population of about one and a half million.

Except for the five years of the Italian occupation (1936–41), Emperor Haile Selassie, the 'king of kings', ruled the country from 1930 until 1974. The feudal political system maintained by the Emperor imposed an unbalanced mix of different forms of production in the economy, and an extremely uneven development between the cities and the countryside. The severe famine in 1973–74 was only the final and most visible outcome of economic and ecological mismanagement, and triggered off a peasants' uprising, violent student riots, workers' strikes, and an internal army revolt which finally ended with army units seizing political power. The *Provisional Military Administrative Council* (PMAC) suspended Parliament and the Constitution after dethroning the Emperor in December 1974.

The revolutionary government, whose slogan was 'Ethiopia Tikdem' (Ethiopia onwards), attempted an Ethiopian way to socialism, introduced central planning, and brought large sectors of the economy under direct state control. Efforts were particularly made to modernize the rural sector. However, until now this strategy has not brought the intended results, and similarly, as in most other developing countries, between 60 per cent and 90 per cent of the population remain living within the subsistence economy outside the modern sector. Moreover, industrialization attempts have destroyed many aspects of the traditional economy and have thus further reduced the substance base of the rural population.

Eritrea, which had been under Italian rule since 1890, was federated into Ethiopian sovereignty in 1952, and after 10 years of formal autonomy became the country's

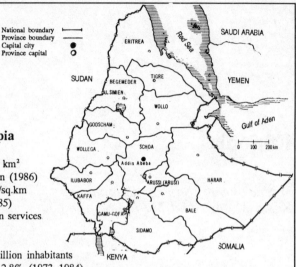

National boundary
Province boundary
Capital city
Province capital

Country Profile: Ethiopia

National territory: 1,221,900 km^2
Population: 44,930,000 million (1986)
Population density: 37 inhab/sq.km
Labour force: 19,182,000 (1985)
   77% in agriculture, 13% in services
Unemployment:
Urbanization rate: 18%
Capital: Addis Ababa; 1.5 million inhabitants
Average natural growth rate: 2.8% (1973–1984)
Life expectancy: 44.1 years for men; 44.6 years for women
Infant mortality: 17.2%
Illiteracy rate: 55% (1981)
Religion: Coptic Christians 41%, Muslim 40% (esp. in Eritrea), indigenous religions 10%
Language: Amharic (official), English and more than 100 local languages
Educational expenditure: 11.3% of budget
Military expenditure: 28% of budget (1984)
Export products: coffee 62%, hides and skins 10%, petroleum products 8%, vegetables 8%
Major markets: US 18%, Djibouti 11%, Italy 10%, Soviet Union 9%, FRG 8%
Foreign assistance: $ 915.3 million (1985); sources: OECD 46%, CMEA 21%, EEC 10.3%

Some important dates:

1st century	Creation of kingdom of Aksum in northern Ethiopian highlands
16th century	Arab, later Turkish occupation
1890	Eritrea becomes Italian colony
1930	Haile Selassie become Emperor of Ethiopia
1936	Occupation of Ethiopia by Mussolini's troops
1941	End of Italian occupation, Eritrea becomes British mandate (until 1952)
1950	The UN decides that Eritrea should become a federated state within Ethiopia
1958	Foundation of the *Eritrean Liberation Front*
1962	Eritrea is fully incorporated into Ethiopian empire
1974	Severe famine. Successful coup against Haile Selassie, military take power through *PMAC = Provisional Military Administrative Council*, also known as *'DERG'* ('committee' in Amharic), proclamation of 'Ethiopian socialism'.
1975	Radical land reform, nationalization of land & foreign owned industries, banks...
1977	*Red Terror,* conflict between different Marxist tendencies, over 5,000 dead. US arms embargo, increasing co-operation with Soviet Union.
1984	Foundation of *Workers' Party of Ethiopia* under pressure from USSR. Proclamation of *Peoples' Democratic Republic of Eritrea*
1984–85	Severe drought, famine kills more than 450,000

Sources: Die Länder der Erde, Köln: Pahl–Rugenstein, 1982. Third World Guide, Montevideo: Third World Editors, 1988. Politisches Lexikon Afrika. München: C.H. Beck, 1985.

fourteenth province in 1962. Since that time, separatist movements have been fighting for Eritrean autonomy, and so large proportions of the government budget have been absorbed by the apparently endless war. Ethiopia's closest allies were the Soviet Union, to which the country owes $4 billion for military expenses, and Italy. Cuba also contributes military and development aid.

Ethiopia is still a predominantly rural country with agriculture contributing up to 50 per cent to the entire economy, generating some 90 per cent of export earnings (mainly coffee) and employing 85 per cent of the economically active population. Manufacturing industry remains a small sector of the economy due to the extremely low investment capacity. With an estimated GNP per capita of $110 (1985) and with a vast proportion (60 per cent) of the population living below the absolute poverty level, Ethiopia figures among the poorest countries in the world. Nevertheless, the revolutionary government's health and education policies have considerably improved the people's life.

A very recent policy shift departed from orthodox Marxist thought and aims at re-incorporating the private sector more strongly into the economy. In his speech to the *Workers' Party of Ethiopia* (WPE) Central Committee, in November 1988, President Mengitsu, head of the government since 1978, outlined a series of reforms, the most important of them being the removal of investment ceilings to private sector investments, the opening of other sectors of the economy which were reserved for the state monopoly, and the extension of certain privileges previously only granted to foreign investors. However, at the same occasion he reaffirmed the government's basic socialist orientation.

In response to the reforms, the World Bank, which had stopped loans to Ethiopia in April 1987, agreed to resume support in 1988, with a loan of $85 million from the IDA. A further three World Bank credits are currently under negotiation. European donors were also said to be pleased with the President's speech – and have indicated their willingness to increase development aid in the near future. (E.I.U. 1989)

Housing and National Development

If we speak about national incomes and investment priorities as part of a government's economic and social policies we usually refer to the monetary share of the 'formal' economy. In Ethiopia, as in many other Third World countries, there is a split between the monetary and subsistence economies. In rural areas the *subsistence economy* is still predominant, and this is the traditional form of production of shelter, stables, roads, bridges, stone walls dividing different estates, and so on. There is no monetary value set to this economic output, but estimates suggest that the *non-*monetary sector contributes 70 per cent, or 940 million Birr, to the 'real' GNP, whereas the monetary sector only contributes 30 per cent, or 403 million Birr (Wendt & Wendt, n.d.). The *monetary economy,* on its own, is divided into the formal and the informal sector. The *formal sector* is officially recognized, pays the official minimum wage to its employees, and offers a certain job security. The *informal sector,* in relation to building development, includes both self–help builders and small scale general contractors: the latter ones, in most cases, are one–person companies that hire additional labourers on a day–to–day basis, as the jobs require.

Given the tight economic situation of the country when the *Provisional Military Administrative Council* (PMAC) took power in 1974, a radical change of the socio-economic system, which aimed at reducing internal economic and social disparities, was deemed necessary. First priority was attributed to agricultural and agro–industrial development, followed by (industrial) investments in the urban economy, which nonetheless have shown minimal growth since 1974. The construction sector is ranked third. In 1980, only 10 per cent of the national income was reinvested, and 57.4 per cent of this investment went into the building sector. Of course, within the building sector, housing is a minor item, representing only 1.2 per cent of GNP in the mid–1980s. It has been calculated, however, that a minimum of 4 per cent spending of the national plan 1984–1994 would be necessary to satisfy the calculated housing deficit applying very 'minimal standards', and assuming stable prices in the construction sector.

There are regional imbalances and set priorities too: for example, of industrial investment, 72 per cent is located in the central province of Shoa, with 25.6 per cent of that concentrated in the capital Addis Ababa. However, in respect to building materials (both imported and those produced locally), the largest share is reserved for rural areas, in line with the government's regional development programmes. One unintended consequence of this policy, though, is that those areas where the housing problem is worst, namely in the major towns, receive the smallest proportion of the available building materials.

Land Policy

In 1974, the newly installed military government inherited a feudal land tenure system in which power was concentrated within a small number of families. On the eve of the revolution, the king and his immediate family, the landed aristocracy and the clergy of the Ethiopian Orthodox Church owned more than 70 per cent of the productive agricultural land. Some 80 per cent of the peasant population were tenants on this land paying *'one quarter to one third, or sometimes one half of their annual production*[1] to the landlords. Property structures in urban centres showed similar figures: in 1966, 95 per cent of the land in the capital city was owned by a mere 5 per cent of the population (Mariam, 1970; Bereket Habte, n.y.; Pankhurst, 1962). Land speculation constituted one of the main sources of income for the urban aristocracy (AID,1965). In the period 1961–1974, prices for inner–city land in Addis Ababa skyrocketed from 25 cents to 200–300 Birr per square metre, or 1,200 times (Zeresghi, 1981; Galperin, 1981). Extensive areas situated in the centre of the capital city were left undeveloped in expectation of high profits. This land ownership situation brought about land use patterns, by which, for example, only 10 per cent of

---

1) In the southern regions of Ethiopia, conquered during King Menik's rule at the end of the 19th century, peasants were compelled to concede even 70% of their harvest (Mesfin Wolde Mariam, 1970).

the Addis Ababa population occupied 30–50 per cent of the entire urban area, while the majority of the urban poor lived in very limited, extremely crowded districts, in dwellings often built and owned by minor landlords. Except for luxury apartments, villas or office buildings, landlords did not develop their land, but used to subdivide their urban properties into minute plots which would then be leased to individual families at exorbitant rates.

By implementing one of the most radical land reforms in African history, it took the PMAC only a few months to eliminate the traditional system of land tenure. By mid–1975, the PMAC had abolished feudalism and stopped land speculation by nationalizing urban land along with 'extra' houses (proclamation No. 47 of 1975).

After the reforms affecting rural and urban land ownership, each Ethiopian citizen was given the right to occupancy of up to 500 square metres land (in urban areas) for residential use, while the land itself remains the property of the state. According to the guidelines of the *Ministry of Urban Development and Housing* (MUDH), an institution founded in 1975 in order to centralize regional and urban planning, plot sizes should correlate with the surface of the house. Thus, for a house of 40 square metres, a typical size for houses built in Addis Ababa, the corresponding plot would be 200 square metres. However, several studies have shown the actual plot sizes as being considerably larger, and frequently exceeding 300 square metres (Scattoni & Chinaglia, 1984; Scaramella, 1984). Particularly in Addis Ababa, where houses often do not exceed 30 square metres, the achievable densities in newly built up areas are low. Infrastructure provision is expensive and subsequently lags far behind the alloca-tion of sites. At the same time, the municipal planning authorities face a scarcity of residential land and cannot, within its present administrative boundaries, accommo-date even the most optimistic estimated population growth.[2]

Although land itself is provided free of charge, distributed by the Town Planning and Land Administration Department of the Ministry of Urban Development and Housing (MUDH, *TPLA Dept.*), the applicants must furnish proof of a deposit at the *Housing and Savings Bank* – supposedly to prove their ability to afford to build a · house – before they are accepted on the waiting list. The land is divided into four tax categories, reflecting the level of services and its location, and the allocated category exclusively depends on the amount of the deposit. There is, however, no relation established between deposit and the size of the plot, which would reflect the higher cost of providing infrastructure to larger plots. In order to qualify for the two higher categories of land a deposit of 20,000 to 30,000 Birr is required. For those areas with poorer services, plots of the third and fourth category, a deposit of 15,000 to 7,500 Birr is sufficient. Thus, lower income groups who cannot afford better serviced inner city sites not only suffer disadvantages regarding services, but also have the disadvantage of lengthy, time–consuming travel and subsequently higher transportation costs. There can be no doubt that the allocation requirements for land and credit provoke social segregation.

---

2) As early as 1981, Mach stated: *'According to information obtained from TPLA Dept., 14 out of 25 Keftegenas – all located in the central core of the city – are completely closed for residential use, some areas even being overpopulated (target 100 persons/ha.). In the remaining 11 Keftegenas, 35 out of 289 kebele still have some residential land reserve.'* (Mach, 1981)

Political Administration and People's Organizations

One of the supposedly most important outcomes of the revolution was the institution of mass organizations, today a deeply rooted element in Ethiopian society. Every Ethiopian citizen belongs either to a Peasants' Association, if he lives in a rural area, or to an Urban Dwellers' Association, also called 'urban co-operatives' or *Kebele,* if he lives in an urban area. In Addis Ababa there are, for example, 284 Kebeles which are assigned to one of 25 *'Keftegenas'* (Higher Urban Dwellers Associations)[3], which again are subordinate to the City Council Administration. These Associations, embedded in the PMAC's concepts of 'democratic centralism', are the basic political and organizational units of civic administration, and intended to contest the 'remaining traces of feudalism, imperialism, bureaucracy and capitalism' (Ethiopia, 1976). Their role is extremely important in almost all aspects of political, social and economic life, and all government policies, programmes and regulations are implemented through them.

In 1976, during the first months of the PMAC's rule, the Kebeles were given important responsibilities for a broad spectrum of activities in urban development. Within their boundaries, they are in charge of keeping civil registers; protecting public property; establishing judicial tribunals for cases of minor importance; running of basic grocer's shops; conducting hygiene education activities and campaigns to eradicate illiteracy, and also assisting small scale industries or producers' co-operatives. The Kebele and its residents are also supposed to engage in collective physical work such as developing forest resources, preventing soil erosion, 'beautifying' the neigbourhood and participating in the construction of schools, clinics, infrastructure and social facilities (Markakis & Ayele, 1978:104; Koehn, 1980:93).

Rapid Urbanization

Although as a traditional rural society the average rate of urbanization is still very low, amounting to only 14 per cent, Ethiopia's urban centres are growing fast, at a rate of 8.1 per cent annually. Such rapid urban growth is mostly due to rural–urban migration which accounts for 5.5 per cent[4], and a natural increase of 2.5 per cent (Central Statistical Office, 1980; Ethiopia 1982). Urban hierarchy is still dominated by the capital city of Addis Ababa, a typical primate city, which hosts three times the population of the second largest city, Asmera (425,000 inhabitants in 1980) and yet disproportionally absorbs the country's economic and social infrastructure (Kebbedé & Jakob, 1985). Nevertheless, the results of the latest available Central Statistical Office's (CSO) survey indicate substantial changes in the pattern of distribution of urban population. Owing to the government's regional development policy, but also

---

3) Each Kebele covers an area of approximately 8 to 12 ha. and accommodates 5,000 to 7,000 inhabitants. Addis Ababa, for example, is divided into 284 Kebeles.
4) 55.7 per cent of the population in Addis Abeba was not born within the city (Bishow, 1982).

*Fig. 1:   Addis Ababa Grand Market Area. Sixty to ninety percent of the built–up area is 'unplanned'
and outside the formal economy.*   *(Foto: Sabine Wendt)*

due to its villagization programmes (see below), the number of second–ranging
centres and smaller urban settlements has increased notably.

According to Table 1, Addis Ababa's and Asmara's share of the total population
declined from 43.4 per cent to 40.5 per cent between 1970 and 1980. There is also
a remarkable shift in urbanization towards the Southern and Western provinces, due
to the ongoing civil war and famine experienced in the northern and eastern provinces
of Eritrea, Tigrai, Welo and Hararge, where early urban development took place.

Table 1: Distribution of the urban population by size and category: 1970 and 1980.

Size	Category	No. of urban centres		Population (000s)		Percentage of total urban population	
		1970	1980	1979	1980	1970	1980
I	100,000	2	2	1,014.3	1,617.6	43.4	40.5
II	50 — 100,000	1	6	60.9	410.4	2.6	10.3
III	20 — 50,000	11	19	366.2	564.3	15.7	14.1
IV	5 — 20,000	63	113	544.0	995.6	23.7	24.9
V	2 — 5,000	108	119	342.5	405.1	14.6	10.2
Total		185	259	2,337.9	3,993.0	100.0	100.0

*Source: Compiled from Central Statistical Office, Urbanization in Ethiopia. Statistical Bulletin No 9, 1972 and
Central Statistical Office, Ethiopian Statistical Abstract, 1980, quoted in: Kebbedé & Jacob, 1985.*

Table 2: Urban population change by administrative region, 1979–1980. Source: see Table 1

Administrative region	Urban population 1970 (000s)	Urban population 1980 (000s)	Urban percentage 1970	1980	Increase 1970–1980
Ardsi	43.9	105.2	5.8	9.2	114 %
Bale	24.3	49.9	3.5	5.7	106 %
Gonder	84.5	162.2	5.3	7.9	92 %
Eritrea	386.5	107.7	20.4	29.2	83 %
Gemu Gofa	32.5	46.9	4.2	4.7	44 %
Gojam	81.6	190.1	5.1	9.3	133 %
Hararge	163.9	272.5	6.7	8.7	66 %
Ilubabor	23.4	54.1	3.8	6.7	132 %
Kefa	66.4	132.7	5.3	8.2	100 %
Shewa	1,073.7	1794.9	21.1	30.0	73 %
Sidamo	112.3	212.9	4.7	7.6	90 %
Tigrai	123.3	193.5	7.3	8.9	57 %
Welega	48.2	118.7	3.1	5.9	146 %
Wela	103.8	183.6	5.3	10.0	77 %
Total	2,337.4	4,224.9	7.9	13.6	81 %

Rural–urban migration is continuing and has not ceased during the post–revolution period (Table 2). Despite the abolition of feudal landownership and regional development policies, regional disparities are still noticeable and political and climatic conditions fuel migration. There is no systematic migration control since every Ethiopian has the right to own a house in a town of his choice (Eghzibar, 1985:16), but access to subsidized food requires registration with a Kebele. In some cases socially unwanted migrants such as beggars and prostitutes were reported to be sent back to their places of origin.

Table 3: Estimated Housing Need for Ethiopia 1984–1994

Source of housing need	units	%
Population growth	563,758	69.2
Overcrowding	177,510	22.8
Replacement of dilapidated stock	61,804	8.0
Total	776,072	100.0

Source: Belay, 1985, Table 3

These spatial–economic disparities find their material expression in the built environment of the cities: the most apparent effect is the growth of new, large, residential areas in the periphery, without appropriate services and infrastructure, and the densification and deterioration of existing popular neighbourhoods. With population densities of up to 418 inhabitants per hectare, and an average density of 231 inhabitants per hectare (in Addis Ababa), overcrowding is a serious problem (Belay, 1985). Seventy-five per cent of all dwellings have a surface area of less than 50 square metres, but are occupied by 5 to 9 persons. In the 1984–1994 ten year plan the housing deficit was calculated at 776,000 dwellings (see Table 3). In addition, there is an urgent need for maintenance and modernization of the existing housing stock (Bishow, 1982):

- 93 per cent of all houses have corrugated iron roofs
- 87 per cent are of timber construction, and only 13 per cent of so-called durable materials (4.1 per cent brick buildings, 4.6 per cent stone houses)
- 79 per cent have only pit latrines
- 77 per cent of all houses lack ceilings
- 74 per cent have outdoor kitchens only
- 72 per cent have no water connection
- 71 per cent lack electricity
- 63 per cent share kitchens with their neighbours
- 46 per cent of all houses have no foundation
- 36 per cent lack organized garbage collection
- 22 per cent share these latrines with neighbours

Most of the popular settlements – which are often hidden behind high corrugated iron fences[5] – are unplanned. Master plans do exist (usually prepared by foreign consultants) for most major urban centres, but generally these did not foresee the construction of low-income housing or provide for public facilities; occasionally popular settlements were even demolished (as in the early 1980s in Addis Ababa to make place for a 'party palace'). If implemented at all, the execution of the plans tends to be poor, due to the lack of municipal funding and inadequate legislation (Koehn & Koehn, 1979:226).

Housing Policy

Speculation in land, the lack of tenant protection, poor incomes and high rents marked the housing situation for low and middle income earners in Ethiopia before the revolution. No specific government policy regarding housing had ever been formulated, and the government did not feel responsible for supplying shelter for low-income groups. Only one low-cost project, the *Kolfe* scheme, financed from funds by a Swedish Non-Governmental Organization, had been constructed in the late 1960s.

The fact that 67.7 per cent of all the buildings in Addis Ababa are defined as *'attached houses'* reflects the pre-revolutionary land pattern. In the popular settlements, small *chika,* the traditional mud dwellings, were attached to a main building thus saving one of the four walls, and even smaller *chikas* were added to these. Between these conglomerations of shelters there would rarely be enough space for even a narrow path. Only the main buildings, often inhabited by minor landlords,

---

5) A kind of facade syndrome is traditional in Addis Ababa. Historically, on the occasion of official events, such as the Emperor's birthday or the Crown Jubilee, at the government's instigation, all buildings along the main roads were freshly painted. Certain dilapidated buildings which could not be given a more favourable appearance were briefly hidden behind high corrugated iron fences. For certain events these fences would also be 'beautified' by repainting – the last occasion was the celebration of the 10th anniversary of the socialist revolution. See: Akesson, 1965:8, Markus, 1977:467.

were supplied with water, latrines and electricity. As a result of such uncontrolled and unplanned urban growth, Addis Ababa has the highest percentage of slums of all the capital cities of Africa. According to World Bank figures only 10 per cent of the city is not considered as such (World Bank, n.d.:175).

PMAC, the revolutionary government, which recognizes housing as a social right, also never declared housing to be a government responsibility. For the last 20 years the housing sector has been regulated by a set of proclamations and norms issued from time to time while proposals for a comprehensive housing policy are still being studied. Measures taken immediately after the revolution to tackle the urban housing problem included not only the nationalization of land and the reduction of rents on existing houses, but also provisions for setting up *housing co-operatives,* the founding of the *Housing and Savings Bank* (HSB), and administrative reorganizations like the creation of the *Ministry of Urban Development and Housing* (MUDH).

The supposedly most important policy document was the proclamation No. 47 of 1975, known as *'Government Ownership of Urban Lands and "Extra" Houses Proclamation',* which aimed at three different results simultaneously:

1. prevention of land speculation by shifting all urban areas under its direct control;
2. the facilitating of appropriation of property claimed by the planning authorities for public need, and
3. a rental reduction, benefiting 60 per cent of the households in Addis Ababa

(Table 4).

Table 4: Reduction of Rents of Nationalized Units by Proclamation No.47, 1975

Rent (Birr) before 1975	Reduction as a percentage
25	50
25 – 50	40
50 – 100	30
100 – 150	25
150 – 200	20
200 – 300	15

Source: Proclamation No.47 of 1975, In: Negarit Gazeta, 34th year, July 1975.

As the Military Government assumed that the poorest population occupied the dwellings with the cheapest rent, these were reduced proportionally more than other housing. In fact, in Addis Ababa alone, nearly 90 per cent of the residents benefited from the 50 per cent reduction in rents. Of course, in absolute figures, high and middle income families saved much more through the rent reduction.

According to this proclamation, private ownership of land and houses for the purpose of renting was outlawed. The equities belonging to the royal family, to foreigners, and to the church were nationalized, and the same happened to any property owned, but not personally used, by nationals and their families. As a principle it was intended to compensate former owners of the expropriated stock in case they had not sufficient other income apart from the rents, and if the houses had not been built from the state's funds or those of the imperial family. However, there

Table 5: Revenues of Kebeles and Monthly Compensation Payments

Number of houses owned by Kebeles	135,347
Monthly revenues from rents	61,740,110
Monthly compensation payments/Birr	831,417
Number of households drawing compensation	17,823
Average of compensation/Birr	47
Share of compensation payments in revenues from rents	48%

Source: Calculated from statements in "Report on Addis Ababa Housing Census",
Ministry of Urban Development and Housing, MUDH, Addis Ababa, 1984.

were no cash compensations paid in one go; instead 18,000 ex–owners continue to receive pensions of up to 250 Birr per month, which represent a substantial part of the rents that the authorities collect on their behalf.[6] It has been suggested that these payments would be better used for the construction of new houses and thus help to solve the country's housing problem (Cabannes, n.d.:15), but a comparison with today's construction costs shows that the achievable number of new houses is negligible, and does not justify the expected internal and international political complications.

The management of the nationalized houses was, depending on their standard, transferred to one of two newly established state organizations: houses of a high standard under the *'Agency for the Administration of Rented Housing'*, RHA (4 per cent of the total stock)[7]. Houses with a rental value of less than 100 Birr per month were assigned to the Kebeles (57 per cent of the stock). The remaining houses are still under owner occupation (Scaramella, 1985).

The fragmentation of the housing stock between two management organizations implies a division by standards. The worst houses and the meagre rents collected from these Kebele houses are rarely sufficient to pay for maintenance and moderniz-ation, not to mention the construction of new units. This is particularly true since 50. per cent of this income is earmarked for payments to the previous owners (Cabannes, n.d.:14). Since the rental reduction in accordance with proclamation 47, 70 per cent of the population still pays less than 10 Birr per month. On the other hand, the rents of RHA administered units, which constitute the best part of the city's housing stock, and which are mostly rented to foreigners, almost tripled in 1978, and have contributed to the considerable profits that the organization has accumulated (80 millon Birr in 1983 alone).

---

6) Proclamation No. 47 states *'the government shall pay fair compensation in respect of houses transferred to government ownership...'* Beneficiaries are defined as:
○ Families and minors who have no income other than the rent they collect from their extra house(s) subject to nationalization. Until they earn income by working, such persons will be paid an amount up to 250 Birr per month.
○ Persons, former owners of 'extra' houses, whose income does not exceed 200 Birr per month, are paid amounts up to 100 Birr monthly.

7) RHA has controls 16,000 housing units, has 3,500 staff of which 1,000 are reserved for maintenance only (Cabannes, n.d:14).

Like the RHA, each Kebele collects taxes on urban land and rent for the houses it owns to compensate the former owners, and pay for maintenance, repair, modernization, and supposedly also for new construction of economical housing. Unfortunately, unlike building costs, the Kebeles' rents and taxes have not increased since 1975. Furthermore the collection of taxes and rents by the Kebeles is often inefficient, resulting in considerable losses, with virtually no income left to spend on new construction (*Table 5*).

Housing Construction

The most significant among the government's interventions in the housing sector were legislative measures including the nationalization of land and 'extra' houses, the reduction of rents, and the implementation of the Kebeles. Apart from the legal reforms, the central government also engaged in housing construction programmes, to be executed through the Rental Housing Association, the Ministry of Urban Development and Housing, the *Kebeles,* the *Ministry of Agriculture* (MOA) and nationalized industries (staff housing).

There are not many figures available on the volume of housing construction in Ethiopia on the whole. However, for Addis Ababa a construction of 1,588 housing units was recorded for the year 1978/79, or 2,000 on average in the period 1969–1984 (Cabannes, n.d.:5) when the housing deficit was calculated at 280,000 units by Cabannes. Set in relation to the number of citizens, this represents an output of 1.1 units per 1,000 inhabitants, which is considerably less than the average in other African nations, and far below the recommendation of the *United Nations,* which suggests a figure of 8–10 units per 1,000 inhabitants. In all urban centres (with a total population of 4.7 million, out of which one third is concentrated in Addis Ababa), slightly more than 5,000 new units were built annually since 1975.

Apart from financial constraints, which the Kebeles have faced since revolution, there are a number of reasons that may explain why both private and state sector have invested very little in housing: the nearly total freeze on wages since 1975, the country's deteriorating financial situation, the huge losses in human and physical resources brought about by civil war, and recurring famine, are all a constant drain on Ethiopia's investment capacity (E.I.U., 1989:25).[8]

The measures undertaken to encourage private investment in housing remained cumbersome, and scarcity of building materials, high cost of construction, rigid bureaucracy in land allocation and building permit procedures characterize the sector. Private house building is basically divided into four categories: housing co-operatives, assisted self–help projects, 'pure' self–help construction, and individual

---

8) In a speech to the WPE (Workers' Party of Ethiopia) Central Committee in November, 1988, President Mengitsu exposed details of Ethiopia's current economic situation. He confirmed that performance had been particularly poor in the agricultural sector, which suffered a 0.4% annual decline in production between 1980 and 1988. He further noted that the war in the north absorbed 15% of the GNP and 50% of the government's budget. Military expenditure had been rising at a rate of 19% annually since 1974, increasing from 105 million Birr to the current level of 3.5 billion Birr.

Fig. 2:   *Low–cost housing in Addis Ababa, built of locally produced cement blocks and Eucalyptus roof trusses.*   *(Foto: Sabine Wendt)*

building. The *Housing and Savings Bank* (HSB) and the *Ministry of Urban Development and Housing* (MUDH) function as support agencies to this sector.

Individual builders can obtain a standard house plan and land free of charge. The construction is usually done through small contractors operating in the informal sector. Provided the monthly family income does not exceed 250 Birr, they may obtain a loan from the *Housing and Savings Bank* at an interest rate of 9–11 per cent; the repayment period varies between 15 and 30 years, and is calculated in such a way that the annuities will not exceed 25 per cent of the family income (Proclamation No. 60/1975). The applicants must provide a certificate from their employer confirming their income. In practice however, given the large number of people working in the informal sector or periodically unemployed, this requirement excludes the majority of the population. A survey made in *Kebele 41* in Addis Ababa revealed that only 24 per cent of household heads had a regular income, 21 per cent were self–employed in the informal sector, and 50 per cent were unemployed or without a regular income (Bishow, 1982). For the Addis Ababa region, 6,900 individually built houses have been reported for the period 1976–1984 (Cabannes, n.d.: Table 3).

'Pure Self–Help' schemes are intended for the lowest income group working in the informal sector, with nominal incomes of up to 250 Birr. Participants of such schemes may obtain the plans for their houses, with a surface area of 26 square metres, from the MUDH, but have to generate their own funds, which is mainly achieved through an informal lottery savings system known as *Equb,* whereby a group of 10, 15 or more friends put together the same amount of money every week, and once every fortnight or month the accumulated sum is taken out by one of them (Egziabher 1985:20). For the period 1976–84, the completion of 1,550 'pure self–help' units (730 of them low–cost) was reported (Cabannes, n.d., Table 3). Since 1986, 'pure self–help' groups were offered the same assistance as normal Housing Co–operatives, except that they do not qualify for loans and have no minimum or maximum income limits (Alder, 1989:5).

Table 6: Income distribution per household and month

Income bracket ..	Population
0 to .... 50 Birr	30.0 per cent
50 to ... 99 Birr	29.3 per cent
100 to ... 149 Birr	13.4 per cent
150 to ... 199 Birr	7.6 per cent
200 to ... 299 Birr	8.2 per cent
300 to ... 499 Birr	6.1 per cent
500 to ... 699 Birr	1.9 per cent
700 and ..... more	3.5 per cent

Source: Ethiopia, 1982

The **'Assisted Self–Help'** programme focuses, in theory, on those with an income between 100 and 200 Birr, and is directed by the *Ministry of Urban Development and Housing.* The applicants may obtain plots, technical supervision, skilled contractors and loans at an interest rate of 6 per cent from the state, but must contribute their own unskilled labour. However, due to high building costs and limited related credit, families earning less than 160 Birr per month are practically excluded from this pro–gramme (Belay, 1985). Even the next income bracket of 160–500 Birr have found it increasingly difficult to qualify for the scheme, because of inflation in building costs: in 1979, the cheapest house built in Addis Ababa was at a cost of 3,493 Birr (Ethiopia, 1982). Set in relation to income distribution (*see Table 6*), we can see that 70 per cent of the population does not have an income sufficiently high to reach the affordability line drawn by the credit regulations. In Addis Ababa, 99 self–help groups of 20 families each had formed by 1985, and built almost 2,000 houses; another 1,200 units were constructed (with EEC funding) in other towns (Eghzibar, 1985:18).

Co–operative housing, the fourth scheme, caters for an upper income group of 250 Birr and above (70 percent of participants earned more than 500 Birr per month, see Egziabher, 1985:20) but was presented as a specifically 'socialist' model by the military government. No attempt was made to incorporate the positive experience of the traditional mutual assistance associations, the so–called *Edirs,* which existed prior to the revolution and assumed important community development functions, such as the construction of infrastructure, social facilities and dwellings.

Members of registered housing co–operatives can apply for a building site, a standard house plan and a loan from the *Housing Savings Bank* (HBS). Construction

Table 7: Housing Production by Co-operatives and Private Enterprise

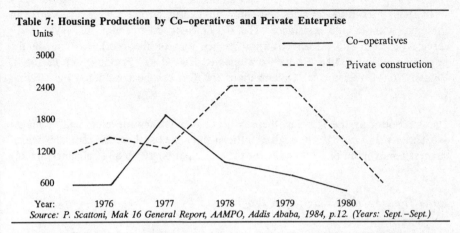

Source: *P. Scattoni, Mak 16 General Report, AAMPO, Addis Ababa, 1984, p.12. (Years: Sept.–Sept.)*

is mostly performed by informal sector artisans, but some people also employ official contractors (Egziabher, 1985:20; Alder, 1989:5). In Addis Ababa, with an average of 500 units built per year over the last decade, the co-operatives produced more houses than the two 'self-help' options. But despite the Government's propaganda this pro-gramme attracted fewer housebuilders than expected in its first phase 1975–1986. In fact, the number of co-operatives have diminished significantly over the years, see *Table 7*. This trend is understandable given that membership in a co-operative housing scheme used to bring more disadvantages than benefits, to the house builder. Apart from the apparently unavoidable hassle in fulfilling all requirements requested by the local bureaucracy (e.g., obtaining co-operative status, certificate of repayment capacity for all members of the co-operative, etc.), the registration process usually took up to three years to complete. Once that point was reached, the *Town Planning and Administration Department* did not have enough contiguous plots at its disposal for co-operatives within the city, and so members were allocated plots in the periphery, with bad transport and fewer services. Furthermore, one of the most praised advantages of a co-operative, namely cheaper supply of building materials through bulk purchase, could not be realized since such quantities are simply not available. Subsequently co-operatives have to either halt construction, or try to find materials individually from all sorts of suppliers, at substantially higher cost.

The new urban housing policy introduced in 1986 attempted to revitalize the co-operative movement, and provided new guidelines for finance, plot size, and the support of the MUDH and HSB. There is now a vast range of technical assistance services available to the co-operatives free of charge, and the interest rate of HSB loans has been reduced from nine to four-and-a-half per cent – lower than the inflation rate which is between seven and eleven per cent. Since then, and until 1989, 1,424 new co-operatives with a total membership of 37,129 persons have been organized, but less than a third of them managed to finalize registration procedures. Only 1,346 houses have been completed and allocated in this period. Building materials are still in desperately short supply, which can delay the completion of a house for several years (Alder, 1989; Ashenafi et al, 1989).

In 1985, **sites–and–services** and **slum–upgrading projects** were also started in Ethiopia, with foreign assistance. The *World Bank* co–operates in a sites–and–services scheme (IDA loan covering 70 per cent of the cost), whereas in the upgrading schemes, like the well documented *Kebele 41* (Egziabher et al, 1988), foreign Non–Governmental Organizations (NGOs) can be considered the striving force.

Due to control by the Kebeles, there is no substantial new development of **illegal settlements** *(squatters)*. Although no official figures exist there are estimates which suggest a maximum of 5,000 units for the entire period 1975–83 (Cabannes, n.d.:4)

Rural Housing and Villagization Programmes[9]

One of the most important revolutionary changes that has taken place since 1974 includes the socialization of rural land, which was handed over to the peasant associations, producers' co–operatives, and service co–operatives as part of the government's rural development policy. Implementation is the responsibility of the *Engineering Service Section* and *Rural Development Units* of each administrative region within the *Ministry of Agriculture* (Egziabher, 1985:4).

The variety of Ethiopia's natural environment and corresponding climatic differences has traditionally contributed to a concentration of population in the highlands, which only cover some 20 per cent of the national territory. Whereas deforestation and ecologically inappropriate land use have dramatically reduced fertility in this zone over the last decades, other areas are thinly occupied and offer supposedly untapped development opportunities. Therefore – but also because of strategic considerations related to the civil war in the north – the government launched a 'villagization programme' which since 1984 has moved more than three million peasants from previously isolated hamlets into planned settlements of at least 500, on average 1,400 persons, and situated mostly in the south and south–west (i.e. in the Asossa region, near the Sudanese border).

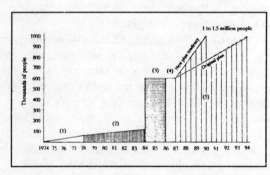

Fig. 3: Magnitude of Resettlement Programme

Although similar population transfers were recurrently ordered by Ethiopian kings and emperors prior to the revolution, the present *resettlement* policy, now operated through the Ministry of Agriculture (MOA), was first presented and tested as a *relief* programme to the drought. It was then managed through the Ethiopian Relief and Rehabilitation Commission (RRC) which

---

9) This section was partly taken from Cabannes, 1987.

had relatively easy access to foreign humanitarian assistance. Cabannes (1987) distinguishes five distinct phases of population transfers since the revolution (see *Fig.1*):

- **Phase 1:** *'Early resettlements (1974–1978) were originally directed towards people affected by national or manmade disasters but interestingly concentrated on other than drought victims as social categories: urban unemployed, nomads, charcoal makers. The principal displacements took place at a regional scale.'*

- **Phase 2:** *'Transfer from drought prone areas (1978–1984) increased with the spread of the drought. Special settlements were implemented in the famine free, potentially fertile and sparsely populated areas. Transfers were mainly from Wollo and Tigray towards Welega and Somali Plateau on the foothills of the highlands. At the end of this phase in 1984, 85 settlements were established and occupied by 120,000 inhabitants approximately....'*

- **Phase 3:** Massive transfers occurred: *'from 1984 (date of the much celebrated 10th anniversary of the revolution) till mid–1986, 300,000 people were transferred mainly to Welega province. The conditions of selection, transport, choice of sites were poor and their consequences often not controlled. This coincided with the maximum peak of the drought.'*

- **Phase 4:** An interruption of transfers could be observed from mid–1986 to 1987. *'Apparently international campaigns, reduction of support from foreign aid agencies, and the decline in famine ... might explain the sudden interruption.'*

- **Phase 5:** *'Future transfers: 1987 onwards. Although the plans are not totally clear, it seems that a target of 300,000 to be transferred every year might be a planning reality. The initial target fluctuating from 1 to 1.5 million people would then be achieved within three years'.*

Eventually, the settlers were supposed to organize themselves into peasant organizations, although some adopted the status of a 'producer's co-operative' as an intermediary step. Some of the settlements, such as the Assossa scheme, were able to achieve self-sufficiency in food production after only a few years, and to diversify their economies with forestry schemes, home

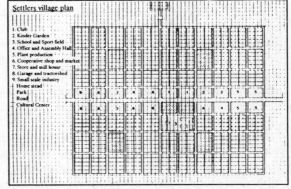

Fig. 4: Settlers Village Plan in the Asossa Region

economics, cottage industries, beekeeping, etc. On the other hand, the villages have often further destroyed the existing fragile environment in order to survive. Settlers nowadays walk from 7 to 12 hours to get firewood when initially it was available in the immediate surroundings. In urbanistic terms, the design of new settlements is usually poor and has followed a monotonous and rigid grid pattern, not offering private or semi–private open spaces (*Fig. 2*).

Building and Building Materials Industry

Building technology is not very advanced in Ethiopia. Similar to the situation in most developing countries, the installed building capacity is low, the number of qualified professionals and artisans is minimal, building materials are expensive and continue to rise due to inflation. The cost of building one square metre of a 'low–cost' house is eight to ten times the minimum monthly salary – whereas the ratio in most other Third World countries is 1:1 (Cabannes, n.d.:22).

Apart from purely politically motivated cases all private building firms with a staff level higher than 100, and those with a high rate of capital investment (machinery), were expropriated during the nationalization campaign after 1974. Since then the construction sector has almost exclusively belonged to the state, except for the very small units which operate in the informal sector. All state owned building materials enterprises belong to the *'Ethiopian Building Materials Corporation'*, which is responsible to the *Ministry of Industry*. Building construction enterprises, however, are dependent on the *Ministry of Construction*. Malfunctioning co–ordination between both ministries used to cause considerable delays in the completion of buildings in the past. To reduce these problems, there are plans to concentrate all responsibilities within the Ministry of Construction.

The output of the building materials industry is far below the need of the country, and many modern materials such as glass, tubes, sanitary fittings, certain plastics and electrical installation material must be imported. The first national (10–year) plan had envisaged import substitution by increasing local production or using locally available substitutes, and in the case of very basic materials like cement blocks and bricks this was achieved to a certain extent, but at the cost of inferior quality. The national production of cement – probably the aggregate in highest demand – has rapidly fallen since revolution: whereas the annual production reached 203,000 tons in 1973, the figure was 126,000, or 36 per cent, in 1983. One important reason behind this drop probably lies in outdated equipment, originally installed in 1936 in the case of the *Dire Dawa Cement Factory,* or in the mid–sixties in the case of the *Addis Ababa Cement Factory* and the *Eritrea Cement Factory*. The completion of a fourth cement factory with an installed capacity of 300,000 tons per year was scheduled to be completed in 1985, thus multiplying the total output almost by four. However, provisions laid down in the 1984 ten–year plan did not foresee using this additional capacity for housing and, unfortunately, there are no up–to–date figures available on the present production and its use.

The modest production of cement affects the availability and quality of the cement based building components, cement blocks in particular. Reported official production – excluding the informal sector which is relatively active – was only 1.5 million blocks in 1982, just enough to build 926 houses at a surface area of 50 square metres

(Ethiopia, 1982).[10] Furthermore, in order to increase production, many producers of concrete blocks, private and state enterprises alike, stretch the use of cement – the most expensive component – thus critically affecting the durability and stability of the houses built.

Clay bricks, in Ethiopia the second most important building material after cement, are of relatively low standard, in spite of recurrent attempts to improve quality. In quantitative terms, production output has also declined by 14.8 per cent between 1973 and 1980, probably due to the increased cost of crude oil, which is used in its production. The ten–year plan of 1984 envisaged multiplying brick production ten times by 1992, in relation to the last available figures referring to the year 1982.

A third building material of major importance is corrugated iron sheeting, locally known as *corcoro*. Corcoro was first introduced to Ethiopia in 1902, when the Addis Ababa–Djibouti railroad was completed. By 1911, 555 tons of corrugated sheets had been imported, and only 40 years later, Addis Ababa was christened the 'city of corrugated iron'. Today practically all new buildings, except flat roofed office and apartment buildings, are covered by '*corcoro*' – and this not only because it is the cheapest alternative available. At the beginning of the century corrugated iron used to be put up as fences by the rich as protection against the hyenas, and acquired a high social status.

Given that the country suffers from serious problems in both quality and quantity of building materials, and from poor performance in the construction industry due to the emigration of technicians after the revolution, outdated machinery, lack of spare parts, loss of instruction manuals, etc., the few available resources are mainly used for urbanistic embellishment and the construction of official buildings in Addis Ababa. Within the housing sector, most modern materials are being reserved for the provinces, so that most urban housing construction has to rely on the informal sector and on traditional materials and techniques, which are, however, unpopular, not specifically promoted by the authorities, and increasingly expensive due to the lack of wood.

Housing design and architecture

Although foreign to the traditional Ethiopian culture the typical urban house form of today is the attached house, representing 67.7 per cent of the existing stock – a consequence of speculative development practices before the revolution.

State–built houses, constructed by the *Ethiopian Building Corporation* and distributed through the MUDH or the RHA, are turn–key multi–storey flats or so–called 'low–cost' bungalows made from concrete blocks with water and electricity connections. Within the co–operative and aided self–help sector there exist a large variety of standard designs which bear, however, little relevance to the needs of the prospective users. For example, in 1985, among some 68 different types available

---

10) About 13 blocks are needed to construct 1 square metre of wall, therefore 1.5 million blocks would be sufficient to build 120,000 square metres of wall.

Fig. 5: Block of flats being built in Addis Ababa (Bole Road) (*Foto: Sabine Wendt*)

(always one type assigned to a particular income level) only two were of a surface area of less than 30 square metres, although the majority of the population does not have the financial capacity to afford houses which are larger than that. On the other hand, there were several designs of international style houses, as large as 200 square metres, with wrought iron gates and marble floors (there is no national production of marble). More than half of the models envisage concrete construction. Cheaper alternatives, such as terraced or two storey houses, are completely lacking in the catalogue. No provisions are made to accommodate income earning activities within the house, nor for further extensions – which would be a useful suggestion with fertility rates being high.

Conclusion

Although not impressive in their physical output of newly built houses Ethiopian housing and settlement policies contain a number of important innovations for the majority of the population with respect to the situation before the revolution. The *nationalization of land* halted speculation and made land free and accessible to more people who need to build a house, but affordability still influences the quality of flats that can be occupied. There is real *security of tenure* – there is no threat that any owner occupier or tenant will be evicted or otherwise displaced against his will. There is *no strict migration control* as in some other socialist countries but this causes part of the problem of *rapid urbanization* in Addis Ababa. There are few squatter settlements, but nevertheless the proportion of slums in the capital is greater than in other Third World states (Cabannes, n.d.).

Less successful have been attempts to develop the building materials and construction industry. Therefore many building materials must be imported which results in extremely expensive cost of construction. Upgrading of existing housing or additions to the present housing stock are minimal and far from satisfying new and accumulated need. Traditional solutions, both technical (local building materials) and social (Edirs, Equb), are not taken up to mobilize the population. Official urban planning and housing design solutions bear little relation to the population's traditions and needs. Particularly critical are some aspects of the villagization programme, the ignorance of ecological considerations, the lack of investment capacity as a consequence of the war. It is too early to assess the very recent acceptance of 'western' recommendations and credits, but it appears that not all 'indigenous' options have been tried first.

References and further reading

AID (United States Agency for International Development), 1965: *A Survey of Housing in Ethiopia – with Special Emphasis on the Capital City of Addis Ababa,* Addis Ababa 1965, p.80
Akesson, Torvald, 1965: *Low Cost Housing in East Africa, Survey of Housing Conditions in Tekle Haimanot and Lidetta,* Survey I, May 1962, the Ethio–Swedish Institute of Building Technology, Addis Ababa.
Alder, Graham, 1989: Co–operative Housing in Ethiopia. In: *Sina Newsletter No. 19.* Nairobi: Mazingira Institute. Pp 3–7.
Ashenafi, Sisay et al, 1989: SINA Ethiopia National Workshop and Study Tour on Housing Co–operatives. Working Group Reports. In: *Sina Newsletter No. 19.* Nairobi: Mazingira Institute. Pp 8–14.
Belay, Tariku, 1985: *Housing Conditions and Problems in Spontaneous Urban Settlements in Addis Ababa, Ethiopia.* Dissertation. Weimar (GDR).
Bishow, Makonnen, 1982: *Social Development Needs in Addis Ababa.* Addis Ababa: Ministry of Urban Development.
Cabannes, Yves, 1987: Settlements: An Ethiopian Answer to Drought. *23rd Congress of the International Society of City and Regional Planners,* New Delhi, 5–11 December. Paris: GRET.

Cabannes, Yves, n.d. (probably 1985): *Low Cost Housing: A top priority for Addis Ababa.* Mission Report to the 'Ministère de l'Enseignement Supérieur et de la Recherche', Paris (Décision d'aide N° 83 L 0438. Paris: GRET.

E.I.U., 1989: *Economist Intelligence Unit Country Report* No. 1.

Egziabher, Axumite G., 1985: *Housing in Ethiopia.* International Conference 'Shelter Policies in Socialist Third World Nations', Kleve (RFA).

Egziabher, Axumite G. et al, 1988: Kebele 41 – Community Upgrading in Ethiopia. In: Turner, Berta (Ed.): *Building Community*, London. Pp. 25–32.

Ethiopia, 1975: Proclamation No. 47 of 1975, in: *Negarit Gazeta 34th year, No. 4l,* Addis Ababa.

Ethiopia, 1976: Proclamation No. 104 of 1976, 'Urban Dwellers Association Consolidation and Municipalities Proclamation', in: *Negarit Gazeta 36th year, No. 5,* Addis Ababa.

Ethiopia, 1981: *10 Year Urban Development and Housing Perspective Plan – Broad Objectives and Strategies.* Addis Ababa: Central Planning Supreme Council.

Ethiopia, 1982: *Statistical Abstracts 1980.* Addis Ababa: Central Statistical Office.

Ethiopia, 1984: *Report on Addis Ababa Housing Census,* Ministry of Urban Development and Housing, Addis Ababa: MUDH.

Galperin, George, 1981: *Ethiopia: Population, Resources, Economy*, Moscow, p. 98.

Kebbede, Girma & Jacob, Mary, 1985: 'Urban Growth and the Housing Problem in Ethiopia'. In: *Cities, August 85.*

Koehn, E. & Koehn, P., 1979: 'Urbanization and Urban Development Planning in Ethiopia`, in: R.A. Obudho, S. El–Shaks, *Development of Urban Systems in Africa,* New York, 1979.

Koehn, P., 1980: An Urban Perspective, in: Scaritt, J.R. (ed.), *Analyzing Political Change in Africa, Applications of a New Multidimensional Framework,* Boulder, Colorado, 1980.

Lindhal, Bernard, 1970 (Ethiopian Calendar): *Architectural History of Ethiopia in Pictures.* Addis Ababa: The Ethio–Swedish Institute of Building Technology.

Mach, W., 1981: *Assessment of Problems Pertaining to Private and Co–operative House Construction Activities.* Ministry of Urban Development and Housing, Housing Research Department, Addis Ababa.

Markakis, J, & Ayele, Nega, 1978: *Class and Revolution in Ethiopia,* Nottingham, 1978.

Markus, Harold, G., 1977: 'T'Sehai Negus (Sunking)', in: *Proceedings of the 5th International Conference of Ethiopian Studies,* Nice.

Pankhurst, Richard, 1962: 'The Foundation and Growth of Addis Ababa to 1935', *Ethiopia Observer, Vol.6, No.* l, S.52.

Bereket Habte, Selassie, n.y.: 'Political Leadership in Crisis, The Ethiopian Case', in: *Summit,*Vol. 3, No. l, New York

Scaramella, Matteo, 1984, *Proposed National Urban Housing Policy* (2nd Draft), AAMPPO, Addis Ababa, 1984

Scaramella, Matteo, 1985: Urban Housing in Ethiopia, Ten Years after Revolution. In *TRIALOG No. 6.,* Darmstadt.

Scattoni, P. & Chinaglia, P., 1984: *Mak 16 Project – General Report Addis Ababa Master Plan Project Office* (AAMPPO) Addis Ababa 1984

Wendt, J. & Wendt, Sabine, n.d: *Planen, Projektieren, Bauen in Äthiopien. Expertise über das Äthiopische Bauwesen.* Weimar: unpublished manuscript

Wendt, Sabine, n.d.: Selbsthilfe im Wohnungsbau im konkreten sozialen, ökonomischen, und kulturelen Kontext Äthiopiens. In: *Proceedings of the 9th Bartlett International Summer School.*

Wendt, Sabine, 1987: Zur Wohnungsproblematik in Entwicklungsländern (Ethiopia). In: *Wissenschaftliche Zeitschrift für Architektur und Bauwesen, vol. 33/3.* Weimar (GDR).

Wolde Mariam, Mesfin, 1970: Problems of Urbanization, in: *Proceedings of the Third International Conference of Ethiopian Studies, 1966,* Institute of Ethiopian Studies, Addis Ababa, p.28.

World Bank (IBRD), n.d., *Background Paper on Housing,* Washington.

World Bank, 1978: *Addis Ababa Urban Development Project. Phase 1. Preliminary development Proposal,* Addis Ababa: MUDH

World Bank, 1982: *Addis Ababa Urban Development Project, Staff Appraisal Report.* Eastern Africa Projects Department. Washington D.C.

Zerezghi, T. M. 1981: 'Self–help and Co–operative Construction in Ethiopia since 1974', Paper for the conference on *Teaching Materials and Training Programmes for Co–operative Modes of Participation in Slum and Squatter Settlements,* 28.9–9.10.81, Nairobi.

Algeria

Djaffar Lesbet[1]

Introduction

The history of independent Algeria is one of 30 years of sporadic trial and error amid efforts to tackle the various key sectors of the national economy. Over and above the urban problems encountered in all the cities of such countries, in the case of Algeria, the problems are magnified still further and attempts to find solutions complicated by another particularity: Algeria was the country which experienced the most significant and radical severance from the existing system. Its urban population underwent an almost complete turnover in less than 4 months, between 19th March and 5th July 1962. The cities of other – this time Portuguese – colonies (Mozambique, Angola), were to witness the same phenomenon. Algeria might have served as an example on which to draw, but the country itself has not yet absorbed all the lessons to be learnt from its own case. How can cities which have been created by others be managed? How can flats designed for others be occupied? How can accommodation which had been occupied without it really belonging to one be maintained? How can confidence be restored to a rural population who have seen their villages destroyed, their inhabitants resettled in guarded camps, their agriculture abandoned and their land rendered infertile as a result of being liberally sprinkled with napalm?

These considerations apart, our aim is to review the issues raised by the housing shortage in both towns and cities, the problems resulting from failure to control the urban areas and the consequent imbalances, compared with the limited contribution of sophisticated and expensively imported solutions. In this context, planning is more akin to a list of good intentions than a coordinated succession of interventions.

The approach we have adopted is to describe the first three decades of the young Algerian state. The colonial past is evoked in order to be able to trace the path which has led to the country's urbanism being such as it is, a key characteristic in its social

---

1) Translated from French by Claire Norton

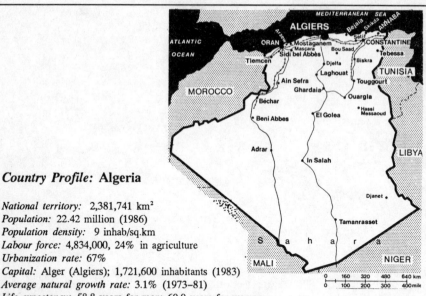

Country Profile: Algeria

National territory: 2,381,741 km^2
Population: 22.42 million (1986)
Population density: 9 inhab/sq.km
Labour force: 4,834,000, 24% in agriculture
Urbanization rate: 67%
Capital: Alger (Algiers); 1,721,600 inhabitants (1983)
Average natural growth rate: 3.1% (1973–81)
Life expectancy: 58.8 years for men; 60.9 years for women
Infant mortality: 8.2%
Illiteracy rate: 55.3%
Religion: Muslim
Language: Arabic (official), Berber in some areas, French also known
Educational expenditure: 24.3% of budget (1984)
Military expenditure: 4% of budget
Major export products: crude oil 43%, petroleum products 31%, gas 24%
Major markets: US 48%, France 13%, FRG 12%, Italy 6%, Netherlands 5%
Foreign assistance: $ 191.8 million (1985);
  sources: 82% OECD, 7% EEC, 5% OPEC, 1% CMEA

Some important dates:
1830 Invasion by French troops
1873 France decides to expropriate land for French settlers
1945 45,000 Algerians killed in a spontaneous uprising against the French
1954 Beginning of armed liberation struggle through *National Liberation Front* (FLN)
1962 Ceasefire signed by De Gaulle, agreeing to free elections in Algeria
1962 Independence declared and Constituent Assembly elected, Ahmet Ben Bella head of new
      government. 600,000 Frenchmen left Algeria taking everything they could with them
1965 Internal political crisis, revolutionary council under Houari Boumédienne took power.
      Algeria assumes leading role among non–aligned nations, and grants asylum to African
      and Latin American revolutionaries
1967 First (local) elections
1971 Nationalization of petrochemical industry
1976 Boumédienne elected State President (died 1978), followed by Chadli Bendjedid
1979 Political reforms implying, among others, removal of prohibition on private housing,
      crackdown on bureaucracy and corruption
1986 New constitution passed, this time omitting special references to socialism, and emphasizing
      instead Islam and Arab–Islamic culture.

Sources: Die Länder der Erde, Köln: Pahl–Rugenstein, 1982. Third World Guide, Montevideo: Third World Editors, 1988.

and economic policy, rather than as the sole cause of all the difficulties the country is currently experiencing.

How indeed could one otherwise consider the production of the built environment in a country which was once an integral part of the developed world but which was reclassified as a developing country as soon as it gained Independence! Once a minor and therefore colonial state, it gained its majority but simultaneously became underdeveloped. This game of classifying and reclassifying gives little idea of the extent of the country's backwardness in the fields of education and professional training and of the enormity of the tasks which would be required to bridge the gap. To this day this gap still weighs heavily on national production. The sporadic and particularly violent demonstrations of October 1988 are symptomatic of the current social and political unease.

There is nothing unusual in the fact that the lack of any supporting structure means that one has to manage situations which require long training and generations of experience with the means available. The petrol boom provides substantial revenue in a relatively short time; the same cannot be said where the training of an individual is concerned. Financial capability has all too often been confused with the ability to implement. "You can do anything with money", is the repeated cry, but housing is different, it is like a garment worn by a family; if it is the wrong size, if it doesn't fit their way of dressing, it will inevitably be badly worn and feel uncomfortable. The (urban) fabric will split on all sides, and the 'tramp' ethos will set into life, the city and its inhabitants, unable to live decently there.

The Present State of Affairs

Algeria emerged from its long colonial night on 5th July 1962 after 132 years of foreign domination which left deep scars on both men and their environment. The final seven years of Algeria's status as a French department before gaining independence were to prove particularly painful and bloody. The French administration left behind it a considerable number of poorly-housed people, and an urban fabric fragmented by the preceding strategies of the occupying army. Shanty towns which had sprung up under colonial rule flourished under the pressures of war. If we consider only Algiers, it is noteworthy that as early as 1954, that is to say the year in which the national liberation war broke out, the population of the city was 30 per cent Algerian, and of these 41.5 per cent lived in shanty towns.

Algerians made up nine tenths of the population of the country, but were very poorly represented in the cities. Urban centres were in practice virtually a privilege reserved for foreign residents. Only the native labour force needed by business and for various urban chores (maintenance, cleaning etc...) were allowed in.

Before the second forced displacement of the Algerian population in the course of the national liberation war (1954–62) barely 18 per cent of the urban population as a whole were Algerian; only one Algerian in five had any experience of city life. The independence struggle triggered bloody repression and the introduction of new procedures of 'urbanization in uniform' resting essentially on a policy of controlling freedom of movement.

To ensure that they retained control of the outlying areas and to cut the combatants off from the rural population, where most of them had their roots, the French army proceeded to round up peasants and their families in so–called group centres. There they were to be kept in enforced idleness on survival rations for seven years. This humiliating concentration led to the exodus of some sections of the rural population to the cities where they helped to swell the extent of shanty towns, whilst others preferred to flee daily extortion and seek refuge at the borders of neighbouring states (Tunisia or Morocco). As a result of different measures, one Algerian in two was displaced from his place of origin, a fate common to all wars of liberation.

'Normal' wars in which the opposing sides are countries, usually capitalist powers, essentially affect the urban areas where the industrial means of production are concentrated; popular guerilla warfare on the other hand is mainly waged in the countryside. The direction in which the population moves is in fact highly significant; in the course of the last world war Europe for example witnessed vast numbers of the population moving into the countryside which was thought to be less dangerous than the cities.

A colonial war follows a different logic. The countryside is the territory selected for national liberation struggles. This leads a section of the peasantry, caught between the contradictory pressures of the colonial army and the liberation army, to abandon their land and take refuge in towns and cities, seeking a frequently illusory protection. For the occupying troops it is also essential to make the land unproductive and to deprive the groups of combatants of logistical support. The forces of the colonial army need not concern themselves with their own food which is almost entirely imported from the mainland. There is therefore nothing to stop them from destroying villages and agricultural land as they wish.

Deprived of their land, the peasantry find themselves completely at the mercy of the 'liberality' of the colonial system. It was the peasant population, far more than the city–dwellers, which suffered during the war. Driven off their land, transported or interned haphazardly according to where military groups happened to be stationed, enrolled by force into the army, stripped of all they had, watched, numbered, reduced to food hand–outs, they were left essentially with no defences. And the land left fallow and often completely destroyed by napalm or soil erosion was to prove hard to cultivate.

We have seen the same process unfold in Vietnam and Cambodia. Successive waves of rural inhabitants driven out of the countryside expanded Saigon, later renamed Ho Chi Minh City, and Phnom Penh beyond all proportion. The cities were like huge parking lots containing an ever–growing number of unproductive arms and mouths to feed. When the occupying force withdrew, this pseudo–economy crumpled like a house of cards. The responses of the new powers confronted by this massive break–down, however, differed.

The Vietnamese government opted for a determined policy of recultivation of abandoned paddy–fields as the answer to reducing urban pressure, reviving agriculture and breaking up the mechanisms which underlay the huge market of unproductive consumers which the cities had become. Cambodia, more radical, used force. The cities had to be rid of whatever might recall the preceding period; hence cities were razed to the ground, their inhabitants slaughtered, to stimulate the rebirth of the countryside. Algeria chose to follow a policy of *laissez–faire,* a policy which in the long term also implies the need for greater effort and means to achieve it than a successfully implemented voluntarist option.

The housing left empty before the country regained effective independence was taken over by Algerians. Population movements did not wait upon the sanction of arms or of the ballot–box. Two months before the results of the self–determination vote which was to bring to an end over a century of colonial domination were out, the housing stock already had new tenants, a new character and above all a new rate of occupancy.

The departure of nine out of ten foreign nationals was to have two unexpected results: it provoked a destabilization of the urban order well–established in Algeria. The capital and other cities attracted peasants exiled from their land with no experience of urban life, but the capital also had some special fascination. It was here that power had been seized. Rural migrants were joined by salaried and administrative staff, more active and above all more able to adapt to the urban mores of the impending new society. The number of Algerians whose home or place of origin no longer existed was very great. Arriving from the borders or fleeing certain group camps these uprooted people flooded the roads all sharing a common destination: the city, often synonymous with the capital. Settling in the urban centres was the act which gave reality to the reconquest of their country. These hostages of war were to become the prisoners of a particular kind of city life. Algiers thus became one of the few examples in the world of a city which suddenly 'made' its inhabitants city–dwellers.

A singular piece of behaviour emerged during this period, a most rare urban phenomenon disproving the prejudiced notion of 'original sin' which constantly hangs over the inhabitants of shanty towns. They are systematically perceived as individuals with little regard for private property, unrepentant outlaws. The events at Algiers and the mass exodus of foreigners which followed showed that the very same people who are most excluded from urban society are also those with the greatest respect for order, despite the fact that they are often the first to suffer from it even when it is no longer in force. They break the law only insofar as the constraints of the law weigh too heavily on them, forcing them to adopt a position of 'self–defence'.

The inhabitants of Algiers' shanty towns were paradoxically the first to respect other people's property. For the most part they stayed in their huts while the city emptied around them, only to see it fill again and overflow onto them. Today most of them would explain or attribute their remaining in the shanty towns to their sense of civic duty. They would claim not to have dared transgress the order issued by the National Liberation Front calling for restraint and discipline.

The Algerian state could not but dispense justice and once installed in its functions and peace restored, would proceed with an equitable distribution between Algerians alone, since all the others had gone. There was therefore no hurry, no need to break the law. To each according to his deserts and his needs. Many believed this. The call to order was transmitted by the urban resistance movement using the same channels as during the national liberation struggle and reached the same population, those in permanent contact with the resistance. The others "didn't know anything"...! Totally unaware, or almost, of the situation, they moved into vacant properties without waiting for a share–out.

Neighbourhoods filled up haphazardly, or following chance encounters. The new occupants found it difficult to adapt to the distribution and internal organization of outward–looking flats with monofunctional rooms, having up till then lived for the most part in inward–looking housing in which they felt relatively at ease, however inconvenient or uncomfortable it was. The housing they had left behind contained multi–functional rooms; the courtyard, if there was one, was indispensable for allowing various daily activities. The new flats were more cramped even though they had more rooms. Ignoring the way a standard flat was designed to be used, they gave free rein to their imagination. The spaces had elastic sides. Multiple transformations subjected the built environment to rude and brutal treatment for which it was not intended. Hence the rapid deterioration of buildings and installations. Unable to remove all trace of the conquered, as the latter had done in their time, they settled for profaning and mutilating what they had left behind, rendering it unusable, even if this was later to rebound on them.

The diffident acts of reappropriation which we have rapidly reviewed deserve greater attention. Why did the shanty town population not rush to take over empty housing as they did for the spaces they occupied often illegally? Why did large families 10 to a room occupy only a 2 or 3 room flat for the most considerate, when the choice was wide open? Breaking the law for 3 to 6 room accommodation doesn't after all double the gravity of the fault. Why did young couples of modest income occupy bed–sitters rather than a big flat which could have held their large future family?

The housing stock freed in the capital by the mass exodus of the foreign population was sufficient to satisfy the needs of all badly–housed families. The housing stock abandoned by expatriates as a whole was at that time public property. Thus the new state (in Algiers) inherited 102,195 housing units and 11,996 professional premises. Responsibility for this housing stock was to be assumed in the most confused political, economic and judicial circumstances and managed by an inexperienced administration, leading to much abuse of power and a remarkable degree of indifference which accelerated the process of deterioration of the built environment.

The Phenomenon of Rapid Urbanization

On gaining Independence, Algeria found itself confronted with the complete disorganization of public services; technical and administrative records had been destroyed or removed by the boatload to France. The mass departure of the foreign minority nearly provoked a radicalization of the political situation. It also helped to strangle the economy, suddenly deprived of any technical infrastructure and of capital.

In the space of a few months, 900,000 foreigners living in Algeria left, including 33,000 heads of companies, 15,000 senior administrators, 35,000 skilled workers and nearly 200,000 people engaged in jobs requiring technical training or advanced–level education. The fall in investment, credit restrictions, dramatic price rises, the deserting

Ill. 1: Popular neighbourhood in Algiers (Foto: U. Opitz / TRIALOG)

of the countryside, the choked cities, industrial unemployment, and lastly the sabotaging of means of production by extremists characterized the transition period.

Moreover the economic development path selected by Algeria resulted in agriculture taking second place behind a supposedly 'industrializing' heavy industry. Bringing an abandoned plot of land back into use requires that the means of production of the villages be reappropriated and that a minimal subsidy be provided so that the peasants can survive until the first harvest and until they can once more take their place in their villages and in the national economy. None of this was done. Every effort was directed towards what had up till then been unthinkable: *the exclusive cities and heavy industry,* which while absorbing a great deal of capital provided but few jobs and many illusions.

Legal and illegal occupation was followed by a spate of moving. Repeatedly entering properties either to occupy them or to take what one wanted to set up house elsewhere, or to supply the second–hand stalls sprouting on every street corner, meant that violation of the privacy of the home no longer meant anything. It had lost all meaning in Algeria. For seven long years people were dragged from their homes at any hour of the day or night. Their homes were ceaselessly occupied without any justification by various civil and military uniforms. This was a time when if a family left their home for more than a few days, they ran the risk of finding some–one else installed there and no longer being able to reoccupy their own home. Moreover, how to prove that it belonged to them? An end had to be put to this urban mobility over which the State exercised little control.

Even today, this instinct has not totally disappeared. Anyone occupying a fine property will not go on holiday or even an overseas posting, until he has installed a 'trusted friend' until his return. One never knows.

The city of Algiers saw its population treble in less than two years after Independence. Having been declared the capital, it had to confront the many obligations to be fulfilled in the light of this new role. A section of the housing stock was allocated to diplomatic staff, another was requisitioned for the offices of a top-heavy administration, of a developing army, of ministries in full spate, of a party being reorganized, of any number of burgeoning national companies, etc. etc. These many functions proportionately reduced the availability of the housing stock and heralded the advent of an urban crisis which already needed solving and which had failed to be prevented.

The human and economic toll was to prove heavy. It was in circumstances that were new to everyone and in a particular atmosphere that the new authorities had to legislate, take decisions, and launch initiatives which would allow the management and growth of the cities against a background of the overall restructuring of the national territory.

In 1962, planning in Algeria was taking its first tentative steps, but it has nevertheless taken its place in the developmentalist mythology which considers it to be an indispensable recipe for stimulating development, in the course of which the objective sought is to focus the economy inwards and to break once for all with the colonial legacy of extroversion.

In the great surge of enthusiasm which followed the gaining of Independence urbanism might have looked like a poor relation in a country suddenly endowed with the manna of 'vacant premises'. Attention focused primarily on urban unemployment which was creating an explosive situation. Thousands of resourceless men just emerged from the djebel or recently arrived from the douars were waiting for the revolution to reach their daily lives. With this objective in mind, efforts were concentrated on the industrialization already set in motion in the context of the 'Constantine Plan'[2] the dogged pursuit of which was to lift the country out of under-development, and on education. Here then were the two widest wounds left gaping by a recent colonial past. The priority given to industrialization, and the insolvency of agricultural activities, was to release wave upon wave of human tide flooding into the cities. Driven from the countryside, and/or drawn by the mirage of the urban centres, this was the peasants' way of expressing their dissent. By their unwelcome presence in the city, they demanded their share of well-being and their right to the advantages of city life.

The response to this situation was merely to revise the existing urbanistic legislation. The period 1962–1974 confined itself to recalling French legislative texts. The principle of the ZUP (Urban Priority Zones) was adopted but its name given a more Algerian ring. The Algerian Bank for the Development of the Territory (CADAT), originally created in 1956, was reinstated. Later, in 1968, the presidential council set up a Permanent Committee for the Study, Development and Organization of Algiers (COMEDOR) to monitor directly the evolution of the city's urban fabric,

---

2) The Constantine Plan is a kind of mini-Marshall plan proposed by de Gaulle in 1955 in a speech made during his stay in Constantine. The basic idea was to convert the struggle for independence into a trade union claim.

demonstrating the importance accorded in high places to the management of space in the country's first city.

A great avalanche of abbreviated names came tumbling down to give the use of space a national flavour. Urban Development Plan (PUD), Urban Priority Plan (PUP), New Housing Zone (ZUHN), Urban Modernization Plan (PMU), Communal Development Plan (PCD), Property Development Plan (PAF) etc. ... without leading – and small wonder – to a genuine code of urbanism which would lay the foundations of a new long–term spatial distribution and which truly integrated the new political direction.

It was not possible to apply progress in stages in Algeria. Growing needs and a failure to grasp all the parameters, notably demographic and rural depopulation, encouraged the importation of inappropriate solutions, difficult to apply outside the social and economic contexts in which they had emerged. This new kind of consumerism deepened the sense of rejection of a system unable to apply solutions already tested (elsewhere).

Having seen the dangers of centralization, decentralization was put into effect in order to fragment the problems and make them accessible to local solutions.

Redistribution of the Urban Population

The new policy rested mainly on the collaboration of local collectives. But the problematical distribution of the national infrastructure meant that many communes were unable to play the role assigned to them in the second plan. They found themselves quite unable to define needs and to put into place the necessary infrastructure, or indeed to assume responsibility for undertaking or ensuring their operation. A map showing the distribution of the national infrastructure would provide a very useful indication of the partial implementation of the plans.

Lack of mobility of the skilled work–force is invariably linked to lack of housing and this restricts the freedom of industry to choose where to locate: the 1966 census estimated the population of Algeria to be 12,096,347 and the housing stock to be 1,979,888 units of which 1,423,253 were in durable materials, 352,652 in non–durable materials, and 203,983 of undeclared type, that is to say housing presenting a health hazard. Overall nearly one unit in two (45.8 per cent) was built before 1945. The older the construction, the more characteristically uncomfortable. Two thirds had no interior running water and no mains drainage and a similar proportion had neither piped gas nor electricity. Apart from this lack of services, the housing units were very small. One–room and two–room units each represented one third of the total. The habitable area moreover varied between 34 and 45 m². This tiny accommodation already housed more than 6 people (rate of occupancy = 6.1). These facts did not unduly alarm the supporters of the first two plans in the course of which not a single significant or concrete measure was envisaged to shore up the housing crisis apparent behind the figures.

If we compare the capacity of the housing stock and the number of jobs, we find that in 1966 there were 1.8 million housing units and 1,720,000 jobs, or a proportion of 1.04. In 1978, with 2,200,000 housing units and 2,830,000 jobs, this figure falls to 0.77, and if we compare the increase of 400,000 in the housing stock over the intervening 12 years with the number of jobs created in the same period, 1,100,000 (which is more accurate), the proportion becomes absurdly low, at 0.36 per cent. These figures show that while the accent was on employment, housing failed to keep up with industrial programmes.

The gap between the number of jobs created and housing units built hints at the (unstated) notion according to which housing problems relate to a sector generally restricted to assisted sections of the population and thus non-priority. To have regarded the sector as self-integrating, which in a crisis situation results in a whole series of consequences, is a strategic error on the part of the planners which has led amongst other things to the failure to control inter-sectorial relations and links and has resulted in the uncontrolled and uncontrollable fluidity of populations seeking urban housing options above all else.

Emergency Pre-fabricated Units

By 1970, the accent was on the industrialization of the building industry and 50 heavy pre-fabrication units had been created. Between them they had a production capacity of 35,000 units per year. The arguments used to justify their importation, savings of time and economical implementation, have never been substantiated. The average duration of site-work is 4 years and the units operate at some 30 per cent capacity. In the face of this inability to reach the theoretical production capacity of the systems, or to remove the obstacles to their being reached, foreign companies were called upon to deliver 'key-ready' housing. As for industry, the failure of this formula did not seem to dismay the promotors of this repeat performance. The outside 'helping hand' was to increase production, remove difficulties and address from the outset the problem of maintenance which they feigned not to be aware of at the time and which was to emerge in all its acuteness forthwith.

Ill. 2: A mass housing scheme attempting to respond to traditional Arab living patterns, and offering family privacy in spite of increased densities and modern technology   (M'sila, TRIALOG archive)

The programmes attracted the migration of individuals for whom building represents one of the best ways of becoming integrated into city life. It is the foot in the door which leads to a steady job, better paid and less dirty. Office corridors are jammed with desks behind which are entrenched 'former builders'. Those who have 'pulled off' their urban integration have got a place for life in these human parking lots. The urgency of the need to reduce the housing shortage resulted in projects being undertaken without the least preliminary survey, hence the badly located housing programmes disfiguring the landscape.

Villagization policies

The revival of rural Algeria demanded the political will and means equal to the questions it raised both with regard to housing and food. It was here that the effective fall-out of well-being on the Algerian people could be verified. The majority of the population was still concentrated in the rural world; it was there also that was to be found the greatest imbalance in the provision of collective services and the deepest poverty.

Long-neglected, rural Algeria manifested its dissatisfaction by regularly allowing its human surplus to overflow into the cities and choke them. It even threatened to cancel out the first results of the then current industrialization policy. Returning the land to the disinherited rural population to halt the flow into urban centres and giving them decent housing with facilities and services, in the framework of socialist villages, was now an urgent priority (Lesbet, 1984). This new organization was political (the Party providing the framework for the socialist village), economic (the integration of poor peasants into state cooperatives), as well as being spatial. It required the rational distribution of human groups with a view to restructuring the rural world and leading to a new redistribution, but this time planned, of the peasantry in relation to the creation of state cooperatives and the installation of services and infrastructures to be built at the same time as the villages.

After Independence the authorities chose to follow the example in this respect of fellow socialist countries who opted for development based on heavy industry at the expense of the agricultural sector, leading to a growing dependence on imports of basic foodstuffs. In a peasant household, all the active members, men and women (especially for growing vegetables and raising animals on a small scale), contribute to building up the family revenue. In the socialist villages, as soon as he has moved in the beneficiary of the housing must face up to the increased demands on his family. The house is supplied free, provided he is engaged in agriculture for five years; it has the two minimal features of domestic comfort (running water and electricity). The inclusion of these elementary signs of well-being implies a certain standard of social and economic behaviour, a specific rationale without which they would become a source of constraint and frustration. Moreover, one of the conditions for obtaining a 'modern house' was that the peasant beneficiary should live apart from his animals for hygienic reasons; this measure contributed to reducing the family's resources. Thus unable to submit to the obligations implied by this new life-style, the peasants attempted to adapt their 'modern' house to their modest condition. It is no

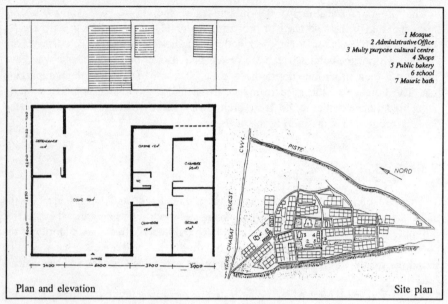

1 Mosque
2 Administrative Office
3 Multy purpose cultural centre
4 Shops
5 Public bakery
6 school
7 Mauric bath

Plan and elevation   Site plan

Ill. 3: Socialist Village 'd'Aurès el Meida', commune de Hammam Bou Hadjar

longer a case of a makeshift hut being improved, closely following increases in family income, ultimately to become transformed into a house in durable materials, but rather the 'modern house' being 'shantified' because of lack of means. A plastic bag fills in the gap left by a broken window pane that it is too expensive to replace; water no longer runs through the tap no-one understands how to repair; the broken tile which no-one knows how to make any more and which is too dear to buy is replaced by makeshift materials. Only the neat rows in which the houses were aligned recall the ambitious project this once was. It all happened as if one had tired of watching this peasant walking so far behind progress, and had given him a car to help him catch up, but in the haste to do so omitted to teach him how to drive, or to give him the wherewithal to obtain petrol for it, or to provide petrol and service stations along his way to ensure that he could maintain 'his' car. The existence of collective facilities, however necessary, remain insufficient to fill the void or the gap revealed by planning so long as the social and cultural dimensions so often indispensable to a smooth functioning are neglected.

The Agrarian Revolution and in its aftermath the creation of 1000 Socialist Villages completed an economic and political project based on a (tardy) ideological justification founded on social justice and national solidarity. The new territorial improvements organized, without preliminary study, the 'democratic' location of the rural population. This was presented as in line with the wishes of the poor peasant masses – for the authorities, it was a case of changing the 'peasant mentality', of transforming his relationship with the earth and of modifying the make-up of the social group to which he belonged in response to predominant urban values. The new village organization rendered obsolete his production methods, his previous home and his attachment to his place of origin.

The state dispossessed him of his values and transformed him into a worker-peasant, the model beneficiary of a housing type. In these circumstances, model projects and architectural languages are all equally foreign, be they French, Spanish, Soviet, Romanian ... or even Algerian. The points they share in common are:

- universality in time and place;
- designed by the same social level;
- for the same class, that of the dispossessed – the byword is beware – in a so-called underdeveloped country claiming to be guided by socialism.

Amongst the rural population of Algeria active participation in the creation of the living space, rather than any legal status granted, favours appropriation thanks to the links forged with the environment. Architecture which turns its back on the group's lifestyle is condemned to extinction or subjects the group which has to suffer it to destruction.

Access to 'decent' housing in the rural world (or even in cities) is the culmination of a complex economic process. It reflects an increase in revenue, but can be neither the starting–point nor the spring–board for an improvement in living habits, or if so only for the duration of a political season. This will be the case so long as housing programmes intended for low–income groups continue to be determined by:

- a theoretical life–style
- technical prowess, and
- magic words.

As a general rule, these suppositions are most often proved right at the expense of the very people whose standard of living one wishes to improve whilst taking account of their low economic capacity.

Today the houses offered to peasants in the context of socialist villages are simply places to live accommodating the beneficiaries. The latter attempt to adapt them to their low economic means, an activity which cannot be confused with the local life-style. The numerous adaptations (in self defence) which they undertake individually give the lie to the basis on which the theoretical life–style projected upon them was made.

The rapid deterioration of the villages today shows that the inhabitants are actually paying at inflated rates to put right the work that was hastily done in the name of respect for political deadlines to the detriment of serious workmanship. The villages could have been used as genuinely collaborative laboratories to launch a housing programme based on the massive use of local materials and drawing widely on the know–how of the rural population (Lesbet, 1988a). This approach, to which political lip–service was paid at the beginning of the operation, would have reduced costs, raised the rate of production and above all put into place or restored the family building maintenance system. In the few villages where the 'risk' of associating the peasants with their village project in the fields in which they were proficient was taken, these rare results were amply borne out.

Magic words, or political speeches, have been at the root of real social evils. The promises made at the time of the implementation of the Agrarian Revolution and the Socialist Villages damaged credibility and revealed the limits of real power of the political authorities in the face of their conservative detractors (political and religious).

The many kinds of cooperative set up at the same time as the villages have been largely disbanded. The Agrarian Revolution barely resembles a timid reform, the socialist villages have now been relegated to mere agricultural villages with no ideological connotations and have lost any political flavour.

The state's abandonment of a project which was to have transformed the future of the rural world heralded radical change and a fundamental re-evaluation of the nature of Algerian socialism. This failure in the countryside was to have an impact in the cities.

Urban policies

Much hinged on the outcome of the 1970s and 1980s: the country was anxiously waiting for the realization of the hopes raised by the implementation of an industrial policy which was supposedly industrializing. This was to stabilize the urbanized populations, or even provoke a return to the countryside, modernized and equipped with public facilities.

The lack of coherence and the inefficiency of the Agrarian Revolution accelerated still further the movement between country and city. The shockwaves caused by this flight to the cities were felt in the first urban centres (Lesbet, 1985).

The new migrants overwhelmed the ancient town centres, less able to resist them than other parts of the city. Oran, Constantine, Annaba and many more lost the greater part of their architectural heritage as a result. The qasbah of Algiers was in its death throes. In 30 years, more vernacular houses of great architectural interest were allowed to collapse than had been actively destroyed in nearly a century and a half of colonial rule.

Algiers had difficulty in absorbing the large numbers flooding in. The combined effects of demographic growth, amongst the highest in the world, of the premature aging of the housing stock as a result of lack of maintenance and critical over-occupation leading to an acute housing crisis were more and more apparent. Unable to hold out for long, the qasbah failed to survive the loss of its native inhabitants. Abandoned by its own, it was left to the uncertain mercies of supervisory administrations. It was also a victim of its own prestigious history; its ruins, formidable in the past, now give cause to fear the worst. The evacuations on which any thorough intervention is based obey reasons of state rather than respecting the architectural and urbanistic value of the dwelling.

Since Independence, nearly a thousand houses had collapsed or been demolished. Only 1,700 remained of which a mere 1,200 predated the French occupation. In 1987, a thousand houses were still standing and habitable. Amongst these one third are a health risk, another third are on the verge of crumbling; the remainder consist of houses well-maintained or in an acceptable habitable condition. The qasbah shelters within its walls 70,000 people, in other words nearly twice as many as were noted in

1830[3], and this in three times fewer houses. The qasbah is overpopulated. In certain areas there are more than 4,000 inhabitants per hectare.

During the period 1970–1986, the state allocated nearly 2,000 houses to the various disaster victims of the qasbah (the official figure was much higher) but these population transfers, sometimes on a huge scale, failed to achieve their objectives, which were to lower densities, or to allow the inception of planned operations. Moreover, this fleeing before the tide allowed rural people expelled from the countryside and drawn by the bright lights of the city to gain entry.

The squatter–occupied palaces and houses broke under the sheer weight of numbers. These population turnovers made of the qasbah a transitional space where it had once been a place of permanence and urbanity for generations. The qasbah ended up by being no more than a reflection of the marginal economic circumstances of its occupants, accelerating the decay of the built environment. The external interventions which followed sought above all to avoid the consequent social unrest. But in giving rise to occasional reactions to a continuous process over which they exercised no control, these interventions forged the links between the stages of a now classic scenario:

a) progressive deterioration of the built environment
b) collapse of the building
c) rehousing of the occupants of all the houses where there had been a victim, often regardless of the priority list established by the 'Atelier–Casbah'.

This process in effect promotes the demolition of the very sector which one wants to save, penalizes families who continue despite everything to maintain their homes, now overloaded (by natural growth), and who find themselves condemned to perpetual promiscuity precisely because they maintain their homes.

Analysis of the mechanics of the process shows that there is another approach which would restore a climate of confidence between inhabitants concerned with the future of their city and the Public Authorities. This cooperation is indispensable to the launch of any rescue programme equal to the task of putting a stop to demolitions for 'safety' reasons. What is needed is to put local know–how and the collective maintenance system, thanks to which the architectural heritage has been transmitted from one generation to the next, firmly back on the agenda. Instead of rehabilitating the engineering aspects of the locale (Lesbet, 1988b) renovation techniques more appropriate to bureaucratic workings than to the difficulties of the terrain have been imposed. Thus for over two decades now the absence of any clear and well–defined perspective on the destiny of this urban enclave has resulted in failure to confront the numerous rescue projects of the qasbah with the complexities of daily life.

Restoring the ancient town centres encourages long–established city families to stay in the urban centres. The latter then become once more the disseminating points from which radiate authentically local city habits. This is all the more important given that the country's cities, now choked, have not ceased to ruralize themselves.

---

3) According to Klein (Feuillets d'El Djazaï, p. 30, note 2) there were 40,000 inhabitants in 1830.

Thus 30 years after Independence, housing problems in general have not ceased to grow. Today we are forced to admit that the urban situation as well as the rural one shows that as they have continued to grow these problems have greatly overtaken the existing capacity to contain them.

To emerge from this dead–end, a number of measures have been adopted, the principal ones being:

- the creation of private building plots to increase the capacity of the housing stock;
- the sale of state assets to prolong the life of blocks of flats;
- the mobilization of savings plans to relieve public finances;
- and the latest hatched recipe, personalized housing.

Building Plots

Henceforth, communes will be held responsible for making their real–estate reserves viable and for selling land to citizens who have formed housing cooperatives. The objective of this operation is to put an initial 50,000 building plots onto the market and later to reach 100,000 plots (*El Moudjahid,* 1980), the magic figure targeted and never reached for the production of collective housing with pre–fabricated building systems. This achievement is now the target for individual houses, which is why communes are obliged to parcel out at least 200 plots per year.

The consequences of this policy risk being catastrophic. Fifty thousand building plots per year would have to be organized, i.e. 50,000 x 500 m² per plot = 25,000,000 m² not including space for infrastructure and services which would use 5,000 hectares. Thus to house 50,000 families, at 50 housing units per hectare, which represents a population density nearly 100 times lower than that of certain areas of central Algiers, it would be necessary to use a real–estate establishment 10 times greater.

This kind of promotion of individual housing would give rise to a multitude of private building companies. They would in turn compete with public programmes at all levels. They would greatly increase demand for skilled labourers, already scarce on the market. This is likely to encourage more pilfering of building materials from public sites for individual private projects.

Thus the population as a whole indirectly subsidizes a housing 'policy' from which the majority are debarred. Public prices are restricted to those who have building consent, the remainder obtaining their supplies at second, third or fourth hand and paying their materials 5 to 10 times their worth according to how many 'hands' they have passed through since they left the official market. In sum, whilst paying for their own houses, the poor are also financing 5 or 10 other dwellings for the rich.

In these circumstances, the approach of parcelling off plots has not 'democratized' access to housing. The building plots have allowed those whom the system privileged to hold onto their lead, to achieve their own housing while increasing the global capacity of the housing stock. They have also helped to reduce the dramatic and political tone of the housing crisis, by transforming this national issue into an individual problem. It has become normal, or at least 'democratically' acceptable, for those with several sources of income (it is virtually impossible to build an individual house in a city on a single salary, even that of a senior civil servant) to satisfy their desire for a detached house.

Paradoxically the fall-out from these actions as a whole, planned or otherwise, encourages the promoters of non-regulated housing and all who cannot gain housing by known (official) channels nor obtain their building material supplies at public prices, to seize their share of urban land directly and illegally. The latter subsequently will establish their own clandestine title to the urban land and thus direct official urbanization. New individual plots and collective housing programmes regularly spring up on the site of former shanty towns.

Evidence of this could be easily obtained by undertaking a simple quick survey to classify the social categories of those who have been able to build their homes either with their own means or with state help since Independence! It is not even necessary to compare the construction norms of builders belonging to social levels which are well-off and close to the government and others, always supposing there are any 'others' (Benamrane, 1984, p.103).

At the same time as the supply of housing was accelerating, new urban problems appeared resulting in disorderly growth in cities already scarcely controlled by the existing measures. Between 1966 and 1977 the number of private constructions (entaa-achaab: belonging to the people as they are known in popular language) illegally built has been estimated at over 45,000 in urban areas alone and the number of 'unplanned' public buildings, therefore equally outside the law, erected thanks to arbitrary credits drawn on the treasury funds of the fund companies of local collectives, at not less than 37,000 (Benamrane, 1984, p.79). Overall the number of illegal buildings put up in 1988 is estimated at 300,000 (Dossiers Constructions illicites, 1988).

The omnipresent housing crisis meant that the city municipalities were not always able to take the necessary time to do an overall study of the areas and the parcelled land in order to integrate them into the existing urban fabric or to make them correspond to current urbanism plans. All sorts of pressures put on the elected members of the commune made them allocate plots hastily, plots which were subsequently precipitately constructed. The result is often anarchic extensions which have unbalanced the city peripheries and accentuated the chronic deficit in collective facilities and services. Today, urbanism is re-active rather them pro-active ... the evident imbalances, anarchic development and the progressive loss of urban control on the part of the public authorities pose the serious problem of the management of the built environment of the population.

The Housing Finance System

The sale of housing simultaneously with building plots should in principle have enabled the state to get back a certain number of housing units. Each beneficiary of a plot had to commit himself to handing over the keys of his existing accommodation as soon as his individual house was completed. But this restriction was soon lifted given the size of the stakes at risk. Today, anyone can become a home-owner without any restriction other than having to pay for it.

The state had hoped in this way to relieve itself of an aged and mostly dilapidated housing stock. This operation met with a certain degree of success to begin with. Above all it allowed the occupants of detached houses to become home–owners. Tenants from collective housing blocks were less enchanted by the formula, apart from those who lived in well–maintained blocks.

The remainder prefer to (ir)regularly pay their modest rent.[4] Confusion with regard to rent is such that it is the inhabitants, the workers, who pay proportionately the highest rent (up to 50 per cent of their salary). "It is the minority occupying detached houses, at rents of 1 per cent of their salary, who scoff at socialism and produce the most active militants in favour of privatization." Some people are not convinced of their good fortune, particularly as in becoming the owner of old–fashioned housing, one also became responsible for its upkeep. The state sale of assets operation goes on in slow motion. The measure was enlarged to cover all of the public housing stock. But faced with dogged failure, every state housing beneficiary was obliged to sign an agreement to buy before the keys were handed over to him! Yet another 'specificity' of Algerian socialism. It is the state which incites to private property in order to make the citizen participate in the construction effort.

The state cannot continue to take financial responsibility for the accumulated housing deficit. On the other hand all the successive plans have never exhausted the budget limit set for housing, despite which savings are being mobilized.

In the national savings bank CNEP (Caisse National d'Epargne) it is not liquidity which is in short supply, but the utilization circuits to procure housing for the savers. A decree had to be promulgated to oblige other more powerful public administrations to allow the CNEP the possibility of allocation for a few savers who were not spared by the housing crisis. The CNEP collects several thousand millions each year, enough to house more than 50,000 savers annually. Savings amongst families in Algeria follows the market trend: the worse the shortages, the higher the savings. Never was the fall in savings so great as when the anti–shortages plan (PAP) was in force. One could find (almost) everything in the shops. Households then had (almost) nothing left to put on their savings accounts. In 1980 for example, a fine period of shortage, household savings totalled 3,671.4 million Algerian dinars. In 1981, when the PAP came into force, savings shrank dramatically, falling to 1,784 million dinars. And when PAP came to an end they shot up again reaching 4,154 million dinars in 1982 and 5,293.9 million in 1986. Savings had never been so high at a time of record shortages.

The accumulated savings had reached 44,545 million dinars by 30 September 1987, enough to finance several thousand houses. This money lies dormant in the form of bank bills in the coffers of the CNEP. If we add deposits on post–office savings (unremunerated other than by inflation) to these unused sums of money, the amount reached represents a considerable financial asset left unproductive in the various coffers of public organisations.

Thus savings in Algeria are a kind of barometer measuring the transformation of the poor distribution which regularly feeds the vicious circles of shortages rather than

---

4) In 1985, rent arrears totalled 1,000 million centimes.

reflecting the state of health of family finances. The clear improvement in standard of living of the population as a whole is another particularity of the Algerian system compared with other countries in the Maghrib. As far as Algeria is concerned, the problem is not how to finance housing but how to transform the money available in the state coffers and with the individual into housing!

Irregular cycles of supply result in circumstantial or chronic shortages. The launch of numerous special programmes and the implementation of plans have considerably increased demand for construction materials. Moreover the significant delay in development in this sector had not allowed supply to follow the demand curve and this despite massive recourse to importations. The response is to 'personalize to the maximum extent possible' (Lesbet, 1984).

This programme has theoretically been designed to avoid wastage of already scarce building materials caused by the fact that every new tenant carries out changes to his new home before moving in. It was suggested that the housing should be handed over to future occupants without paint–work, wood–work, tiling and plumbing so that the latter could adapt these to his own taste. But everyone knows full well that it is not to suit their taste that tenants undertake work under these four headings. They take on these jobs because in general doors and windows are badly made, tiling comes off the walls within a matter of days, taps drip etc... It is the finishings which leave a great deal to be desired. Unfinished sites are (obliged to be) handed over in the name of urgency and to avoid putting state companies in difficulties; (de)personalized housing is another way of side–stepping the serious problems which have multiple consequences and which have existed in an acute form for nearly twenty years: the shortage of building materials at the root of many interruptions in site work and the corollary of this, the poor quality of the finished product. So it is up to the future tenant to put up with poor workmanship, delays and additional costs since he is forced to obtain his supplies on the black market.

All the reasons given to explain delays in site work relate to obstacles which could be entirely removed particularly in a planned economy. No report mentions bad weather, strikes or other occasional and unpredictable impediments.

Housing: More Means than Ends

Building essentially relates to factories. Housing continues to be left to one side from the point of view of realization. But where finance is concerned, there are in fact problems in using all of the allocated budget! The finances available for housing were three times higher than expenditure utilized: 13,200 million dinars out of 32,500 million authorized (Table 1).

For urban housing, 44.6 per cent of the allocated budget was spent, but only 25.9 per cent of the programme was completed. This disparity can be explained by the difficulty public companies experience in managing the two contradictory objectives of the programme at once: to stay within planned charges and costs of implementation on the one hand, and on the other to guarantee full salaries to all employees regardless of the length of frequent interruptions in site work caused by machinery lying idle due to lack of spare parts, out–of–stocks due to lack of transport. Erratic

Table 1: Urban housing: spending and products at 31.12.1978

	Expenditure authorized	Expendit. taken up	%	Remaining amount	%	Housing units registered	Housing units handed over	%	Housing Units in progess	%	Housing units not started	%
Programmes agreed before 1974	3106	2640	85	466	15	47042	36441	77.5	9408	20.0	1193	2.0
Programmes agreed between 1974 and 1978	17834	6507	36.5	11327	63.5	147589	13893	9.5	100750	68	32946	22.5
TOTAL	20940	9147	44.6	11773	56.4	194631	50334	25.8	110158	56.6	34139	17.6

supplies are undoubtedly one of the greatest obstacles. The absence of building materials on site is often the pretext for costly down–time, for laying off workers, for interrupting the rate of progress. Some public companies are therefore forced to turn to the 'black market' for supplies to avoid overshooting deadlines, whilst at the same time keeping within the price per m^2 fixed in the plan.

Faced with problems in obtaining re–evaluations which take account of real costs, the operators prefer to reduce the number of housing units planned rather than take the risk of embarking on a re–evaluation process. Meanwhile, as the rate of implementation stagnates or lowers, the birth rate continues to rise and exert unrelenting pressure.

Outlook

Between the census of '66 and that of '77, the active urban population doubled, rising from 1,017,000 to 2,195,000. Jobs more than trebled from 682,000 to 2,020,000. The number of unemployed fell by half from 335,000 to 175,000 and in percentage terms unemployment went from 33 to 8 per cent. What the statistics fail to show is that only the active male population is taken into account. The overall population growth rate was 3.2 per cent over the last decade, whereas that of the urban population was over 5 per cent.

In 1977, the population rose to 17,386,484 and the number of housing units to 2,808,912. The rate of occupancy (ROA) also rose, reaching 7.9. The 1977 census showed that nearly 3 out of every 4 housing units belonged to the private sector.

In 1979, the population rose to 18,500,000 and 120,000 additional housing units were built. The ROA was then approximately 8 people. Using 1986 as a base, the deficit was already 700,000 housing units. This shortfall grew despite the huge amounts of money made available. It emerged during the 1980s that 91 per cent of the population live on 14.5 per cent of the surface area of the country. The urban population was already 43 per cent. If current growth continues, the urbanization rate will reach 60 per cent by 1990 and 75 per cent by the year 2000 (Lesbet, 1988a).

It is no easy task to find out the number of housing units in habitable condition as defined in the national charter. The overall housing stock was estimated at 2,785,000 in 1980, out of which half should be deducted as being in a state of decay, leaving some 1 million housing units for the country's 18 million inhabitants.

Table 2: Distribution of housing stock 1977

Left: by nature of occupancy (in % terms)		*Right: by construction type*
Moderate rent public housing ('HLM')		34,059 housing blocks
and public bodies	6%	3,153 commercial blocks
State–owned companies	2%	1,743,170 detached houses
Civil service	2%	139,856 traditional houses
State assets	16%	174 hotels and similar
Private housing	72%	9,768 other ordinary buildings
Undeclared	2%	75,381 mud/thatch houses and wooden sheds
		7,652 other improvised constructions
TOTAL	100%	440 'undeclared'

Between 1977 and 1979 150,000 housing units were built, 100,000 by the state and the remainder by the private sector, bringing the stock of decent housing units to 1,650,000 (Lesbet, 1985). In other words to have an ROA of 6, some 1,360,000 housing units would be required.

If we compare population growth projections with figures for the progression of the housing stock, there is cause for concern at the way the situation is evolving. During the first three plans (1966–1977) annual production was at 25,000 housing units; this then rose sharply to 97,000 units per year during the last 5–year plan (1980–1984), peaking at 100,000 in the last year. If we add to these figures private construction estimated at 125,000 housing units over the same period we reach a total of 428,871 housing units built between 1978 and 1984.

If we average the production figures for these ten recent years, which it will be recalled are the record, we get an annual production rate of 71,478 housing units. Albeit three times higher than that obtained during the decade 1966–1977, this figure remains woefully inadequate compared with what needs to be achieved by the year 2000.

Population growth alone already requires the building of 68,000 housing units per year, if only to catch up on accumulated shortfalls. At this very moment, more than one and a half million urban housing units are probably needed. Even if these were built, they would barely contain the situation, and to reduce the ROA to 7, more than 2 million would be needed. And yet during the period 1970–1985 only 425,000 urban housing units were built, equivalent to not even 30 per cent of the potential demand for the same period. There is an urgent need to consider how the 33 million Algerians who will be present at the end of the century will be housed.

Conclusions

The heavy toll of 130 years of colonial presence has resulted in the legitimate wish to make the national economy more inward–looking, to work for regional equilibrium, to give the country the heavy industry it lacked and to achieve a better distribution of agricultural land. These priorities were emotional imperatives rather than economic calculations worked out on the basis of the actual means available for completely achieving them.

Immediately following Independence, the active population of the country was predominantly agricultural. Rural inhabitants made up nearly one third of the population. Industrial potential was embryonic, the cities had emptied. The scale of the vacant housing stock relegated the production of the built environment to a later stage.

Industrial settlements reinforced the existing urban framework. Most investment was concentrated on the east–west axis along the coast. This manifested itself in a mass exodus on the part of the rural population to the extent of reversing the rural/urban ratio. This is a continuing trend. By the year 2000 nearly two–thirds of the population will be urban. 'Roadside' urbanization has bounded ahead and has far more impact than the urbanists' recommendations, leading to haphazard city sprawl to a greater or lesser extent.

The overflow from the larger overloaded towns and cities regularly floods into the small and medium ones located within their radius of influence until they are eventually absorbed into the perimeter. Towns and villages then become mere neighbourhoods or dormitory suburbs. Until now they have enabled the big conglomerations to flee before the tide by saving them from seizing up. But today, they too have reached saturation point. This combination of circumstances often elevates a simple village to the rank of the chief town of the commune or that of Daïra (sub–prefecture district) as a result of the ten–year reorganization (1974–1985). Special plans ('PS', 'PMU') then in turn sanction this political promotion. Such reclassification regularly results in practice in a series of investments, new public buildings (various civil service offices, education, health, police, justice, party etc...) and in the arrival of many civil servants. All this serves to start the site snowball rolling again. *Urbanization thus becomes for a longer or shorter period of time the driving force of local development,* of which it is alternately a symptom and a cause of regional growth.

The shortage of housing in urban areas results in an inability to accommodate all who aspire to city life. New arrivals (demographic or immigrant) occupy the tiniest spaces in housing blocks (permanently pushing up the ROA) or settle on 'free' ground, continually widening the spread of these unregulated neighbourhoods. This is the weak link in the cities' chain, making them unpredictable; where 20 years ago they absorbed new arrivals without distinction, today they impose a strict segregation on those aspiring to live in them.

Shanty towns, considered by some to be a sign of dynamism amongst an economically weak social class, and to represent the failure of an over–ambitious economy by others, progressively urbanize the peripheral land with each successive invasion.

Ill. 4: Housing project in Maader, near M'sila, using local building materials. The plan, incorporating central courtyards, was designed with participation of the users. *(1980, TRIALOG)*

A plan to clean–up the urban centres launched three years ago aimed to improve the cities' image. It consisted in expelling all the inhabitants who had not managed to find accommodation in a building not (yet) declared a health hazard during their stay in the city, and returning them to their place of origin with a promise not always honoured of housing for the family, jobs for those of working age, and school places for children at school.

This city clean–up operation has revealed that the greater part of the work–force responsible for relieving the city of *household rubbish* lived in this *urban 'rubbish'*. The vast majority of the wholesalers employed on the sites intended to improve the appearance of the capital live in the shanty towns. All building works were therefore slowed down. Paradoxically, in throwing the shanty town inhabitants out beyond the perimeters of the old town centre the image of the city suffered even more. This (un)expected result then resulted in expulsions being made selectively. Only the households whose working members were not indispensable to the running of the city were removed. This shows the important part played by standardized housing in stabilizing the labour–force indispensable for urban management.

Simply making the materials and tools needed for the maintenance and repair of housing blocks available on the market would encourage the formation of small businesses of which there are not enough at present. This would usefully mobilize the army of unemployed stationed in the cities.

The constant imbalance between supply and demand regularly adds to the list of 'scarce' products making maintenance prohibitively expensive and therefore selective whilst increasing the influence of the informal sector on the national economy.

But in the case of Algeria (as in other socialist countries) the informal sector is more a reflection of the purchasing power of households (great money availability) than the result of their inadequate supplies. Speculation on rarity value relates to 'extras' (cars, videos, records, imported clothing) and essentially building materials whereas in developing countries with so–called liberal economies the informal sector is maintained mainly by basic foodstuffs.

The efficiency of the informal sector in socialist countries is due not to the skill of the actors but rather to their position in the (bureaucratic) hierarchy of the distribution chains. The informal sector for luxury goods drains household savings mainly so that they can acquire some distinguishing sign, a rarefied 'superficial' product, but this is only possible because the state takes almost complete financial responsibility for the three heaviest and most important budget items, health, education and housing. The first two are free (care completely covered even abroad for serious illnesses and grants for further education studies either within the country or abroad);[5] as for the third, rents are widely state–subsidized. The state does not take account of the real cost of the accommodation; for example in Algeria the cost per habitable m^2 is twice as high as in France although the minimum wage is half that of France, whereas rent for medium–sized accommodation (a three–roomed flat) is approximately ten times lower. In the final analysis it is the political system rather than the shadowy world of the black–market circuit which ensures the 'performance' and the 'efficiency' of the so–called informal sector in so–called socialist countries.

The city harbours an important potential of workers trained on–the–job now qualified and familiar with public building works. These can be efficiently used to launch a gigantic essentially urban housing programme which should be implemented in the course of the next decade and above all to start the work of repairing the cities showing signs of overall decay.

The accumulated housing shortage precludes the efficient management of space and contributes to the disorganization of the land system. Urgency is the by–word for every activity. The 'specificity' of the situation permits all possible architectural and urbanistic aberrations. Real–estate control is proportionate to the importance of the housing crisis. This is what conditions the weight of pressure exerted on local elected representatives, actors and practitioners.

The provisional urban plans (PUPs) have been made definitive. The master–plans are often called into question after they have been approved. In this context, control over land can only succeed fully if the direct and indirect injunctions, largely in response to the housing shortage, and which contribute to urban confusion are greatly reduced. It is for these reasons that we have chosen housing production in the approach we have adopted to review issues relating to urbanization in Algeria.

Taken together the facts show that the solution to the problems of the city is more than ever conditioned by property control and urban management. In vain might we seek to find a makeshift solution through an illusory return to the countryside by forced expulsions from the urban centres to the birthplaces of a section of the most dynamic of the active population. The latter have assumed responsibility for their own housing problems by finding a 'solution' in keeping with their skills and according to the possibilities offered by settlement area. They have often been behind a (pragmatic) officious urbanism. Trained in various building trades they participate fully in urban maintenance and the growth of the ancient town centre.

---

5) The drop in crude oil prices in the world market forced the Algerian state to cut down the number of students sent abroad with a government scholarship.

References

Benamrane, Djilali (1984), *Crise de l'Habitat. Perspective de développement socialiste en Algérie, 1945–1980,* Algiers, O.P.U.
'Dossiers Constructions illicites, régulariser oui, mais ...' (1988), *Algérie Actualité,* no. 1185, 30 June.
El Moudjahid (1980), (official daily national newspaper), 6 May.
Klein, Henry (n.y.), *Feuillets d'El Djazaïr.*
Lesbet, Djaffar (1984), *Les 1000 Villages Socialistes en Algérie,* Paris: Editions Syros.
Lesbet, Djaffar (1985), *La Casbah d'Alger,* Edition CNRS, O.P.U., May.
Lesbet, Djaffar (1988a), *Les coûts d'un logement gratuit,* O.P.U., September.
Lesbet, Djaffar (1988b), 'La Casbah d'Alger entre réhabilitation et réanimation', *Revue Peuples Méditerranéens, numéro spécial, 'Les Urbanistes dans le doute',* no. 43, Paris.
'Logement à prestations réduites, les économies qui coûtent cher', *Algérie Actualité,* no. 1183, 16 June 1988.
Review of urbanism sector by the Ministry of Urbanism, Building and Housing (1980), Algiers.

Further reading:

El Kadi, Galila (1984), 'La démocratisation du logement en Algérie', Burgel, Guy et al. (Eds.), in: *Le logement, l'état et les pauvres,* Talence: CNRS, 37–58.
EPF-Z / Imesch, H. (Ed.) (1978), *Villages Socialistes Agricoles en Algérie* (2nd ed.). Zürich: Verlag der Fachvereine an den Schweizer Hochschulen.
Maurer, G. (1979), 'Les villages socialistes en Algérie', in: Equipe de Recherche Associée no. 706, Urbanisation et nouvelle des campagnes au Maghreb, *Fascicule de Recherche no. 5,* Poitiers: Centre inter-universitaire d'études méditerranéennes, p. 107.
Mutin, Georges (1986), 'Aménagement et développement d'Alger', *Bulletin de la Société Languedoc-ienne de Géographie* (20), 2–3, Montpellier, pp. 299–318.
Nacer, M'Hamed and Sutton, Keith (1987), 'Regional Disparities and Regional Development in Algeria' in: Forbes, Dean and Thrift, Nigel (eds.), *The Socialist Third World. Urban Development and Territorial Planning,* Oxford: Basil Blackwell, pp. 129–167.
Opitz, Ursula (1984), 'Partizipation in Algerien: Anleihe bei alten Traditionen?', in: *TRIALOG* 4 (October), pp. 12–15.
Sutton, Keith (1982), 'The Socialist Villages of Algeria', in: *Third World Planning Review,* vol. 4, no. 3, 247–264.

Vietnam

Ngyên Duc Nhuân and Kosta Mathéy

The Two Vietnams[1]

Vietnam's history is marked by repeated wars and long periods of foreign occupation. This fate probably helped in the spread of communist and liberation movements: the first nationalist organizations were founded in the 1920s under French occupation, and a Marxist–Leninist party appeared in 1929, joining with similar movements in neighbouring countries in 1930 into the *Indochina Communist Party*. Its founder, Ngyen Ai Quaoc, adopted the name Ho Chi Minh, under which he became the symbol of the liberation war in the 1960s and 1970s. When the Kampuchean and Laos sections of the party split away in 1951, it adopted the name 'Workers' Party' in Vietnam, until it was changed again into the *Communist Party of Vietnam* at its fourth congress in 1976.

Ho Chi Minh founded a people's army known as the *Viet Minh* (League for Independence) including workers, peasants and the petty bourgeoisie in the Second World War to fight Japanese occupation, which was overthrown in 1945. An independent *Vietnamese Democratic Republic* was subsequently proclaimed but not allowed a peaceful life since the French troops tried to recover their former colony. It was only after another nine years of fighting that the French were eventually conquered in 1954. A peace plan was drawn up in Geneva foreseeing free elections in the whole of Vietnam, and requesting the *Viet Minh* troops to withdraw north of the 14th parallel. However, once the freedom fighters had fulfilled that condition a shadow regime was installed in the South with foreign help without holding elections, in breach of the Geneva treaties. This regime, however, failed to win the necessary popular support to sustain life on its own. With increasing US intervention the

---

1) Most information in this introductory section was taken from the *Vietnam* chapter in the *Third World Guide 1989/90*.

275

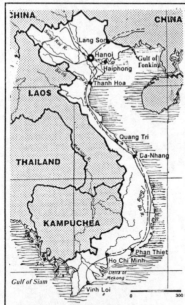

Country Profile: Vietnam

National territory: 329,556 km²
Population: 60,920,000 inhabitants (1986)
Population density: 174 inhab/sq.km
Labour force: 28,755,000; 62% in agriculture, 19% in services, 10% in industry.
Urbanization rate: 26%
Capital: Hanoi; 2,570,905 inhabitants (1979)
Average natural growth rate: 2.6% (1973–84)
Life expectancy:
    55.7 years for men; 59.2 years for women
Infant mortality: 5%
Illiteracy rate: 16% (men 9.5%, women 21.7%)
Religion: mainly Buddhist, also traditional religions, Catholics, sects.
Language: Vietnamese (official), ethnic dialects
Major export products: wood, minerals
Major markets: USSR, Japan, GDR, Hong Kong, France
Foreign assistance: $ 1,392.8 million (1985); sources:
    82% CMEA, UNDP 11%, OECD 4%, OPEC 1%

Some important dates:

207 B.C.	Kingdom of Nam Viet
938	Independence obtained from China. Formation of *Dai Viet* dynasty
1804	*Dai Viet* is renamed *Viet Nam*
1858	French colonization, fragmentation into three 3 parts: Tongking, Anam, Cochinchina
1920	First nationalist movements were created
1929	Marxist–Leninist parties appear in different parts of Vietnam
1930	Communist parties unite into *Indochina Communist Party* under Ho Chi Minh
1940	In World War II Japan occupies Vietnam
1945	At Japan's surrender the Vietnamese resistance alliance under Ho Chi Minh takes control of the country and declares independence. Renewed attempts by France to recover former colony. Continuation of armed resistance struggle.
1954	Final defeat of French army. Geneva Agreements provide for elections in 1956, provided that the revolutionary troops withdraw to the north
1955	The USA reinstates a puppet regime in the South, violating the Geneva Agreements. Beginning of the 'second liberation war'.
1964	Beginning of open US war in Vietnam
1969	US troops in Vietnam reach 580,000. Beginning of Paris peace talks
1969	Death of Ho Chi Minh
1974	Peace treaty signed in Paris
1975	Military victory of revolutionary army over US troops in South Vietnam. Exodus of 'boat people' starts
1976	Re-unification of Vietnam under the name *Socialist Republic of Vietnam*, general elections held.
1979	Chinese invasion of northern Vietnam. Number of 'boat people' increases
1980	Six severe typhoons devastate Vietnam, then a drought, then floods; resulting in famine
1981	US president Ronald Reagan declares an embargo on grain shipments to Vietnam and blocks UNDP emergency help programme
1984	Sixth party congress confirms policy of self-sufficiency in key sectors
1986/87	Resignation of several old political leaders. New leadership starts with campaign against corruption and incompetence.

Sources: Die Länder der Erde, Köln: Pahl–Rugenstein, 1982. Third World Guide, Montevideo: Third World Editors, 1988.

liberation war escalated to a horrifying scale destroying South and North alike. After another fifteen years of fighting Saigon, the capital of the South, fell in 1975. Elections were eventually held in 1976, unifying the country under the name of the *Socialist Republic of Vietnam.* Reconstruction was begun with international aid from the East and the West alike.

However, peace did not last for very long. In 1979, Vietnamese troops entered Kampuchea, and Vietnam was invaded itself by Chinese troops from the north. The country became politically isolated with the consequence of almost all foreign development suspended save for that from the USSR, which remained one of the few allies. Apart from the military expense the economy was hit by several natural disasters, and suffered a US trade embargo imposed by President Reagan.

The devastating economic situation called for imaginative emergency policies. The sixth party congress in 1984 put the main emphasis on self-sufficiency in the key sectors. The party leadership, however, most of them elderly and associating themselves with orthodox communist principles, continued to follow a centrally planned austerity policy, until most of them died or resigned around 1986. In the same year, at the December 1986 congress, the new leaders started an attack against corruption and bureaucracy, and introduced radical reforms in all sectors of the economy. A surprising step was the proclamation of a so called *'market socialism'.* This implied the legalization of private enterprise in almost all sectors, self–financing of state enterprises and provisions for joint public–private ventures. Credit now became accessible, at least in theory, to all kind of enterprises including private firms and co–operatives.

Particular effort was made to attract foreign capital which may now freely invest in Vietnam, for example in the construction of hotels and holiday homes. Most earnings from foreign exchange are expected to come from the large numbers of Vietnamese living abroad but which still have part of their family inside the country. These people used to send home consumer goods such as sewing machines, TV sets etc. As an alternative they were now given the opportunity to build and own individual houses for their relatives inside Vietnam, paying in dollars but relying on local resources. Special savings banks were set up, and some of them draw up to 40 per cent of their revenue from abroad.

The turn towards 'market socialism' was also applauded by most foreign and international donors which had interrupted their aid after 1978 as a response to Vietnamese military involvement in Kampuchea. The World Bank, for example, has sent a mission and is negotiating terms for new development projects in Vietnam.

Housing and National Development

Like most revolutionary and Marxist regimes Vietnam concentrated its reconstruction and development efforts in the production sector, to which some 90 per cent of the budget was dedicated, and specific emphasis was laid on heavy industries (particularly prescribed in the First Five–Year Plan, 1960–1965). Housing and urban policies were attributed to the sphere of consumption and received no more than 2 per cent of the budget, at least before 1986.

But even the combined budget for production and consumption together was obliged to operate on a shoestring because of increasing military expenditure representing 20 per cent of the budget in 1975–1979, but rising to about 40 per cent thereafter. Before unification in 1975, the military share was, of course, much higher still, reaching 60 per cent of the budget, but most of that expense was then reimbursed by other socialist states, the Soviet Union and China in particular. Linked to the preoccupation with industrial military investment rural development was not given much attention. Agriculture only obtained directly a fifth of central budget spending, although the population of the country was 74 per cent rural. The only exceptions were isolated big projects such as dams or mining projects, but by their very nature these kind of investments did not directly benefit the rural population.

Inside the consumption sector priorities were given to health and education services. For housing, again the biggest share went to the urban areas, since self-building with local resources continued to be common practice in the countryside. To this should be added, however, that traditionally Vietnam has a relatively rather decentralized administrative structure with rather high local budgets, which may be distributed according to local priorities.

The policy reforms after 1986 also marked a U–turn in Vietnamese housing policies, by attributing housing and infrastructure provision the fourth priority after agricultural production, consumer goods, and exports. In March 1989 special (region-al) co–operative savings banks were set up with the objective of specializing in hous-ing finance and to serve projects proposed by the central or local government, nation-al or foreign private investors. As far as foreign funds for housing are concerned, the majority are invested in towns in Southern Vietnam and the countryside in the North, since these are the overpopulated areas from where most Vietnamese working abroad originate. There are no attempts, for the time being, to channel foreign investments into particular sectors or regions; such a policy would be difficult to implement, and the prime interest is earnings for foreign exchange anyway.

Spatial and Political Organization

In line with traditional habits local government has been relatively decentralized and autonomous since 1955 in the North and since unification in 1975 in the South. Formal administration is based on urban *boroughs (arrondissements)* in the towns and *rural districts* in the countryside (including the green belts), both comprising some 100,000 to 200,000 people on average. The boroughs are subdivided again into *quarters* and *blocks* (neighbourhoods or housing estates). All these units, except for the *blocks* as the smallest units, are organized in so called *'popular committees'* with directly elected deputies at the quarter and district/boroughs level. In theory this system of local self–administration is separated both from the party[2] and government,

---

2) The Communist Party is the only legal party in Vietnam. Until a few years ago there were a number of smaller political parties registered as well, like the Socialist Party or the Democracy Party, but in practice they depended on the Communist Party, to which their leaders (presidents, secretaries, etc.) also belonged.

but in practice it is not: the president and vice president of these committees tend to be members of the Communist Party too. *Street committees* and *block committees* are more informal today. Before 1986 they were formally established entities and used as a main instrument of political control and policing by the state. Due to that function they became most unpopular and practically ceased to operate.

As in other socialist countries there also exist a number of *mass organizations* that have an increasingly decisive role as compared with the people's committees. Noteworthy examples among these are the women's association, the trade unions, the youth clubs, the old people's associations, the intellectual patriots, the Buddhist patriots, the Catholics Association. Among all the mass organizations the women's organization appears to be the most active one. It takes care of families which suffer extraordinary housing problems, runs kindergartens for women who are at work, and – in recent years – has fought for equal rights including greater representation in the administration of the workplace and the right to live alone or together with other women without a male head of household.

The mass organizations, too, are often led by party members, but are more linked to day–to–day concerns of the people, including neighbourhood tasks related to the upkeeping to the habitat. For example, the running of the local library or the health station, and keeping them clean, are typical responsibilities apart from vigilance at night. On the so called *'red Saturdays'*, or *'communist Saturdays'*, they engage in voluntary clean–up campaigns in the street, tree planting, anti–erosion measures and similar activities. All residents are supposed to take part in these exercises: farmers in the countryside are obliged to work some 50 days per year in voluntary collective labour to complete infrastructure work; in the cities only 20 days are required from each person. This obligation is, however, not personal and many people send a (paid) deputy.

In the countryside the collectivization of the productive forces and the concentration of the population in co–operatives following the Chinese model was promoted by the government from 1958 onwards, but took a long time to complete. "The co-operatives were also a measure for promoting political integration. The personnel resources of the Workers' Party were insufficient to oversee the daily workings of the co–operative, which were thus entrusted with responsibility for ensuring public participation in day–to–day decisions affecting individual welfare." The co-operatives' network was to play a crucial part in the war effort, for it provided a form of territorial organization that maximized the possibilities of achieving local-level economic self–sufficiency and assisted decentralized political decision–making. Both were critical ingredients in the ultimate success of the 'people's war' (Forbes & Thrift 1987:105–6, referring to Elliot, 1975, and White, 1982). Some of the agricultural co–operatives were dissolved after 1986, allowing them to devote more time to work for their individual income, and lessening the obligation to participate in collective work – with the result that infrastructure is deteriorating.

Land Policy

In socialist Vietnam the land belongs to the state, both in urban areas and in the countryside, but user rights are granted to individuals. After the revolution private land owners had been expropriated without compensation in the North, and after unification in the South. However, this measure was not considered to be a particularly harsh policy, since temporary user rights over the soil were customary in Vietnam and used to expire after five years of not cultivating or living on the ground. The Roman law and its concept of private property over land had only been introduced by the French colonizers.

Until the reforms of 1986 the transfer of land use rights could not made directly between individuals or corporate owners such as co-operatives, but needed to be handed back to the local authorities which would handle registration and authorization of landownership through its *'offices of land and housing'*. The surface of houses, however, could be traded, and this implied user rights over the land. But there was no land market as such, and no land speculation. Following the anti-bureaucracy crusade in 1986, the state legalized the exchange of sites between individuals. However, since no mechanisms to control the prices have been found or implemented so far, speculation is on the increase again: within two years prices for prime sites in *Ho Chi Minh City* (the former *Saigon*) have gone up 10 to 15 times; in *Hanoi* increases were smaller but still reached 300 or 400 per cent.

There are certain *minimum* standards set for urban plots to be developed for housing. In respect to the maximum sizes it is rather the people themselves who are hesitant to exceed a certain limit, and do not dare yet to visibly expose any excessive capital they were able to accumulate. In the countryside the typical plot sizes including a vegetable garden range between 100 and 300 square metres.

Urbanization and Deurbanization

The classic communist discourse about the structural imbalance between 'consumer towns' and the 'producing' rural areas was also found in Vietnam, at least until 1985. But unlike in certain other socialist states, such as Kampuchea, there was not a wholesale refusal of cities as such; the objective was rather to urbanize the countryside, and to achieve a rational and balanced population distribution among the different provinces. In this sense it was an explicit policy to reinforce the provincial administrative centres and some 600 district towns (the latter with a target population of around 10,000). All towns, from the two big cities of Hanoi and Ho Chi Minh City down to the district towns, were surrounded with agricultural *'green belts'* permitting at least 30 to 40 per cent food self–sufficiency. Inside the cities, however, there was no declared policy to promote urban farming, but the worsening economic situation, particularly after 1979, forced many citizens to supplement the official food supply with small livestock and vegetables which they could grow in their gardens – even within the middle of Hanoi. The reforms after 1986 also affected the green belts: farmers in the green belts are now allowed to diversify their crop production to include vegetables and fruits, for example, whereas before the policy was to produce staple food – such as rice and cereals. The peasants may now also sell their products on the market, with the effect that periurban farmers have become the most affluent section of society over the last few years (and build the most expensive houses).

There was, however, much concern not to allow the biggest cities to grow any further. One of the instruments to serve this purpose is the refusal of credits for new buildings or for repairs in the city centres of Hanoi and Ho Chi Minh City.[3] There was, however, considerable rebuilding in the periphery (satellite towns) of Hanoi after 1975, to repair war damage. Another measure limiting the uncontrolled growth of the big cities was strict migration control until 1986, requiring special permits to travel between the countryside and the urban areas, or even between rural areas of different provinces. As free movement is now possible everywhere in the country, urbanization rates are bound to increase sharply. As a counter–policy the government is promoting the development of medium–sized cities, in addition to the previous district town strategy. Unfortunately there are no special employment programmes linked to this effort thus thwarting its effect; the main incentives for the population to move are better accessibility to services, rationing vouchers, and legal status.

The objective to achieve a more even distribution of the population over the whole country, and to restrict the growth of the major cities, also implied massive resettlement, and various programmes – not only directed to the urban population but also for moving the rural population away from densely populated areas – can be identified in specific periods (namely the Second and Third Five Year Plans, 1976–81, and 1981–86). In total about three to four million people were moved in these resettlement programmes, or 6 per cent of the entire population. About half of this number, two million, came from the big cities, the rest from the overpopulated rural areas or from within the same provinces.

Between 1975 and 1979 there were large scale transfers of population from the big cities towards so–called *model villages* and *new economic zones*. This measure affected small businessmen in particular. In the South they had benefited from the war situation before but were not considered economically useful elements once commerce had been monopolized by the state. This resettlement process was, however, much less violent than in Kampuchea, for example, since many of the urban poor were of rural origin. They had only come to the city because of the war, and were happy to return to the countryside. If there was pressure exerted upon the people to move then this happened in an indirect manner, through the (non–) allocation of food rationing vouchers, schooling, health and other social services. Sometimes migration was the only way to benefit from these services.

The model villages programme was started around 1976, representing some 20 to 30 per cent of all transfers. The new settlements were relatively well equipped due to international aid including aid from the World Bank and UNICEF. But since this aid dried up in 1978 the programme has been discontinued.

The establishment of *New Economic Zones* started slightly later and concentrated on the north and south west. "A number of New Economic Zones were established

---

3) Unlike the smaller towns which enjoy a certain autonomy in their investment policy, the biggest cities, like Hanoi and Ho Chi Minh City, are directly dependent on the central government, allowing it to control building and other investment here.

along the Kampuchean border, primarily composed of soldier–civilian settlements, and designed to act as a buffer. Another focus of resettlement was the central Highlands, again with security reasons in mind for this is an area where non–Vietnamese minorities have long been active in resisting centralized rule" (Forbes & Thrift, 1987:116). Many of the New Economic Zones have become a disaster due to bad planning, lack of finance, and other reasons. Because of this some of the settlers returned to the cities as small businessmen, or left the country among the so–called *'boat people'*. After 1982, the resettlement slowed down considerably because of the economic sanctions on behalf of the international community. Transfers from the cities towards the countryside were stopped in 1986, but they continue from overpopulated areas to other rural zones.

Housing Provision

Due to over 30 years of war economy and direct destruction there is an extreme shortage of housing in Vietnam, but conditions vary widely from one place to another. For example, whereas in Ho Chi Minh City in 1976 some fourteen square metres of living space per person was usual, there was only 1.5 square metres in Hanoi (Forbes & Thrift, 1987:126), with the target to increase the standard to 6 square metres by the year 2000. Also among different parts of the same city there can be a significant variation in the quality of services, particularly health and education. In the countryside the picture is characterized by the traditional arrangement of privately built and owned farmhouses and huts of moderate standard.

The Public Sector

The constitution states that everybody has the right to housing, education, health etc. but there is no explicit obligation by the state to provide this. Nevertheless, in the urban periphery the state has built housing for renting in large collective estates since the 1960s, now representing about 30 per cent of the urban, or 3 per cent of the total stock. A similar proportion of rented accommodation is managed by the state on behalf of former big landlords. The previous owners were never expropriated, but the state retains the maintenance costs, which were always higher than the rents, which are very low at one to three per cent of income (the same as for state built housing). Therefore many owners preferred to sell their property to the state to receive a meagre compensation at least. The share of the state–controlled sector varies according to region; in the big cities, including Hanoi, it is about 30 per cent of the stock. In the smaller cities the provincial governments also build housing for rent.

Access to state or municipal housing is largely reserved for civil servants and members of the army, who have a statutory right to a two bedroom flat, and who, in order to top up their salaries, tend to sublet these units to others if they do not use them themselves. At the end of a tenancy the occupant is supposed to hand back his apartment to the state so that it can be allocated to the next applicant on the waiting

Ill. 1: Multi-storey housing is being built in spite of lack in modern equipment
(Foto: Lars Reuterswärd)

list. But more common is the practice of presenting subsequent tenants to the rent officer who is prepared to bend the rules in exchange for a bribe, and there is no secret about the widespread corruption in all aspects of exchange of public housing.

With the reforms of 1986, there is also public house building in the countryside reflecting the new priority to develop the agricultural sector, but the most radical innovation is house–building for sale by the state. This activity happens in addition to the state's commitment to build for rent, which remained at the same volume as before. The increase of the total production volume was possible because this new programme does not imply such huge subsidies as renting does (at the ridiculously low rents). It is almost self-financing.

Since 1986 collective housing can also be built by housing co–operatives – an innovation. These co–operatives may be formed by enterprises for the purpose of staff housing or by individuals. Both categories obtain credits from the housing bank. Private co–operatives often use self–help for construction, whereas the enterprises which operate a housing co–op may also exchange products and labour in kind with other enterprises if they do not happen to employ their own construction unit. Occasionally their own staff also contributes unqualified labour to the construction of these units in periods of work stoppages (through interrupted supply of raw materials, spare parts or other reasons). The dwellings are handed over into owner occupation after termination, and their monthly cost (repayment of the credit) is considerably more expensive than state rented housing, but it is available much quicker. In fact, the cost may reach 90 or 100 per cent of the (official) income; but since the monetary income is so low and supplemented by the social wage (i.e. in the form of supply vouchers) and by the secondary informal sector incomes it remains within the affordability of the owners.[4]

The Private Sector

Private subletting is common practice and represents maybe 20 per cent or more of urban housing supply. It is tolerated by the state, though not explicitly permitted. There are of course no contracts or price control (and no taxes) for this kind of tenancy, but due to the extralegal situation subletting is usually an arrangement between relatives or friends and implies reasonable levels of rents.[5]

Owner occupation is estimated at about 40 per cent in the cities, but up to 100 per cent in the countryside. Owners can sell their houses freely and are not restricted by any price controls. There is no established mechanism for the exchange of dwellings; people normally make use of the advertising sections in the newspapers, and official documents about the ownership of the dwellings are issued at the ward or city committee.

In theory individuals can also build new houses for owner–occupation, but in practice this has remained an exclusively rural phenomenon – at least for the last few years. One reason for this being so is the high costs involved, and the appearance of housing co–operatives which are offered much more favourable terms for credit than individuals. For example, a three bedroom house with a small shop at street level would cost 1.6 million *Dong* in 1987–1988, at a time when a good salary was 20,000 Dong. (House price = 6.6 yearly incomes.) Self–builders may buy the formal occupancy right for a building plot from the state, and recently some serviced sites were made available for this purpose. There is no official building code prescribing certain minimum standards for new construction; and building control is at the discretion of the local planning office.

Squatting

Squatting, although officially not existing, has become a recent practice particularly in Hanoi (5–10 per cent of households). A large proportion of squatters are ex-servicemen who engage themselves in small scale business production or services, such as repair shops, restaurants etc. In Saigon, of course, some 15 per cent of residential areas are squatter settlements inherited from the colonial system before unification. There the government attempted to demolish these slums but gave up after violent opposition by the settlers, and now even avoids entering certain districts in the urban periphery. Pavement dwellers, specifically in and around the railway

---

4) In the past there was no policy of taxes on private incomes (but there was for business) since wages were low and paid by the state anyway, and the proportion of the social wage was consider-able. Since the reforms in 1986, when private business was allowed again, the government realized that is was losing a good proportion of income and decided to levy taxes on incomes in mid–1989.

5) There are of course no legal mechanisms to enforce rent payments or to evict these tenants, therefore nobody rents rooms to people they do not know very well.

stations, are a common feature since the removal of migration control in 1986; also as a very recent phenomenon the municipal parks are being used for living. Most of these squatters are people coming back from the new development zones or are emigrants returning from abroad. There are no figures available, but a rough estimate would be 100,000 for Saigon, and maybe 10,000 or 20,000 in Hanoi.

Building Industry

Until 1986 the building industry was controlled by state enterprises which opted, in housing, for prefabricated concrete systems, without paying too much respect to the local climatic and social conditions. There is, however, increasing criticism of this technology, and its outcomes, by the users themselves, and the elevated cost of this kind of construction tends to put it beyond the means of the recently formed co-operatives anyway. Therefore the share of prefabrication has decreased automatically. Municipal (not state) building brigades, small family enterprises (serving individual private owners) and the informal sector have continued to use more traditional materials. In the countryside there used to be the general habit of building with organic materials. However, fast growing species of rice have now been introduced and their stalks are too short for thatching, forcing peasants to turn to inorganic materials, in which, at least, there is a limited experience in small scale lime production.

The technical quality of the housing stock is also affected by poor quality and short supply of all building materials, therefore the buildings age very quickly. After 1986, building quality has slightly improved, because quality control and account-ability is easier for the co-operatives with their decentralized structure.

Now, with the reforms, larger private builders may operate in the construction sector again and employ hired labour. Up to 1989 the number of staff was limited to 20, but there are no restrictions now. In practice, however, there are no builders with more than 100 employees.

House Forms

In the first years of the revolution there was a short period, until 1976–77, in which experiments in 'communist' forms of housing consumption were started, advancing, for example, collective kitchens and other amenities for joint use. The users, however, were not so excited about the idea, preferring to deposit garbage in the communal kitchens and use their individual balconies for cooking.

In the following period, Eastern European standard designs were imported, together with heavy construction methods. In the South, however, the occupation by the US has influenced the common taste, and imported videocassettes (smuggled from Thailand or sent from relatives abroad) continue the very same tradition. The 'Californian bungalow' including its private swimming pool is still a dominant pattern in people's minds today, although there is little chance to turn these dreams into reality for the time being.

House forms have also been affected by the recent policy changes in Vietnam. High rise buildings, for example, are built increasingly less, whereas smaller and more decorated houses are becoming popular. In the countryside one and two storey houses have always been most prevalent and best liked anyway. There are plans to restore the historic centre of Hanoi, possibly also central areas of Ho Chi Minh City, but up to now there are only local funds and no foreign aid available for such schemes.

Ill. 2: International co-operation with Vietnam: Design for a self-help housing project prepared at the University of Weimar / GDR in 1984.   (Jürgen Arnold, Folke Dietzsch, Ingo Gräfenhahn)

Assessment

In assessing Vietnam's housing policies we must take into account the ongoing war situation over several decades. We do not know what the government's approach would have been under 'normal' conditions. As an indication we can refer to the proclamations that the state acknowledges the right to certain minimum standards of housing for every family. And, unike the experience in almost all other countries (communist or capitalist alike) which have included similar statements in their constitution, this right was guaranteed – though at low standards –in North Vietnam until the late seventies, even in the big cities. Nobody was forced to sleep in the street. The very recent policy changes seem positive and negative at the same time. Housing conditions have greatly improved for those who have some money available. At the same time, the very poor – still not a majority like elsewhere in the developing world – cannot rely upon the assistance of the state, and even have to face, in the central avenues of the big cities, clean–up exercises by the police.

References and further reading

Cao, A.D., 1978: 'Development Planning in Vietnam: A Problem of Postwar Transition'. In: *Asia Quarterly*, 4, 263–76.

Elliot, D., 1975: Political Integration in North Vietnam: The Co–operativization Period. In: Zasloff, J.J. and Brown, M. (Eds.): *Communism in Indochina*, Lexington.

Ngyên, duc Nhuân, 1978: Désurbanisation et Développement Régional au Vietnam (1954–1977). Paris: Centre de Sociologie Urbaine.

Ngyên, duc Nhuân, 1984: *Do* the Urban and Regional Policies of Socialist Vietnam Reflect the Patterns of the Ancient Mandarin Bureaucracy? In: *International Journal of Urban and Regional Research*, 8 (1), 78–139.

Ngyên, duc Nhuân, et al (Eds.): 1987, *Le Vietnam Post–Révolutionnaire.* Paris: l'Harmattan.

Forbes, Dean and Thrift, Nigel, 1987: 'Territorial Organization, Regional Development and the City in Vietnam'. In: Forbes, D. & Thrift, N., *The Socialist Third World,* Oxford: Basil Blackwell.

Lang, M.H. & Kolb, B., 1980: 'Locational Components of Urban and Regional Public Policy in Postwar Vietnam: The Case of Ho Chi Minh City (Saigon)'. *Geo Journal,* 4 (1) Pp. 13–18.

Reuterswärd, Lars; Nyström, Maria; Roslund, Hans, 1985: 'Shelter Policies in Vietnam'. In: Mathéy, K. (Ed.), *Socialist Housing?. TRIALOG Special Issue,* No 6. Darmstadt.

Third World Guide 89/90, 1988: (Vietnam: pp. 563–566), Montevideo: Third World Editors.

Thrift, Nigel, 1987: Difficult Years: Ideology and Urbanization in South Vietnam, 1975–86. *Urban Geography,* 7, pp. 420–439.

Thrift, Nigel & Forbes, D. 1985: 'Cities, Socialism and War: Hanoi, Saigon and the Vietnamese Experience of Urbanization'. In *Society and Space,* 3 (3), 279–308.

Thrift, Nigel & Forbes, D.: 1986: *The Price of War: Urbanization in Vietnam 1954–1985.* London: Allen and Unwin.

White, Christine, 1982: *Debates in Vietnamese Development Policy*. University of Sussex Discussion Paper 171, Falmer: IDS.

White, Christine, 1983: 'Recent Debates in Vietnamese Development Policy'. In: White, G.; Murray, R.; White, C.: *Revolutionary Socialist Development in the Third World.*

Van Tap, Dao, 1980: 'On the Transformation and New Distribution of Population Centers in the Socialist Republic of Vietnam'. In: *International Journal of Urban and Regional Research,* 4 (4), Pp. 503–15.

White, Christine, 1985: 'Agricultural Planning, Pricing Policy and Co–operatives in Vietnam'. In: *World Development,* vol. 13, No.1. Oxford. Pp. 97–114.

China

Richard Kirkby

Forty years ago, the Chinese Communist Party (CCP) found itself on the threshold of nationwide power. That the Party's leaders viewed their new, urban–centred tasks with trepidation was no secret (Mao, 1981, pp. 361–75). They were ill prepared for their new role as arbiters of industrial and commercial complexities in the great cities. They were fearful of dealing with urban class relationships which bore scant resemblance to those which had become familiar, and manageable, in the countryside. And they had in the long years of rural exile given next to no thought to the question of the city as a physical and spatial entity.

In many ways, the sheer chaos of the newly liberated cities, and the evident remedies immediately required, hindered the emergence of any grand philosophy of urbanism for the new age. The response demanded by the vast squatter areas, the miles of stagnant ditches, and the millions of tons of street debris of decades of national decay, was self–evident. On the other hand, even more obvious was the necessity of restoring and mobilizing the machinery of production, circulation and communication; it was these over–riding tasks that figured large in the communist programme for national reconstruction. We will recall that Mao's strategic prescription for the cities was to transform them from slothful, corrupt centres of consumption (*xiaofei chengshi*) to purposeful socialist 'producer cities' (*shengchan chengshi*). With this productionist ethos in command, speculation about the form and spatial weave of urban society appropriate to the new socialism was not ruled out of order – it simply never arose in the China of the Mao era.

The new regime immediately inaugurated vast programmes of slum clearance and housing construction, especially in the large coastal metropolises. These efforts stemmed from a subjective desire on the part of the leaders of New China to better the lot of the urban masses; but in terms of socialist ambition, of the kind suggested by the great debates on the urban question which had been a feature of the Soviet Union of the 1920s, they were unremarkable. The CCP in power evidently regarded urban planning and urban construction as identical. As for urban citizenship,

289

Country Profile: China

National territory: 9,596,961 km²
Population: 1,100 million
Population density: 114.6 inhab/sq.km
Labour force: 617,906,000, 28% in agriculture
Urbanization rate: 50% (1988 — Kirkby), 27% (Third World Guide)
Capital: Beijing (Peking); 5,670,000 inhabitants
Average natural growth rate: 1.93 (1949–82); 1.4 (1973–1984)
Urban growth rate: 3.14% (1949–82); 0.64% (1976)
Life expectancy: 69.4 years for men; 72.3 years for women
Infant mortality: 3.6%
Illiteracy rate: 34.5% (men 20.8%, women 48.9%)
Religion: Buddhism, Taoism, Confucianism. Muslim and Christian minorities.
Languages: Chinese (official), Ethnic minorities with own languages.
Educational expenditure: 8.1% of budget (1984)
Military expenditure: 12% of budget
Major export products: agricultural products (rice, peanuts, cotton, tobacco, tea, skins...); textiles, silk, industrial products (bicycles, sewing machines, tools, enamel...); minerals (coal, iron, crude oil, graphite...)
Major markets: Japan 73%, US 16%, Austria 10%, Switzerland 4% (capital inflow)
Foreign assistance: $ 963.4 million (1985); sources: IDA, OECD, OPEC

Some important dates:
551 B.C. Birth of Confucius ('Master Kung') — died 479 B.C.
220 B.C. Today's Chinese territory, which has existed already for 2,000 years of uninterrupted self–government, achieves territorial unification. Construction of the Great Wall (5,000 km)
1295 First Chinese products imported to Europe by Marco Polo
1415 The Portuguese open maritime route to China
1839 England declared the 'Opium War' in the name of free trade, when China tried to impede drug trade by the English *East India Company*. China lost the war in 1842, and with it, Hong Kong.
1856 Anglo–French troops conducted another war against China: fall of Beijing in 1860.
1895 China lost part of its territory, including Korea, Taiwan (Formosa) to Japan.
1898 Anti-imperialist rebellion led by members of the *'Boxers' Society'*, which was defeated by joint English, Russian, German, French, Japanese and US military intervention.
1911 Several nationalist groups, supported by the Emperor's army, proclaimed the Republic, but the result was chaos and fragmented the country.
1921 Creation of Chinese Communist Party (CCP). When the Chinese general Chiang Kai–Shek massacred communists in Shanghai, a 22–year civil war began. The communists were defeated in the south, and began the Long March north under the leadership of Mao Tse–Tung and established a 'Red Republic' in the north.
1949 With help from the Soviet Union, communists defeat the US–backed Chiang Kai–Shek's troops. People's Republic of China was proclaimed, Chiang Kai–Shek fled to Formosa and established Chinese exile government.
1961 First official controversies with the Soviet Union and withdrawal of Soviet experts.
1966 Mao inspired the Cultural Revolution, aiming at political mobilization and criticism of non–Communist practices, but causing an economic setback.
1976 Death of Mao, followed by a *de–Maoization* campaign; principles of Cultural Revolution denied. The new constitution makes the People's National Assembly the supreme state body. Economic emphasis on consumer goods rather than heavy industry.
1886 First big students' demonstration in Shanghai calling for democracy and free press.
1989 Renewed student demonstration following Gorbachev's visit was brutally suppressed.

Sources: Die Länder der Erde, Köln: Pahl–Rugenstein, 1982. Third World Guide, Montevideo: Third World Editors, 1988. R. Kirkby, Urbanization in China, Beckenham: Croom Helm, 1985

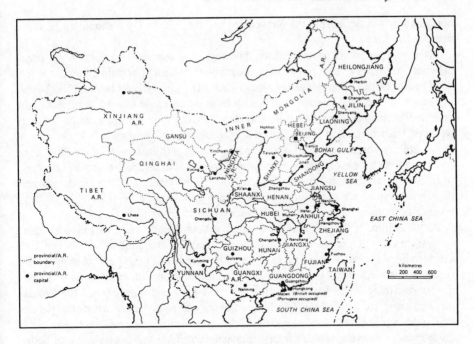

throughout the Mao era, a reductionist equation was to predominate: urban citizen equals urban producer.

Interpretations by Western observers that the PRC's development process was 'anti-urban' are no longer tenable: the Chinese experience has been – and to a lesser degree, remains – a variant on the theme of urban–industrial bias (Leeming, 1985; Kirkby, 1985, pp. 1–20). Within the dominant ethos of the Mao era, central to which was the hegemony of production and of accumulation over consumption, all those in the tightly delineated and controlled urban sphere have been beneficiaries of this bias. The early adoption of the eight–grade wage system, the almost unbreakable 'iron rice–bowl', was the underlying guarantee of urban supremacy. Welfare in the broad sense (*shehui fuli*), including employees' health care, preschool care, and, most costly of all, the provision of basic shelter, was to be part of a social wage in an economy which was expressly 'low–wage' as far as monetary remuneration was concerned. Workers' welfare was essential to the grand purpose of rapid industrialization, the *raison d'être* of Communist Party power.

From the early 1950s on, therefore, urban housing provision was considered the responsibility of the state. This, of course, was a novel departure in China; now the government, through local municipal housing bureaux, or through the urban enterprise system, would take on the primary responsibility for housing investment, construction and rehabilitation, allocation, maintenance and repair and general management. By 1956, 95 per cent of urban land had become state property and less than 5 per cent of rented sector accommodation remained in private hands (Yu Xinyan, 1981, p. 45). Though owner occupation was upheld (in the mid–1950s comprising just over two–thirds of all the private sector), by and large it was assumed that private urban

292 *Housing Policies in the Socialist Third World*

housing was a residue from the old society and that ultimately it should all be taken over by the state.

As a component of state welfare, housing provision was to follow the broad principle of equity in supply. This meant that within a certain range, unequal distribution of the social wage was sanctified: officials, technicians, and the 'higher intelligentsia' were to be treated differently from the common masses. A survey of the mid–1950s demonstrates this mild inequity – while only 17 per cent of ordinary workers' households had four or more square metres of 'living space', 40 per cent of white–collar workers (including government officers) had more than this.[1] And appropriations for new housing construction for those of a superior station in society were considerably differentiated. For example, in the Nanjing of the 1950s, workers received apartments at around 30 *yuan* per four square metres while college professors' housing cost more than 60 *yuan* (Howe, 1968, p. 80).

At the bottom of the pile were the single workers, usually male, recruited by urban units from the villages. In the early days, the People's Republic vowed to eradicate the dormitory system – seen as a hangover from the feudal craft guild culture and the foreign–imposed factory system. But the temptations of continuing – indeed institutionalizing – the dormitory idea were too great. At a time when the Soviet–inspired norm for newly built family apartments was nine square metres per person, the 2–2.5 square metres of the dormitories represented a considerable saving in investment – a saving which factory managers considered they could put to better, more productive uses (Kwok, 1973, p. 241).

In short, by the mid–1950s, the parameters of urban housing policy had been established. Housing had become primarily the responsibility of the state, either directly through municipal government, or indirectly through the enterprise or institution. Just as for health care, educational and recreational services, the consumer was to pay only a nominal fee for housing, a basic element of the collective welfare system which was the concomitant of the low wage economy.

However, in the 1980s, the economic reformers at the apex of the Party (at least until June 1989) overthrew many of the previously inviolable tenets of China's post–1949 policy. Urban housing did not escape their attention. The overriding objective was a drastic transformation of the immediate supply basis of housing, premised upon a revolution in macro–economics which put aside the Stalin–Mao model and its ruling nexuses.[2] The transformation demanded a dramatic increase in non–productive capital investments as a part of all capital construction funds. Despite the huge increase in the building programme resulting from this measure, the housing crisis remained as intractable as ever. The reformers were thus driven to challenge the entire edifice of China's urban housing provision.

We will next, therefore, consider the crisis in housing supply which was the legacy of the Mao years, and which has occasioned radical measures in the housing field. The subsequent sections describe the revolution in the housing supply picture. Largely

---

1) *Juzhu mianji* – the general Chinese measure which excludes corridors, kitchen and lavatory space, etc.
2) Namely, high accumulation rate, low consumption rate in the national income, heavy industry over light industry, productive investments over non–productive.

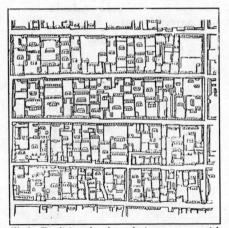

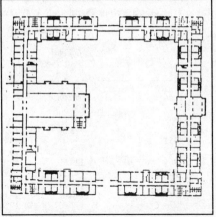

Ill. 1: Traditional urban design pattern with inward oriented extended family court-houses, built up to two floors.   (Source: TRIALOG 4)

Ill. 2:   Design for an urban 'Peoples' Commune' for collective living in Hong-Shen (Tientsin), period of the 'Great Leap Forward', 1956

because of its limited impact in the face of extraordinary urban population growth (as indicated in *Table 1*) new, more market-oriented policies began to appear in the early 1980s, with their inevitable ideological justifications. The final section speculates on the future for housing policy, and for the basic provision of urban shelter in a period of development which promises enormous expansion of China's non-agricultural population.

The Emerging Housing Crisis under Mao

The extensive industrialization programme of the First Five-Year Plan (1953–57, hereafter: 1FYP) was accompanied by considerable attention to the question of housing the new cohorts of factory workers. Yet even with 9.1 per cent of total 'basic capital construction funds' *(jieben jianshe touzi)* annually devoted to housing (SYB, 1948, pp. 333, 339), the sheer scale of urban population growth outpaced housing supply. On the eve of the 1FYP, China's global urban population stood at almost 72 million (*Table 1*). Average per capita floorspace available was 5.4 square metres. Just seven years later, in 1960, because of the injudicious migration policies of the 'Great Leap Forward' and a neglect of housing after 1957 (in the 2FYP it averaged only 4.1 per cent of total capital construction funds), the hugely swollen urban population of around 130 million enjoyed a per capita housing space of just 3.5 square metres (Kirkby, 1985, p. 173; RMRB, 8 May 1981). There is evidence that the larger the urban place, the less available housing space there is per person (Chao Kang, 1966, p. 393).

The ensuing fifteen years saw a more marked neglect of non-productive urban capital investments – utilities, roads and above all housing. It is not surprising in view of the anti-consumption ideology of the Cultural Revolution that the 3FYP (1966–70) saw all time lows in both housing investment (4 per cent of all capital

Table 1: China's Urban Population 1949–1988: An Acceptable Series

	Urban Population				Urban and Rural Population
	Official Post 1982 Series		Acceptable Series		
Year	No.(m.)	%	No.(m.)	%	(m.)
1949	57.65	10.6	49.00	9.1	541.17
1953	78.26	13.3	64.64	11.0	587.96
1957	99.49	15.4	82.18	12.7	646.53
1960	130.73	19.7	109.55	16.5	661.07
1964	129.50	18.4	98.85	14.0	704.99
1969	141.17	17.5	100.65	12.5	806.71
1976	163.41	17.4	113.42	12.1	937.17
1977	166.69	17.6	116.17	12.2	949.74
1978	172.45	17.9	122.78	12.8	962.59
1979	185.95	19.0	133.57	13.7	975.42
1980	191.40	19.4	140.28	14.2	987.05
1981	201.71	20.2	146.55	14.6	1000.72
1982	211.31	20.8	152.91	15.1	1015.90
1983	241.50	23.5	160.08	15.6	1027.64
1984	331.36	31.9	174.42	16.8	1038.76
1985	384.46	36.6	188.90	18.0	1050.44
1986	441.03	41.4	200.90	18.9	1065.29
1987	503.62	46.6	214.98	19.9	1080.73
1988e	550.00	50.0	230.05	20.9	1100.00

Notes

Urban figures for 1949 to 1976 are to be found in some recently published Chinese sources. From 1977–88, the urban population totals are estimates based upon a smaller official series, which is for the total non–agricultural population in China's designated municipalities (*shi*) and towns (*zhen*).

The broad reason for the huge proportions of China's official urban population (1987 figure, 503.62 million, or 46.6 per cent of China's total population designated as urban) relate to changes in urban population criteria in the 1980s. Thus:

- *Firstly*, the municipal data which go to make up this total is inflated by the inclusion of large numbers of rural persons who happen to be resident in *jiaoqu* (suburban city districts) of municipalities, especially where *jiaoqu* boundaries are arbitrarily drawn far into the countryside.

- *Secondly*, the town data which are incorporated in the grand total include vast numbers of agricultural persons.

Note that all figures are in millions and at year–end.

Sources:

Acceptable series for urban population

1977–82:	Kirkby, 1985, Chapter 4, Tables 4.2, 4.6, 4.9.
1983:	up 4.69 per cent on previous year (a rate derived from L.J.C. Ma and Cui Ganghao, 'Administrative Changes and Urban Population in China', *Annals of the Association of American Geographers* '77 (3), 1987, pp. 373–95, Table 7, p. 40).
1984:	up 8.69 per cent on previous year (Ma and Cui, op. cit.).
1985:	up 8.3 per cent on previous year (derived from *China City Planning Review*, Vol. 3, No. 4, Dec. 1987, p. 40. Note that the official non–agricultural urban population for 1985 year–end is 175.46 million.
1986–88:	Figures are derived on the basis of annual increase of 7.01 per cent, which is the average increase over three years 1983–85 for the relevant series.
1988's	urban total in the official series (col. 1) is an estimate, as is the total population at the end of 1988.

Official post–1982 urban series, and total population of China:

Figures for China's total population and the official 'urban' population: State Statistical Bureau of the People's Republic of China, China Statistical Publishing House, *Zhongguo tongji nianjian 1988* (Statistical Yearbook of China), Bejing, 1988, p. 97.

1988 total population figure is an estimate.

construction funds) and in floorspace produced (annual average of 10.8 million square metres). This gross neglect of urban infrastructure and housing coincided, of course, with a retardation of urban growth due to mass expulsions of city youth and other sections of society. From 1964 to the end of 1976, it is estimated that China's urban population grew only around 12 per cent (from above 99 to 113 million). With increased resources devoted to housing during the 4FYP (1970–75), the overall average at the end of 1978 had increased to 5.3 square metres per capita (Kirkby, 1985, p. 176).

Yet this figure concealed much variation, principally between the smaller, non–municipal urban settlements (almost all of which were under 100,000 in population), and the designated municipalities. A survey in 1978 of these municipalities (at the time numbering 192) found that here the average space was only 3.6 square metres per person, in contrast to the 4.5 square metres of 1952. Further, this survey discovered that of the approximately 23 million households in the 192 municipalities, around one–third had severe housing problems. For example, 1.83 million families were housed in warehouses, corridors, factory workshops, classrooms and offices; 1.89 million families had three generations sleeping in the same room and several million young people were unable to marry because they had no place to live (Zhang Jun, 1985, p. 32). In Shanghai 800,000 people of a total urban population of around five million were judged to be in severe housing difficulty, with per capita housing space under 2 square metres, or grown–up children of different sexes sharing the same room, or young people of marriageable age (at that time twenty–seven for men and twenty–five for women) still on the housing waiting list (Wang Fengwu, 1985, p. 22).

As for the condition of the urban housing stock, a wander off the main highways in any city would reveal the parlous state of housing after decades of neglect. The absence of routine repairs and maintenance during the Mao years was partly the result of lack of funding and of building materials for the domestic sector and partly of peasant attitudes to the city. Between 1949 and 1980 the official figures show that the gross urban housing floorspace stock grew by 469 million square metres. Yet 675.4 million square metres of the new housing was put up in these 31 years. With very little being deliberately demolished to make way for new projects – for this was definitely not the policy of the urban authorities – we can estimate that upwards of 150 million square metres was lost due to neglect of simple repairs (Kirkby, 1985, p. 173).

A survey in 1955 had shown that 50 per cent of all municipal housing stock was in need of rehabilitation (Kwok, 1973, p. 226). While in certain cities (particularly *Beijing*) much effort was put into repairs in the 1950s, the ravages of time meant that the overall physical state of China's urban housing by the end of the Mao period was much worse than in the mid–1950s. It was especially bad in the fifty or so cities of over 500,000 in population, where over 40 per cent of all China's urban population resided (Kirkby, 1985, p. 150). Take the example of the great metropolis of Wuhan in central China: here, of the 6.37 million square metres of housing floorspace administered by the municipal housing bureau, some 9 per cent was in a 'highly dangerous' state, 77 per cent was broken–down or damaged and only 14 per cent was considered up to standard (He Gongjian, 1980, pp. 13–14).

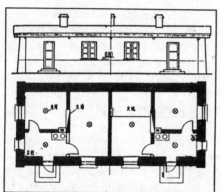

Ill. 3: Model design no. 6502 for workers' housing to be built with local materials (about 1970).

1 Primary scool
2 Shops on ground floor
3 Nursery
4 Playground
5 News stand
6 News stand
7 Bath house

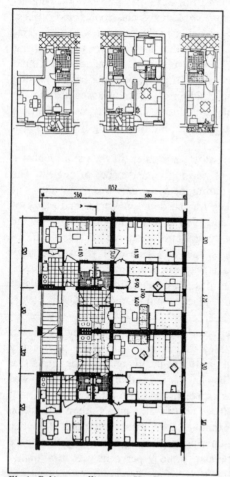

Ill. 4: Peking satellite town Xin Fu: model designs based on the norms established 1957

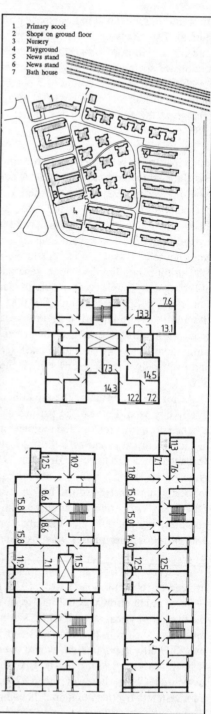

Ill. 5: Shanghai satellite town (Fan Gua Long), site plan and flat plans (size in sq.m.), 1964

City housing managers complained that they neither had the financial resources nor the trained staff to cope with matters more efficiently. In 1977, a national housing conference heard that in all the then 187 designated municipalities *(she shi)* as a whole, the average annual repair bill (let alone management, maintenance and additions to the housing stock) per square metres of public housing stood at 2.1 *yuan*, whereas the rental income was a mere 1.09. For Wuhan, on average in the 1970s, 830,000 square metres (roughly 13 per cent) of the municipal housing stock required 'large or medium-scale' repairs. Yet the funds available for repairs could only be stretched to just over one third of this area (He Gongjian, 1980, p. 14).

This problem of disparity between costs and rental income continues. The extraordinary expansion of the housing programme (described in the following section) has seen a large rise in unit cost of construction. Some of the first of the new wave of building in China was along Beijing's Qiansanmen A venue. But here, the disparity between relatively high rental income and the costs of running the new multistorey buildings was even more remarkable. One report claimed that while the annual rental income for the nineteen high-rise blocks of the project came to 500,000 *yuan* in 1980, the cost of maintaining and running the lifts alone came to 750,000 *yuan* (RMRB, 8 May 1981). It was calculations of this order and the despair among those responsible for administering a housing finance system that had become almost inoperable, which provided the political basis for a complete rethinking of the housing supply system in recent years.

The Post-Mao Housing Programmes and their Impact

Mass Problems and Mass Solutions

The transformation of many aspects of economic life in China over the decade after 1978 had, of course, its accompaniments in the realm of theory. Often these have seemed rather hollow justifications for pragmatic action. A rather more edifying debate, however, centred on the proper objectives of work and life in a socialist society. While the new regime by no means eschewed stark output targeting, there was now general agreement that the purpose of socialist production was not simply to enhance future production. At first, the discussion was couched in Mao's own terminology and directives - specifically his observation that planners must not give way to the temptation to build up the 'skeleton' *(gutou)* at the expense of the 'flesh' *(rou)*(RMRB, 8 May 1981). But the Cultural Revolution rule of thumb, *xian shenghan, hou shenghuo* ('first production, then livelihood') came under heavy fire. In urban policy, complaints against the neglect of the Mao years began to be aired. The concept of the cities as primarily places of production, in which consumption aspects were regarded as unworthy of attention by socialist planners, was thoroughly rejected.

All this presaged a change in those policies which most closely determined the state of the physical fabric of urban China. In September 1978, during the last days of the Hua Guofeng interregnum, the State Capital Construction Commission convened a special conference on housing. Here it was declared that in the coming seven years (1979–85), more urban housing was to be built than in the previous twenty–eight years, that is to say at least 550 million square metres (*Ta Kung Pao,* 28 September 1978). In the five years before the conference, a mere 28 million square metres per annum had been achieved (Kirkby, 1985, p. 173) and the prospect of increasing annual output by a factor of three seemed most unrealistic. Targets such as these would demand the mobilization of millions of construction workers, an enormously expanded construction materials industry and a rebirth of rudimentary urban planning at central and municipal levels. But most difficult of all, they demanded a revolution in central investment policies.

That this revolution actually occurred is one of the unsung achievements of the reform decade which began in 1978. In that year, non–productive funds constituted 20.6 per cent of all capital construction investments, and housing took 7.8 per cent. A dramatic climb in these figures peaked in 1982 at 45.5 per cent and 25.4 per cent respectively. That is, one–quarter of all capital investments in 1982 went to urban housing construction, compared with the historical low of 4 per cent per annum in the early years of the Cultural Revolution (SYB 1985, p. 304). As *Table 2* illustrates, the amount of housing floorspace produced in China's towns and cities reflected this staggering escalation in funding – from 37.5 million square metres completed in 1978 to around 90 million square metres in 1982.

We will only briefly comment on the nature of the housing produced in this enormous programme of construction. On the whole it has meant an abandonment of previous building methods and designs (principally the four/five storey walk–up block using a mixture of traditional and modern structural techniques). The revolution in housing output has necessitated the adoption of the mechanized construction techniques which were seen in the West in the late 1950s and 1960s. Much of what has been produced is, of course, of dubious structural and social quality. But as a mass solution to an immediate problem of vast proportions, the post–1978 develop- ments have been an outstanding achievement. At first, a key organizational factor was the re–institution of the approach developed in the 1950s – tongyi (*tongyi jianshe*) – 'integrated construction'. The 'six integrateds' cover planning, investment sources, design, construction, allocation and management. The results – extensive high–rise estates – are to be seen today in every city in China.[3]

This mass construction programme was intended to help those in greatest need. But with housing the most pressing problem of urban existence, it inevitably created ample opportunity for abuse of official position. Newspapers and radio broadcasts of the early 1980s regularly featured cases of corruption in the housing sphere; commissions of enquiry were set up in many localities, and most cities promulgated special by–laws in an attempt to curb the worst excesses. In 1984, the Party's Central Consolidation and Guidance Commission issued a directive stating 'the distribution of housing should be decided by honest and upright people with no leading Party cadre allowed to make decisions if personally involved'. One immediate outcome was the releasing of tens of thousands of purloined flats around the country by Party

---

3) For instance the Beijing *Tuanjie Hu* scheme on the east side of the city, visited in August 1979. Tuanjie Hu is an integrated neighbourhood development of 300,000 square metres in total, 260,000 being for housing.

Table 2: China's Urban Housing:
Non-productive Investment, Investment and Floorspace produced, 1949-1990

Period	Non-Productive Investment (a)	Housing Investment	Urban Housing floorspace (million m²)
Rehabilitation			
1950–2	34.0	10.6	04.5
1st FYP 1953–7	33.0	9.1	18.9
2nd FYP 1958–62	14.6	4.1	22.0
Readjustment 1963–5	20.6	6.9	14.2
3rd FYP 1966–70	16.2	4.0	10.8
4th FYP 1977–5	17.5	5.7	25.2
5th FYP 1976–80	26.1	11.8	47.0
1976	18.8	6.1	24.2
1977	20.6	6.9	28.3
1978	20.9	7.8	37.5
Readjustment 1979	30.3	14.8	62.6
1980	35.7	20.0	82.3
6th FYP 1981–5	42.7	21.9	84.9
1981	43.0	25.1	79.0
1982	45.5	25.4	90.2
1983	41.7	21.1	82.5
1984	40.3	18.1	77.0
1985	43.1	20.0	96.0
7th FYP 1986–90	37.0	13.5	85.8
1986	39.4	16.1	89.0
1987	34.5	13.5	65.0
1988	32.0e	13.0e	95.0e
1989	33.0e	12.0e	90.0e
1990	34.0e	13.0e	90.0e

a) Non-productive investment *(fei shengchanxing touzi)* is that part of the state's 'basic capital construction' funds devoted mainly to urban utilities, cultural, educational and social services installations, public buildings, commercial enterprises, transport, communications construction and housing. Here, the figures in the first column represent non-productive investment's proportion of all capital investments (where years are grouped, per annum averages). Column 2 is that part of all basic capital construction investments going to housing. Column three is the average annual output of urban housing floorspace *(juzhu mianji)* in millions of square metres. In the period rows, all data are annual averages for the respective period. 1988–90 figures are estimates (e).

Source: *SYB, 1984, pp. 323, 339, 357; SYB, 1985, pp. 304, 331; SYB, 1988, pp. 559–561, 563.*

officials *(Ta Kung Pao*, 23 February 1984).

Nevertheless, in the short term at least, and in quantity if not quality, the brave and unprecedented efforts on the urban housing front had tangible results. But these were far less than anticipated in 1978, for the transformation in the sphere of housing coincided with a considerable wave of rural–urban migration and an upturn in the natural rate of increase of the urban population. At the end of 1977, China's global urban population stood at 116 million. By the end of 1982 it was up to 153 million (see *Table 1*). Had there been no net migration to the urban areas during this period, a natural rate of increase of eleven per thousand would have meant a total increment on the 1977 figure of just 6.5 million rather than the actual 37 million (Kirkby, 1985, p. 121). A low order of urban increase (consonant with the experience in the previous fifteen years) would have brought considerable improvements in the average per capita space standards – from the 5.2 square metres of 1977 to 7.8 square metres of 1977 to 7.8 square metres at the end of 1982. Instead, the improvement was confined to just 1.1 square metres per person on average (1982, 6.3 square metres).[4] By 1987, with a much expanded urban population of 215 million, the official per capita floorspace figure was 8 square metres. However, this figure was inflated by the inclusion in the urban population count of large numbers of newly designated small settlements, whose housing conditions are generally above average. The situation in the larger centres, particularly the 170 prefectural–level municipalities, had hardly improved and in many cases had actually deteriorated.

The Ideological Shift and a New Housing Policy

The Development of the Debate on the Housing Question

By 1980, the ideological climate had veered further towards the concepts of market guidance and market regulation in the planned economy. This was a natural development of the reforms inaugurated in rural production after 1978; it was considerably spurred on by outside advice. In 1980 China became a member of the World Bank; an examination of the Bank's latest overview, *China: Long Term Issues and Options*, and comparison with current policy directions as enshrined in the recently published Seventh Five–Year Plan indicate a high degree of correspondence between the official Chinese view and outside opinion.

By the mid–1980s, housing had become one of the most important spheres of the urban economy in which radical new measures were now being tested. There were particular reasons for this: first, despite the efforts described above, the outcome in terms of overall betterment of urban housing conditions has been marginal. In the largest cities there was no end in sight to the housing crisis; while the average urban per capita floorspace at the end of 1982 stood at 6.3 square metres, for the twenty so–called million cities, it was just over half this figure. Indeed, official statistics show that for Lanzhou, Chengdu, Shenyang, Chongqing and Tianjin the average was well under 3 square metres per person (Kirkby, 1985, p. 275).

After three decades in which central bureaucratic planning had become overrigid, unwieldy and in many areas of the economy a deadening influence on productivity, the market backlash of the early 1980s was hardly unexpected. In a climate in which the market was suddenly invested with almost magical powers, this theoretical reassessment was soon to encompass the intractable problems of urban housing supply. The immediate catalyst was the enormous state budgetary deficit which

---

4) See Kirkby, 1985, Table 6.3, p. 176; these figures differ somewhat from those of *BR*, no. 40, 7 October 1985 in which it is stated that per capita living space at the end of 1984 was 6.32 square metres compared with 1980's 4.96 square metres. The disparity probably arises because these figures refer to the municipalities only; around a hundred small cities with relatively good housing conditions were designated as municipalities in the four years concerned. Also, see *Zhonghua renmin gongeheguo xingzheng quhua jiance, Administrative Divisions of the People's Republic of China* (Beijing, Ditu Chubanshe, published annually).

confronted the nation in 1979. Major causes were the downturn in enterprise profits remitted to the government, which resulted from changes in management and accounting requirements, and the unparalleled increase in agricultural procurement prices which were implemented without due consideration of the ability of urban wage–earners to absorb them. In 1979, the government was obliged to subsidize these transfers in part by a supplement to the urban wage packet *(BR, no.* 12, 25 March 1985, pp. 16–17).

Economists calculated that in 1981, on average each urban resident paid 0.1 *yuan* per square metres for housing; the actual cost (taking into account depreciation, repair, maintenance and management) came to 0.38 *yuan.* Thus the state subsidized each square metre to the tune of 0.28 *yuan.* The total call on the state budget by the existing housing stock (not including new construction) was therefore 3.5 billion *yuan* – a figure greater than the entire national budget deficit for 1982 *(BR,* no. 39, 25 October 1982).

Housing ownership rentals in the early 1980s

At this point let us summarize the overall situation regarding housing ownership and rent levels. By 1980, 250 million square metres (31 per cent) of the total urban housing stock of 810 million square metres was owned and managed directly by municipal housing bureaux (variously titled, but most usually *fangchan guanli ju*). Urban enterprises held 360 million square metres – 44 per cent of the total. Two hundred million square metres (25 per cent) remained in private hands, the majority of this being in owner occupation, but with a significant part still in the private rented sector. As for the most important urban centres, the municipalities, the situation in 1981 is shown in *Table 3.* From this table, we can see that the state, either directly or indirectly, owned around 82 per cent of all municipal urban housing stock, somewhat more than for all urban areas (75 per cent) and rather less than in the largest cities. For example, the figures for Shanghai in 1981 were 42 per cent under the Municipal Housing Bureau and 43 per cent under the enterprise, giving a total state ownership of housing of 85 per cent (Zhang Jun, 1985, p. 27). The general picture, then, is that the larger the urban settlement, the greater the proportion of state–owned housing stock.

Table 3: Housing and Rentals in 200 Municipalities, 1981

Ownership	Total floorspace (million m²)	Percentage	Average monthly rent (yuan/m²)
Municipal housing bureaux	203.4	28.7	0.08–0.12
Enterprises	380.3	53.6	under 0.08
Private	125.8	17.7	0.10–0.14 (rented sector)
Totals	709.5	100.0	---

Source: Zhang Jun, 1985, Table 2, p. 27.

In the years immediately after the liberation, household rents were relatively high (e.g. in Wuhan they represented 14 per cent of household income. See *JHLT,* no. 5, 1980, p. 31). This was deemed too great and in the mid–1950s leading economists proposed that the appropriate level for rents in the New China should be 6 to 10 per cent of household income (He Gongjian, 1980, p. 14). There were two factors, however, which made rentals a diminishing proportion. First and most importantly, the labour participation rate in the urban sector climbed dramatically, from around 20 per cent in the early 1950s to almost 60 per cent by the 1980s (municipalities only. See SYB, 1984, p. 470). Second, rents experienced a real fall, mainly but not exclusively because of the expanding enterprise welfare sector. For example (again in Wuhan), in 1974 all municipal housing bureau stock had rents cut by one–third. In that city, therefore, rents fell from 14 per cent of household expenditure immediately after Liberation, to 8 per cent in 1957 and 5 per cent in 1970: by 1978 they represented just 2.3 per cent. Now they had become merely 'token rents' (*xiangzhenxing fangzu*), though the situation described earlier of declining per capita space standards and deterioration of the housing fabric must, of course, be borne in mind (*JHLT,* no. 5, 1980, p. 31). More recent data for China's urban population as a whole indicates this steady decline in rents, though starting at a lower point altogether (*Table 4*).

Table 4: Rents and Household Utilities as a Proportion of Household Expenditure

Year	Rent (%)	Water and Electricity (%)	Food (%)
1957	2.32	1.46	58.43
1964	2.61	0.97	59.22
1981	1.39	0.97	58.66
1983	1.52	1.14	59.20

Regarding the upturn after 1981 in rental and utilities proportions, the World Bank Report (1985, Annex E, p. 88, Table G2a) puts urban rentals and fuel/power proportions higher, at 4.9 per cent and 4.5 per cent respectively of household expenditures.

Source: SYB, 1985, pp. 463–4.

The ideological onslaught on low rents

The year 1980 saw an early and influential attack on the traditional housing supply system, in an article by Su Xing, published by the Party's theoretical journal, *Hongqi* (Red Flag). Having reviewed the problems at the end of the Mao era, and roundly criticized their causes, Su Xing then endeavours to develop a theoretical case to prove that under the socialist system, housing is a commodity. In doing so he enlists Engels to his cause, for in his arguments with Proudhon Engels refuted any suggestion that the relationship between landlord and tenant was equatable with that between capitalist and worker. Therefore,

In a socialist society, housing is an individual consumer item and remains a commodity. What is different is that here it is no longer a transaction between individuals; instead, the state, representing the system of ownership by the people, rents or sells the houses to the individual labourers, making this a form of the principle of to each according to his labour ... The difference between housing and other consumer goods is that the duration of its consumption is relatively long ... Is it permissible to sell some of the housing to workers and staff? It should be.

Su Xing then goes on to praise the Romanian state mortgage system, which requires down–payments of 20–30 per cent and repayments over 15–25 years at low rates of interest (3–5 per cent). He argues that in theory, rent levels should be based on the total value of the labour power expended in the creation of a given housing unit. He concedes that in practice, given the structure of incomes in urban China and the 'low-wage' policy, the average difference between household incomes and expenditures is very small. Therefore immediate all round increases in family housing budgets would be impracticable. Nevertheless, he asserts, rents should not be further reduced, and excessive low and 'irrational' rents should be raised forthwith:

In the current stage, the rental should at least cover depreciation, maintenance and management expenses and land taxes. Otherwise, it will be impossible to retrieve not merely the cost of reproduction of housing, but also the cost of minimum maintenance.

Su Xing recommends the removal of housing from welfare and from the control of enterprise. The public housing stock should be placed under the control of special corporations, with their own internal profit–and–loss accounting, thus creating the 'reproduction and expanded reproduction' of housing through their own income generation. Only in this way will the 'objective economic laws' of socialism be honoured.

The editor of *Hongqi* chose in the ensuing issues of the journal to carry a number of articles which were more or less in favour of Su Xing's proposals (e.g. *HQ*, no. 7, 1980, p. 49; no. 9, 1980, pp. 27–8). Meanwhile, however, an obscure Wuhan social sciences publication, the *Jianghan Luntan (JHLT)*, became a forum for both the pro–commodification *(shangpinhua)* position and, more interestingly, for well argued appeals in favour of maintaining the status quo in China's urban housing system.

The *JHLT* debate was initiated by Gu Zhiming, in an article entitled 'Housing's Fundamental Character and the Problem of Return on Investment' (*Zhuzai de xingzhi he touzi shouhui wenti* in *JHLT*, no. 5, 1980, pp. 3–7). The case which Gu rehearses here is much the same as that of Su Xing, except that his contribution endeavours to be more theoretical, liberally referring to the Marxist classics and their critique of housing under capitalism. Indeed, the entire *JHLT* housing debate was couched in highly theoretical formulae, in many cases to justify quite prosaic conclusions. Since the official case for commodification has already been reviewed, we will concentrate here on the opposing viewpoints, which rest on both 'theoretical' and practical lines of argument. Those extracted from a number of issues of *JHLT* between 1980 and 1983 are summarized below.

1. It is broadly accepted that in the era of socialism, commodity production is still the rule rather than the exception; however, commodity production is of a special nature and is subordinate to planning. It should therefore not be regarded as an end in itself, or as an article of faith.

2. Though housing may be a commodity, it is no ordinary one, for its period of consumption is very long, and, if privately owned, it represents a form of personal wealth and savings, and is thus a basis for speculation or private gain incompatible with socialism.

3. Various contributors resurrected the Mao bogey of a 'return to the small peasant economy' (i.e. 'capitalism' in the Cultural Revolution polemics) which the communists had been trying to eliminate for three decades. If the present housing supply system were privatized, it would not be in keeping with the social progress demanded by a society which called itself socialist. Indeed, generalization of the commodity principle could threaten the very basis of China's socialist system.

4. Other writers against commercialization ridiculed their opponents' use of 'theory'. They pointed out that theoretical arguments by their nature must maintain consistency. Thus, if state support to housing were to be withdrawn, so should the myriad of subsidies provided by the central and local state, including many granted by work units. For example, heating allowances, the whole range of supports to urban food prices, health, cultural and educational facilities, and so on and so forth (with many of these areas now, in the mid–1980s, receiving the attention of the commercializers, proponents of this line of argument may now wish they had held their fire).

5. One writer hi–jacks the theoretical underpinnings of the commodifiers and turns these against them. He notes Engels' opposition to home ownership under capitalism, on the grounds that it fetters the working class to one place, thus preventing labour mobility and the full development of capitalism, in which socialism is seen as immanent. Since the new economics of the 1980s claims that the current stage is one of almost universal commodity production, it must acknowledge the necessity of a mobile labour force to the further development of China's productive forces.

6. Technical reasons are also highlighted, principally the practical difficulties of splitting up existing publicly owned apartment blocks into private units.

7. The most forceful arguments rest on the universality of the low–wage system. One writer examines both household income and expenditure, and finds that the balance between the two (with the latter comprising universally acknowledged necessities) is very narrow. In Wuhan in 1977, for example, the municipal authorities determined the per capita basic subsistence requirement to be 22.74 *yuan* monthly. Yet 40 per cent of the employed population (including their dependents) had less than 20 *yuan* per head. As one commentator remarked, if the government did not want a mass rebellion, it would have to raise urban incomes to pay for higher rents. This would be a pointless exercise, taking money out of one pocket of the state and simply placing it in another.

Despite frequent use of highly contrived positions, on the whole this grand controversy over housing policy represented a healthy departure from the 'one–line' debates of the 1970s. Yet given the 'gale of commodification' which began to sweep the board in the early 1980s, the opponents of commercialization were unlikely to prevail. By May 1984, the whole debate was effectively foreclosed through the direct intervention of Deng Xiaoping himself. The *People's Daily* (15 May 1984) reported Deng's exchanges with the 'central comrades responsible for the construction industry and housing policy' of the previous month. Here, Deng called for an enhanced role in the economy for the construction industry, noting that in the western capitalist nations it constituted one of the 'three main pillars' of the economy, and that it should therefore be capable of making good profits. Housing should be built for sale, and existing public housing privatized or at least made to return realistic revenues. Individual savings should be put into housing, and land and housing costs should be made to reflect differential locational attributes that should continue to enjoy state housing subsidies for the time being. Deng's own declared views in fact reflected developments towards commercialization which were already well underway.

Commercialization in Practice

By the end of the 6FYP (1985), there had been no fundamental change for the vast majority of urban dwellers in traditional parameters surrounding housing supply. Rents remained more or less at the same level, though price rises for domestic electricity and water had been implemented in selected areas.[5] Yet as the policy changes heralded by the great debate began to be realized, for a rapidly growing minority, the all important factor of shelter in the cities was taking on a novel character.

A precursor of this experiment lay in the revival of the 'overseas Chinese new village' arrangements of the 1950s. In order to secure foreign exchange, and more importantly, to play for the allegiance of the overseas Chinese communities, the government now made possible the extensive involvement of Hong Kong and Singapore property companies in the development of housing projects. These were in their native areas. For example, in 1979, the Dongshan development in Guangzhou was placed on the market, and demand was such that prospective purchasers had to draw lots for the 150 flats of its first phase (Ta Kung Pao, 22 October 1979). By 1985, Shanghai had completed several luxury developments and had plans for fifty large blocks to be built in conjunction with overseas Chinese interests. Such projects have been used not only as a test bed for new high–rise construction methods; they have also provided many localities with an exposure to the technicalities of financing and marketing of a commercialized housing project.

Like all the policy innovations of the reform decade, the commercialization of housing for citizens of the People's Republic was initially started on an experimental basis and without great fanfare, in a small number of selected localities. The earliest reported pilot projects were begun in 1979 in Shenyang and in Fuzhou. In the latter, the emphasis was on the use of private resources for the construction of new housing; the experiment was conducted on some scale, for it was reported that in

---

5) *XH*, 8 April 1983, stated that before the end of that year, fifteen cities would abolish the system whereby electricity, water and gas were heavily subsidized by work units: in future, charges would be paid directly by households and each flat would have meters installed.

1980, as much new private housing was constructed as under Fuzhou's public municipal programme *(BR,* no. 32, 10 August 1979, pp. 7–8; no. 42, 20 October 1980, p. 5). It is probable that a good proportion of the funds for this private construction came from relatives abroad. In Shenyang, however, where such possibilities are limited, the experiment took the form of selling off existing public housing stock to individual purchasers. According to newspaper reports, demand greatly outstripped supply (e.g. *Ta Kung Pao,* 9 October 1980).

In April 1980, Gu Mu (then Vice–Premier) announced that in Nanning, Xi'an, Fuzhou, Wuxi and a number of other cities, schemes for the sale of public housing would be initiated. Both outright purchase and instalment plan methods (fifteen years, at 1–2 per cent interest) would be utilized *(BR* no. 21, 26 May 1980, p. 7). Encouraged by the popularity of such schemes – at least amongst the minority of urban households that had accumulated sufficient savings to find the scheme attractive – in late 1981, the National Housing Construction and Development Corporation *(Zhongguo fangwu jianshe gongsi,* hereafter CHCDC) was established.[6] The CHCDC selected the four cities of Zhengzhou *(Henan),* Changzhou *(Jiangsu),* Shashi *(Hubei)* and Siping *(Jilin)* as testing grounds for an expanded scheme. Today, the experimentation in these four centres is generally acknowledged to be the first serious effort to change the basis of China's housing supply. The package offered by the CHCDC was a repayment period of from five to twenty years at interest rates of up to 5 per cent. Where outright purchase was opted for, a 20–30 per cent discount on market price would be offered. Significantly, the standard purchasing arrangements represented a considerable retreat from the more extreme commodification proposals suggested by Party theorists. In CHCDC projects, only 30 per cent of an apartment's cost was to be repaid by the purchaser, and that through instalments if necessary, with low rates of interest. The *danwei* (work unit) and the local municipal government would undertake joint responsibility for the balance of the purchase price. After the amortization period, a flat would become the property of its occupier; it could not legally be sold, but could be passed on to children (Ta Kung Pao, 1 March 1984, p. 6; 26 July 1984, p. 6).

Between 1983 and 1985, there was abundant reportage of the growing influence and stature of the CHCDC in tackling China's housing problems. By its second year of operation the Corporation had established itself in nineteen cities. Its activities were supplemented by both the People's Bank of China and the Industrial and Commercial Bank, which began to experiment with the issuance of housing repair and purchase loans. In 1984, the State Council approved the CHCDC's extension to eighty more cities, including the three metropolitan centres of Beijing, Shanghai and Tianjin. There was provision for some flexibility in the application of the three–way division in investment (state, work unit, individual) 'depending on the financial situations of the buyers and their work units' (Ta Kung Pao, 25 October 1984). By its third national conference at the end of 1984, the CHCDC had become a nationwide institution, with branches in over one hundred major cities. Nineteen eighty–five

---

6) Under the general aegis of the newly formed Ministry for Urban–Rural Planning and Environmental Protection.

appears to have been the Corporation's high point: its 102 branches completed a total of 18 million m² floorspace nationwide (cf. 1984's figure of less than one million m²). This was one fifth of all urban housing constructed in 1985; 350,000 households were thereby provided for, and at high space standards of 12 m² per head (XH, 15 December 1984; *China Daily,* 26 November 1985).

Oddly, the activities of the CHCDC seemed to drop gradually out of sight after the mid–1980s. In the event, problems with the first major experiment in home purchase on which it based its activities – attempted after 1981 in Zhengzhou, Changzhou, Siping and Shashi – were not acknowledged until some years after they had been quietly abandoned. The obvious difficulty lay in their investment composition. The formula whereby the individual was required to finance only one–third of the purchase cost of a housing unit (the remaining two–thirds being divided equally between the central state and the work unit) left a burden on public funds far higher than could be supported under the prevailing fiscal regime. The central state budget was no healthier in the mid–1980s than it had been in the late 1970s. And further, in shifting the responsibility partly to the enterprise, the central authorities were imposing an enormous tax on their newly won right to retain a proportion of self–generated income. The antipathy towards the new scheme by factories, commercial and service enterprises (let alone schools, hospitals and other cash–starved non–production units) must have spelt its early demise *(Beijing Review,* 14 November 1988; *China Reconstructs,* August 1988).

It was soon evident, however, that official enthusiasm for the commercialization of housing had not been diminished by the setbacks of the first experiments of the reform decade. The determination to press ahead was spelt out in October 1985, when a special national conference of the CCP laid out the programme for China's 7th Five Year Plan (1986–90). According to then Premier Zhao Ziyang, the commercialzation of urban housing was to be one of the strategic principles of the Plan. At the same time, echoing one of Deng Xiaoping's personal preoccupations, the construction industry was to become a 'pillar of the national economy'. Once again, the state's low return on housing investments was bemoaned, and 'well considered methods....to gradually commercialise housing' were promised (BR no. 40, 7 October 1985). Meanwhile, the reformers realised the need to base their plans for urban housing on a firmer footing as far as data was concerned. Using one million enumerators, 31 December 1985 saw China's first nationwide census of housing, which by the completion of its detailed analysis provided ample evidence of the huge scale of the problems which persisted and which cried out for a radical solution.

Soon, therefore, the focus was shifted to a completely new pilot scheme, for which the rich coastal city of Yantai (Shandong Province) was assigned the role of test–bed. In contrast to the earlier experiments, the Yantai scheme was intended in the first instance to introduce commercialization of public sector rents rather than home––ownership. The Yantai model rests on the notion that the state housing subsidy should continue, albeit at lower level in global terms. While in the past it had been indirect, resulting in only notional rental transfers by tenants, now it should be paid directly to wage earners as an income supplement. The corollary would of course be a considerable increase in rental levels. Such methods had been previously applied in 1979 when staple food prices were dramatically increased as a result of sudden hikes in agricultural procurement prices. At that time, each wage earner received a standard monthly supplement, which could be used to offset grain price increases or alternatively (in theory at least) to diversify consumption to non–staples.

The official argument in favour of the new method of state subsidy to housing was that it increased consumer sovereignty, each household now deciding its requirement for housing in terms of the rented or owner–occupied sector, age, style, floor, location and, most crucial, the number of square metres it wished to occupy. The proponents of the new scheme were especially eager that it should release onto the market a large quantity of floorspace currently underused and surplus to the needs of the occupiers. Many of those obliged to relinquish floorspace by moving to smaller units would of course be Party and state cadres. We have already remarked that housing has been one of the most prominent areas for abuse of position: while on the whole official salaries are modest, their perquisites may be considerable. Thus the introduction of a more market–oriented system would, it was argued in the classic liberal capitalist mould, have a levelling effect which bureaucratic planning could never achieve.

In the Yantai scheme, it was decided after considerable research that housing vouchers should be issued with monthly pay, and they should have a value of 23.5 per cent of salary. The Yantai experience, introduced over 1986–7, was quickly deemed a great success and was formally approved by the State Council in August 1987. Already in July 1987 it had been decided to extend the experiment to a dozen more cities throughout the land in early 1988. In March 1988, the State Council's 'Leading Group on the Reform of the State Housing System' (an increasingly prominent segment of the central government's bureaucracy of reform) held an important meeting which sanctified the Yantai approach. It laid out a ten–year programme for completion of the housing reform nationwide which was somewhat surprising in its level of detail. For instance, by the end of the first five years, it was stipulated that average rents should have risen to 1.56 yuan per square metre (over ten times the mid–1980s level). Within this projected figure was taken into account the precise contributions of depreciation, costs of repairs, management, interest on capital and land tax. During the initial period, the Yantai system should be followed – that is, housing vouchers paid alongside salary, their value set at some 25 per cent of an individual's basic pay. The second stage should see a further increase in rental levels, which would reflect the introduction of two items currently foreign to the Chinese system. These would be property insurance and (notional) land–rent (*China Reconstructs*, August 1989). By the end of the 1990s, housing supplements would no longer be separated from monthly income but would be absorbed within it.

Thus China's reformers, through a process of experimentation lasting almost a decade, appear to have arrived at their definitive model for the market transformation of the nation's 2,400 million square metres of urban housing floorspace. We will comment in the concluding remarks to this chapter on the liklihood of success of their grand vision of a vibrant housing property market as the cornerstone of the urban economy.

Conclusion

With the advent of the Communist Party to power in 1949, it is no exaggeration to say that urban housing supply in China underwent a revolutionary transformation. The basic guarantees of life were for the first time offered to the masses of urban Chinese, and these included the right to shelter. Huge squatter and slum areas were quickly eradicated, and in the large cities such as Shanghai, where two–thirds of all housing units had been owned by 10 per cent of the population, the ravages of landlordism were quickly removed. The First Five Year Plan placed housing firmly on the agenda of national development strategy.

Yet in the ensuing years of the Mao era, the momentum of the 1st FYP was lost and housing and urban infrastructure sorely neglected. The reductionist philosophy of the Maoist planning apparatus, which saw China's cities as no more than the fulcrum of growing industrial production, became the order of the day. Basic shelter continued to be provided, but the quality of urban life was not a concept acknowledged by the authorities. During the periods of Maoist ascendancy in the Party, and especially during the last eleven years of his life, there was enforced restriction of urban population growth, regular induction of large numbers of single peasants into the urban wage economy, and drastic sanctions against anyone foolish enough to complain about urban living conditions. Without these factors it would have been impossible to countenance such neglect of the urban fabric year in, year out.

While the Chinese urban housing system did not permit the urban squalor and misery associated with most industrial revolutions, or with those processes of 'development' such as have been seen in the post–colonial world, at the same time it ceased to have any revolutionary dynamism. Once basic shelter was guaranteed, the transformation of the early years ossified into a highly bureaucratized and in many ways corrupt stasis. Above all, for all those in the state or enterprise rented sector, housing was a 'top–down' system allowing no room for individual control or initiative. The debates on urbanism and the socialist society seen for a short period in the Soviet Union of the 1920s were never to emerge in People's China.

The post–Mao regime was faced with all the decrepitude of urban decay bequeathed by twenty years of neglect. Its social and economic policies also meant vast numbers of new urban dwellers to house, employ and feed. Nonetheless, the reformists were able both to understand the need to change the balance between consumption and accumulation and dramatically change their equation. Housing and associated urban amenities were the greatest beneficiary, and their share of national investment in capital projects rose from the derisory levels of the Cultural Revolution to over one–quarter of the national total. Yet the system remained centralized and unwieldy, and the new urban environment of the huge high–rise estates which now mark every city are of limited quality, in both physical and social terms. In the more enlightened times which one hopes will come to China, the vast housing programme which began in 1979 will surely be regarded as a questionable achievement.

With the relentless rise in overall urban population (there are more than 100 million more urban Chinese today than a decade ago), in per capita floorspace terms it has been a case of running very hard just to keep still. The net effect of the decade of construction is that each urban resident today has on average around 8 square metres of living space. However, this overall figure is inflated by the inclusion as urban places of many small settlements of a semi–rural nature. Here, space standards have traditionally been far superior to those of the metropolitan centres. In Shanghai, Tianjin, Wuhan, Shenyang, Guangzhou, and many other provincial capitals the average available floorspace has increased little from the three or four square metres of the late 1970s. The 1985 national housing census revealed, for example, that while one–fifth of all urban households had over 10 square metres per capita, one quarter still had less than 4 square metres. Nationwide the census indicated that 10.45 million families (almost 50 million persons) urgently required rehousing. Even in the showcase of Beijing, around one third of the urban households were 'without proper homes' (*China Reconstructs*, August 1989).

The ideology of the reform of the 1980s invested a profound belief in the utility of market solutions to situations in which supply is hopelessly outmatched by demand. It is not surprising therefore that along with deregulation of food supply, urban housing was regarded as an ideal arena for *shangpinhua* – commodification. The early hope was for a generalization of home ownership. The pilot schemes having this objective foundered because of the obvious lack of disposable income of China's urban masses. Certainly in the case of the larger cities, where new flats have been offered at prices in excess of 1500 yuan per square metre, it is difficult to envisage the advent of large scale home ownership. It should be remembered that average annual industrial wages hardly match the cost of one square metre of housing at these inflated prices. Yet despite all this it was surprising to learn that as much as 30 per cent of all new urban housing completed in 1988 was for private sale (*China Daily*, 15 August 1989). This figure surely reflects the emergence of a privileged and moneyed stratum of urban Chinese after a decade of economic reform, and social polarization.

By the mid–1980s the focus had shifted away from home ownership schemes and towards the *Yantai*–type model, where 'market rents' was the objective in the hope that this would gradually relieve the state of its 30 billion *yuan* annual subsidy to housing. The Yantai model has only been operational for a short period; official reports of 1989 claim of course that it has already proved an undoubted success. For example, the majority of Yantai's homeless have now found a solution to their problems because of the release of (probably low grade) property by the hidden hand of the market. Yet even here, we are told that almost half the households of Yantai are having to supplement their housing vouchers with cash. This notwithstanding, the Yantai experience is in the 1990s to be generalized throughout the nation.

On past experience, official appraisals of socio–economic models set up by the Chinese system cannot be accepted with a great degree of confidence. For instance, the initial reports on the home ownership experiments launched in the four medium–sized cities in 1980 were highly enthusiastic. In late 1984, the *People's Daily* somewhat prematurely suggested that China's housing difficulties would thus soon be solved. It was stated that the rate of return on capital in one CHCDC home ownership programme was as high as ten to one (17 December 1984). Yet commercialization of housing principally through the means of home–ownership was not promoted with anything like the same enthusiasm after the mid–1980s.

Therefore we should remain sceptical about the Yantai model's accomplishments, and the possibility of generalizing them throughout urban China. A *World Bank* study has concluded that should direct state housing subsidies be entirely removed, the required urban income increases would range from 30 per cent for the more affluent sectors of society and up to 50 per cent for the poorer groupings *(China,* 1985, p. 150). China's planners have resolved that housing vouchers should be equivalent to no more than 25 per cent of wage packets. The majority of Chinese households may be able to cope at this level, as the labour participation rate in urban China is high. But if the market rent scheme is implemented nationwide there will be tens of millions of losers: those with less than average working members per household, those outside the state employment system, and those on low salaries. This last group will certainly include the majority of the intelligentsia: in the early 1980s this group, which had suffered great discrimination during the Mao period – was promised positive action as far as living standards were concerned. Some progress was made towards honouring the Party's promises, particularly in the area of housing and to a certain extent in salaries. But this advance now seems certain to be brought to a halt; in the political disturbances of the first half of 1989 the intellectuals played a leading role, and they must now reap their reward from a much angered Party hierarchy.

How do China's urban masses view the prospect of removal of housing from the realm of the social wage? One only has glimpses of their inchoate response. One survey of 1988 did however find that 85 per cent of those balloted were in favour of preserving the status quo *(Beijing Review,* 14 November 1988). This corresponds with the impressions gained by the present writer from a number of discussions in China. While the reforming zealots – with the encouragment of the international financial agencies – see the low–wage and high subsidy economy as an anachronism and an impediment to 'modernization', China's citizens are firmly attached to their achievements on the social welfare front. They are fruits of the revolution not to be passed up in exchange for vague promises of the urban good life. Before the mid–1980s, price inflation of daily necessities, particularly food, had been unknown to a whole generation of Chinese. Its reappearance, and at annual rates of 20–30 per cent, has created a severe psychological malaise. The prospect of officially–induced hyper–inflation of rents, whether or not alleviated by income supplements, is now another, inescapable challenge to the collective psyche. The mass disenchantment with the regime, so visibly demonstrated to the world and so harshly suppressed by the leadership in June 1989, certainly arises in part from the disquiet which the new plans for housing have aroused.

So what of the future? While the events of 1989 have removed political reform from the agenda at least until the expiry of the present old–guard leadership, it is highly unlikely that the economic edifice of Maoist days will be restored. Yet there will be a degree of decentralization and a removal of those aspects of market regulation of the economy which truly threaten the hegemony of central control. This will be mainly in the realm of production, distribution and foreign economic relations. Close observers of China are currently waiting for the dust to settle before they hazard firm predictions concerning China's future. The post–June official position on the housing reform is that it should go ahead according to plan. Yet to quote one recent overview of the situation, 'Housing reform has reached a crucial stage' (*China Reconstructs*, August 1989).

Despite their apparent remoteness from the reality of the masses, the present commanders of the nation are bound to understand that concessions to public opinion will have to be made. There is therefore every likelihood of further significant modification of the plans to introduce market–oriented reforms to China's urban housing. That is, the political forces which come to the fore in the early 1990s may well see the wisdom of preserving urban housing as a social welfare good rather than pressing it into the arena of stark commodity relations. With the overwhelming problems of population and food supply which remain a feature of China in the late twentieth century, China's leaders will have much else to occupy them.

Bibliography

Chao Kang, 1966, Industrialization and Urban Housing in Communist China. In *Journal of Asian Studies 25* (3).
China 1985: Long Term Development Issues and Options. The World Bank, Washington and Johns Hopkins Press, Baltimore.
Gu Zhiming, 1980. Housing's Fundamental Character and the Problem of Return on Investment (in Chinese). In *Jianghan Luntan* (Jianghan Review) *5,* Wuhan.
He Gongjian, 1980. The Realities of the Housing Problem and Ideas for its Solution (in Chinese). In *Jianghan Luntan* (Jianghan Review) *6,* Wuhan.
Howe, C., 1968. The Supply and Administration of Urban Housing in Mainland China: The Case of Shanghai. In *China Quarterly, 33*
Kirkby, Richard J.R., 1985. *Urbanization in China: Town and Country in a Developing Economy 1949–2000 AD.* London, Croom Helm.
Kwok, R.Y., 1973. *Urban–Rural Planning and Housing Development in the People's Republic of China,* Ph.D. Thesis, Columbia University. Ann Arbor, Xerox University Microfilms.
Leeming, F., 1985. *Rural China Today.* London, Longman.
Mao Zedong, 1981. Report to the Second Plenary Session of the Seventh Central Committee of the Communist Party of China. In *Selected Works of Mao Tse–Tung,* vol. IV. Beijing, Foreign Languages Press.
Su Xing, 1980. How to Solve the Housing Problem More Quickly. In *Hongqui* (Red Flag) 2, January.
Wang Fengwu, 1985. *Urban Planning in Britain and China.* Unpublished Ph.D. Thesis. University of Wales, Institute of Science and Technology.
Yu Xinyan, 1981. Some Views on the Housing Question (in Chinese). In *Jianghan Luntan* (Jianghan Review) *1,* Wuhan.
Zhang Jun, 1985. China 1980–2000: *Urban Construction and Financing.* Unpublished background paper prepared for The World Bank. Washington, D.C., October.

Further reading

Jüngst, Peter; Peisert, Christoph; Schulze–Göbel, Hans–Jörg (Eds.), 1985. *Stadtplanung in der Volksrepublik China. Entwicklungsstand im Spiegel von Aufsätzen und Gesprächen (1949–1979).* Urbs et Regio, vol. 35/1984. Kassel (Germany): Gesamthochschulbibliothek.
Eplan, Leon et al., 1984. Urban Planning in China. Report of an American Delegation of City Planners. In: Blair, Thomas (Ed.), *Urban Innovation Abroad,* New York: Plenum, p. 212–250.
Hahn, Ekhart, 1979. China heute: Tendenzen und Entwicklungen in Städtebau und Stadtpolitik. In *Bauwelt* No. 12, p. 414–426.
Hahn, Ekhart, 1983. *Umweltbewußte Siedlungspolitik in China.* Frankfurt/Main: Campus.

Hahn, Ekhart, 1984. Wohnungszusammenhänge zwischen Siedlungspolitik, Umweltpolitik, und Entwicklungspolitik in der VR China. In *TRIALOG* 4, Darmstadt, p.29–34.

Howe, Christopher (Ed.), 1981. *Shanghai – Revolution and Development in an Asian Metropolis.* Cambridge – London – New York.

Gavinelli, Corrado, and Gibelli, Maria Cristina, 1979. *Ciudad y Territorio en China.* Madrid: H. Blume.

Küchler, Johannes, 1976. Stadterneureung in der VR China. In: *Stadterneuerungsprozeß – Stadt-entwicklungschancen: Planung in Berlin, Bologna. und in der VR China.* Göttingen (Germany).

Maxwell, Neville, and McFarlane, Bruce (Eds.). *China's Changed Road to Development.* World Development Special Issue (vol. 11, no. 8).

Oertl, Christian, 1984. Wohnungsbau und Stadtentwicklung in der Volksrepublik China. In: *TRIALOG* 4 (Okt.), Darmstadt (Germany), p. 26–39.

Suifang, Li, 1989. Residence Planning for Towns: On the Improvement of Residence and Living Environment. In *TRIALOG* 20, p. 42–44.

Albania

Lena Magnusson[1]

The National Setting

Albania represents a particularly interesting case because it is considered to be the most isolated, and hence, the most independent socialist country in the world. Unfortunately, but not surprisingly, the political isolation, which even closed borders to tourists and journalists for long periods, also implies that there is little accessible information about housing policies. However, the few facts we know are arresting enough to investigate the issue further. The country has been following certain austere policy measures which other governments certainly considered but never dared to enforce.

Among the developing countries, Albania is one of the oldest socialist regimes. In the second world war, when the country was occupied by the Italians, 'anti-fascist resistance turned into a guerilla war directed by the communists under the leadership of Enver Hoxa (born 1908). On 29 November, 1944, the occupation forces withdrew from the country and the following year a People's Republic was declared' *(Third World Guide,* 1988). The society is organized strictly in line with the Marxist-Leninist ideology, and responded to reformist policies in Yugoslavia (1948), in the Soviet Union (the de-Stalinization period), and in China after Mao (1981) by cutting off diplomatic relations with these countries. Albania is a one-party state, and almost 5 per cent of the population are members of the *Partia e Punes e Shqiperisie* (PPSH or Labour Party of Albania), but a much larger number belong to such mass organizations as the Central Council of Albanian Trade Unions (400,000 members), the Working Youth Union, the women's organization, or the association of writers and artists of Albania. All these organizations are part of the party system, just like the

---

1) This chapter is based on research carried out at the National Swedish Institute for Building Research in Gävle, Sweden. It was reproduced here with kind permission of Jozsef Hegedüs, Ivan Tosics, and Beng Turner – the editors of a forthcoming book *'Housing Reforms in Eastern Europe'* where an expanded version of the paper will be published.

Country Profile: Albania

National territory: 28,748 km²
Population: 3.02 million (1986)
Population density: 101 inhab/sq.km
Labour force: 1,398,000 (1985)
    51% in agriculture, 25% in industry, 14% in services.
Urbanization rate: 39%
Capital: Tirana; 206,100 inhabitants (1983)
Estimated natural growth rate: 2% (1973–84)
Life expectancy: 69.3 years for men; 72.2 years for women
Infant mortality: 4.4%
Illiteracy rate: 28%
Religion: Religious cults are illegal. Islam used to be the majority religion
Language: Albanian (official)
Military expenditure: 11% of budget

Some important dates:
1478 Turkish occupation
1912 Liberation from Turkish occupation, declaration of independence
1928 President Ahmet Zogu proclaims monarchy after signing a treaty with Italy
1939 Italy occupied and formally annexed Albania, guerilla resistance led by the communists
1943 Occupation by German army
1944 Occupation forces withdrew
1946 Proclamation of *People's Republic of Albania*
1948 Breaking diplomatic relations with Yugoslavia, which was labelled revisionist
1955 Entry into *Warsaw Pact*
1968 Exit from *Warsaw Pact* and closer ties with China
1976 New constitution and renaming of the country *Socialist People's Republic*
1981 Albania cut off relations with China following de–Maoization move
1985 Death of Enver Hoxha, head of state, with Ramiz Alia, his successor, slowly easing Albania past political isolation.
1986 Announcement that diplomatic relations will be resumed with Germany (after payment of war reparations); also USSR offers to resume relations.
1987 Parliamentary elections

Sources: Die Länder der Erde, Köln: Pahl–Rugenstein, 1982. Third World Guide, Montevideo: Third World Editors, 1988.

people's assembly which constitutes the government at the local and departmental level.

In the year 1976, Albania adopted a new constitution, which reinforces the socialist orientation:

> *"The people's socialist republic of Albania is the state of the dictatorship of the proletariat which expresses and defends the interests of all workers. It is based on the unity of the people and has its roots in the alliance of the working class with the co-operativist peasantry, under the leadership of the working class" (Berxholi et al., 1986).*

Albania's centrally planned economy aims at agricultural self-sufficiency, which it achieved in wheat and is expected to attain in cotton, sunflower, sugar and other crops. It also attempts to build up an independent domestic industry and has made impressive economic progress. For example, according to government statistics, industrial output has increased 125 times, electricity 322 times, and building materials production 236 times over the post-war period *(Third World Guide, 1988)*.

Despite a claimed economic growth of 6 per cent per annum in the 1981–85 five-year plan, with a gross national product of US$930 in 1986, the country still ranks among the poorest in Europe. The major constraints to economic growth are low productivity levels due to weak investment capacity and shortage of skilled labour. The major producer is agriculture, employing over 60 per cent of the labour force; 80 per cent of agricultural output is produced by the 420 agricultural cooperatives (Chamberlain, 1988).

Albania is also Europe's most collectivized society, in which private property in most objects, including cars, is banned as a matter of principle. In 1945–6, the property of all capitalists was expropriated, and the large land holdings were distributed among 70,000 landless farmers as part of the agrarian reform. The last private land was nationalized in 1976. However, among the few exceptions from the ban on private property are livestock and housing, which can be built and owned privately. Also, private vegetable trading is tolerated in small amounts.

All direct taxation and levies were abolished in 1969, but wages are low. There is a policy to reduce to a minimum wage differentials between distinct occupational groups and between town and countryside. The difference between the lowest and the highest wage has been reported to be in the area of 1:2 (Chamberlain, 1988; Utrikespolitiska Institutet, 1988).

Anti-Urbanization Policies

One of the key principles of Albanian home politics is to develop rural areas and to restrain urbanization. On the whole this policy has been successful. Although the share of the urban population has increased between 1945 and 1960, the distribution has stabilized thereafter at a level of about one-third urban and two-thirds rural population. Less than 7 per cent of the population live in the capital, Tirana.

One of the instruments used to control urban growth was the establishment of a border around every city, beyond which it was not allowed to expand. This so-called

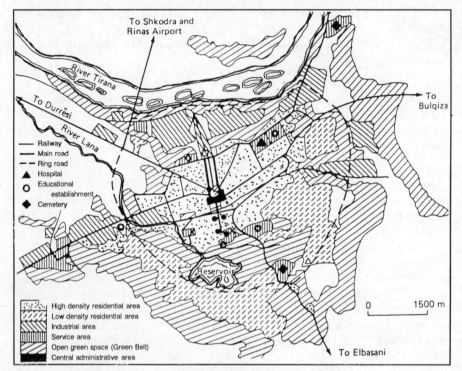

Ill. 1: Tirana Development plan. The green belt concept is clearly visible.
Adapted from: Ministry of Construction, Tirana, reproduced in 'Cities', Oct. 1986)

'yellow line' constitutes the division between rural and urban territory. Most cities have now reached the yellow line. Any other people who want to live in such cities are directed to other new or existing cities. Special permits are necessary for those who want to move to the city, but they must show proof of a job and a place to live.

Demographic Development and Housing Demand

Albania with about 3.2 million inhabitants (1989) has the fastest growing population in Europe. The average annual growth rate was 2 per cent in the last decade (1973–84, *Third World Guide,* 1988). As a consequence, the population is relatively young, with a mean age of 26 years *(Table 1).* The household pattern reflects traditional agrarian society. Household sizes are comparatively large; due to overcrowding and culture, it is rather common for more than one couple to share a dwelling. It is accepted that the eldest son should take care of his parents and share his dwelling with them (Proko, 1989).

The number of families is increasing even more steeply than the population as a whole *(Table 2).* Between the census of 1969 and 1979 the number of families grew by 35 per cent, but the population only by 25 per cent. The main reason for this phe-nomenon is a tendency to smaller families of four to five persons *(Table 3).* How-

Table 1:   Age composition in Albania
Under 15 years 35%
15–39 years 43%
40–59 years 15%
over 59 years 7%

Source: Misja and Vejesiu, 1985

Table 2: Families by couples

	1950	1979
One couple	61.5%	71.4%
two couples	26.9%	24.8%
three couples and more	11.6%	3.8%

Source: Misja and Vejesiu, 1985

ever, the number of one and two person households is decreasing and is now less than 10 per cent, a trend that is much different from the rest of Europe where this group represents between 30 and 55 per cent. Apart from an obviously increasing demand for housing, the strong traditional values of marriage and family, which imply that children stay with their parents until they get married, are reflected here. No young single–person families enter the housing market.

Table 3: Structure of families by number of persons in 1950, 1960, 1969, and 1979

Family size	Number of families			
	1950	1960	1969	1979
1 person	8.9%	6.1%	3.8%	3.3%
2–3 persons	21.2%	16.7%	16.1%	17.2%
4–5 persons	27.0%	26.9%	28.3%	33.9%
6–8 persons	28.3%	34.7%	36.4%	33.4%
9 or more persons	14.5%	15.6%	15.4%	12.2%
Total	99.9%	100.0%	100.0%	100.0%

Source: Statistical Yearbook of P.S.R. of Albania, 1988

State Housing Policies

As no official statistics on housing production and exchange are available, the analysis is bound to be tentative. However, certain basic facts can be confirmed.

Basically there are three tenure forms in Albania: flats rented from the state, co-operatively owned flats, and privately owned one–family houses. In the cities, most of the dwellings are rented flats in prefabricated multi–family blocks, which are owned by the state. The share of government–built dwellings, including those belonging to state farms, has increased from 10 per cent in the late 1940s to about 50 per cent in the early 1970s and thereafter. In the countryside, where some 300,000 families live, the majority (235,000 families) live in co–operatives and state farms. The remainder (approximately 65,000 families) seem to be owner occupiers (Hall, 1987).

In total, about 300,000 dwellings have been built within all three sectors between the end of World War II and 1980 (Table 4). In economic terms, investment into housing increased from 4.3 to 6.7 per cent of total investments over the past forty years.

Table 4: Number of dwellings built by the state, by voluntary work, and by individuals 1946–1987.

Years of construction	Total number of dwellings	Built by the state	Built by voluntary work	Built by individuals
1946–1950	12,114	1,114		11,000
1951–1955	26,110	7,596		18,514
1956–1960	47,413	11,734		35,679
1961–1965	44,693	15,808		28,885
1966–1970	73,213	16,587	12,458	44,168
1971–1975	61,908	9,106	22,932	29,870
1976–1980	56,390	16,144	10,182	30,064
1981–1985	75,362	25,569	15,618	34,175
1986	15,049	4,742	3,319	6,988
1987	13,863	4,118	3,152	6,593

Source: *Statistical Yearbook of P.S.R. of Albania, 1988*

The state builds its flats in urban areas both through its own organization in direct labour, and through voluntary campaigns. The latter method had first emerged in 1968 when a pioneer programme was inaugurated in Tirana during the country's cultural revolution. Voluntary labour implies that the state provides building materials and technical assistance, and the future residents contribute their own labour force (Sjöberg, 1989b). This policy became an important resource for housing construction particularly after the two earthquakes in 1967 and 1979 (Albania, 1982)

State–owned flats are allocated through the neighbourhoods people's councils, which are part of the party system. The main criterion for assignment is the size of the applicant's family (Proko, 1989). The rents paid are very low, approximately equal to the income from one or two workdays (Sjöberg, 1988).

The Private Sector and Housing Standards

Since 1950, those who want to build their own houses have been able to obtain loans from the state to cover the cost of construction. These loans are available to everyone, and have to be paid back over twenty to twenty–five years, at an interest rate of only 0.5 per cent (Sjöberg, 1988). The reason for such a favourable interest rate is Albania's claims to have overcome inflation.

The size of the plot to be allocated to a house builder depends on its location. In urban areas, 150 square metres are the standard for a single–family house; in the countryside it is 200 square metres, and 300 in the mountains. A special state office is in charge of preparing construction plans for all types of buildings. Single–family houses which are being built in Albania today belong to one of three standardized types, with a surface area of about 60 to 80 square metres. Once a house plot and the construction plans have been handed over to the prospective user, it usually takes two or three months to obtain the allocated building material, but additional supply through the informal sector is common practice (Sjöberg, 1988, 1989b).

In the countryside many people still cook on open fires and heat with traditional hearths. In the state–built blocks of flats, maintenance problems have been reported, which is particularly true for the post–war high–rise buildings. But on the whole, standards are improving. Refrigerators and washing machines, which have to be imported, are becoming common, being promoted with the argument that they alleviate housework and permit women to participate in so–called 'productive work'.

Concluding Remarks

Not unlike the development in other socialist states, Albania has started to establish trade and political exchange with other, and not exclusively socialist, countries in recent years. And in home politics, Albanians have 'opted for a mild glasnost of their own' (Chamberlain, 1988). Incentives and decentralization are being promoted, incompetence denounced, and cultural relaxation called for. However, so far signs of a housing reform are not easy to find.

References and Further Reading

Albania, 1982: *Portrait of Albania,* The 8 Nentori Publishing House, Tirana.

Berxholi, A. and P. Quirizani, 1986: *Albania – A Geographical View.* Tirana: The 8 Nentori Publishing House.

Carrière, P. and M. Sivignon, 1982: Les rapports ville–campagne et l'urbanisation de l'espace et de la société en Albanie. In *Villes et Parallèles,* no. 6, p. 158.

Carter, F.W., 1986: Tirana City Profile. In *Cities* (November), p. 270–281.

Chamberlain, D.R., 1988: *Albania.* The Europe Review, 1988.

Hall, D.R., 1987: 'Albania', in A.H. Dawson (ed.), *Planning in Eastern Europe.* London: Croom Helm.

Misja, V. and Y. Vejesiu, 1985: *Demographic Development in the People's Socialist Republic of Albania.* Tirana: The 8 Nentori Publishing House.

Proko, P., 1989. Personal interview, 12 April.

Sjöberg, Ö., 1988: *Rural Change in Albania: A Survey of the Evidence.* Unpublished dissertation, Department of Social and Economic Geography, Uppsala University.

Sjöberg, Ö., 1989a: *A Note on the Regional Dimension of Postwar Demographic Development in Albania.* Unpublished paper.

Sjöberg, Ö., 1989b: Personal interview, 8 May.

Statistical Yearbook of P.S.R. of Albania, 1988. Tirana.

Third World Guide 89/90. 1988. Montevideo: Third World Editors.

Utrikespolitiska Institutet, 1988: *Albanien.* Stockholm.

Index

Access to housing 3, 16
Addis Ababa 227, 232, 235, 238,
    239, 247
Administrative structure 172
Adobe 90, 110, 127, 141, 172, 184,
    212
Affordability 3, 16, 222, 284
Afghanistan 21, 29
African Socialism 8, 21, 24, 107, 185
Agrarian reform 22, 38, 260
Ajuda barrio (Bissau) 100
Albania 10, **315–321**
Aldeamentos 106
Aleta (hurricane) 85
Algeria 9, 10, 13, 15, 21, 26, 102,
    249–273
Algiers 253, 256
Allende, Salvador 21
AMLAE = Women's organization
    (Nicaragua) 78
Angola 7, 17, 21, 28, 100, 123, **129–
    145,** 249
Anti-consumption ideology 293
Anti-urbanization 317
APIE = *Administração de Parque
    Inmobilario* (Mozambique) 152,
    168
Appropriate technology 17, 46, 89,
    127, 140, 156, 166, 171
Architectural heritage 263
Ardhi Institute Conferences 192
Arusha Declaration 26, 185, 189
Asbestos 212

Assimilados 118
Assossa scheme (Ethiopia) 243
Avant–garde strategy 220, 223
Bairros 156, 166
Bamboo 90, 110
Barlavento (Cape Verde) 121
Basic needs 143
Benin 21
Berlin Congress 1885 99
BIN = *Banco Inmobiliario de
    Nicaragua S.A.* 88
Bishop, Maurice 21
Black market 9, 27, 28, 53, 54, 60,
    88, 268, 272
Block committees 279
Boat people 282
Bohíos (Cuba) 37, 40, 52, 59
Brain drain 91, 129, 152, 254
Brazil 121, 138
Britain 100, 165
Building brigades 8, 15, 45, 165, 197,
    209, 213, 218, 285
Building industry 244, 258, 285, 307
Building materials 88, 90, 110, 128,
    140, 159, 162, 172, 174, 230, 238,
    244, 247, 264, 267, 268, 271
Building materials banks 83
Building permits 108, 126, 238
Building regulations 60
Building technology 46
Bulldozing 211, 222
Bureaucracy 15, 135, 142, 176, 194,
    241, 272, 280, 300, 308

Burkina Faso 21
Burma 6
Cabral, Amilcar 97, 100, 101, 105, 107, 117, 123
CADAT = Algerian Bank for the Development of the Territory 256
Cambodia 21, 252
Cape Verde 7, 10, 21, 97, 99, **121– 128,** 122
Casas de vecindad 40
Cash-crop farming 187
Catholic Church 118
Cazenga (Angola) 137
CBS = *Comité de Barrio Sandinista* (Nicaragua) 79
CCP = Chinese Communist Party 20, 289
CDR = Committees for the Defence of the Revolution (Cuba) 51
CDS = *Comité de Defensa Sandinista* (Nicaragua) 78
Cell-system 183
Cement 90, 111, 127, 134, 165, 172, 244
CEOPCU = State Commissariat for Public Works (Bissau) 115
CHCDC = National Housing Construction Corporation (China) 306
Chika 235
Child care centres 62
Chile 21
China 10, 14, 19, 20, 23, 24, 28, 29, 30, 76, 277, 278, **289–314,** 315
CIDA = International Development Agency 119
CINVA-RAM 141
CITA = Centre for Appropriate Technology (Nicar.) 90
Ciudadelas 40
Civil servants 194
Clandestine urbanization 265
Clay bricks 172, 245
CNEP = Caisse National d'Epargne (Algeria) 266
Co-operatives 8, 16, 42, 45, 53, 57, 60, 102, 111, 112, 116, 119, 126,

131, 143, 155, 164, 165, 175, 177, 189, 210, 214, 218, 232, 238, 240, 242, 245, 259, 279, 283–285, 286, 317, 319
Coca-Cola 29
Collective construction 141
Collective facilities 260
Collective kitchens 285
Collectivization 131, 279
COMEDOR = Committee for the Development of Algiers ... 256
Comintern 20, 21, 24
Comités de base (Guinea Bissau) 116
Commercialization 304, 305, 307
Commodification 10, 303, 310
Commodity production 304
Communal services 89
Communal villages 157, 159, 175
Communist Manifesto 22
Communist Saturdays 279
Community facilities 44, 46, 186
Community organization 116
Community participation 60, 65, 79, 114–116, 125, 139
Complejos Habitacionales (Nicaragua) 83
Comprehensive Development Zones 49
Concrete 110, 161, 171, 285
Congo 21, 25
Constantine Plan 256
Construction brigades 137, 138
Construction co-operatives 164, 172
Construction industry 170, 307
Construction materials 134, 152, 167, 170
Construction standards 170
Consultants 235
Consumer cities 107, 135, 280
Consumer sovereignty 308
Consumerism 14, 29, 257
Consumption of housing 285
Contras (Nicaragua) 73, 85
Corcoro (corrugated iron) 245
Cordon sanitaire 132
Core housing 83, 163, 205

Corrugated iron sheets 245
Corruption 27, 52, 53, 61, 283, 298
Cost recovery 203, 207, 310
Cost rents 10
Council housing 207
COVIN = State Building Companies
(Nicaragua) 77
CRALOMBA = *Comité Regional de
Asignación* . . . (Nicaragua) 79
Credits 57, 82, 154, 156, 181, 183,
191, 265, 283, 284
CSO = Central Statistical Office
(Ethiopia) 232
CST = Central Sandinista de Trabaja-
dores (Nicaragua) 79
Cuarterías (Cuba) 40
Cuba 4, 6, 8, 13, 15, 17,
19–22, 24, **35–70**, 90, 102, 114,
123, 133, 135, 137, 138, 209, 229
Cultural Revolution 293, 297
Dar es Salaam 181, 183, 191
DCU = Construction and Urbanization
Directorate (Mozambique) 164
Decentralization 28, 39, 45, 62, 64,
75, 134, 141, 142, 159, 171, 257,
270, 279, 311, 321
Deficit of housing 87, 91, 162
Deforestation 121
Demolition 108, 211
Densification 219, 234
Densities 49, 63, 231, 282
Depreciation 169, 301, 303, 308
Deregulation 66
Design of housing 46, 245
Destabilization policies 29
Deurbanization 144, 280
Development plans 77
Development Workshop 140
Direct labour 15, 45, 119, 170
Distribution of housing 16, 52, 79, 85
Djebel (Algeria) 256
DNH = *Direção Nacional de Habi-
tação* (Mozambique) 155
Domingos rojos 143
Dormitory suburbs 270
Dormitory system 292

Douars (Algeria) 256
Dynamizing groups 8, 156, 164, 167,
166, 169, 177
Earthquakes 49, 171
Eastern Europe 4, 10, 15, 65, 285
Ecology 30
Edirs (Etiopia) 240
Electrification 41
EMEC = *Empresa Estadal de Con-
strução* (Cape Verde) 124
EMPA = *Empresa Pública de
Abastecimento* (Cape Verde) 124
Employment generation 119
Enabling policy 177
Engels, Friedrich 3, 302
Epworth (Zimbabwe) 212
Equb (Ethiopia) 240
Eradication 108
Eritrea 227
Ethiopia 9, 21, 26, **227–248**
European Community 107, 240
Eviction 89, 284
Evictions 58
Exchange of housing 55
Experts 86, 114
Exploitation 3, 13, 22, 123, 207
Expropriation 80, 88, 136,
280, 282
Facade syndrome 235
Famine 238, 243
FFYDP = First Four Year
Development Plan (Bissau) 103
Fibre cement 91
Finance of housing 16, 77, 117, 265,
278
FNA = *Faction Nito Alves* (Angola)
135
FNLA = National Front for the Liber-
ation of Angola 129
Food aid 103
Fordist industrialization 29
Foreign assistance 173, 243
Foreign debt 74
Foreign exchange 90, 106, 278
Fourier 29
France 121, 251, 254

Frelimo party (Mozambique) 24, 25
    153, 154, 166, 167, 175, 177
FSLN = *Frente Sandinista de Libera-
    ción Nacional* (Nicaragua) 78
FYP = Five-Year Plan (China) 293
Gabu 101
Garbage collection 44
Garden city 203
Gender democracy 200
Gender issues 194
Geneva treaties 275
Germany 158, 171
Ghana 21
Gigantismo 25, 28
Gorbachev 28
Grass roots democracy 15, 79, 91
Great Leap Forward (China) 293
Green belt 143, 164, 278, 280, 318
Grenada 21
GRET = Groupe de Recherche et
    d'Echanges Technologues 5
Group camps 253
Group of 77 26
Growth poles 43
Guerrilla war 100, 315
Guerrilla movements 123
GUHRLM = *Gabinete de Urbaniza-
    ção* ... (Mozambique) 151
Guinea Bissau 7, 21, 30, **97–120,**
    121, 123
Guinea Conakry 99, 106
Guyana 6
Gypsum 127
Habana del Este 46
Haile Selassie 227
Hanoi 282, 284, 285
Harare 201, 215, 220
HDD = Housing Development
    Departments (Tanzania) 193
HDF = Housing Development Fund
    (Tanzania) 193
High-density 49
High-rise 44, 46, 49, 57, 169, 170,
    201, 286, 297, 298, 305
Historical town centres 263
Ho Chi Minh 275

Ho Chi Minh City 282
Holland 121
Home ownership 40, 66, 207, 301,
    310
Homelessness 4
Hong Kong 305
Housing Bank 77
Housing finance, private savings 17
Housing production 208
Housing reform 308
Housing rights 136
Hungary 16
Hurricanes 85
ICRC = International Committee of
    the Red Cross 132
IIED = International Institute for En-
    vironment and Development
    5, 119
Illegal building 60
Import subsitution 134
Improvement programmes 80
In-fill housing 49
Income differentials 92
Indigenous architecture 111
Industrial settlements 270
Industrialization 23, 29, 197, 258
Industrialized building and construc-
    tion 10, 17, 46, 50, 90, 114, 138,
    161, 173, 298
Inflation 14, 81, 255, 266, 311
Informal sector 88, 108, 111, 117,
    205, 230, 242, 271
Informal settlements 124
Infrastructure 44, 60, 62, 77, 86, 89,
    109, 116, 134, 142, 154, 162, 232,
    240, 259, 309
Infrastructure improvement 79, 125
Inheritance 55
INPF = National Institute for Physical
    Planning (Mozambique) 159
Inquilenatos 88
Institution-building 113
Interest on loans 3, 57, 241, 308
Intermediate technology 46
International assistance 118
International Labour Office 107

International Monetary Fund 7, 26, 27, 132
International Year of Shelter for the Homeless 165
Invasions 89, 123
Italy 122, 125, 138, 227
Japan 275
Kampuchea 276, 277, 280, 281
Kebele 232, 237, 238, 242
Kebele 41 (Addis Ababa, Ethiopia) 239, 242
Keftegenas = Higher Urban Dwellers Associations (Ethiopia) 232
Kerala (India) 20
Khmer Rouge 29
Khrushchev 23
Kleve 5, 224
Kolfe scheme (Ethiopia) 235
Korea (North) 6
Kulak farmers 187
Kuwadzana (Zimbabwe) 213
Labour unions 80, 183
Labour-intensive construction technology 17, 111
Laissez-faire policy 253
Lancaster House Agreement 199
Land 13, 14, 37, 52, 80, 106, 107, 123, 167, 187, 206, 230, 234, 247, 264, 280, 303, 308
Land banking 54, 168
Land reform 199, 231
Land reserve 206
Land use control 60, 165, 167
Land use pattern 230
Landlordism 3, 223, 231
Landlords (absentee) 7
Laos 21
Large-scale development 62, 117
LCHS = Lund Committee on Habitat and Development Studies 5
Leasehold 56
Legislation for housing (Nicaragua) **92**, (Mozambique) **177**
Lenin 23, 24
Liberalization 104, 114
Liberation struggle 13, 21, 251

Lime 128, 172, 285
Literacy campaign 74
Loans 43, 55, 57, 117, 127, 188, 213, 229, 240, 242, 306, 320
Local autarchy 10
Local building materials 125, 127, 247, 261
Local government 45
Local self-administration 278
Lottery savings system 240
Low-cost housing 53, 152, 188, 207, 245
Low-rise 49
Low-wage policy 303
MAC = *Empresa Pública de Materi-ais de Construção* (Cape Verde) 124
Maintenance problems 17, 48, 51, 82, 161, 169, 235, 237, 261, 295, 303, 321
MALU = *Ministério da Administração Local e Urbanismo* (Cape Verde) 126
Management 303, 308
Managua 75, 91
Mandinga invasion (Guinea Bissau) 99
Manuals 141, 218
Mao 293, 302, 309
Market economy 27, 29, 300
Market socialism 10, 176, 277
Márquez, Gabriel García 129
Marx 22, 29, 229
Mass housing 9, 10, 38, 83, 297
Mass organizations 78, 80, 116, 232, 279
Master plans 77, 272
Maxaquene 155, 165
Mazingira Institute 165
MCA = Ministry of Construction and Water Affairs (Mozambique) 165
Messica (Mozambique) 165
MICONS = Ministry of Construction (Cuba) 44
Microbrigades 6, 15, 38, 39, 40, **44**, 47, 52, 56, **60**, 63, 209

MIDINRA = Ministry of Agriculture (Nicaragua) 78
Migration 4, 10, 41–43, 58, 121, 124, 132, 136, 201, 203, 234, 247, 253, 257, 259, 262, 285, 299
MINVAH = Ministry of Housing and Human Settlements (Nicar.) 74
Mixed economy 88, 131, 199
MLHUD = Ministry of Lands, Housing ... (Tanzania) 191
MOA = Ministry of Agriculture (Ethiopia) 238
Model villages 281
Modernization 235, 237, 257, 311
Módulos básicos (Nicaragua) 85
Monoculture 121
MOPH = Ministry of Public Works and Housing (Mozambique) 155
Morocco 132, 252
Mortgages 56, 88, 168, 169
Mozambique 8, 17, 21, 24–26, 28, 100, 123, 144, **147–180,** 249
MPLA = Movement for the Liberation of Angola 129
MPLA–PT = Labour party of Angola 143
MPS = *Militia* (Nicaragua) 78
MUDH = Ministry of Urban Development and Housing (Ethiopia) 231
Mugabe, Robert 199
Multi-storey flats 245
Multinationals 199
Musseques 137, 143
Mutual Aid 38, 54, 240
Mwenge housing co-operative (Tanzania) 189
Namibia 132
Napalm 252
National Liberation Front (Algeria) 253
Nationalization 7, 37, 103, 106, 107, 123, 131, 133, 136, 152, 154, 168, 168, 187, 231, 238, 247
Neighbourhood architects 62

Neighbourhood committees 52, 78, 79, 116
New development zones 285
New economy zones 281
New society 253
New towns 42, 53, 56, 213
NHC = National Housing Corporation (Tanzania) 188
Nicaragua 4, 6, 7, 13–15, 17, 21, 37, **71–96**
Non-Governmental Organizations 6, 87, 117, 126, 164, 165, 166, 235, 242
North Korea 20
Nyerere, Julius 181
O.E.C.D. 22
Optimum strategy 220, 222
Orthodox Church 230
OTM = Mozambican trade union 25
Overcrowding 65, 108, 110, 170, 201, 234, 295, 318
Owner occupation 16, 50, 81, 82, 222, 237, 239, 284, 301, 308, 319
Pacification 99
PAF = Property Development Plan (Algeria) 257
PAIGC = African Party for Independence (Cape Verde) 121; (Guinea Bissau) 97
Parasite cities 10
Paris Treaty 1886 99
Participation 15, 28, 115, 117, 137, 166
Party hierarchy 311
Pavement dwellers 285
PCD = Communal Development Plan (Algeria) 257
Peasant economy 26, 304
Peasant mentality 260
Peasants' Association (Ethiopia) 232
People's Councils 64
Perestroika 4, 10
Permuta (Cuba) 56
Petrol boom 251
Petty bourgeoisie 219
Plan techo (Nicaragua) 85

PMAC = Provisional Military Admin–
   istrative Council (Ethiopia) 227
PMU = Urban Modernization Plan
   (Algeria) 257
Poder popular (Angola) 131, 136,
   143
Policy silences 218
Political administration 232
Popular committees 278
Popular mobilization 8, 15, 106, 156,
   166, 212, 247, 278
Popular participation 59, 64, 78,
   113–115, 117, 124, 139, 166
Population growth 41
Portugal 37, 100, 106, 107, 117, 121,
   123, 136, 138, 147
Portuguese Guinea 97
Pozzolana 127
PPI = *Plano Prospectivo Indicativo*
   (Mozambique) 157
PRC = People's Republic of China
   290
Prefabrication 9, 46, 49, 90, 114,
   127, 134, 135, 138, 158, 161, 171,
   258, 285, 319
Preservation of buildings 50
Primate cities 75, 135
Private construction 117, 210, 264,
   306
Private enterprise 264, 284
Private ownership 10, 81, 88, 207,
   236
Private renting 57, 81
Private sector 151, 217, 283, 291,
   320
Privatization 10, 266, 283
Producer cities 289
Production of housing 16, 83
Productive investment 14, 75
Progressive Urbanization 85, 88
PROHABITA = *Gabinete de
   Programas de Habitação* (Mozam–
   bique) 160
Property insurance 308
Prostitution 211
Proudhon 302

Public housing (see 'State housing')
Public sector 282
Public services 254
PUD = Urban Development Plan
   (Algeria) 257
PUP = Urban Priority Plan (Algeria)
   257
Purchasing power 271
Qasbah (Algiers) 262
RCHU = Rural Constructions and
   Housing Units (Tanz.) 188
Reconstruction 277
Rectification (Cuba) 40, 61
Recultivation 252
Red Cross 132
Red Saturdays 143, 279
Reforestation 79
Reformism 176
Refugees 132, 211
Regional development plans 158
Regional priorities 74
Rehabilitation 52, 61, 169, 177, 178
Rent arrears 266
Rent control 37, 58, 203
Rent pooling 3
Rented accommodation 16, 51, 66,
   136, 168, 169, 170, 175, 203, 217,
   282, 291, 301, 308, 319
Rents 56, 266, 297, 301, 302, 304,
   310, 320
Repairs 43, 51, 57, 61, 82, 295, 308
Resettlement 106, 243, 257, 281
RHA = Agency for ... Rented Housing
   (Ethiopia) 237
RHCU = Rural Housing and
   Construction Units (Tanzania) 193
Rhodesia 147, 199
ROA = Rate of occupancy 268
ROB = Registrar of Buildings
   (Tanzania) 192
Rojo y negro 79, 143
Roof loans programme 188
RRC = Ethiopian Relief and Rehabili–
   tation Commission 242
Rural depopulation 257
Rural housing 42, 77, 193, 242, 259

Rural population 252
SADCC = Southern African Confer-
ence on Co-operation . . . 26
Saigon 277, 284, 285
Salisbury 201
San Judas (Nicaragua) 78
Sandinistas 71, 80
Sandino system 46, 135, 170
Satellite towns 281
Savings 117, 266, 305
Sectoral priorities 74
Security of tenure 57, 66, 136, 162,
212
Self-administration 15, 128, 135, 278
Self-building 38, 39, 40, 43, 45, 50,
51, 53, 56, 59, 63, 66, 84, 157,
163, 171, 194, 205, 211, 229, 278,
284
Self-determination 21, 176
Self-financing 39, 283
Self-help 7, 8, 10, 16, 17, 38, 54, 83,
90, 113, 114, 116, 118, 126, 127,
134, 135, 138, 139, 141, 142, 151,
152, 154, 155, 158–161, 163–167,
171, 175, 189, 193, 207, 208, 210,
213, 229, 238, 239, 241, 245, 283
Self-reliance 5, 21, 26, 27, 185, 193
Self-sufficiency 7, 10, 24, 25, 74,
143, 243, 277, 279, 280, 317
Senegal 99, 121
Service centres 186
Services 86, 109, 167, 231, 259
Shanghai 295, 305
Shanty towns 37, 38, 51–53, 251,
253, 265, 270
Shortage of housing 142, 205, 207,
257, 266, 282, 295
Singapore 305
Sites-and-services 15, 84, 86, 151,
155, 156, 158, 160, 162, 189, 191,
193, 242
Slums 40, 52, 187, 236, 251, 253
Slum clearance 187, 289
Slum-upgrading 15, 242
Small-scale enterprises 125
Social consumption 30

Social expenditure 74
Social facilities 232, 240
Social housing (see 'State housing')
Social microbrigades **44,** 52, 61
Social mobilization 10
Social right strategy 220, 221
Social segregation 8, 136, 201
Social services 14, 91
Social wage 311
Social workers 212
Socialist villages 259
Socio-cultural patterns 135
Soil erosion 252
Solares (Cuba) 40
Solidarity groups 80
Somoza 71, 80
Sotavento (Cape Verde) 121
South Africa 7, 25, 28, 100, 131,
132, 136, 147, 199
South-South cooperation 26
Soviet Union 19, 29, 30, 229, 278,
289, 309, 315
Space standards 49
Speculation 3, 4, 14, 37, 54, 60, 61,
80, 88, 167, 197, 230, 231, 235,
247, 271, 280, 304
Squatting 9, 10, 51, 88, 91, 136, 137,
142, 143, 187, 194, 201, 205, 211,
222, 242, 263, 284
Stalin 24, 292
Standards 154, 170, 187, 207, 220,
223, 237, 280, 284, 285, 300, 310,
320
State brigades 61
State housing 8, 38, 44, 53, 57, 83,
87, 124, 137, 161, 169, 222, 282,
292, 319
Strategic hamlets *(aldeamentos)* 101
Strategic territorial planning 101
Street committees 279
Structural adjustment programme 97
Structure plans 158
Subdivision of land 80, 88, 212, 265
Subletting 38, 57, 88, 170, 205, 209,
219, 282, 284
Subsidies 301, 307, 308, 310

Subsistence economy 229
SUN = *Sistema Urbana Nacional* (Nicaragua) 75
Superblock 46
Swahili house 184, 189, 192
Sweden 102, 138, 221
Tabancas 105, 111
Tanga 183
Tanganyika 181
TANU = Tanganyika African National Union (Tanzania) 181
Tanzania 8, 9, 21, 26, **181–196**
Taxes 238, 284, 303, 309
Technical assistance 142, 152, 157, 173, 241
Technology 16, 43, 89, 170
Tenure forms 16, 50, 81, 319
Thatched roofs 212
THB = Tanzania Housing Bank 191, 193
Tied accommodation 51
Town planning 77
TPLA = Town Planning and Land Administration Deptartment (Ethiopia) 231
Trade embargo 38, 46, 277
Trade unions 25, 26, 52, 79, 279
Traditional architecture 154, 194, 262
Traditional building materials 134, 285
Traditional construction 111, 161, 167, 171
Training programmes 137, 141, 154, 160
TRIALOG 5
Tribal land ownership 107
Tunisia 252
Ujamaa 8, 21, 26, **185**
UNCHS = United Nations Centre for Human Settlements 163
Unemployment 17, 27, 40, 61, 111, 121, 210, 212, 255
UNESCO 50
UNICEF 281
UNITA = National Union for the Total Independence of Angola 129

United Nations 4, 102, 106, 107, 126, 153, 154, 157, 158, 163, 173, 238
University (Managua) 91
Upgrading 86, 126, 156, 163, 165, 194, 211, 212, 243, 247
Urban Development Planning 105, 257
Urban Dwellers' Association (Ethiopia) 232
Urban growth 42, 106
Urban housing 291, 307
Urban reform 38, 57, 80
Urbanizaciones Progresivas (Nicaragua) 15, 81, 85
Urbanization 74, 107, 124, 135, 137, 143, 160, 200, 232, 247, 251, 254, 262, 268, 270, 280, 309, 317
USA 7, 22, 24, 35, 37, 73, 121, 132, 213, 217, 277, 285
USAID = United States Agency for International Affairs 212
USSR 102, 277
Vaccination campaigns 79, 133
Venice University 5
Vernacular architecture 155, 194, 262
Vietnam 4, 9, 20–22, 24, 29, 37, 252, **275–287**
Village commune 23
Villagization 8–10, 25, 26, 85, 101, 143, 153, 159, 185, 242, 247, 259, 281, 305
Voluntarism 176
Voluntary labour 61, 63, 279, 320
Waiting list 207, 210, 215
Walk–up blocks 298
Water supply 112, 136, 186
West Bengal (India) 20
Women 52, 62, 78, 116, 169, 194, 205, 214, 217, 279, 321
World Bank 7, 9, 27, 83, 90, 97, 104, 114, 117, 132, 174, 176, 177, 191, 206, 217, 229, 236, 242, 277, 281, 300, 311
World cultural heritage 50
World War II 24, 37

WPE = Workers' Party of Ethiopia
229
Yellow line (Albania) 10, 318
Zaire 132
ZANU–PF = Zimbabwe African
National Union – Patriotic Front
199

Zanzibar 181
Zaramo house 191
Zimbabwe 8, 21, **197–226**
ZUHN = New Housing Zone
(Algeria) 257
ZUP = Urban Priority Zones (Algeria)
256